Financial Development in Latin America and the Caribbean

Financial Development in Latin America and the Caribbean

The Road Ahead

By a team led by Augusto de la Torre,
Alain Ize, and Sergio L. Schmukler

THE WORLD BANK
Washington, D.C.

ISBN: 978-0-8213-8847-1
eISBN: 978-0-8213-8936-2
DOI: 10.1596/978-0-8213-8847-1

Library of Congress Cataloging-in-Publication data have been requested.

Cover design: Naylor Design, Inc.

Cover photo: SVLuma and Ash Design/Shutterstock.com

Contents

Foreword . . . . *xi*

Acknowledgments . . . . *xiii*

Abbreviations . . . . *xv*

1   **Overview** 1
    The conventional view on financial development and its limitations 2
    Revisiting financial development. 4
    Where is LAC? 5
    Promoting the bright side 7
    Dealing with the dark side 8
    Notes 12

2   **Financial Development: Bright Side, Patterns, Paths, and Dark Side** 15
    The bright side 16
    The patterns 19
    The paths 22
    The dark side 24
    Can there be too much finance? 25
    Notes 26

3   **Domestic Financial Development: Where Does LAC Stand?** 29
    Methodology 30
    Main findings 31
    Banking 32
    Bond markets 32
    Equity markets 35
    The new players 39

Alternative markets and products 48
Notes 56

4 Financial Globalization: Where Does LAC Stand? 59
The two dimensions of financial globalization 60
Financial diversification 60
Financial offshoring 67
Notes 76

5 Financial Inclusion: Where Does LAC Stand? 77
Methodology 78
Supply-side evidence 78
Demand-side evidence 80
The role of government 88
Notes 92

6 The Banking Gap 95
Is the banking gap real? 96
Supply or demand? 98
Are these the ghosts of a turbulent past? 102
Where is LAC now? 104
Notes 106

7 The Equity Gap 107
Effects of globalization 108
Free float 111
Market concentration 111
Institutional investors 112
Corporate governance 114
Other factors 115
Conclusions 116
Notes 118

8 Going Long 121
What are the issues? 122
What are the options? 123
Where is LAC? 125
What are the key policy challenges? 133
Notes 136

9 Risk Bearing by the State: A Collective Action Perspective 141
The role of the state in the pure agency paradigms 142
Adding collective action frictions 144
Adding risk aversion 145
The question of private or state guarantees 147
Systemic risk 149
LAC's policy swings—a play in four acts 150
Toward a rebalanced policy 152
Notes 155

10 Prudential Oversight: Where Does LAC Stand? 159
Methodology 160
The progress and the remaining gaps 163
The systemic oversight challenges ahead 168

Annex 10.A Methodology for the econometric analysis of BCP Ratings 171
Annex 10.B Highlights of the 2007 World Bank survey of supervisory
practices 172
Annex 10.C Joint World Bank–ASBA survey on systemic oversight 175
Annex 10.D Financial concentration in LAC 176
Notes 178

11 Macroprudential Policies over the Cycle in LAC 181
Macroprudential policy and the dynamics of the dark side 182
LAC's cycles and vulnerabilities: Lessons from the past? 184
Some key macroprudential policy design issues 192
The path ahead 196
Notes 199

12 Microsystemic Regulation 203
The rationale for prudential regulation 204
The outer boundaries: Illuminating the shadows 205
The inner boundaries: Silos versus universal licensing 209
The SIFI problem 211
Systemic liquidity: Norms and access 213
Financial innovation: Did LAC have it right? 214
The regulatory agenda ahead 215
Annex 12.A Challenges posed by large, complex financial conglomerates:
The case of CL Financial in the Caribbean 216
Notes 218

13 Systemic Supervision 221
The new connections 222
A new approach 223
New tools 225
Getting there 226
The agenda ahead 229
Notes 230

14 Summary of Policy Directions for the Road Ahead 233
Where is LAC? 233
The tough issues to think about 235
Policy directions: The bright side 236
Policy directions: The dark side 239

References 243

Boxes

3.1 The bond market in Chile 41
3.2 The equity market in Brazil 50
4.1 Costs and benefits of the participation of foreign banks in
domestic financial systems 73
6.1 A brief history of housing finance in LAC 99
7.1 Corporate governance and equity market development 115
8.1 Covered bonds versus mortgage-backed securities: LAC's recent experience 131
8.2 LAC's indexation experiences in housing finance 133
9.1 Welfare criteria in the theoretical literature on state guarantees 142

12.1   The Mexican Sofoles 206
12.2   Reforming the regulatory perimeter: United States versus the European Union. 207

Figures

2.1   Frictions, paradigms, and failures 17
2.2   Appearance, convexity, and returns to scale of FD indicator paths 20
2.3   Paths for government debt: External and domestic 21
2.4   Banking indicators' paths: Retail and wholesale funding and private credit 21
2.5   Financial depth indicators: Dynamic and cross-section development paths. 23
3.1   Domestic financial systems. 31
3.2   Banking indicators relative to global benchmarks 33
3.3   Bank credit. 35
3.4   Foreign ownership and concentration of banking systems. 36
3.5   Total banking assets as a percentage of GDP, within LAC. 37
3.6   LAC-7 financial indicators against benchmark 38
3.7   Primary bond markets 39
3.8   Domestic bond market turnover 40
3.9   Average maturity of bonds at issuance in local markets. 42
3.10   Currency composition of bonds at issuance in local markets. 43
3.11   Equity market size 44
3.12   Equity markets. 45
3.13   Stock market turnover relative to global benchmarks 46
3.14   Concentration in equity markets 47
3.15   Within LAC: Trading activity and number of listed firms in domestic
        equity markets 48
3.16   Equity market capitalization as a percentage of GDP, within LAC 49
3.17   Pension fund, mutual fund, and insurance company assets 51
3.18   Composition of pension fund portfolios 52
3.19   Mutual fund portfolio holdings 53
3.20   Derivative and factoring markets. 54
3.21   Financial cooperatives, credit unions, and exchange-traded funds 55
4.1   Foreign assets and liabilities and gross capital flows 61
4.2   Within LAC: Foreign assets and liabilities and gross capital flows. 62
4.3   Valuation effects. 63
4.4   De jure and de facto financial globalization measures 64
4.5   Net foreign assets as percentage of GDP: Equity and bonds 66
4.6   Within LAC: Net foreign assets as percentage of GDP: Equity and bonds. 67
4.7   New capital-raising issues in foreign markets 68
4.8   Relative size of foreign capital markets 69
4.9   Average maturity of bonds at issuance. 70
4.10   Within LAC: Average maturity of public and private bonds in foreign markets
        at issuance 71
4.11   Ratio of foreign currency bonds to total bonds at issuance 72
4.12   Equity trading in domestic and foreign markets 73
4.13   Concentration in foreign bond and equity markets 74
4.14   Foreign-owned bank assets as a percentage of total banks assets 75
5.1   Number of branches, ATMs, and deposits and loan accounts 79
5.2   Actual versus predicted number of deposits per 1,000 adults 82
5.3   Actual versus predicted number of loans per 1,000 adults. 82
5.4   Annual fees 83

5.5   Firms' use of bank accounts and credit products 85
5.6   Fixed assets and working capital financed by banks 86
5.7   Percentage of firms that consider access to finance as a severe obstacle 87
5.8   Governments' commitment to financial inclusion 89
5.9   Governments' commitment to financial inclusion: LAC-7 versus other
        LAC comparators. 90
5.10   The adoption of correspondent banking and mobile branches. 91
5.11   The adoption of correspondent banking and mobile branches:
        LAC-7 versus rest of LAC 91
5.12   Index of credit information and legal rights. 92
6.1   Offshore versus onshore credit to the private sector, LAC-4 97
6.2   Evolution of private credit by type of credit across LAC-7 countries 98
6.3   Real lending rate, real deposit rate, and EMBI: differentials between
        LAC-6 and the United States 100
6.4   Net interest margins: Contribution of different factors in explaining
        differences between Latin America's average and that for
        developing countries. 101
6.5   Real credit to the private sector and the compounded real deposit rate
        index, LAC-6 103
7.1   Percentage of LACs that implemented capital market reforms, various years 108
7.2   Onshore and offshore equity markets 109
7.3   Average of residuals of domestic and foreign turnover, 2005–09. 110
7.4   Trading activity in domestic equity markets during the 2000s 112
7.5   Domestic turnover and concentration 113
7.6   Domestic turnover and institutional investors 114
7.7   Domestic turnover and corporate governance 116
10.1   BCP assessments, LAC-6 162
10.2   BCP assessments, Caribbean 162
10.3   BCP assessments, rest of LAC 163
10.4   Compliance to BCP principles by LAC countries. 164
10.5   Financial regulation and supervision progress in nine LAC countries 165
10.6   Complexity index. 165
10.7   Selected soundness indicators. 169
11.1   Unconditional probability of booms and crises 185
11.2   Synchronization between real output and financial cycles. 187
11.3   Behavior of credit during downturns in real economic activity:
        Are financial cycles leading real cycles? 188
11.4   Unconditional and conditional probability of lending booms 189
11.5   Real exchange rate behavior during downturns in real credit 190
11.6   Foreign capital and credit downturns. 191
11.7   Main features of the credit cycle over time 193
11.8   Reserve requirements and reference rates. 195
12.1   Average number of banks with more than 10 percent of total banking
        assets, 2006–09. 212
12.A.1 CL Financial annual report, 2007 217

Tables

2.1   A simple typology of paradigms. 16
3.1   Countries analyzed, by region 30

3.2   Benchmark model for LAC's financial development indicators 34
5.1   Regressions of indicators of financial inclusion on income,
        population density, and country-group dummies............................. 81
5.2   Regressions for deposit and loan fees....................................... 84
6.1   LAC-7 credit gap by type of credit, 1996 and 2007.......................... 96
6.2   Real lending rates by type of firm, 2007 97
6.3   LAC bank net interest margins, bank overheads, and private credit 101
6.4   LAC-7 private credit gap: A decomposition by source 102
6.5   Number of crises by type, 1970–2007.. 103
6.6   LAC banks' interest margins, financial soundness, enabling environment
        indicators, and credit history—growth and crashes.......................... 105
6.7   LAC private credit, financial dollarization, and inflation, 2005–08 105
7.1   Benchmarking model 111
7.2   Domestic equity turnover and enabling environment indicators 117
8.1   Mutual fund fees in selected Latin American countries...................... 127
8.2   Share of deposits in portfolios of Chilean mutual funds 128
9.1   Development banks in Latin America and the Caribbean: Operative
        modality of development banks at the beginning of 2009 150
10.1   Econometric analysis of BCP ratings 161
10.2   Capital adequacy requirements for selected LAC-6 countries 166
10.A.1 BCP consolidation into groups.. 171
10.B.1 World Bank survey of supervisory practices 173
10.D.1 Market share of largest companies and funds in selected LAC countries.......... 176
10.D.2 Ownership concentration in selected Latin American countries 177
11.1   Main features of real and financial cycles 186
11.2   Size of financial booms and the probability of crisis: Probit analysis............. 192

Foreword

During the 1980s and 1990s, financial sectors were the Achilles' heel of economic development in Latin America and the Caribbean (LAC). Since then, these sectors have grown and deepened, becoming more integrated and competitive, with new actors, markets, and instruments springing up and financial inclusion broadening. To crown these achievements, the region's financial systems were left largely unscathed by the global financial crisis of 2008–09.

Now that the successes of LAC's macro-financial stability are widely recognized and tested, it is high time for an in-depth stock-taking of what remains to be done.

For starters, despite this stability, the dividends in terms of output growth and greater social equity still remain to be fully realized. It is broadly accepted that the effective operation of financial systems is key to reaching these goals. But as evidenced in this flagship report, the region continues to face some core financial development gaps and challenges.

In particular, banks in the region generally lend less to the private sector compared with banks in comparable countries around the world, and they do so under generally higher

interest rates. Also, equity markets across the region continue to suffer from a chronic lack of liquidity. These financial indicators are precisely those most closely connected to economic growth.

In addition, the global financial crisis has brought to the surface a new set of issues that LAC must address, along with every other region around the globe. The crisis has shown that financial development and financial stability interact intensely—something that the international financial architecture continues to ignore by almost single-mindedly focusing on the latter.

The crisis has also highlighted the need for the state to keep the process of financial development on a safe track, while also accepting that, once a major crisis hits, the state is the risk absorber of last resort, a role that requires additional thinking and institution building. In LAC, the important countercyclical role played by public banks in the crisis also reopened the debate over the development role of the state in finance, and this report sets out useful pointers to help further the discussion.

These are hard policy questions that will keep the world and LAC occupied for many years. Fortunately, LAC benefits from its rich historical experience in managing systemic risks. But there is little time to spare. The policy decisions of today will shape LAC's financial world of tomorrow. As global turbulences continue to impact the region, quality financial development and financial oversight policies that can adapt to a rapidly changing environment will be essential to securing its future.

Pamela Cox
Regional Vice President
Latin America and the Caribbean
The World Bank

Acknowledgments

This report was produced by a core team led by Augusto de la Torre, Alain Ize, and Sergio L. Schmukler. Other members of the core team include: Deniz Anginer, Luis Martín Auqui, César Calderón, Francisco Ceballos, Mariano Cortés, Tatiana Didicr, Katia d'Hulster, Miquel Dijkman, Erik Feyen, Eva Gutiérrez, Socorro Heysen, Eduardo Levy-Yeyati, María Soledad Martínez Pería, Claudio Raddatz, Steve Seelig, and Luis Servén.

The report benefited from very detailed and substantive comments on the entire document by Martin Cihak and Roberto Rocha (both of the World Bank), as well as from most helpful insights and comments at various times and on various parts of the study by other peer reviewers and discussants, including Stijn Claessens (International Monetary Fund [IMF]), Tito Cordella (World Bank), Luis Cortavarria (IMF), Asli Demirgüç-Kunt (World Bank), Eduardo Fernández-Arias (Inter-American Development Bank), Marialisa Motta (World Bank), Aditya Narain (IMF), Andrew Powell (Inter-American Development Bank [IDB]), Robert Rennhack (IMF), Liliana Rojas Suarez (Center for Global Development), Pablo Sanguinetti (CAF), Sophie Sirtaine (World Bank), and Rodrigo Valdés (IMF).

The flagship report was also guided by an advisory group of Latin America and the Caribbean (LAC) countries' financial policy makers, many of whom provided substantive comments at an authors' workshop in December 2010. The members of the advisory group are as follows:

- From Brazil: Alexandre Tombini (Governor, Central Bank) and Luis Pereira da Silva (Deputy Governor for International Affairs, Central Bank)
- From Chile: Luis Céspedes (former Head of Research, Central Bank)
- From Colombia: Ana Fernanda Maiguashca (Regulation Director, Ministry of Finance)
- From Costa Rica: Francisco de Paula Gutiérrez (former Governor, Central Bank)
- From Jamaica: Brian Wynter (Governor, Bank of Jamaica) and Brian Langrin (Chief Economist, Financial Stability Unit, Bank of Jamaica)
- From Mexico: Guillermo Babatz Torres (President, National Banking and Securities Commission) and Carlos Serrano (Vice President of Regulatory Policies, National Banking and Securities Commission)
- From Peru: Javier Poggi (Chief Economist, Superintendency of Banking, Insurance,

and Private Pension Funds) and Manuel Luy (Head of the Economic Research Department, Superintendency of Banking, Insurance, and Private Pension Funds)
• From Uruguay: Mario Bergara (Governor, Central Bank)

The report also benefited from written input by Olivier Hassler, as well as from conversations with experts in the field, including Aquiles Almansi, Timothy Brennan, Anderson Caputo Silva, Jorge Chan-Lau, Loic Chiquier, Joaquín Gutierrez, Tamuna Loladze, Heinz Rudolph, Ilias Skamnelos, and Craig Thorburn.

We thank Francisco Ceballos and Tatiana Didier for invaluable help in coordinating and putting together the documents that constitute this 2011 Regional Flagship Study. Outstanding professional editing was provided by Judith Goff. We benefited from excellent research assistance at different stages of the project provided by Matías Antonio, Mariana Barrera, Patricia Caraballo, Francisco Ceballos, Luciano Cohan, Juan Miguel Cuattromo, Federico Filippini, Ana Gazmuri, Julian Genoud, Laura Malatini, Lucas Nuñez, Paula Pedro, Virginia Poggio, Juliana Portella de Aguiar Vieira, Gustavo Saguier, Mauricio Tejada, Patricio Valenzuela, Luis Fernando Vieira, Tomas Williams, and Gabriel Zelpo. For competent administrative assistance, we thank Erika Bazan Lavanda and Ruth Delgado.

The main output of the 2011 Regional Flagship Study consists of this flagship report and a companion edited volume with specialized chapters drafted by different members of the team. While both the flagship report and the papers in the edited volume result from a team effort, the responsibility for their content ultimately remains with their drafting authors. Thus, the views expressed in this flagship report may at times differ slightly from those expressed in the supporting papers of the edited volume.

The documents of the 2011 Regional Flagship Study are posted on the website of the World Bank's Office of the Chief Economist for Latin America and the Caribbean (http://www.worldbank.org/laceconomist).

Abbreviations

ALIDE	Latin American Association of Development Finance Institutions
ALM	asset-liability manager
ASBA	Association of Supervisors of Banks of the Americas
ATM	automated teller machine
BCP	Basel Core Principles for Effective Banking Supervision
CAF	Corporación Andina de Fomento
CEBS	Committee of European Banking Supervisors
CGD	Center for Global Development
CPI	consumer price index
DR	depository receipt
DTI	debt service to income
EU	European Union
FD	financial development
FDI	foreign direct investment
FDIC	Federal Deposit Insurance Corporation
FHC	financial holding company
FSA	Financial Sector Authority
FSAP	Financial Sector Assessment Program
FSOC	Financial Stability Oversight Council
GDP	gross domestic product
IDB	Inter-American Development Bank
IMF	International Monetary Fund
LAC	Latin America and the Caribbean
LCH	Letras de Crédito Hipotecario
LCR	liquidity coverage ratio
LLR	lender of last resort
LTV	loan-to-value ratio
MOU	memorandum of understanding
MBS	mortgage-backed securities
NGO	nongovernmental organization

NSFR	net stable funding ratio
OTC	over-the-counter
PCG	partial credit guarantee
PEVC	private equity and venture capital
PFA	pension fund administrator
PPP	public-private partnerships
ROA	return on investment
ROSC	report on the observance of standards and codes
SAP	Sociedades de Ahorro y Préstamo
SBPE	Sistema Brasileiro de Poupança e Empréstimo (a housing finance system)
SHF	Sociedad Hipotecaria Federal (Federal Mortgage Society)
SIFI	systemically important financial entities
SME	small and medium enterprises
TBTF	too-big-to-fail
UDI	Unidad de Inversión
UF	Unidad de Fomento

Overview | 1

The financial systems of the Latin America and the Caribbean region (LAC) are at a crucial juncture. After a history of recurrent instability and crisis (a trademark of the region), they now seem well poised for rapid expansion. Since the last wave of financial crises that swept through the region in the late 1990s and early 2000s, financial systems in LAC have continued to gain in soundness, depth, and diversity. The size of banking systems has increased, albeit from a low base; local currency bond markets have greatly developed, both in volumes and in reach over the yield curve; stock markets have expanded; and derivative markets—particularly currency derivatives—have grown and multiplied. Institutional investors have become more important relative to banks, making the financial system more complex and diversified. Importantly, much progress has been made in financial inclusion, particularly through the expansion of payments, savings, and credit services to lower-income households and microenterprises.[1] As evidence of their new soundness and resiliency, financial systems in the region, except in some Caribbean countries, weathered the recent global financial crisis remarkably well.

The progress in financial development in LAC no doubt reflects substantial improvements in the enabling environment, lower macroeconomic volatility, more independent and better-anchored currencies, increased financial liberalization, lower currency mismatches and foreign debt exposures, enhanced effectiveness of regulation and supervision, and notable improvements in the underlying market infrastructures (for example, trading, payments, custody, clearing, and settlement).[2]

For all the gains, however, many challenges remain. There is still a nagging contrast between the intensity of financial sector reforms that LAC implemented over the past 20 years (including aggressive financial liberalization and vigorous efforts to adopt internationally recognized regulatory and supervisory standards) and the actual size and depth of the region's financial systems. In many respects—notably bank credit to the private sector and domestic equity market liquidity—the region's financial services industry is underdeveloped by international comparison. The expansion of bank credit has been biased in favor of financing consumption rather than production. The provision of long-term finance—whether to households, firms, or infrastructure—remains problematic.

Thus, as LAC enters a new phase of financial development, encouraged by more supportive enabling environments and a more stable macroeconomy, the time is ripe for an in-depth stocktaking of LAC's financial systems and a forward-looking assessment of the region's main financial development issues and policies. Such an assessment is particularly important considering that the challenges of ensuring sustained development in a more globalized and possibly more turbulent world are likely to mutate, giving rise to complexities that may have little to do with the traditional challenges of the past. Latin American and Caribbean policy makers will face in the years to come a range of novel issues for which they need to prepare.

This regional flagship report aims at providing such a stocktaking and forward-looking assessment of the region's financial development. Rather than going into detail about sector-specific issues, the report focuses on the main architectural issues, overall perspectives, and interconnections. The value added of the report thus hinges on its holistic view of the development process, its broad coverage of the financial services industry (not just banking), its emphasis on benchmarking, its systemic perspective, and its explicit effort to incorporate the lessons from the recent global financial crisis. The book builds on and complements several overview studies on financial development in both LAC countries and the developing world that have been published in the past decade, including studies by the World Bank.[3] The book, moreover, is part of a wave of financial sector development studies appearing in 2011 that the World Bank has undertaken in other regions, including the Middle East and North Africa, and Sub-Saharan Africa.[4] Finally, this study is highly complementary to the recent flagship report of the Corporación Andina de Fomento (2011), which focuses on financial access.

This chapter describes the structure and scope of this regional flagship report. First, however, it reviews the current state of thinking in LAC regarding financial development policy, because that will further help to set the stage for the scope, structure, and focus of the report.

The conventional view on financial development and its limitations

Two major LAC-specific historical experiences stand behind what became over the past decade or so the conventional wisdom on financial development in the region. The first one is the state *dirigisme* over the financial sector that dominated the continent during the epoch of import-substitution industrialization, especially in the 1960s and 1970s. That experience ended up leaving a bad taste in the region. It resulted in atrophied financial systems and large fiscal costs associated with mismanaged public banks that paved the road for a major swing in favor of market-based financial development. The second experience is the painful recurrent and often devastating currency and banking crises that hit the region, particularly during the 1980s and 1990s. These crises confirmed the dangers that poor macroeconomic fundamentals pose for open financial systems. Crises thwarted and set back financial development by years at a time, with major adverse implications on growth, employment, and equity.[5] As the 1990s unfolded, moreover, the wave of financial liberalization that heralded the shift away from state interventionism interacted in perverse ways with underlying macrovulnerabilities, exacerbating financial instability. This led the reform agenda to put an increasing emphasis on regulatory frameworks and the institutional enabling environment—an agenda on which LAC countries embarked with great vigor, particularly since the second half of the 1990s.[6]

These experiences—together with a worldwide intellectual shift in favor of free market economics—gave rise to a relatively strong consensus in the region on a financial development policy agenda based on four basic endeavors: getting the macro right, letting financial markets breath, converging toward Basel-inspired standards of prudential regulation and supervision, and promoting the broadening of access to financial services.[7] The first, *getting the macro right*, reflected the conviction that unlocking the process of financial development had necessarily to start with macrostability. This aim entailed, in particular, the cultivation of the local currency as a reliable store of value that can underpin financial contracts. Over the past 20 years or so, therefore, ensuring stable and low inflation became the first order of business toward unleashing financial development. Fiscal reform and the development of local currency public bond markets were viewed as natural complements to monetary reform.

The second endeavor, *letting financial markets breath*, was initially manifested mainly in a rapid process of financial liberalization.[8] Subsequently, it incorporated efforts to strengthen the multiple facets (institutional, informational, and contractual) of the enabling environment. All of this was also naturally accompanied by efforts to enhance market discipline, which included a sharp reduction or elimination of the direct intervention of the state in financial activities, including the state's tendency to quickly bail out troubled institutions.[9]

The third endeavor, *converging toward Basel-inspired standards of prudential regulation and supervision*, focused, prior to the global financial crisis, on idiosyncratic risks and ignored systemic risks. It also favored limiting the perimeter of prudential regulation to deposit-taking institutions. The underlying assumptions were that the soundness of individual financial intermediaries implied the soundness of the financial system and that the well-informed and sophisticated players outside the core banking system would discipline each other.

The fourth endeavor, *promoting the broadening of access to financial services* for the underserved (that is, small farmers, microentrepreneurs, small and medium enterprises [SMEs], and low-income households) was added to the policy agenda vigorously but more recently (around the beginning of this millennium). It was spurred by enthusiastic support from multilateral development banks, nongovernmental organizations, and foundations (such as the Bill and Melinda

Gates Foundation). It was also boosted by the microfinance revolution, in which LAC played a salient role.[10]

It is clear that the overall thrust of this (precrisis) regional consensus on macrostability and market-friendly policies is enduring and should not be ignored going forward. The reforms undertaken under that consensus paid off handsomely during the recent global crisis.[11] Indeed, in a break with history—and with the possible exception of the Caribbean, where a few large financial conglomerates failed—no domestic banking system crisis was registered in LAC.[12] The region avoided domestic financial crises even as financial systems in the G-7 spiraled down into near-total collapse, averted only by unprecedented, massive bailouts.

It is also evident, however, that the global financial crisis invites a serious reassessment, not just of the policy agenda but, perhaps more important, of the conception of financial development that supported it. The crisis raised questions about each of the region's four basic endeavors mentioned above. It illustrated that apparent *macroeconomic stability* (for example, the "great moderation" of low inflation and output volatility, accompanied by low interest rates) can contribute to unsustainable financial development. It showed that *market discipline* can fail miserably, even more so, paradoxically, in the land of well-informed and sophisticated agents (commercial bank treasurers, investment bankers, fund managers, stock brokers, derivatives traders, rating agencies, and so forth). The crisis provided evidence that market discipline may actually tighten with financial development, instead of being boosted by it.

The crisis also demonstrated that the *Basel-inspired oversight program* had major flaws, including that this program was based on a great fallacy of composition—as the soundness of the parts does not guarantee the soundness of the whole. It demonstrated that the links between financial stability and financial development are much more complex than believed. Finally, the crisis raised red flags regarding policies that seek too aggressively to broaden *financial access*. It showed that there can be significant tensions between financial inclusion (for example, the drive to make a homeowner out of every household) and financial sustainability.

Therefore, to chart LAC's financial development going forward requires, on the one hand, a careful stocktaking of where the region's financial systems are now with respect to their development dimensions (as regards depth, diversity, access, degree of internationalization, and so forth), as well as to the enabling institutional and regulatory environment. On the other hand, it calls for a reassessment of the financial development paradigm that has been in effect to date. As the global crisis has demonstrated, the reassessment needs to take into account two fundamental themes: that the financial development process itself can lead to financial instability and that, to avoid such instability, the relationship between financial markets and the state needs to be reframed.

Both of these themes are of significant and increasing relevance to LAC. The region's financial systems are experiencing strong expansion pressures, not least owing to surging capital inflows, and this situation poses risks of financial excesses and bubbles—the "dark side" of financial development. In turn, this pressure raises the premium on the quality of financial development policies, thereby highlighting the need for a more effective complementation between the role of markets and that of the state.

The 2011 Regional Flagship Study research project aims at meeting this dual challenge—stocktaking and reassessment of the financial development paradigm—to set on firmer ground the financial development agenda for LAC going forward. This summary report synthesizes the results of a comprehensive analysis of the status, prospects, and challenges of sustainable financial development in the region. Much of the background research for this report can be found in a companion book.[13] This report starts by presenting a general conceptual framework of financial development that provides the key lines of intersection and organization for the rest of the report, including links between

financial development and financial stability. The report then takes stock of where the region's financial development lies by (a) analyzing in more detail some of the reasons and policy implications underlying its banking depth and equity liquidity gaps and (b) revisiting two themes that are central to its financial development: long-term finance and the role of the state in risk bearing. The last part of the report deals with issues of prudential oversight, first taking stock of progress in the region and then analyzing the challenges faced by the region as regards three main facets of systemic oversight: macroprudential policy, microsystemic regulation, and systemic supervision.

The following sections present the main threads that bind together all the chapters in the report.

Revisiting financial development

The flagship report starts in chapter 2 by revisiting the concept and process of financial development, something on which surprisingly little has been written. Financial development is all about the gradual grinding down of two basic classes of frictions—*agency frictions* and *collective frictions*. Agency (information asymmetry and contract enforcement) frictions limit financial contracting because they induce a misalignment of incentives between the principal and the agent. Collective frictions (action and cognition) hinder financial development because they constrain participation—thereby limiting the positive externalities in immediacy and liquidity that derive from large, interconnected financial intermediaries and deep markets. The constant interplay between these two classes of frictions—as market participants and financial institutions find ways to reduce or circumvent them under the stimulus of competition and innovation—shapes financial structure and makes it evolve over time. The gradual easing of agency frictions helps boost participation (that is, financial inclusion). In turn, by unleashing positive network and scale externalities, the benefits of participation become self-reinforcing. This process provides broad pointers about the order in which various financial activities are likely to emerge, and the shape of the paths they are likely to follow once they emerge.

These patterns are broadly verified through an econometric analysis of a large set of financial indicators. Financial activities for which agency frictions can be resolved more easily develop first. Activities that are the most strongly boosted by participation have the most convex development paths, rising steeply once economic and financial development reaches a certain threshold. Government borrowing emerges before basic banking services, which emerge before capital markets. Institutional investors appear at various stages of the process, reflecting policy factors as well links with other components of the development process. At the same time, the activities that are more tightly linked with market development—and hence benefit the most from the positive externalities of interconnectedness (equities, corporate bonds, mutual funds)—are the most convex.

However, financial development also has a dark side, as the apparently successful easing of agency frictions triggers lethal collective action failures—negative externalities, free riding, or coordination failures—or triggers a second round of agency failures, much as building more highways exacerbates congestion by increasing traffic. Alternatively, the positive externalities of increased market participation in the good times can turn into creeping negative externalities and other collective action failures in the bad times. In either case, the problems arise from wedges between private and social costs and benefits, which markets are unable to handle on their own. Thus, market-based financial development can lead endogenously to crippling financial instability. (Of course, misguided state interventions can also initiate or add to perverse dynamics.)

This interplay of frictions calls for a twin policy response. In designing good financial development policy, the state needs to be aware of the potentially adverse longer-term stability implications. In shaping up prudential oversight, the state needs to do it not just from an idiosyncratic perspective but also from a systemic perspective that makes three types of connections: between the parts and the whole, across time (to integrate the dynamics of the process), and between the forces of the bright side (financial development) and those of the dark side (financial instability).

Where is LAC?

The above narrative sketches the broad conceptual background and main threads on which this flagship report is constructed. Chapters 3 to 5 then offer a comprehensive description of the current state of financial development in LAC. Chapter 3 systematically compares (and benchmarks) LAC-7 with other regions and with other countries in LAC.[14] The chapter concludes that the region's financial systems have become deeper in ways that are consistent with the broad patterns described in chapter 2. There has been a transition from a mostly bank-based model to a more complete and interconnected model in which bond and equity markets have increased in both absolute and relative sizes; institutional investors (mutual funds, pension funds, insurance companies, etc.) play a more central role; and the number and sophistication of participants have increased. At the same time, the strengthening of monetary management has allowed an important shift in the nature of financing, toward the longer term and into the local currency.

However, chapter 3 also concludes that LAC's financial systems remain underdeveloped in some key respects. Even after controlling for a number of possible economic and structural determinants, including size, chapter 3 finds that LAC banks lend less and charge more than they should. The lack of domestic bank credit is only partially offset by other types of financing, particularly cross-border. Consumer credit has expanded at the expense of firm financing and housing finance. Moreover, domestic equity markets in LAC are illiquid and highly concentrated, and insurance is relatively underdeveloped. While institutional investors are sophisticated and large, a large share of their portfolios continues to be allocated to government bonds and bank deposits. Furthermore, there is a large heterogeneity within the region, with the rest of LAC being substantially less developed than LAC-7.

Chapter 4 then looks at some aspects of financial globalization. It finds that although LAC spearheaded a strong process of financial internationalization during the 1990s, its international financial integration tended to stabilize over the following decade, in contrast with other emerging economies. In particular, there has been a significant decline in the share of bonds issued by the public sector abroad and an expansion of local government bond markets. Inversely, however, while equity financing has tended to shift toward home markets, especially in the advanced economies, for LAC it has increasingly gone abroad. Also, in contrast with other emerging economies, LAC's equity liabilities continue to be dominated by foreign direct investment (FDI) rather than by portfolio equity, which is consistent with the shortcomings of the local equity markets. At the same time, LAC's international financial integration has become safer—as debt liabilities have fallen, reserve assets have risen.

Although lack of funding is clearly not an overall issue (in fact, many countries have imposed or are considering controls on capital inflows), there is still progress to be made as regards broadening and deepening participation and financial inclusion, a theme that is surveyed in chapter 5. Most available indicators of financial inclusion suggest that LAC-7 is not obviously underperforming compared to its peers, particularly when it comes to payment and saving services and microfinance. Yet capital markets continue to be highly concentrated, indicating that access is highly unbalanced across firms. Although most LAC-7 countries have adopted comprehensive policy agendas to promote financial inclusion, the attention given to this agenda has been spottier in the rest of the region. Areas that need

a particular focus include financing SMEs, bringing down the cost of financial services, and reforming creditor rights.

Chapters 6 and 7 then explore the severity of, possible reasons for, and potential policy implications of the banking and equity gaps, respectively, that were identified in chapter 3. Chapter 6 argues that, to a large extent, the banking gap simply reflects LAC's turbulent financial history. The region has not yet fully recovered from the repeated credit crashes of its past. This argument puts the spotlight squarely on the dark side and the need for ensuring financial sustainability through a good mix of oversight and development-oriented policies. But limited demand for credit (that is, a lack of bankable projects), possibly reflecting LAC's mediocre output growth, also seems to explain a sizable chunk of the gap. Here, of course, the possible policy responses go much beyond the financial sector. However, growth-inducing financial policies, such as those that facilitate longer maturity loans for SMEs or infrastructure projects, also seem to be called for. Overcoming the banking gap also has to do with addressing the remaining agency frictions. Interestingly, in LAC, the main residual bottleneck is contractual (contract enforcement and creditor rights) rather than informational.

Chapter 7 then switches focus to LAC's gap in domestic equity market liquidity. It concludes that both agency and collective action frictions contribute to explaining the equity liquidity gap. The substitution of domestic equity by foreign markets under the pull of a bigger (more liquid and connected) marketplace is a first obvious reason. The increased trading of the larger stocks that went abroad has in LAC a particularly strong adverse effect on the liquidity of the domestic stock market. Much as for the banking gap, the region's history of macroeconomic and financial turbulence seems to have something to do with this atypical outcome, although for specific reasons that remain to be elucidated. The preponderance of buy-and-hold pension funds, relative to more active institutional traders such as mutual funds, and weaknesses in corporate governance also seem to have played some role.

The policy lessons on how to promote equity markets (thereby facilitating market access) are challenging. Clearly one must deal with the participation externalities, as illiquidity begets illiquidity. Without liquidity, exit is difficult and price revelation is weak, thereby discouraging entry. However, the usual mix of liquidity-enhancing policies (reducing the fragmentation of issues, enhancing securities clearance and settlement, organizing securities lending and borrowing facilities, and so forth), while always welcome, will probably lead to only modest improvements. Efforts to further improve property rights, information, enforcement, and governance can help domestic equity market development, although they may at the same time favor an even greater migration of stock trading abroad. Given the dominant role of size (of markets and of issues) in stock market development, the prospects for small economies are particularly challenging. In this context, a realistic assessment of the costs and benefits of global versus regional integration of stock market activity will be needed. Other key questions are whether, to facilitate the development of the market for primary equity issues, the smaller countries in LAC should go stricter or lighter as regards corporate governance standards, and whether they should, as a result, accept a less liquid secondary market. As yet, there are no clear answers. There is, however, one certainty: the conventional stability-oriented, international standards–laden policy agenda will not suffice.

Promoting the bright side

The next two chapters, chapters 8 and 9, narrow the focus on two basic issues at the core of sustainable financial development: long-term finance ("going long") and the role of the state in risk bearing. While LAC has made much progress in lengthening contracts, notably public debt contracts, considerable progress still can be made. In particular, the hopes initially placed on pension funds to help lengthen maturities and overcome lack of liquidity have not fully materialized. For all their positive contributions to overall financial deepening, defined-contribution pension funds continue to have their portfolios concentrated in public sector bonds, short-duration bank deposits, and liquid equity and corporate debt securities. At the same time, with the demise of the monoline insurers, the public sector remains the only entity able to directly provide, guarantee, or enhance long-term debt finance. All of these factors are taking place in an environment in which the region is awash with investible funds, which is all the more puzzling. Clearly, going long is harder than often believed.

Chapter 8 analyzes the problem of long-term finance and the policy options available to LAC using the same twin lenses—agency frictions and collective frictions—that are used throughout the report. As regards agency frictions, perhaps the most pervasive issue throughout the region (one that is relevant to pension funds as well as mutual funds) is how to better align the incentives of asset managers with those of investors. States will need to find ways that help promote market discipline by facilitating the comparison of asset managers' performance, but without exacerbating the focus on short-term returns. Using life-cycle benchmarks and nudging defined-contribution pension funds into mimicking the investment behavior of defined-benefit pension funds should help. At the same time, states need to find sensible ways to provide more guidance to investors to resolve the problems of consumer protection and bounded rationality that characterize the pension fund industry, but without undermining monitoring incentives or promoting moral hazard.

As regards collective frictions, a first route governments can take is to promote market participation, hence liquidity, by continuing to improve the enabling environment or trading infrastructure. However, LAC policy makers need to be realistic about the feasibility (and desirability) of relying on a U.S.-style solution that uses liquid secondary markets to align investors' desire for an exit option with borrowers' long-term funding needs. As discussed in chapter 7, this solution hinges crucially on size. In addition, it can raise systemic risk. Wedges between private and systemic interests can widen as private agents increasingly free ride on liquidity and relax their monitoring efforts. Alternatively, serious problems of incentive distortions can be created if governments overly commit to being the liquidity providers of last resort. Thus, a second key avenue for dealing with collective frictions is, instead of promoting participation, to mandate it. Indeed, when combined with a vibrant annuities industry, the mandated private pension funds industry provides one of the most promising levers for the development of long-term finance in the region. However, design problems that in many countries currently stand in the way of linking pensions and insurance would need to be removed.

Chapter 9 then proceeds to revisit the role of the state in financial risk bearing, a topic that has risen to greater visibility in the aftermath of the global crisis. Again, the chapter analyzes this theme from the perspective of the underlying frictions. It starts by reminding the reader that over the past half century or so, LAC has undergone large paradigm swings, from state dirigisme to market laissez-faire, and eventually to a more eclectic view. Throughout, agency frictions and social externalities—whether first-tier public banks performed a better or worse agency task in integrating the social dimensions of lending—permeated the debate. A parallel debate developed on public banks' second-tier role in the provision of loans and guarantees.

Thus, chapter 9 reviews in some depth the conceptual justifications for public financial risk bearing. It first concludes that risk aversion, a seldom emphasized factor, is central to guarantees. Without risk aversion, no guarantee program, whether private or public, can be justified. The chapter then concludes that, given risk aversion among lenders, externalities alone justify subsidies but not guarantees; and agency frictions alone justify private but not public guarantees. Thus, public guarantees can be justified only in the presence of risk aversion

and collective action (participation) frictions (that limit the scope for spreading the risk throughout market participants) coexisting with agency frictions (that concentrate risk through skin-in-the-game requirements). Hence, it is the state's natural advantage in resolving collective action (instead of agency) frictions that justifies public guarantees. The state is thus naturally called to play to its strengths to complement markets, rather than substitute them.

Focusing on the role of the state from this perspective raises a policy agenda that is as broad as it is thorny. A key implication is that states, before providing guarantees, should first exhaust efforts to facilitate the spreading of risk through private guarantees and private risk sharing. The state can promote participation without taking risks itself through policies that directly ease the frictions (where, for instance, a development bank acts as coordinator) or through policies that mandate or gently coerce participation, as in the case of the mandatory contributions to privately administered pension funds that were reviewed above. Given the positive externalities, the state can also use well-targeted subsidies as part of this type of intervention.

Chapter 9 then assesses the rationale and scope for public guarantee programs. It emphasizes the need for these programs to refocus their rationale more directly around risk aversion and the agency or collective frictions with which a program interacts. A basic question in this regard is to account for (and price in) the hidden risks that may explain why the private sector cannot itself provide the guarantees. The more the state seeks to push the risk frontier, the more scope in principle the state has to intervene, but also more need for caution. Thus the chapter discusses ways in which the risk to taxpayers can be bounded and public governance enhanced. Clearly this is a rich area for further exploration, in Latin America and the Caribbean and elsewhere.

Dealing with the dark side

While retarding its financial development, LAC's turbulent macrofinancial history has also stimulated efforts to overhaul regulation and supervision—that is, prudential oversight. At a time when many developed-country supervisors were bent on easing intermediation through more market-friendly regimes and less expensive capital and liquidity buffers, many LAC countries went in the opposite direction. Nonetheless, chapter 10 shows that, as much as progress was broad, it was also uneven, both across regions and across areas. In a comparison against an econometric analysis of the Basel Core Principle assessments performed over the past 13 years (an exercise that clearly has many caveats), the LAC-6 countries (LAC-7 minus Argentina) generally perform better than other countries, even after controlling for different levels of economic development. The non-LAC-6 countries perform somewhat worse. There are also important differences across supervision areas, with some issues understandably more difficult to tackle than others.

Two basic issues concerning the legal framework—the *independence of bank supervisors* and *their legal protection*—emerge from a variety of sources as still problematic in many LAC countries. On regulatory issues, there is also some unevenness. Many countries are still not fully meeting the minimum Basel I international standards on capital requirements, and the implementation of Basel II has been thus far limited. However, in many areas, including on the regulation of credit risk, very substantial progress has been made. On basic supervisory issues, LAC-6 countries again tend to perform better than the rest, suggesting that effective implementation might be a problem mostly in the lower-income countries. In any event, important progress has been made across the region, including as regards the shift to risk-based supervision. Finally, as regards *consolidated and cross-border supervision*, a complex issue that to some extent prefigures the challenges of systemic oversight, most LAC countries have had a hard time. Here again LAC-6 exceeds its benchmark; however, opaque conglomerate structures, high conglomeration, high ownership concentration,

and insufficient cooperation and coordination among supervisors combine to make the challenge more difficult. Effective cross-border cooperation also remains a major challenge, all the more so in LAC in view of the importance of foreign banking.

All in all, LAC now has a much better foundation on which to build and deal with the new challenges of systemic oversight. These challenges include connecting the parts and understanding how one may affect the others, building up a proactive capacity to deal with the unstable market dynamics of the dark side, and thinking about developmental and prudential policies as two sides of the same coin. In view of lead times and longer-term dynamics, now is the time for thinking ahead. Moreover, as most of LAC is currently in the midst of a boom resulting from the potentially perilous mix of Asian accelerated growth and the developed world's low interest rates, there is not that much time to ponder anyway. Thankfully, LAC has a leg up. Its prudential buffers are currently high, LAC supervisors have made important strides toward improving traditional oversight, and LAC's numerous past crises have given its supervisors a definite edge.

Chapter 11 then reviews the potential benefits and challenges of macroprudential policy in LAC. The chapter starts with a thorough comparative analysis of financial cycles. It reveals that LAC credit cycles are generally more protracted and abrupt than those in other emerging and industrial countries. Likewise, cyclical fluctuations in bank leverage, housing prices, and real exchange rates also exhibit greater amplitude in LAC, especially in the downturn. The unconditional probability of a banking crisis and the frequency of crash landings following lending booms are also higher. Finally, bigger booms are more likely to end badly. These facts echo the history of macroeconomic instability of the region. They imply that management of financial risks over the cycle represents an even bigger policy concern in LAC than elsewhere.

In considering policies to manage systemic risk over the cycle, the main objective should not be to eliminate the financial cycle but to make the financial system more resilient and to tackle the externalities that amplify the cycles and promote an excessive buildup of risk. A first priority should be placed on setting realistic objectives along various levels of ambitiousness, ranging from removing existing procyclicality in traditional regulations, to building financial system resilience to cyclical fluctuations, to dampening the cyclical fluctuations themselves. Much more research and testing are needed. How to measure the buildup of risk is a particularly difficult challenge. In emerging regions such as LAC, very close monitoring of credit accelerations is likely to be needed to disentangle hazardous credit booms from desirable long-term financial deepening. The quest for developing a robust macroprudential policy framework faces a number of other unresolved issues, including the need to find proper balance between buffering the financial system and dampening the cycle; between institution-specific and system-wide triggers and targets; between price-based and quantity-based tools; and between rules and discretion.

On many of these issues, LAC is not behind the crowd. In fact, many LAC countries have already introduced countercyclical provisioning or capital requirements. And several countries have used reserve requirements proactively to help manage capital inflows and the credit cycle. Finally, many LAC countries have introduced, in the recent past, regulations to limit the risks associated with foreign currency exposures, which are also systemic in nature and similar in spirit to the systemic regulations currently being debated to manage credit cycles.

Chapter 11 also makes the point that reforms in monetary management, as well as in macroprudential management, may be called for. In view of recent evidence showing that low policy interest rates promote the search for yields and encourage banks to push the risk frontier, timely monetary tightening might also contribute to maintaining prudent lending standards in the upswing. This approach might mean allowing inflation to undershoot its target as financial imbalances are building up, and conversely when they unwind. At the same time, however, a more active macroprudential management can help relieve some of the pressure from monetary policy, thereby helping to reconcile inflation and exchange rate targets under open capital accounts—an issue that many LAC central bankers have close to their hearts. Countercyclical deployment of fiscal policy would, of course, also help in achieving financial stability.

Chapter 12 then shifts the focus from connecting the system through time to connecting the parts to the whole—that is, from macroprudential management to microsystemic regulation. The chapter starts by reviewing issues associated with the setting of the outer perimeter of regulation. Although regulatory perimeters are already widely extended in LAC, the issue is nonetheless relevant because boundary problems—the incentive to migrate intermediation to the less regulated domains—continue to exist and because spreading resources too thinly may end up compromising the effectiveness of supervision, providing an unwarranted sense of comfort, and possibly breeding moral hazard.

Thus, to economize on resources, some countries have resorted to auxiliary models of delegated supervision for smaller credit cooperatives. Another form of delegation could involve allowing those entities that fund themselves only from regulated intermediaries to be exempt from prudential regulation. Still another approach is to grant the supervisor statutory authority to readily extend the perimeter as circumstances warrant (as in the Dodd-Frank act). However, exercising such discretionary powers is a particular challenge given the region's administrative law framework. Another daunting task comes from the fact that systemic risk that builds up outside the financial system may end up contaminating the system through its impact on the markets in which both financial and nonfinancial firms participate, or through common ownership.

However, regulatory arbitrage can also take place within the perimeter of regulation when different silos are regulated differently. Indeed, licenses granted to intermediaries in the LAC region tend to have a narrow scope of permissible activities, typically separating commercial from investment banking and insurance from banking. The current silo approach is hindered, however, by the weaknesses in consolidated regulation stressed in chapter 10. One approach to dealing with this issue is to pursue a fully uniform, risk-based approach in which all entities are similarly regulated, ultimately leading to universal licenses. There are, however, potential drawbacks with such an approach. It is technically challenging, it could potentially lead to a loss of diversity that could make the system more fragile, and it could foster the emergence of systemically important financial entities (SIFIs) that are deemed too big to fail.

Indeed, the region has many SIFIs, and there appears to be some consensus on the need to regulate them differentially. Implementing such a differential treatment will be quite challenging, however, in view of data and analytical requirements. The global crisis has also highlighted the need to resolve unviable financial institutions, particularly SIFIs, in a nondestabilizing fashion. While the crises of the recent past have led to the introduction in many LAC countries of sophisticated bank failure resolution frameworks, these frameworks remain largely untested. In fact, crisis simulation exercises conducted in several countries have shown important shortcomings in both tools and processes. Moreover, the development of failure resolution systems for financial conglomerates (including the ones that operate across borders) is in its infancy.

Chapter 13 closes the flagship by discussing systemic supervision, an issue that probably has not received sufficient attention thus far but that is nonetheless central to an effective systemic oversight. The chapter starts by looking at the interface between regulation and supervision. The inherent tensions and complementarities between regulation and supervision are an essential part of the "rules versus discretion" debate. Hence, the main challenge is to build sufficient discretion

into the supervisory process (in a context of appropriate accountability) but without relaxing regulations so much that prudential oversight ends up losing its "teeth." The latter is an even greater challenge in civil law countries, such as those in Latin America, where supervisors tend to be constrained to taking only actions that are specified in laws and regulations.

A second key issue is how best to combine and intermingle a top-down perspective with a bottom-up analysis. Indeed, one of the weaknesses in the financial stability analysis published thus far by central banks has often been the absence of the supervisors' perspective on what is happening at individual institutions. The coordination necessary for this process to succeed, down to the technical staff level, is certainly not trivial, particularly in countries where bottom-up supervision is outside the central bank. A closely related (but conceptually distinct) issue is the relative emphasis on offsite versus onsite supervision. One might think that systemic supervision, because it involves the forest more than the trees, is more about offsite than onsite, but that is unlikely to be the case. Instead, systemic supervision calls for a review of onsite supervision, stressing its complementarities with offsite analysis.

The global crisis also calls for a review of the role of market-based financial indicators and the reliance on market discipline. The key question arising from the crisis is not whether market discipline is good or bad, but instead how supervisors should make better use of market signals. When weak market signals constitute a severe limitation, the key question therefore becomes one of how policy makers can help develop instruments (such as subordinated debt) that help price the risk, thereby facilitating risk discovery. Unless supported in some fashion by the state (and perhaps even subsidized), these instruments may simply be too expensive to see the light of day. An important research agenda for the region, therefore, is to help design, introduce, and support such instruments.

A key requirement for proper market discipline is analysis and information. Because much of information is a public good, there is a good argument that supervisory agencies should provide more of it, including information on (and better analysis of) the system as a whole, how it is wired and interconnected, and what the risks ahead are. When risks are detected, supervisors not only need to inform and guide but also need to take action.

Successfully implementing systemic supervision will require first building up skills, which involves a quantum jump, not a marginal improvement. It also will require suitable organizational arrangements. The need for better coordination between monetary and prudential management with a systemic perspective naturally suggests that the central bank will have to play a leading role. As central banks assume this role, however, care should be taken that their independence is not compromised. What will matter most is to put in place appropriate decision-making and interagency coordinating arrangements. If a systemic oversight or financial stability council is set up, an important element will be to ensure its accountability. Last but not least, staff must be encouraged to work together across agencies. In addition to coordinating at home, supervisors will also need to coordinate better across borders. In LAC, the importance of foreign banks makes this even more of a priority.

Notes

1. LAC was in fact a salient player in the worldwide microfinance revolution, which decisively shifted microfinance from a nongovernmental organization–based, grant-intensive activity to a profitable, commercially viable banking business.
2. Financial sector reform agendas in LAC were often aided by Financial Sector Assessment Program (FSAP) documents undertaken jointly by the International Monetary Fund and World Bank in several countries in the region since 1998, as well as by technical assistance (including in the context of loan operations) provided by these institutions. Comprehensive FSAP documentation, including country reports and reviews of the program, can be found at http://worldbank.org/fsap. A fairly detailed documentation of the capital markets–related reforms undertaken by LAC during the 1990s and early 2000s can be found in de la Torre, Gozzi, and Schmukler (2007a). Chapter 10 of this report documents the progress in LAC with respect to banking supervision.
3. Recent overview studies of LAC's financial sector include the Inter-American Development Bank's (2005) regional flagship report titled *Unlocking Credit: The Quest for Deep and Stable Bank Lending*, which focuses on banking; the World Bank's (2006) regional study titled *Emerging Capital Markets and Globalization: The Latin American Experience*, which focuses on securities markets; the book by Stallings and Studart (2006), *Finance for Development: Latin America in Comparative Perspective*; and the Inter-American Development Bank's (2007) regional flagship report titled *Living with Debt: How to Limit the Risks of Sovereign Finance*. Relevant overview studies of financial sector development issues with a global (rather than a regional) focus include two policy research reports by the World Bank: *Finance for Growth: Policy Choices in a Volatile World* (World Bank 2001) and *Finance for All? Policies and Pitfalls in Expanding Access* (World Bank 2007).
4. See *"Financial Access and Stability for the MENA Region: A Roadmap,"* a World Bank Middle East Financial Sector Flagship, *"Financing Africa: Through the Crisis and Beyond,"* a joint report from the African Development Bank, the German Federal Ministry for Economic Cooperation and Development, and the World Bank, and the *Global Financial Development Report*, a World Bank Flagship Report coordinated by the FPD Chief Economist's Office, forthcoming in 2012.
5. The uncertainty resulting from macroeconomic volatility—particularly high and unpredictable inflation—was deleterious to financial development, most of all at the longer maturities. It corroded the role of money as a store of value, leading to a gradual buildup of currency and duration mismatches. The inflexible exchange rate regimes, which were adopted in part to bring down inflation expectations, ended up exacerbating interest rate volatility and currency mismatches and became vulnerable to self-fulfilling attacks. This experience compounded the region's proneness to currency crashes associated with unsustainable fiscal positions. Widespread (currency, duration, and

maturity) mismatches, for their part, boosted the fragility of financial systems to currency upheavals, interest rate volatility, and runs on banks. In addition, repeated financial crises led to multiple ownership changes. By facilitating the entry of often unfit, improper, or poorly capitalized bankers, some reprivatizations of banking systems in turn compounded the brittleness of financial development. In addition to their major—and well-known—adverse effects on growth and employment, financial crises have proved to be highly regressive for income and wealth distribution (see Halac and Schmukler 2004).

6. For a detailed documentation of the financial sector reforms undertaken in LAC during the 1990s, see de la Torre, Gozzi, and Schmukler (2007a, 2007d).

7. A discussion of the evolution of financial development policy in Latin America and the Caribbean, along with relevant references to the copious literature on the subject, can be found in de la Torre, Gozzi, and Schmukler (2006).

8. A characterization of the financial liberalization sequencing debate, along with the relevant references, can be found in chapter 4 of de la Torre and Schmukler (2007).

9. This microeconomic paradigm underpins World Bank (2001).

10. See, for instance, Armendáriz de Aghion and Morduch (2005); Robinson (2001); Sengupta and Aubuchon (2008); and Yunus (2003).

11. See, for example, de la Torre et al. (2010b), IMF (2010), and Porzecanski (2009).

12. According to the Inter-American Development Bank (2005), in recent history, the LAC region has had the highest incidence of banking crisis in the world. In particular, 27 percent of LAC countries (35 percent excluding the Caribbean) experienced *recurrent* banking crises during the 1974–2003 period, compared to 13 percent in Sub-Saharan Africa, 11 percent in Eastern Europe and Central Asia, 8 percent in East Asia and the Pacific, and 0 percent in high-income Organisation for Economic Cooperation and Development countries.

13. The companion book is a forthcoming edited volume that contains 11 specialized chapters and several appendixes, produced by different members of the flagship team. The chapters of the edited volume are referred to later on, in the sections of this report to which they significantly correspond. The entire flagship study (this summary report, the Edited Volume, and a wider set of graphs and tables) can be found at the website of the Office of the Chief Economist for the Latin America and the Caribbean Regional Vice Presidency (http://www.worldbank.org/laceconomist).

14. The LAC-7 group comprises Argentina, Brazil, Chile, Colombia, Mexico, Peru, and Uruguay. Uruguay is included but República Bolivariana de Venezuela is not, mainly because there is much more data for the former than for the latter.

Financial Development: Bright Side, Patterns, Paths, and Dark Side

2

What is financial development (FD), and how predictable is it? Does it follow a single path or multiple paths? What are the sequences and shapes of the development paths followed by various indicators of FD?[1] In tackling these issues, this chapter introduces the basic threads that run through the rest of this report.[2] It presents a conceptual framework of FD based on a simple typology of frictions. Using this framework, the chapter explores and explains some of the patterns and paths of FD and discusses some of the maladies of FD that justify and shape the state's role and policy response. In this way, the chapter provides the necessary foundations to assess the Latin America and Caribbean region's FD and identify the policy challenges that lie ahead. Main highlights of the chapter are as follows:

- The frictions hindering financial contracting, and hence FD, can be classified into *agency frictions*, which restrict the scope for delegation, and *collective frictions*, which restrict the scope for participation.
- Each of these broad classes of frictions can be analyzed under two paradigms, which the chapter defines depending on the relevant friction and its interaction

with assumptions about the nature of information and the extent of rationality. Thus, the two agency paradigms are *costly enforcement* and *asymmetric information*; the two collective paradigms are *collective action* and *collective cognition*.

- Financial structure reflects economic agents' efforts to find the path of least resistance around the frictions; in turn, FD (the evolution of financial structure over time) reflects the gradual erosion of frictions, quickened by innovation, returns to scale, and network effects.
- It is thus hypothesized that the order of appearance of financial activities should reflect the intensity of the frictions to which they are exposed and should generally correlate with scale effects and the shape (convexity or concavity) of the development paths.
- These patterns are, indeed, broadly verified empirically when a set of relevant financial development indicators is examined. Thus, public debt, banking, and capital markets develop sequentially and along increasingly convex paths. There are, however, some FD indicators whose paths are notable and quite telling exceptions.
- FD indicators do not all follow the same path for all countries, reflecting

country-specific development policies, path dependence, leapfrogging, cycles and crashes, and endogenous quantum developmental jumps.

- The same gradual easing of frictions that underlies the "bright side" of FD can also help breed the tensions and fault lines that may eventually burst into the open in the form of financial crises (that is, the "dark side" of finance).
- The dark side may manifest itself as a result of one (or more) of three processes and their interactions: the easing of agency frictions that triggers lethal collective action failures or breeds second-generation agency frictions; the easing of collective action frictions in good times that unleashes crippling collective action failures in bad times; or the easing of agency or collective frictions that leads to problems of collective cognition.
- Obvious caveats apply, as the analysis in this chapter is, for the most part, an exercise in positive economics with limited data; hence, it is suggestive rather than conclusive.

The first section discusses the conceptual framework (the bright side of FD). The next two sections apply this framework to the empirics of FD, considering the patterns and dynamic paths, respectively. The fourth section explores the dark side of FD. The final section concludes.

The bright side

Financial development is all about the gradual grinding down of the frictions that hinder financial contracting. If economies operated in a frictionless Arrow-Debreu world of complete markets, risks would be fully and efficiently internalized in the price system, suppliers of funds or insurance would deal directly in the market with the users of funds or insurance, and neither of them would have a use for financial service providers. In the real world, however, frictions make the markets and the ability to contract incomplete and imperfect, thereby opening a wide scope for the financial system to add value to society.

Two basic classes of frictions hinder financial transactions—*agency frictions* and *collective frictions*. Each class can, in turn, be subdivided into two categories: one relates to informational frictions (including agents' limited capacity to process and understand information as much as their limited capacity to obtain it); another relates to what can be loosely defined as relational frictions, that is, agents' capacity to agree and to act upon collectively beneficial financial arrangements and to enforce bilateral contracts (table 2.1). Thus, this simple dichotomy underpins four paradigms, two of which—a*symmetric information* and *costly enforcement*—are associated with agency frictions, and two of which—*collective action* and *collective cognition*—are associated with collective frictions. The four paradigms can also be associated with the different stages a financial contract goes through, from preparing the contract to negotiating and enforcing it (figure 2.1).[3]

Agency frictions hinder FD because they limit the capacity of individuals to delegate and contract bilaterally. Asymmetric information frictions lead to a misalignment of incentives between the "principal" and the "agent"—the agent (for example, the banker, the asset manager, the debtor) can use his informational advantage to act in ways that are not in the interest of the principal (for example, the depositor, the mutual fund investor, the lender).[4] This misalignment, in turn, can trigger the commonly known market failures of adverse selection, moral hazard and shirking, and false reporting. Information

TABLE 2.1   **A simple typology of paradigms**

	Full information/ full rationality	**Incomplete information/ bounded rationality**
Bilateral focus	Costly enforcement	Asymmetric information
Multilateral focus	Collective action	Collective cognition

FIGURE 2.1 Frictions, paradigms, and failures

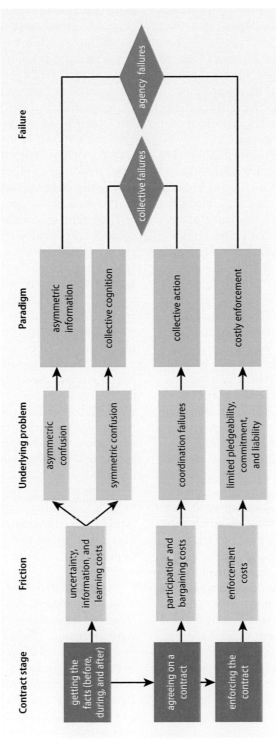

Source: Authors.

asymmetry frictions limit financial contracts to those in which agents have their own resources at risk ("skin in the game") and/or where the principal can adequately screen and monitor the agent. Enforcement frictions lead to a misalignment of incentives due to imperfect pledgeability—a situation where the agent is unable to credibly commit to honor the contract.[5] Imperfect pledgeability thus restricts financial contracts to those that can be effectively collateralized.

Collective frictions, by contrast, hinder FD because they constrain participation—that is, they constrain financial inclusion, broadly defined. Participation can increase along the intensive margin—that is, the same players engaging in more financial transactions—and along the extensive margin—that is, the inclusion of new players in financial activity. Much of the gains from financial activity relate to the reduction in transaction costs and the increase in liquidity and risk diversification benefits that result from multilateral arrangements in which many agents participate. Such arrangements can be either markets, where transactions can be conducted around a simple trading platform, or a financial institution (a bank, an insurance company, a mutual fund) that offers services whose benefits are pooled across a large number of customers. The higher the number of participants, the higher the benefits of participation. However, participation is hindered by cognition frictions—one does not participate in an activity if one does not comprehend it well—as well as collective action frictions, which typically condition the setting up and operation of multilateral arrangements.[6]

Market participants who wish to engage in financial contracting must therefore find the path of least resistance around these frictions and the associated market failures. Once a decision is made to participate in financial contracts, the private responses to coping with frictions can be divided into two subsets: responses aimed at lessening the frictions themselves (acquiring information, using collateral, delegating) and responses aimed at lessening the exposure to these frictions (diversifying and pooling risk, buying insurance and hedges, staying liquid). In turn, the state seeks to facilitate these private responses through a set of progressively more intrusive public interventions: (a) the provision of basic contractual and informational infrastructure (that is, public services that facilitate private contracting); (b) regulation and taxation (internalization of externalities or consumer protection); (c) pure coordination (catalytic involvement, systemic lending of last resort, and mandatory participation); (d) risk absorption and risk spreading (government guarantees); and (e) the direct provision of financial services by the state.

Different components of the financial system help deal with frictions in different ways. Consider, for example, the need for information. Capital markets provide price signals and motivate the supply of hard, public information by borrowing firms. Banks fill the information gap by generating proprietary information. Fund managers do so by monitoring marketable assets. Market facilitators (auditors, rating agencies, credit bureaus) sell specialized information and analysis. As another example, regarding the need for risk reduction through diversification, capital markets allow investors to buy assets with different risk profiles, which banks, insurance companies, and asset managers accomplish through pooling. Finally, as regards the need for liquidity, capital markets provide liquidity by allowing participants to unwind assets at limited cost; instead, banks offer deposits that can be redeemed on demand and at par.

Financial structure is thus a snapshot, at a given point in time, of the actual constellation of financial services aimed at coping with frictions.[7] *Financial development* is, in turn, the evolution of financial structure over time. An early resolution of collective action frictions (including through the introduction of central banks) allows for basic payment and custody services. A steady march from "relationship-based finance" to "arm's-length finance" ensues thereafter.[8] At lower stages of FD, financial markets resolve agency frictions by relying on nontradable and immovable collateral and connections, that is, relationship-based transactions. As the informational and contractual environment improves, private information becomes public and other types of collateral become available and tradable, gradually allowing FD to break free from the tyranny of connections. Similarly, as information becomes more abundant and governance arrangements improve, screening and monitoring costs come down and lenders can increasingly rely on third parties (rating agencies, market analysts, investment advisers, external auditors); statistical methods (scoring systems, value-at-risk calculations); and accounting and disclosure standards.

The gradual easing of agency frictions helps boosts participation. In turn, by unleashing positive network and scale externalities, the benefits of participation (liquidity, efficiency, and so forth) become self-reinforcing. Thus, in the more mature phase of FD, there is a quantum leap in participation as more clients, players, and transactions make markets increasingly deep, dense, and interconnected. The rising participation also increases the degree to which financial institutions and capital markets complement each other. The whole process is quickened by financial innovation, a major driver of FD that reflects and channels the forces of competition, deregulation, and regulatory and tax arbitrage, as well as theoretical or operational breakthroughs.[9]

Financial inclusion follows a process that largely parallels that of FD. Financial exclusion is caused by a mix of agency frictions—in which the marginal investor or borrower faces stronger problems of information asymmetries or lack of collateral—and collective frictions—which limit participation. Should many marginalized investors or borrowers decide to participate, it could bring the costs of participation down and allow participation to increase and financial markets to deepen. Thus, financial inclusion will gradually expand as innovations or a better enabling environment gradually erodes both types of frictions.

The patterns

The gradual easing of agency and collective frictions provides broad pointers about the order in which various financial activities are likely to emerge, and the shape of the paths they are likely to follow once they emerge. The order of appearance of financial activities should reflect the intensity of the frictions to which they are exposed. In addition, since activities that exhibit the highest returns to scale should generally be the ones exposed to the highest collective frictions, scale effects should correlate with the order in which financial activities appear and the shape (convex or concave) of their development path. Of course, deviations from these basic patterns may occur in response to policy choices, market demands, or linkages between the development of various activities and instruments.

Although the time period for which data are available is rather short, these patterns can be broadly verified through econometric analysis.[10] This is what de la Torre, Feyen, and Ize (2011) do, based on a broad benchmarking exercise applied to a battery of financial development indicators.[11] The results on three key patterns—order of appearance, convexity, and returns to scale—are displayed in figure 2.2, where activities are ordered by the per capita income level at which they appear.[12] Overall results conform to what one would expect. Financial activities that are the least prone to frictions emerge and develop first. Activities that are subject to strong frictions require more time. Some activities (such as debt and equity securities markets) are strongly boosted by scale and network effects, which give rise to convexity in the shape of the paths after some threshold level of friction reduction is reached. However, there are also some important outliers—such as domestic public or private debt, for which the returns to scale are not consistent with the order of appearance or the shape of development paths. The main stylized patterns (and possible reasons for deviations from patterns) are discussed in what follows.

FIGURE 2.2   **Appearance, convexity, and returns to scale of FD indicator paths**

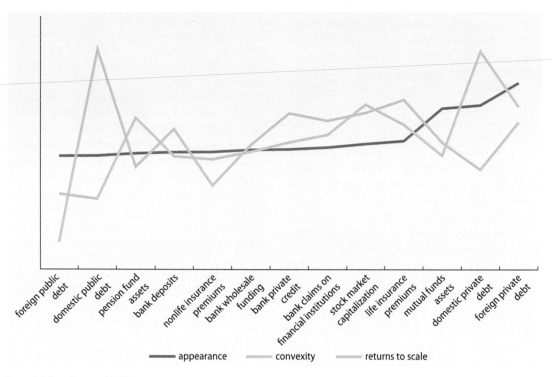

Source: de la Torre, Feyen, and Ize 2011.
Note: This figure represents three important characteristics of selected financial development (FD) indicators and their paths, namely, order of appearance, degree of convexity, and returns to scale. "Appearance" estimates the level of GDP per capita at which the FD indicator becomes relevant. Higher values (along the vertical axis) for the appearance line imply that the indicator starts to develop at higher levels of economic development. "Convexity" captures the speed at which the FD indicator grows as per capita income rises. Positive (negative) values imply that the indicator accelerates (decelerates) at higher levels of economic development. "Returns to scale" is the extent to which the FD indicator benefits from scale effects as derived, for example, from larger population sizes. Higher values for this variable imply that the FD indicator in question gains more from scale effects.

Public debt

Emerging early in the game is government borrowing (figure 2.2), as governments are the first to overcome elementary agency frictions. Given the smallness of domestic markets at low levels of economic development, which reflects collective frictions, government borrowing takes place initially abroad and in foreign currency.[13] As local markets develop and per capita income rises, external public debt declines and is replaced by (mostly local currency) domestic debt. In fact, domestic public debt develops at a relatively earlier stage than would be consistent with the large returns to scale. This may be because governments are willing to pay a premium to meet their financing needs or because a government debt market is a public good that helps conduct monetary policy or develop other financial

markets. Domestic public debt follows an S-shaped path, reflecting solvency constraints that eventually limit its size in relation to GDP (figure 2.3).

Banking services

The next financial activity is banking services (figure 2.2). Retail funding (bank deposits) emerges before credit. Bank deposit services initially respond to an early need for simple custodial and payment services. Banks have a harder time lending than attracting funds. As intermediation evolves from relationship-based lending to arm's-length finance, private credit rises along a convex path—it catches up with deposits over time and eventually exceeds retail funding as wholesale (nondeposit) funding makes up for the slack (figure 2.4). Lending to other financial institutions follows private credit and is highly convex. These features are all related. As agency frictions ease up, retail investors are increasingly able to shift into higher-yielding market instruments or to have their funds managed by asset managers or institutional investors rather than banks. At the same time, banks increasingly lend, including to each other.[14] The high convexity of these activities reflects the externalities-laden reduction of collective action frictions associated with rising participation (more players and the same players engaging in more activity) and denser finance.

Capital markets

After banking is capital markets (figure 2.2). Private debt securities follow equity. The late appearance of capital markets and the strong convexity of their development path are, of course, clear manifestations of the complexity of agency and collective frictions. Notably, private debt markets emerge late in the

FIGURE 2.3   Paths for government debt: External and domestic

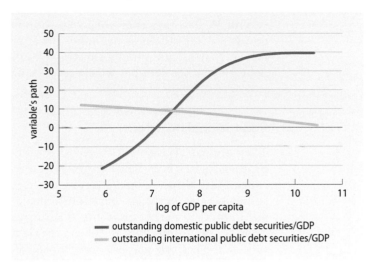

Source: de la Torre, Feyen, and Ize 2011.

game despite involving limited returns to scale, which suggests that, unlike the case of public debt whose growth is primarily constrained by critical mass effects, information

FIGURE 2.4   Banking indicators' paths: Retail and wholesale funding and private credit

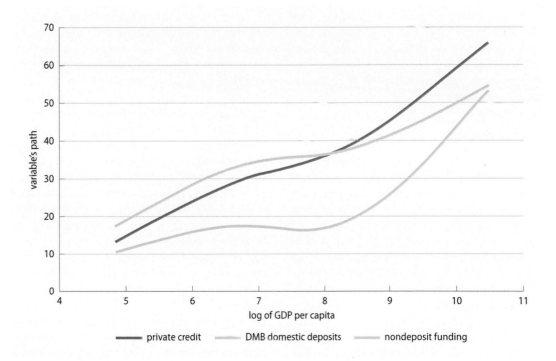

Source: de la Torre, Feyen, and Ize 2011.

and enforcement frictions (rather than collective frictions) are the key binding constraint.[15] The fact that corporate bonds develop after stocks is arguably because growing firms can initially substitute bank debt for market debt but will need to issue stocks at some point no matter what.[16]

Institutional investors

They appear at different stages of the FD process (figure 2.2). Pension funds emerge early, mutual funds late. Insurance arises somewhere in between, but nonlife insurance emerges earlier than life insurance. That pension funds appear early in the data reflects the key role played by recent pension reforms. Mutual funds appear late despite not facing increasing returns to scale (that is, not being constrained by market size) because the availability of marketable assets is a precondition for their development. The later appearance of life over nonlife insurance is in part because the latter is influenced by policy—for example, mandatory insurance for motor vehicles—while the former is dependent on the development of capital markets and, hence, is more subjected to collective action frictions.[17] Life insurance takes more time to bloom because of the need to invest in marketable assets and because of the need for life cohorts to interact intergenerationally; but once it does bloom, it follows a steeply convex path.

The paths

Financial development paths are likely to be unique; that is, the lower-income countries of today are unlikely to retrace precisely the path followed yesterday by the higher-income countries. There are a number of reasons why this might be the case. A first obvious, but still worth noting, reason is *country-specific policies*. These could be policies that affect the financial architecture, such as public sector indebtedness—which mainly reflects fiscal policy—or they could be the assets of pension funds and annuity providers—which reflect policy

decisions concerning the organization of the social security system. But a variety of other public policies can affect the path of a country's FD, including the quality of policies that promote the financial sector and, more generally, the quality and constraints of economic management that, by affecting a country's growth rate, will naturally affect its financial development. In effect, de la Torre, Feyen, and Ize (2011) find that the quality of the informational and contractual enabling environment, as well as average GDP growth over the previous three decades, are important determinants of the actual path of private credit and other key FD indicators.

A second reason for path uniqueness is *path dependence*, which results from the fact that output growth is itself a function of financial development and that institutional rules and arrangements are self-reinforcing (North 1990). Because today's FD depends on today's output, which in turn depends on yesterday's FD, initial conditions matter. Thus, FD trajectories can vary from country to country, especially those financial services that rely heavily on local institutions that are not tradable across borders. De la Torre, Feyen, and Ize (2011) find that contract enforcement institutions account for a significant share of the deviation of individual paths from the cross-section benchmarks, and that the payoffs from better contractual institutions continue to rise with the level of financial and economic development.

A third reason is *leapfrogging*. It is most likely to result from financial innovations that are transferable across borders; therefore, it affects those financial services that do not rely too heavily on (nontradable) local institutions.[18] For example, the dynamic paths followed in figure 2.5, panel e, by banks' net interest margins—which, except for the high-income countries, cross the cross-section path at a sharp angle—are probably a reflection of such leapfrogging at work. Indeed, de la Torre, Feyen, and Ize (2011) find evidence that informational improvements are easy to transfer across borders inasmuch as they rely on importable

FIGURE 2.5   Financial depth indicators: Dynamic and cross-section development paths

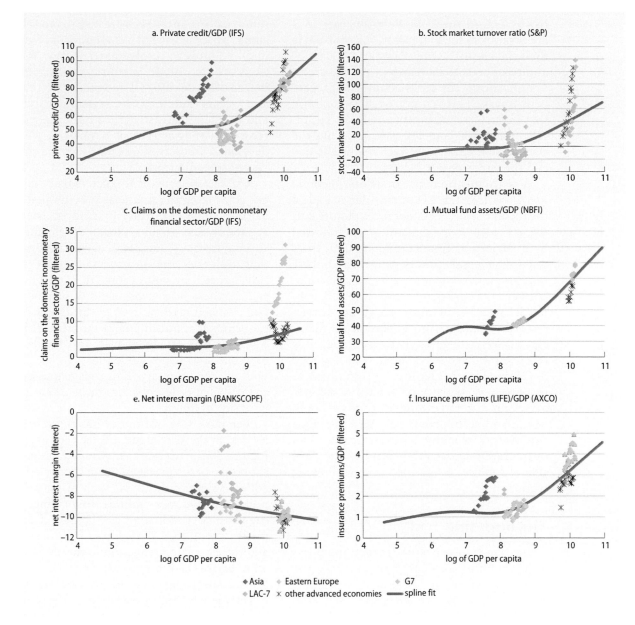

Source: de la Torre, Feyen, and Ize 2011.

technologies. Instead, contractual frictions cannot be solved by technological investments and imports.[19]

A fourth reason for path uniqueness is *financial cycles and crashes*. Credit cycles can give rise to short-term deviations from trend growth paths. As illustrated in figure

2.5, panel a, this was clearly the case of private credit in the low- and middle-income countries, which went through pronounced cycles during the period of observation.[20] Crashes can have an even stronger adverse impact on financial depth, especially credit depth, from which banking systems in particular may take a long time to recover. De la Torre, Feyen, and Ize (2011) find that this is indeed the case. Volatility per se is not a problem for FD; rather, the problem is financial crashes. Remarkably also, the probability of crashes increases as private credit "outperforms" its cross-country aggregate benchmark. This is a noteworthy reminder that financial development and financial stability interact in complex ways, reflecting the ever-present duality between the bright side and the dark side (see below).

A fifth and final reason is *endogenous quantum leaps* in FD at the higher end of the income scale. As illustrated in figure 2.5, this is evident in the dynamic paths followed by a variety of financial depth indicators that follow highly convex paths. For all these indicators, the dynamic paths for rich countries cut the aggregate cross-section benchmark from below and rise along a steep positive slope. Such an "explosion" of financial activity suggests that, once countries reach some stage of economic and financial development, the positive externalities of increased participation "ignite" a secondary chain reaction of financial activity, both inside and across countries. Whether such explosions are stable and sustainable is an open question, given the maladies and dark side of finance, as revealed in the following section.[21]

The dark side

There are two types of finance maladies (that is, failures to complete markets and achieve efficient equilibrium). The first one refers to failures to reduce the basic frictions that hinder FD. This may reflect an inability to resolve agency frictions or collective (participation) frictions. Agency frictions and failures continue to dominate the literature on FD and account for most of the policy debate, but collective frictions and failures are at least as important. Failures to reduce agency frictions may occur at the level of the investor (reflecting his inability to monitor or lack of interest in doing so), at the level of the borrower

(reflecting problems of governance), or somewhere in between (reflecting problems of incentives and "skin in the game" at some level of the monitoring pyramid). Failures to resolve participation frictions are, of course, a routine occurrence in the less-developed financial systems and justify much of the state's catalytic and financial infrastructure-building role. However, they may also happen in well-developed systems, particularly in the process of spreading risk.[22]

The second type of finance malady does not come from the financial system's inability to reduce frictions. Instead, it is the apparently successful financial development ensuing from a reduction of agency and participation frictions—a process that is typically boosted by innovation—that itself may endogenously lead to problems of instability and unsustainability, even in the absence of government-induced social moral hazard. Thus, FD may often take place in a fragile or even self-destructive mode that is in conflict with financial stability. This endogenous outcome is what is described in this report as the dark side of finance.

The dark side of finance has three basic modes. In the first mode, the successful easing of agency frictions is, paradoxically, at the source of the problem. It can trigger lethal collective action failures, such as negative uninternalized externalities, free riding, or catastrophic coordination failures. For example, the availability of public information and the associated reduction in the ability to appropriate the rents from private information encourage investors to free ride. Instead of staying put and investing in analysis and monitoring, they may rather invest short and rely on market liquidity to exit at the first sign of possible trouble.[23] But the easing of agency frictions can also trigger a second round of agency failures, much as building more highways can exacerbate congestion by increasing traffic. For example, as shown in the global crisis, the rising reliance on third party monitors to reduce information frictions, coupled with the ease of exit, can give rise to a complex and opaque chain of transactions, where agents have little or no "skin in the game," thereby creating a new generation of agency frictions.[24]

In the second mode of the dark side, the successful easing of collective action frictions on account of rising participation is, again paradoxically, what triggers the problems. The positive externalities of increased market participation in good times turn into crippling negative externalities and other collective action failures in bad times. While market participation is a "win-win" situation for all, as it enhances depth and illiquidity, market withdrawal in times of stress may be individually optimal but socially harmful as it originates fire sale spirals and self-fulfilling liquidity losses.[25]

In either case, problems arise from significant wedges between private and social costs and benefits, which markets on their own are simply unable to handle. Instead, the financial activities individuals engage in as self-protection for the good times no longer work in the bad times. Individuals and individual institutions do not internalize the adverse social or systemic implications of their actions. For example, insuring oneself by selling risk to others (through, say, credit default swaps) can actually raise systemic fragility through interconnected risk and lead to contagion and accentuated downward spirals in bad times, when default risk becomes highly correlated and the value of collateral collapses. Or else rising participation along the intensive dimension (the same intermediaries engaging in more transactions and becoming financial giants) can boost social moral hazard by vastly increasing the social costs of individual institution failures through the too-big-to-fail or too-interconnected-to-fail syndromes.

But the dark side has yet a third mode in which the successful reduction of agency or participation frictions leads to problems of collective cognition. The bonanza associated with FD feeds a collective mood of optimism that puts the system on a disequilibrium path. This is typically amplified by the far-reaching effects of financial innovations (for example, securitization) that unleash bouts of exuberance, even if the full implications of the innovations are not well understood. The mood swings first accentuate the upswing; once the market sentiment switches and euphoria turns into despair, mood swings worsen the collapse.[26]

All three types of maladies call for policy responses, which is, of course, the central reason for discussing them in this report. The agency frictions that are at the heart of governance and asset management issues are covered in chapters 6–8. The state's role in resolving participation frictions and improving the spreading of risk is covered in chapter 9. The dark side underpins chapters 10–13, the four chapters that conform the prudential oversight section of this report.

Can there be too much finance?

Before closing this chapter, an important additional feature of development paths is worth emphasizing. The counterpart of convex FD indicator paths (for example, that of private credit to GDP) is that *their impact on real development (GDP growth) must necessarily exhibit decreasing returns.* Unless the *rate of growth* of GDP keeps accelerating as the *level* of GDP rises (a clear dynamic impossibility), the impact of finance on growth should necessarily level off at some point. This is exactly the conclusion that several recent papers reach when regressing output growth against financial depth indicators.[27] In itself, this conclusion does not necessarily imply that there might be such a thing as "too much finance." If one reasonably assumes nonsatiation, more finance should always be better. However, unless kept in check by good public policy, the forces of the dark side of finance may gather strength with FD, reflecting the rising potential for financial instability resulting from increasing interconnectedness. If so, the marginal benefits of financial development may at some point become smaller than the marginal costs of maintaining financial stability. Should this occur, it would, of course, throw a whole new light on the FD policy debate.

Notes

1. The literature (particularly the empirical literature) on the process of financial development is relatively thin. That financial structure is shaped by the efforts of market participants to circumvent and reduce the frictions that hinder financial contracting is hardly a new concept (see Merton and Bodie 2004). However, few have attempted to analyze these frictions systematically in terms of how they interact and what this may imply for the dynamics of FD. Interestingly, more work has been done on measuring the impact of FD on economic growth than on exploring how FD is affected by economic growth (see Beck and Levine 2005). When discussing the impact of financial structure on growth, the literature, at least until very recently, generally concluded that function matters more than form (Demirgüç-Kunt and Levine 1999; Allen and Gale 2000). However, more recent papers (such as Demirgüç-Kunt, Feyen, and Levine 2011) have come closer to recognizing that there might be such a thing as an "optimal" financial structure, that is, that form might also matter.

2. This chapter draws heavily on the paper "Financial Development: Structure and Dynamics" by Augusto de la Torre, Erik Feyen, and Alain Ize.

3. For more details on the paradigms, see de la Torre and Ize (2010, 2011) and de la Torre, Feyen, and Ize (2011).

4. This strand of thought follows the insights of Spence (1973), Akerlof (1970), and, especially, Stiglitz and Weiss (1981).

5. This strand of thought is in line with the insights of Holmstrom and Tirole (1998) and Geanakoplos (2009), among others.

6. The collective action frictions of the bright side involve uninternalized positive externalities and coordination failures that prevent agents from moving to a superior equilibrium where everybody would be better off. The collective action frictions of the dark side (discussed below) involve uninternalized negative externalities, free riding, or coordination failures that prevent agents from avoiding falling into an equilibrium that is worse for the group as a whole, albeit possibly better for some.

7. The shape and nature of financial structure is given by the mix (that is, relative weights and composition) and degree of sophistication of markets and products (debt, equity, derivatives); leveraged intermediaries (commercial banks, investment banks, insurance companies, hedge funds, dealers); non-leveraged-asset managers (brokers, mutual funds, pension funds); and facilitators (accounting and auditing firms, rating agencies, investment consultants, mortgage originators).

8. See Rajan and Zingales (2003).

9. Indeed, the history of financial development is marked by major waves of innovation. Consider, for instance, the role in the exponential ascent of finance in the western world, stemming from the invention of Italian banking (based on trade-related bills of exchange) by the Medici in the late 14th century; or the introduction of payments systems based on checking accounts, fractional reserve banking, and central banking during the 17th century; or the development of the government bond market, its seeds already visible in the late Middle Ages; or the invention of the joint-stock, limited liability company in the early 17th century and the associated mushrooming of stock exchanges; or the emergence of marine insurance and life insurance in the second half of the 17th century; or, in the latter part of the 20th century, the development of securitization and derivative products. For an insightful and entertaining rendition of the history of finance in the Western world, see Ferguson (2008). For a recently updated review of the roots and dynamics of financial innovation, see Lerner and Tufano (2011). On the role of competition and deregulation in FD, see Rajan and Zingales (2003). Examples of theoretical and methodological breakthroughs that have dramatically influenced FD include double-entry bookkeeping, probability theory, life expectancy tables and actuarial science, and the Black-Scholes option theory.

10. Remarkably, the sequence derived from this cross-section analysis broadly matches that found in individual countries through historical studies of the process of financial development. The literature on the history of finance in the western world is vast. See Ferguson (2008) and Rajan and Zingales (2003).

11. The authors use a worldwide financial database put together on the basis of publicly available data by the World Bank (FinStats 2009). It covers 40 key FD indicators for

a large number of countries for the period 1980–2008 (country coverage and quality varies). The benchmark paths are estimated by controlling not just for per capita income, as is traditionally done, but also for various factors that are exogenous both to policy and to the FD process itself, including population size and density, age dependency ratios, and certain country-specific characteristics (such as the condition of being an offshore financial center or a major fuel exporter). The paths are estimated using quantile regressions so as to lessen the effects of outliers. To dampen the amplification effects of financial bubbles and downward spirals, rather than performing a traditional panel estimate—which would blend variations across countries and across time—the method used takes the medians of a given financial development indicator for each country and over the entire sample period and estimates a cross-section regression over those country medians. This becomes the benchmark (cross-section) path against which one can compare the paths followed by individual countries or country groupings over time. Some of these comparisons are reported in chapter 3 of this book.

12. The level of gross domestic product (GDP) per capita at which financial services start to appear is measured by the intercept of the cross-section paths with the horizontal axis. To limit lower tail distortions when a nonlinear fit is imposed on the data, for these estimates we use only a linear per capita GDP term. Convexity is measured by the coefficient of quadratic per capita GDP when financial indicators are regressed against both per capita GDP and its square. Scale effects are measured by the coefficient of population size in the controlled regressions.

13. This is, of course, the basic premise of the "original sin" literature, which focuses on the inability of emerging economy sovereigns and corporates to issue long-term debt denominated in their domestic currency. For the relevant analysis and suggestions for "redemption," see Eichengreen and Hausmann (1999, 2002); Calvo and Reinhart (2002); Eichengreen, Hausmann, and Panizza (2005). The fact that the better foreign institutional framework facilitates enforcement is an important component of the "original sin" story (see de la Torre and Schmukler 2004).

14. The high convexity of wholesale funding and interbank lending can be viewed as the growth analogue of the rapid rise of wholesale funding and bank interconnectedness. See Shin (2010).

15. Thus, while market liquidity is crucial to the development of public sector bond markets, it is much less relevant to the development of corporate bond markets.

16. The fact that equity markets have an unlimited upside may also help explain their earlier appearance, even under high agency frictions.

17. The abnormally low (negative) returns to scale of casualty insurance reflect the predominance of foreign trade insurance in the small open economies. It accounts for a disproportionately high share of total casualty insurance. See Feyen, Lester, and Rocha (2011).

18. One may consider, for example, the cases of credit card services and e-banking. These services are now found in most developing countries, and although they cover a smaller fraction of the adult population, their functionality and quality are comparable to those in developed countries. In both cases, developing countries have been able to leapfrog because the associated technology is relatively easy to import and adapt and because the services do not depend heavily on local contractual institutions.

19. De la Torre, Feyen, and Ize (2011) find the quality of the informational environment (credit information) to be *concave with respect to income but subject to scale effects*. In contrast, the quality of the contractual environment (creditor and property rights) is *convex but not subject to scale effects*. This suggests that informational frictions are of a mostly technological nature. Because of fixed costs, they are easier to implement in larger countries. Furthermore, they are solvable with adequate investments and ready-made imports from abroad. Moreover, once the required investments are in place, there are decreasing returns to further informational improvements as developmental levels rise. In contrast, contractual frictions cannot be solved by technological investments or imports. They are mostly institutional and reflect collective action frictions that are trickier to resolve, no matter how large the country. And the payoffs from

better institutions continue to rise with the level of economic development.

20. Although figure 2.5 shows GDP per capita, rather than time, on the horizontal axis, the two variables are highly correlated because GDP per capita generally grows over time. Thus, the steep up and down movements of private credit in Eastern Europe and the LAC region that appear in figure 2.5 can readily be interpreted as pronounced dynamic cycles.

21. Haldane (2010a) and Turner (2010) have suggested that the precrisis explosion of finance in the high-income countries was driven by precisely such dynamics.

22. This is the main theme of chapter 9 of this report.

23. Huang and Ratnovski (2011) show that the dark side of bank wholesale funding dominates when bank assets are more arm's length and tradable.

24. See Ashcraft and Schuermann (2008) and Gorton and Metrick (2010).

25. See Shleifer and Vishny (2011).

26. The importance of mood swings for financial bubbles and panics finds its roots in Keynes's animal spirits and Hyman Minsky's writings on financial crises (see Minsky 1975). More recently, it was popularized by Kindleberger (1989) and Shiller (2006).

27. Deidda and Fattouh (2002) find that FD has a positive but statistically insignificant impact on growth in countries with low levels of economic development and a positive and statistically significant impact on growth in countries with higher levels of economic development. Rioja and Valev (2004) find that there is no statistically significant relationship between finance and growth at low levels of FD, that there is a strong positive relationship at intermediate levels of FD, and that there is a weaker but still positive effect at higher levels of FD. Arcand, Berkes, and Panizza (2011) find that finance actually starts having a negative effect on output growth when credit to the private sector exceeds 110 percent of GDP. This result is congenial to that in de Gregorio and Guidotti (1995), who found that in high-income countries FD was positively correlated with output growth during 1960–85 but that the correlation was negative in the 1970–85 subperiod.

Domestic Financial Development: Where Does LAC Stand? | 3

This chapter describes the state of Latin America and the Caribbean (LAC) region's domestic financial development.[1] It provides systematic evidence on how LAC's financial sector has evolved and where it stands relative to the past and to other regions. The analysis focuses on financial deepening and the provision of financial services. Aspects related to soundness and stability—though clearly linked to financial deepening, as discussed in chapter 2—are covered in chapters 6–10 rather than here. The state of financial globalization and financial inclusion, two key complementary aspects of financial development, are discussed in the next two chapters. Main findings are as follows:

- LAC financial systems have deepened substantially over the past two decades, in ways that conform to the sequencing and paths described in chapter 2.
- In particular, bonds and equity markets have gained ground, institutional investors now play a central role, new markets and instruments have sprung up, maturities have lengthened, and dollarization has been reduced.
- However, significant developmental gaps remain, including the depth and efficiency (as measured by interest rate margins) of banking intermediation, the liquidity of the domestic equity market, and the depth of insurance products.
- These gaps are of concern because they coincide with some of the financial indicators that have been shown to be the best predictors of future output growth and because, except for bank margins, there is little evidence of convergence toward their "benchmark" levels, as determined by the economic development of the region and its basic structural characteristics.
- Other areas of concern include the stubbornly high concentration of issues and trading in the bond and equity markets, and the limited capacity of institutional investors to expand their portfolios beyond the safest and most liquid investments.
- There is also substantial heterogeneity in financial development within the region, with the smaller, lower-income, non-LAC-7 countries generally lagging LAC-7.[2]
- However, many cases of successful development, such as Brazil's equity market and Chile's bond market and annuities industry, may be edifying examples for other countries in the region.

The rest of the chapter is structured as follows: the first section presents the methodology; the second section synthesizes the main findings; the next three sections focus on banking, bond markets, and equity markets, respectively; the sixth section discusses the new players; and the final section considers alternative markets and products.

Methodology

The chapter focuses on LAC-7, although, wherever possible, comparisons with groupings of the smaller LAC economies are provided, namely, the Caribbean countries, Central America (including the Dominican Republic), offshore centers (The Bahamas, Barbados, and Panama), and South American countries.[3] Other emerging regions and countries, such as Asia, China, Eastern Europe, and India, are used for peer group comparisons. The G-7 countries and other developed economies provide broader points of reference (see table 3.1).

To shed light on how funds are intermediated and how broadly they are used, this chapter provides evidence from both sides of the market for lendable funds and focuses on markets as well as financial institutions. It also investigates how financial activity has been evolving qualitatively (currency, maturity, borrower composition, and so on). Two types of cross-country comparisons are conducted. The first provides comparisons of different dimensions of market activity over time and across regions, scaling depth indicators

by gross domestic product (GDP) to enhance comparability. The second is based on a statistical benchmarking exercise that controls, in addition to GDP, for a number of factors that are exogenous to financial development, thus allowing a systematic identification of developmental gaps.[4] To provide a more complete perspective, the results of both types of analysis are presented side by side whenever possible.

This chapter shows evidence on the banking sector, nonbank financial institutions, and capital markets. The analysis of capital markets is particularly relevant because many of the recent reforms were thought to increase competition with banks, reduce the cost of capital, and increase access to finance. Furthermore, the expectation was that capital markets would take off, as banks have been an important player for a longer time. In particular, the chapter documents basic trends in bond (corporate and government) markets and equity markets. It also provides some information on the development of other—newer and less core—markets and instruments, such as derivatives, securitization, private equity, and credit by retail chains. In addition, it documents the evolution of other large financial players, such as pension funds, mutual funds, and insurance companies. Because the developmental efforts aimed at completing financial systems started in earnest in the early 1990s, the focus is primarily on the evolution of financial markets from that period forward.

TABLE 3.1 **Countries analyzed, by region**

Asia	Indonesia, Republic of Korea, Malaysia, Philippines, and Thailand
Eastern Europe	Croatia, Czech Republic, Hungary, Lithuania, Poland, Russian Federation, and Turkey
G-7	Canada, France, Germany, Italy, Japan, United Kingdom, and United States
Other advanced economies	Australia, Finland, Israel, New Zealand, Norway, Spain, and Sweden
LAC	
LAC-7	Argentina, Brazil, Chile, Colombia, Mexico, Peru, and Uruguay
South America	Bolivia, Ecuador, Paraguay, and República Bolivariana de Venezuela
Central America	Belize, Costa Rica, Dominican Republic, El Salvador, Guatemala, Honduras, and Nicaragua
The Caribbean	Jamaica, and Trinidad and Tobago
Offshore financial centers	Aruba, Bahamas, Barbados, Bermuda, Cayman Islands, Netherlands Antilles, and Panama

Source: Authors' compilation.
Note: This table lists all the countries analyzed for each region. Some of these countries might not be used in certain tables and figures because of data availability.

Main findings

In many respects and by several standard measures, LAC financial systems have developed and deepened over the past two decades, much along the sequence predicted in chapter 2. Thus, their overall structure has become more similar to that of developed countries, with bond and equity markets gaining ground vis-à-vis the banking sector. At the same time, institutions and markets are becoming more complete and interconnected, and new markets are taking off, albeit somewhat timidly. Nonbank institutional investors now play a much more central role (particularly in the LAC countries that have introduced Chilean-style pension reforms), and the number and sophistication of participants are increasing (even without taking into account the growing participation of cross-border investors).

The nature of financing is also improving to some extent—for example, the maturity structure of both private and public bonds is longer—but at a slow pace. In addition, the dollarization of loans and bonds has declined.

Despite this general deepening, LAC's financial systems show significant developmental gaps over a number of dimensions. Even more surprising, they do not demonstrate a convergence toward the indexes of financial development observed in the more developed countries, or for that matter, toward the benchmark levels one would expect to find in countries with LAC's characteristics.[5] Figure 3.1 presents a synoptic view of the total size and composition of financial systems. LAC's financial assets, relative to GDP, ranked very close to last among countries examined for 2000–09.[6] The underperformance comes mainly from the very limited

FIGURE 3.1 **Domestic financial systems**

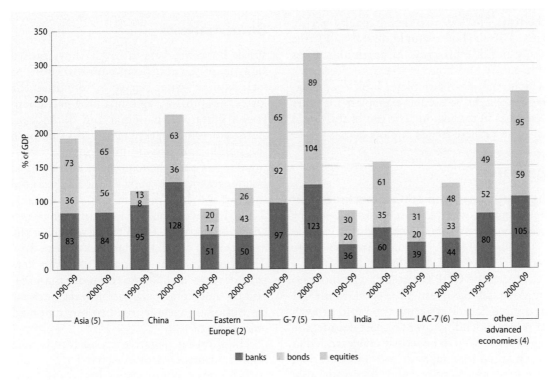

Source: Didier and Schmukler 2011a.
Note: This figure shows the average size and composition of domestic financial systems during the 1990s and 2000s. The figure shows total banking claims, outstanding bonds, and equity market capitalization as a percentage of GDP. Numbers in parentheses show the number of countries in each region.

bank assets, which—at 44 percent of GDP during the 2000–09 period—are below the levels found in any other region.

The underdevelopment of LAC's financial systems cuts across many indicators. As regards banking, private credit underperforms relative to benchmark and, although less now than in the past, so do bank margins. Public bond markets have expanded, but not as fast as those in the rest of the world. Private bond markets have increased in size, and primary markets have somewhat taken off, but markets remain relatively small and illiquid. Equity markets are approximately on track as regards capitalization but lag very substantially as regards liquidity; moreover, they continue to be highly concentrated in a handful of large firms. The development of the insurance industry continues to lag its benchmark. While institutional investors are sophisticated and large, they channel a significant portion of their funds to governments or banks instead of firms. Furthermore, there is a large heterogeneity within the region, with LAC-7 countries being substantially more developed than the rest. There is also heterogeneity within LAC-7 itself. For example, Brazil and Chile show notable progress in particular areas (the equity and bond markets, respectively), which, though incomplete, look encouraging and might be used as exemplars for other countries in the region. The rest of this chapter reviews these trends in more detail.

Banking

Banking systems in LAC lag behind their benchmarks, whether in terms of deposits or credit to the private sector, and this is especially so in LAC-7. The lags are very large (about 20 percent of GDP for deposits and 22 percent of GDP for credit) and show no sign of catching up any time soon (figure 3.2 and table 3.2). Reflecting the rapid growth of personal lending over the past decade, the lags appear now to be mostly concentrated in commercial lending and, even more starkly, in mortgage lending, which is considerably lower than in any other region (figure 3.3, panel a). Moreover, while bank intermediation margins have narrowed substantially (to

just below 1 percentage point in the 2000s decade, down from over 3 percentage points during the previous decade), they remain significantly above their benchmarks (figure 3.2 and table 3.2). LAC-7 banks are also becoming more concentrated, which contrasts with trends in other regions, and LAC-7 systems show the highest penetration of foreign banks (figure 3.4). On the other hand, there has been an important de-dollarization of bank loans (figure 3.3, panel b).[7]

On a country-by-country basis, Chile is the only LAC-7 country that meets its benchmark as regards private credit to GDP. All other LAC-7 countries are widely below benchmark (figure 3.5). When one compares subregions within LAC, the Caribbean countries and Central America show trends similar to those in LAC-7, though South America clearly lags behind its neighbors. However, offshore centers are clear outliers, showing an impressive, almost twofold growth in banking depth between the 1980s and the 2000s (figure 3.6).

Bond markets

While bond markets in LAC-7 have grown significantly, total bond capitalization, as well as new issues per year, remained the lowest in 2000–09 among all the peer countries (figure 3.7, panels a and b). Indeed, statistical benchmarking confirms that both the public and private bond markets continue to lag their benchmarks, albeit public bond markets have made up for a substantial share of the slack over the last decade (table 3.2). Moreover, lack of liquidity remains a key concern, with bond turnover being the lowest of all the peer countries (figure 3.8). This suggests that primary bond markets have developed substantially more than secondary markets, perhaps in part because institutional investors tend to buy and hold (see chapter 6).

These rather negative broad trends hide important success stories in particular countries, however. For example, Brazil and Mexico, and to a lesser extent Colombia, have large and liquid public debt markets with reliable yield curves that can be used to price

FIGURE 3.2   Banking indicators relative to global benchmarks

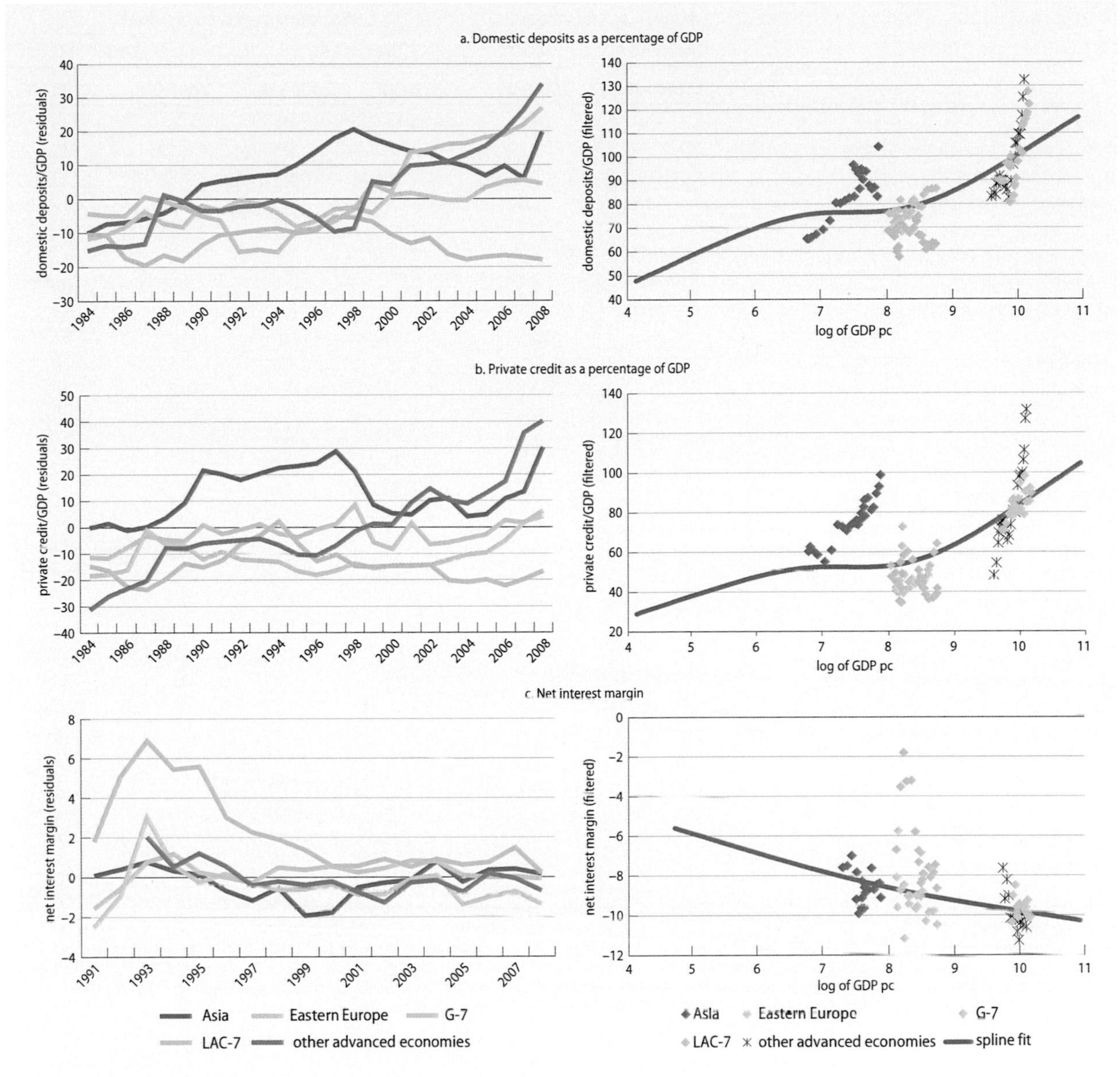

Source: de la Torre, Feyen, and Ize 2011.
Note: This figure shows bank domestic deposits as a percentage of GDP, bank private credit as a percentage of GDP, and bank interest margins across country groups relative to their global benchmarks. The left charts show the evolution of annual median residuals by country group. First, a cross-sectional regression model is estimated on country averages, controlling for GDP per capita, population size and density, young and old-age dependency ratios, a financial offshore center dummy, a transition country dummy, and a large fuel exporter dummy. Annual country residuals are derived from the cross-sectional estimates, which are used to calculate annual country-group medians. The right charts plot annual country-group medians of the filtered variables against the logarithm of GDP per capita. The filtering consists in removing from the actual annual country observations the expected contributions of all factors except GDP per capita, using the cross-sectional estimates from the above model. A four-knot spline approach is used to account for nonlinearities of GDP per capita in the cross-sectional regression.

private fixed income issues and value portfolios and to help develop derivatives markets (figure 3.7, panel c). Indeed, domestic public debt capitalization exceeds its benchmark in both Brazil and Colombia (figure 3.5, panel

h). Also, Brazil, Mexico, and Chile all meet or exceed their benchmarks as regards the capitalization of their private domestic bond markets (figure 3.5, panel g). Chile has a particularly well-established private bond

TABLE 3.2   Benchmark model for LAC's financial development indicators

	Median actual values (%)		Workhorse median residuals			
	Rest of LAC	LAC-7	Rest of LAC		LAC-7	
	2000–08	2000–08	1990–99	2000–08	1990–99	2000–08
Bank private credit	36.0	24.2	–3.9***	–0.8**	–13.6***	–22.5***
Bank claims on domestic financial sector	1.1	2.6	–1.3***	–0.4***	–1.1***	–0.2
Bank credit to government	3.7	10.0	–5.2***	–5.3***	–4.3***	–1.1
Bank foreign claims	8.6	2.5	–0.5	2.0	–4.4***	–5.7***
Bank domestic deposits	37.4	25.4	–10.9***	–4.0***	–13.6***	–20.8***
Bank nondeposit funding	18.4	24.3	–3.1	–1.4	–5.1*	–6.5**
Net interest margin	4.9	4.8	0.0	1.0***	3.3***	0.9***
Noninterest income/total income	25.6	33.5	–9.4***	–4.2***	3.9	1.9**
Total bank financial assets/GDP (excluding reserves)	55.5	65.5	–17.6***	–0.7	–16.7***	–19.5***
Life insurance premiums	0.3	0.7	–0.3***	–0.3***	–0.7***	–0.4***
Nonlife insurance premiums	1.3	1.1	–0.1	0.1***	–0.2***	–0.3***
Pension fund assets	7.5	11.7		–4.3***		–0.7*
Mutual fund assets	1.1	5.9		–9.8**		–5.9
Insurance company assets	2.1	4.0		–2.9***		–7.7***
Stock market turnover	2.3	12.6	–3.7	–10.6***	–18.4***	–28.8***
Stock market capitalization	15.7	33.6	–8.5	–7.7***	–7.7	–0.6
Domestic private debt securities	0.6	9.0	–10.1	–12.3	–1.6***	–3.0*
Domestic public debt securities	28.5	19.7	–17.6**	0.7	–21.3***	–12.2***
Bank foreign claims	17.2	24.5	–2.5**	–3.4	–4.0	0.0*
Foreign private debt securities	1.8	4.0	–1.6*	–2.4**	–1.9**	–2.5***
Foreign public debt securities	9.6	8.9	–3.0	1.3**	0.9	2.6***
Gross portfolio equity assets	0.2	3.1	–4.9***	–0.6***	–0.1	2.4
Gross portfolio debt assets	3.7	1.3	–1.0	1.2	0.1	0.0**
Gross portfolio equity liabilities	0.4	5.4	–2.3*	–2.2***	1.2**	1.8
Gross portfolio debt liabilities	9.2	12.2	16.1***	2.7	–4.9	3.2**
Capital/total assets	10.1	11.5	–0.2**	0.5**	0.6***	2.3***
Liquid assets/total assets	3.6	12.5	–4.8***	–5.9***	2.4***	5.0***
Regulatory capital/RWA (risk weighted assets)	14.1	14.4		0.1		2.0***
Bank capital/assets	10.0	9.8		0.7		2.2***
ROA (return on assets)	1.5	1.3	–0.4	0.1	0.4***	0.5**

Source: de la Torre, Feyen, and Ize 2011.
Note: The table shows the results of a benchmark model for LAC's financial development indicators. It presents the 2000–08 median for all LAC countries and the median LAC residual for the 1990–99 and 2000–08 periods, respectively, derived from the workhorse median regression model of the financial indicator of interest on GDP per capita (squared), population size and density, fuel exporter dummy, age dependency ratio, offshore financial center dummy, transition country dummy, and year fixed effects. The asterisks correspond to the level of significance of Wilcoxon rank sum tests for distributional differences of the residuals between LAC and rest of the world.
Significance level: * = 10 percent, ** = 5 percent, *** = 1 percent

market that can be used as an important point of reference for other countries in the region (see box 3.1). Together with macrostability and the withdrawal of the public sector from debt markets, this illustrates the major role institutional investors can play in promoting market development. The more recent but quite rapid development of the corporate bond market in Brazil is another interesting regional experience worth looking at.[8]

Also worth noting on the positive side, the maturity and currency profiles of bonds in the LAC-7 countries have improved considerably.[9] The average maturity of private sector bonds increased by about a year between the 1990s and the 2000s (figure 3.9, panel a); that of public sector bonds by 35 months between 2000–03 and 2008–09 (figure 3.9, panel b). At the same time, the share of local bonds (corporate and government) denominated in

FIGURE 3.3   **Bank credit**

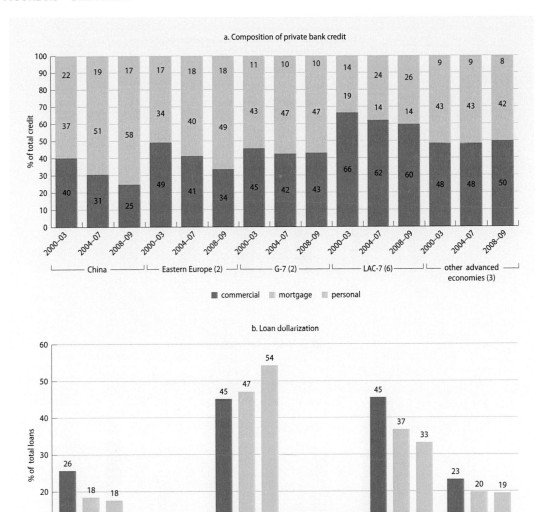

Source: Didier and Schmukler 2011a.
Note: This figure shows in panel a the average share of commercial, mortgage, and personal credit as a share of total banking credit. Panel b shows the extent of dollarization of banking loans. Foreign-currency-denominated loans are shown as a share of total loans averaged between 2000 and 2009. Numbers in parentheses show the number of countries in each region.

(or linked to) foreign currency has declined significantly, from 33 percent during the 1990s to about 25 percent in the 2000s in the case of corporate bonds (figure 3.10).

Equity markets

Equity market capitalization in LAC-7, as in most emerging economies, has grown rapidly

FIGURE 3.4   **Foreign ownership and concentration of banking systems**

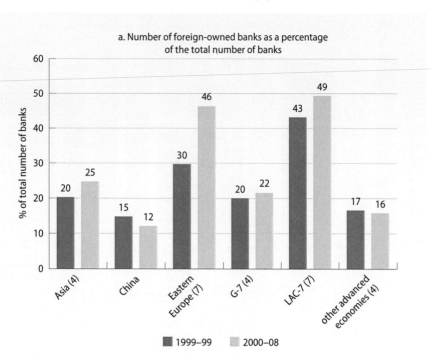

a. Number of foreign-owned banks as a percentage
of the total number of banks

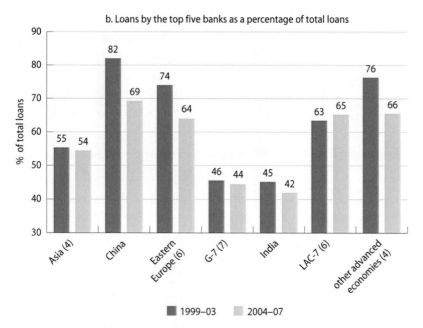

b. Loans by the top five banks as a percentage of total loans

Sources: Claessens and van Horen 2009; Didier and Schmukler 2011a.
Note: This figure shows bank foreign ownership and concentration. Panel a shows the average number of foreign-owned banks as a share of the total number of banks between 1995 and 2008. Panel b shows the annual average of total credit granted by the top five banks as a share of total credit between 1999 and 2007.

FIGURE 3.5   Total banking assets as a percentage of GDP, within LAC

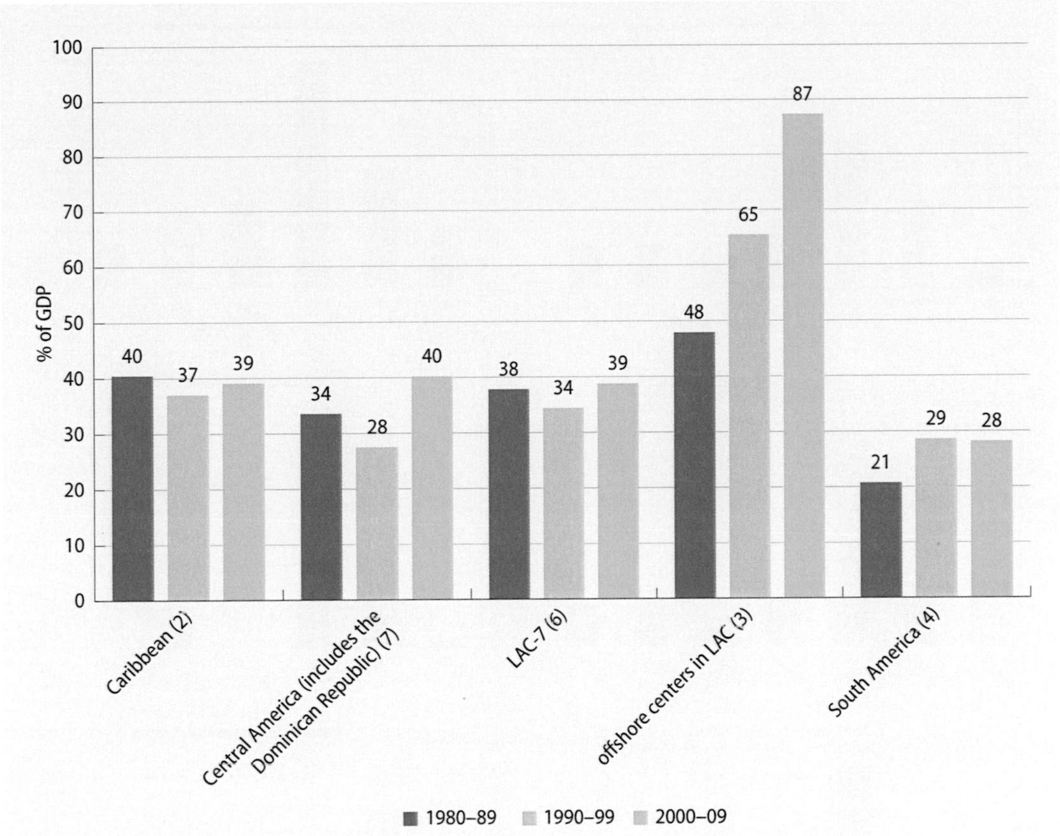

Source: Didier and Schmukler 2011a.
Note: This figure shows average total banking claims as a percentage of GDP between 1980 and 2009 across LAC. Numbers in parentheses show the number of countries in each region.

during the past decade (figure 3.11, panel a). The statistical benchmarking exercise (table 3.2) confirms that the LAC-7 group is on track regarding equity market capitalization (instead, the rest of LAC lags its benchmark). However, when adjusting for changes in equity prices, one observes a much more modest expansion (figure 3.11, panel b). Consistent with the fact that the increase in market capitalization is mostly explained by valuation adjustments, there has been a decline in capital-raising activity that suggests a declining role for equity financing, with equity issuance actually declining by about 70 percent between the 1990 and the 2000 decades (figure 3.12, panel a). The picture

worsens further when one looks at domestic stock market turnover, where the LAC-7 countries lag dramatically behind the global benchmarks (by about 29 percentage points), with the lag growing over time (figure 3.13 and table 3.2). Overall, this suggests, somewhat disturbingly, that the more the LAC-7 equity markets have developed, the more their liquidity has dried up.[10] While the lag in turnover is somewhat less severe in the rest of LAC than in LAC-7, the same story applies for the rest of LAC.

Access to the equity market also remains limited and concentrated in a few firms. The number of listed firms in LAC-7 markets is small and has declined over the past decade

FIGURE 3.6   LAC-7 financial indicators against benchmark

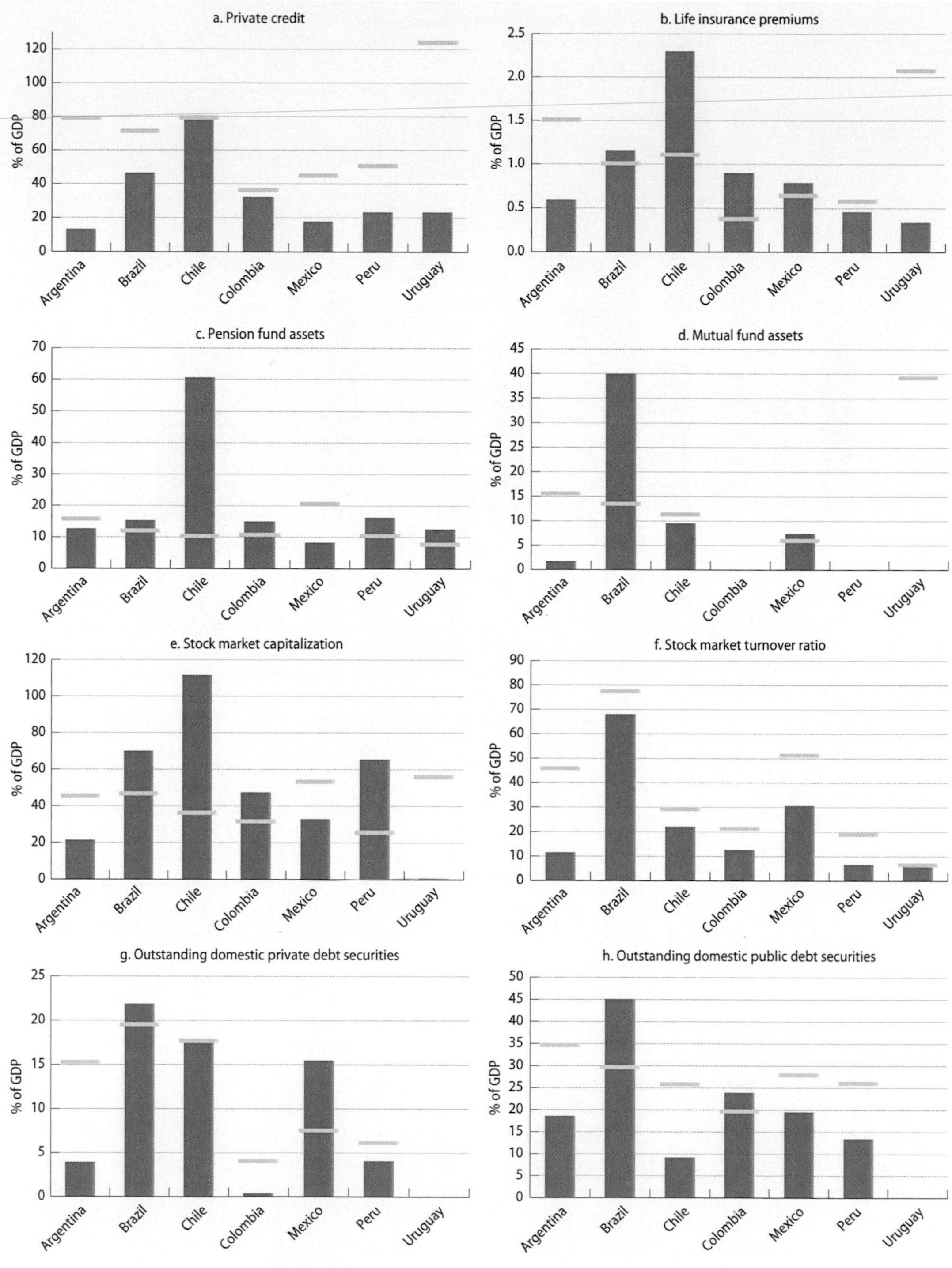

Source: de la Torre, Feyen, and Ize 2011.
Note: This figure shows financial indicators for individual LAC-7 countries against their respective benchmarks (shown as bars).

(figure 3.12, panel b). The number of firms using equity finance on a regular basis is also comparatively small, with only eight firms issuing equity in any given year during the 2000s (figure 3.12, panel c).[11] Moreover, not only do few firms access equity markets on a regular basis, but also the bulk of equity financing is concentrated in few issues. The share of the top five issues has actually increased from 78 percent to 92 percent between the 1990s and the 2000s (figure 3.14, panel a). Lastly, trading in equity markets is also highly concentrated, with the top five firms capturing almost 60 percent of trading (figure 3.14, panel b). Again, there is also wide heterogeneity across the region, with non-LAC-7 countries having generally tiny and illiquid markets—with fewer than 50 listed firms on average and turnover rates below 5 percent of GDP (figure 3.15). In sum, equity markets across the region remain, by and large, small, illiquid, and highly concentrated.

That being said, not all is gloom and doom. Within LAC, the Caribbean and offshore centers show considerably larger and more rapidly increasing market capitalizations (figure 3.16). Within LAC-7, in terms of equity market capitalization, Chile clearly stands out, followed by Peru and Brazil (figure 3.5, panel e). In terms of domestic equity market turnover, except for Uruguay (which just meets its benchmark), all LAC-7 countries fall short of their benchmarks. However, from that group, Brazil is the country that gets closer to meeting it. This relative success is worth noting (see box 3.2). In addition to better governance (boosted by the Novo Mercado), it might reflect the large size and diversity of the private corporate sector and the large size of the mutual fund industry.[12]

The new players

LAC's financial systems have also become more complex from the saver's perspective. While in the past banks captured most of the intermediation between borrowers and lenders, there is now a greater diversity of players, with a broader set of institutions

FIGURE 3.7 Primary bond markets

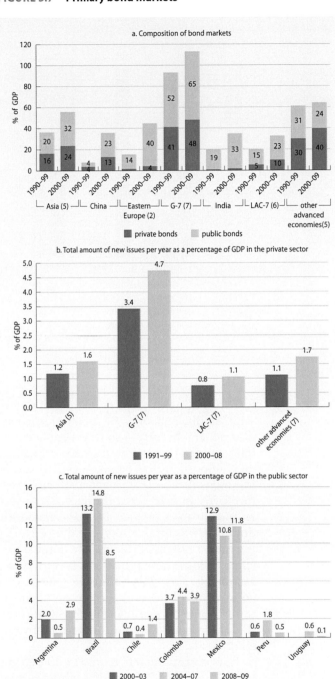

Source: Didier and Schmukler 2011a.
Note: Panel a shows the average size of private and public bonds outstanding in domestic markets as a percentage of GDP between 1990 and 2009. *Domestic bonds* are defined as those issued by residents in domestic currency and targeted at resident investors. Panels b and c show the average yearly amount raised in domestic bond markets as a percentage of GDP. Panel b shows data for the private sector between 1991 and 2008, while panel c shows data for the public sector between 2000 and 2009 for LAC-7 countries. Numbers in parentheses show the number of countries in each region.

FIGURE 3.8   **Domestic bond market turnover**

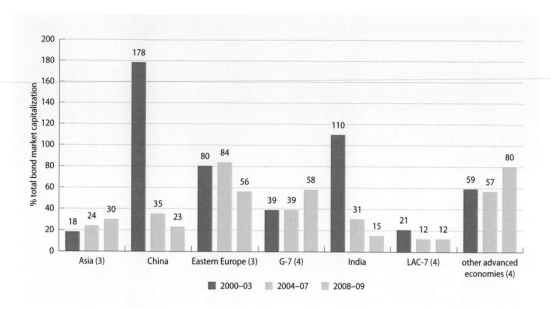

Source: Didier and Schmukler 2011a.
Note: This figure shows the average bond market trading as share of total bond market capitalization between 2000 and 2009. Trading data include domestic private, domestic public, and foreign bonds traded in local stock exchanges. Numbers in parentheses show the number of countries in each region.

intermediating savings, providing economy-wide credit, and offering an ample variety of products. In fact, in some emerging countries, institutional investors have become more important than banks. Given the steady injections they receive from underlying investors, pension funds, mutual funds, and insurance companies provide a stable demand for domestic financial assets and thus have an important potential role to play in the deepening of local capital markets. Nevertheless, as argued below, LAC still has a long way to go in terms of the sophistication of its institutional investors, as most of the savings are still channeled to bank deposits and government bonds.

Pension fund assets represent 20 percent of GDP in LAC-7 countries, while mutual funds and insurance companies represent 10 percent and 6 percent of GDP, respectively (figure 3.17). Compared to their statistical benchmarks, mutual funds and private pension fund assets in the LAC-7 countries are broadly on track; however, insurance company assets are lagging (by close

to 8 percentage points of GDP), and so do life and nonlife insurance company premiums (table 3.2). In LAC, the lags appear to be more severe, with both pension funds and mutual funds also lagging. There is, however, considerable heterogeneity across LAC-7 (and LAC more generally), partly reflecting cross-country differences in the institutional and regulatory environments. Chile has the most developed pension fund system (reaching 70 percent of GDP), while Brazil has the largest mutual fund industry (reaching 42 percent of GDP). When one looks at performance against benchmark, Chile is clearly the star performer as regards pension funds and insurance companies, while Brazil excels as regards mutual funds (figure 3.5). In fact, Brazil is the only LAC country where the size of the mutual funds industry is very large and exceeds its benchmark by an ample margin.

Surprisingly however, institutional investors concentrate a significant fraction of their asset holdings in fixed-income instruments, such as government bonds and deposits,

BOX 3.1 **The bond market in Chile**

The capitalization of the Chilean corporate bond market grew from 13 percent of GDP during the 1990s to 21 percent in the 2000s. Moreover, reflecting fiscal consolidation, the private sector accounts for an increasing share of total outstanding bonds—more than 65 percent in the 2000s. The primary markets for private bonds are highly active, with new bond issues amounting to 3.4 percent of GDP. Moreover, the use of private bonds is growing. In the 1990s, on average, 15 firms issued bonds in local markets in a given year; during the 2000s, this number increased to 63. Concentration is also less of a concern than in other LAC countries. The amount raised by the top five issues during the 2000s was about 30 percent, which is comparable to the G-7 countries (33 percent). Furthermore, firms have been better able to tap into long-term financing, as the average maturity at issuance was 15.2 years, significantly longer than that for other LAC-7 countries or developed countries (with an average maturity of 6.8 years and about 10 years, respectively).[a] These long maturities are generally linked to indexed, high-grade bonds. However, liquidity in secondary markets remains limited.

These developments must be understood in the context of the strong development of institutional investors, mostly pension funds and insurance companies, and, to a lesser extent, mutual funds. These investors, particularly pension funds, provide a stable demand for corporate bonds, given their sheer size (about 65 percent of GDP for pension funds and 20 percent for insurance companies in 2010). Pension funds, for instance, held about 50 percent of the stock of bonds in 2010, and insurance companies held another 32 percent. Because they are such big players, their investment behavior is tightly linked to developments in the corporate bond market. For example, their large size usually induces them to invest large amounts, which limits the potential demand for smaller issues.[b] Moreover, Chilean institutional investors typically pursue buy-and-hold strategies, keeping bonds in their portfolios until maturity, as shown in Opazo, Raddatz, and Schmukler (2009) and Raddatz and Schmukler (2008), which contributes to explaining the low liquidity of secondary private bond markets. In addition, current regulatory restrictions on pension fund investments limit their exposure to noninvestment-grade issues, which helps explain the low fraction of outstanding high-yield corporate bonds. The long maturity of corporate bonds can also be associated with the maturity structure of the liabilities of insurance companies, which allows them to make long-term investments. The nature of their liabilities, mostly indexed to inflation, also implies a significant demand for inflation-linked bonds.

The regulatory changes that took place in the early 2000s also contributed to these developments. In particular, capital market reforms gave pension funds and insurance companies more flexibility in their investments. The consolidation of the macroeconomic and financial frameworks also probably played an important role. Yet, significant challenges remain, including the need to expand access to smaller firms.

a. Bonds with less than one year in maturity (commercial paper mostly) are excluded from these statistics due to data availability.
b. Although large investors do not necessarily make large investments, the data suggest that they typically do so, perhaps reflecting investment practices by institutional investors (Didier, Rigobon, and Schmukler 2011).

thereby limiting their role in the development of corporate bond and equity markets. Thus, pension funds in LAC-7 countries invested on average 32 percent of their portfolios in government bonds in 2009, compared with 40 percent in Eastern Europe, 37 percent in emerging Asia, and only 16 percent in the G-7 countries (figure 3.18, panel a). Nevertheless, the concentration of pension fund portfolios in deposits and government bonds has been slowly declining. There is also significant heterogeneity across LAC-7, with pension funds in some countries heavily invested in government securities (for example, Argentina, Mexico, and Uruguay), while in others, pension funds have a greater share of deposits in their portfolios (for example, Chile and Peru) (figure 3.18, panel c). At the same time, the shares

FIGURE 3.9   **Average maturity of bonds at issuance in local markets**

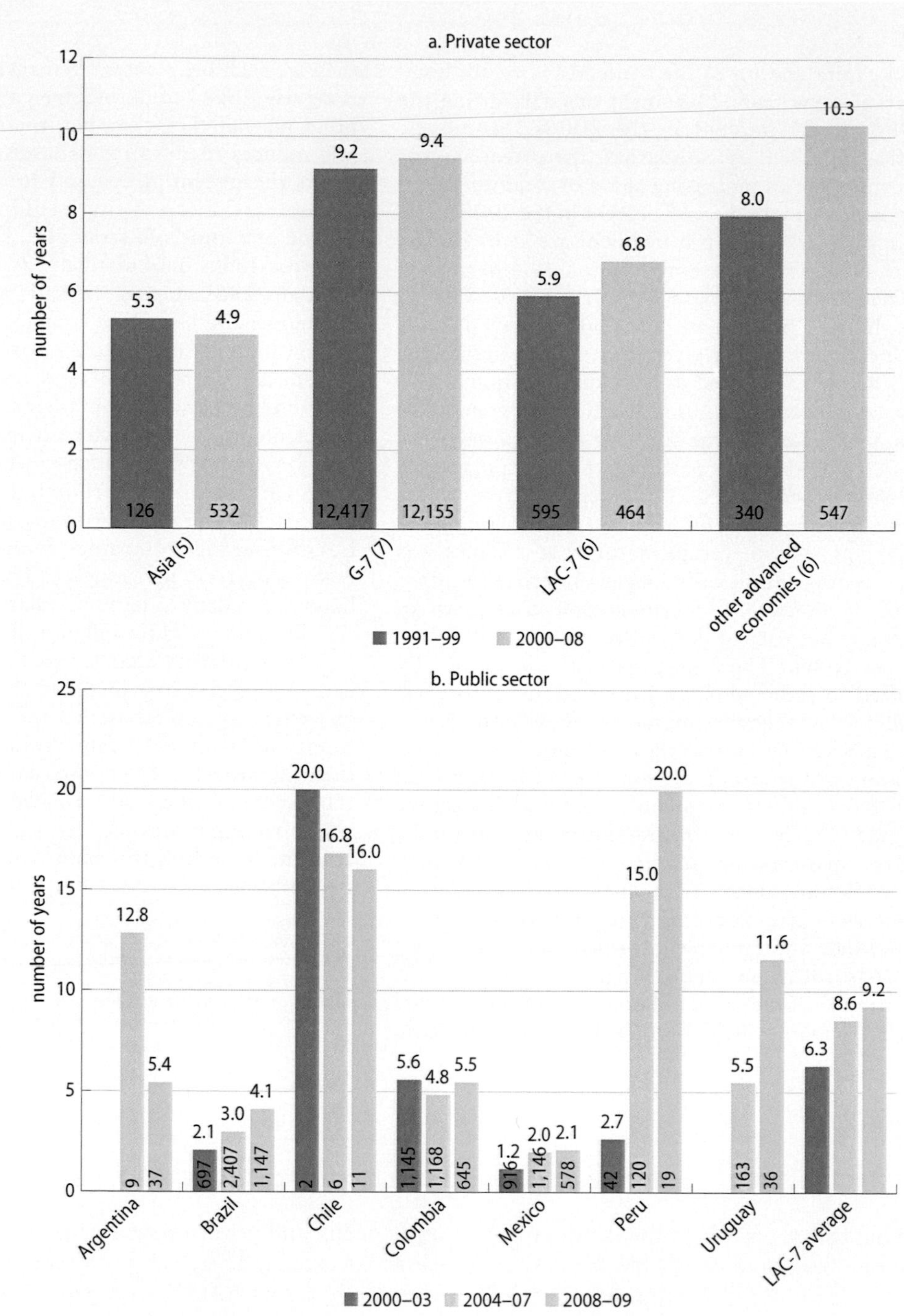

a. Private sector

	Asia (5)	G-7 (7)	LAC-7 (6)	other advanced economies (6)
1991–99	5.3	9.2	5.9	8.0
2000–08	4.9	9.4	6.8	10.3
(n, 1991–99)	126	12,417	595	340
(n, 2000–08)	532	12,155	464	547

■ 1991–99   ■ 2000–08

b. Public sector

	Argentina	Brazil	Chile	Colombia	Mexico	Peru	Uruguay	LAC-7 average
2000–03		2.1	20.0	5.6	1.2	2.7		6.3
2004–07	12.8	3.0	16.8	4.8	2.0	15.0	5.5	8.6
2008–09	5.4	4.1	16.0	5.5	2.1	20.0	11.6	9.2
n (2000–03)	9	697	2	1,145	916	42	163	
n (2004–07)	37	2,407	6	1,168	1,146	120	36	
n (2008–09)		1,147	11	645	578	19		

■ 2000–03   ■ 2004–07   ■ 2008–09

Source: Didier and Schmukler 2011a.
Note: This figure shows the weighted average maturity of bond issuances per year in domestic markets, expressed in years. Panel a shows data for the private sector for the period 1991–2008. Panel b shows data for the public sector for 2000–09. Numbers in the base of the bars represent the total number of issues over the period.

FIGURE 3.10   **Currency composition of bonds at issuance in local markets**

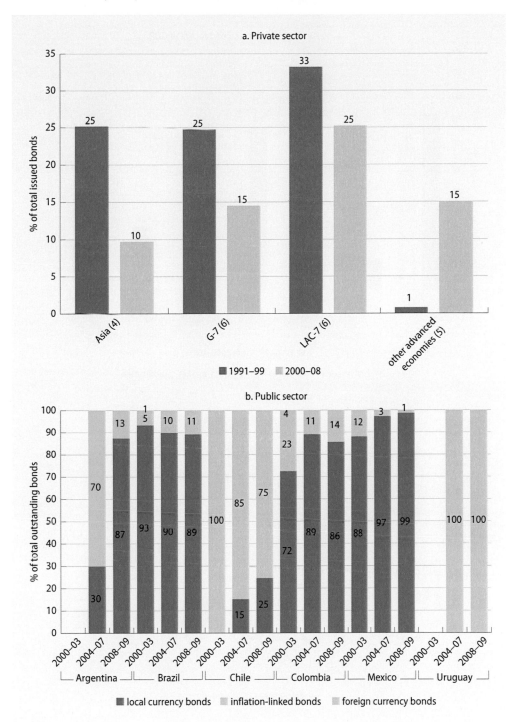

Source: Didier and Schmukler 2011a.

Note: This figure shows the currency composition of domestic private and public bonds at issuance. Panel a shows the average foreign-currency-denominated bonds as a percentage of total bonds issued by the private sector in domestic markets per year between 1991 and 2008. Panel b shows the composition of domestic public bonds issued on average per year (between local currency, foreign currency, and inflation-linked bonds) over the period 2000 and 2009. Numbers in parentheses show the number of countries in each region.

FIGURE 3.11   Equity market size

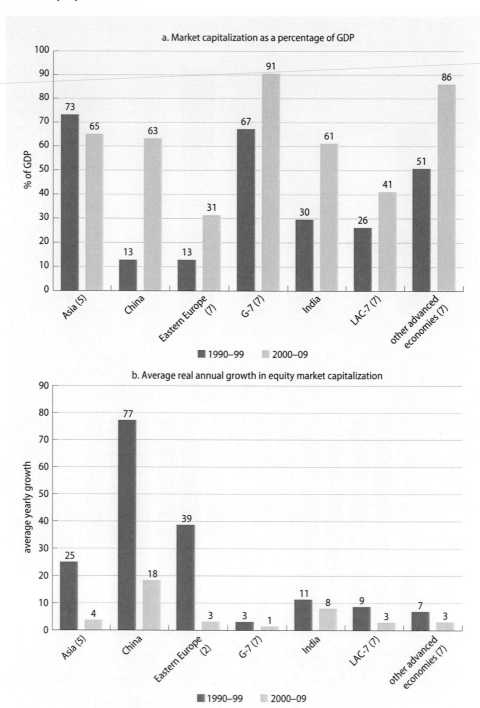

Source: Didier and Schmukler 2011a.
Note: This figure shows in panel a the average market capitalization of domestic equity as a share of GDP between 1990 and 2009. Panel b shows the average annual growth rate in market capitalization of domestic equity between 1990 and 2009. The market capitalization is measured in U.S. dollars and is deflated by local stock market indexes to measure the real growth. Numbers in parentheses show the number of countries in each region.

of equity and foreign securities have been slowly increasing (figure 3.18, panel b).[13]

Comparable patterns are also observed in the portfolios of mutual funds. They invest on average a large fraction of their portfolios in government bonds and money market instruments. However, like pension funds, mutual funds have been gradually shifting their portfolios toward equity investments (figure 3.19). In Brazil, for example, the share of public bonds declined from 73 percent to 48 percent between 2003–04 and 2005–09. In Chile, this fraction declined from 14 percent to 6 percent. However, bank deposits continued to account for a substantial share (63 percent) of the Chilean mutual fund portfolio.

As discussed in greater depth in chapter 8, these trends suggest that the contribution of institutional investors to the development of local markets may not have been as powerful as could have been expected. However, the relatively more successful cases of Brazil and Chile deserve particular attention. In particular, more research is needed to measure the effects that Brazilian mutual funds might have had on the development of Novo Mercado and the Chilean pension funds might have had on the development of primary bond corporate markets.

Finally, private equity and venture capital (PEVC) funds are also becoming significant players in LAC. These funds are particularly important for financing small and medium enterprises (SMEs). Due to limited data availability, only a glimpse of their relative roles can be seen. Unsurprisingly, PEVC funds are still relatively underdeveloped in emerging economies, and particularly so in LAC. Private equity funds raised on average US$4.9 billion per year in LAC, as against almost US$46.0 billion in Asia.[14] Venture capital funds are even less representative, with a total of US$12.0 billion per year raised on average outside the United States and Europe. Nonetheless, although small, PEVC funds have been growing rapidly, particularly in LAC. In the first half of the 2000s, PEVC funds raised US$1.2 billion on average in LAC, and in the second half of the decade, they raised US$7.7 billion. Continued growth will

FIGURE 3.12 Equity markets

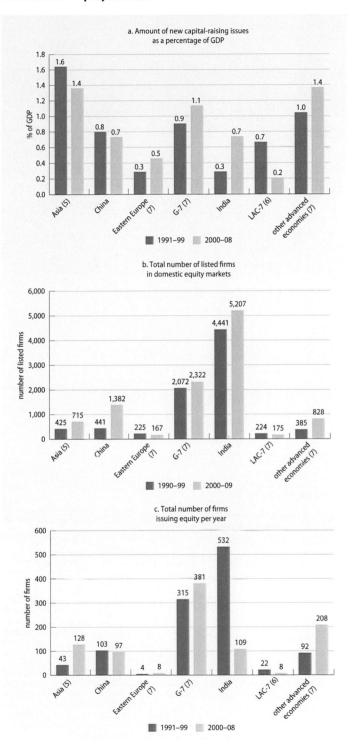

Source: Didier and Schmukler 2011a.
Panel a shows the average amount of capital-raising equity issues as a percent of GDP between 1991 and 2008. Panel b shows the average number of listed firms between 1990 and 2009. Panel c shows the total number of firms issuing equity per year between 1990 and 2009. Numbers in parentheses show the number of countries in each region.

FIGURE 3.13   Stock market turnover relative to global benchmarks

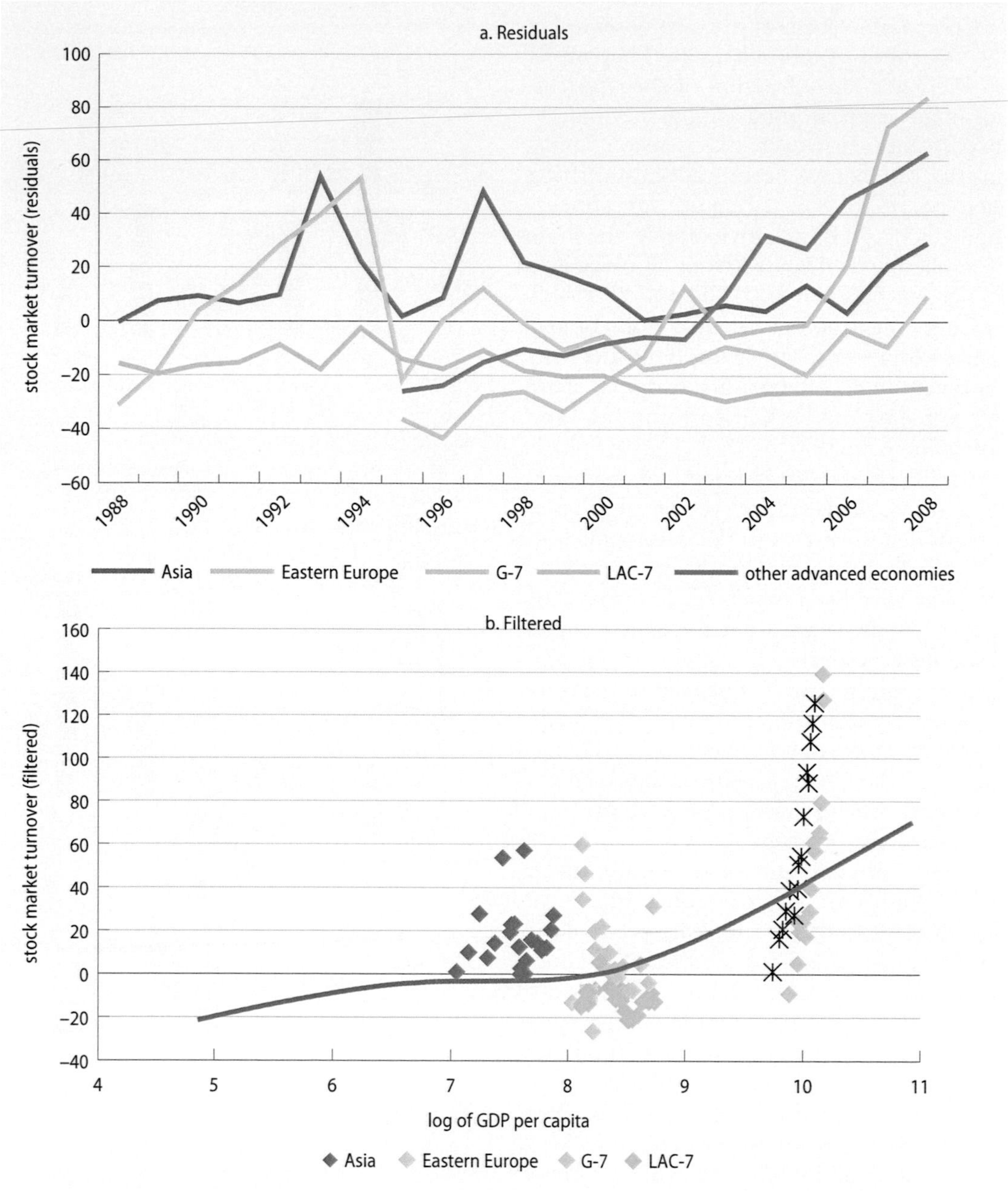

Source: de la Torre, Feyen, and Ize 2011.
Note: This figure shows stock market turnover across country groups relative to their global benchmarks. Panel a shows the evolution of annual median residuals by country group. First, a cross-sectional regression model is estimated on country averages, controlling for GDP per capita, population size and density, young and old-age dependency ratios, a financial offshore center dummy, a transition country dummy, and a large fuel exporter dummy. Annual country residuals are derived from the cross-sectional estimates, which are used to calculate annual country-group medians. Panel b plots annual country-group medians of the filtered variable against the logarithm of GDP per capita. The filtering consists of removing from the actual annual country observations the expected contributions of all factors except GDP per capita, using the cross-sectional estimates from the model. A four-knot spline approach is used to account for nonlinearities of GDP per capita in the cross-sectional regression.

FIGURE 3.14   Concentration in equity markets

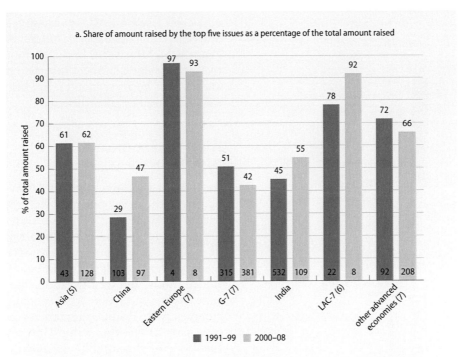

a. Share of amount raised by the top five issues as a percentage of the total amount raised

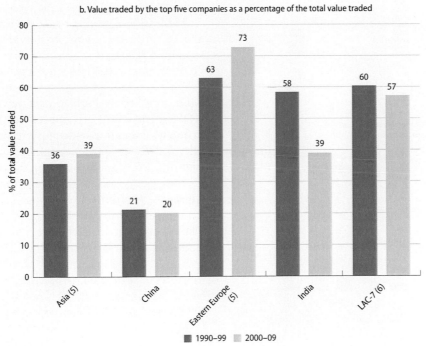

b. Value traded by the top five companies as a percentage of the total value traded

Source: Didier and Schmukler 2011a.
Note: This figure shows the concentration in equity market activity. Panel a shows the average amount raised per year by the top five issues as a share of total issues between 1991 and 2008. Numbers in the base of the bars represent the average number of issues per year. Panel b shows the average share of value traded by the top five companies as share of the total value traded per year between 1990 and 2009. Numbers in parentheses show the number of countries in each region.

FIGURE 3.15   Within LAC: Trading activity and number of listed firms in domestic equity markets

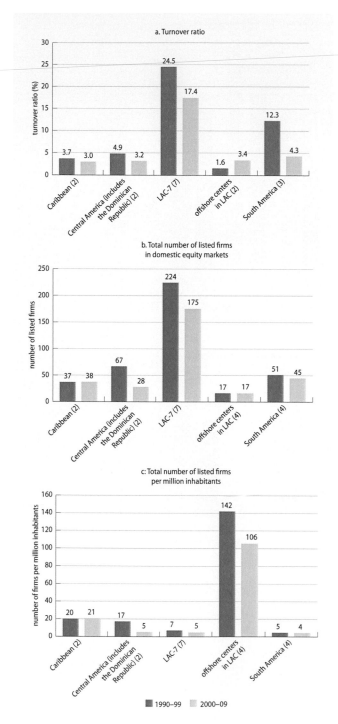

Source: Didier and Schmukler 2011a.
Note: Panel a shows average turnover ratio across LAC, defined as the total value traded per year in domestic markets over total market capitalization between 1990 and 2009. Panels b and c show, respectively, the average number of listed firms and expressed per million inhabitants across LAC between 1990 and 2009. Numbers in parentheses show the number of countries in each region.

require adequate regulation and rigorous disclosure standards. The latter is perceived as a particular issue in LAC, as accessing accurate and objective information for nonpublic firms is not straightforward. In this context, effective ex ante due diligence, valuation analysis, and ex post business monitoring, key for this industry, can be rather difficult.

Alternative markets and products

As part of a global trend, LAC countries have seen the development of less traditional forms of financing. This section briefly reviews some of the most important ones: derivatives, factoring, cooperatives and credit unions, retailers' financing, exchange traded funds, and securitization. These illustrate that financial activity is becoming more complex, with traditional markets capturing only part of the financing. Unfortunately, the scope of this analysis is constrained by data availability.

Trading in exchange rate derivatives has grown in dollar terms, but it has actually remained relatively stable as a percentage of GDP in most countries since the late 1990s. Trading in interest rate contracts, on the other hand, more than doubled as a percentage of GDP in the 2000s compared to the 1990s in most emerging regions, with a growth rate of 213 percent among LAC-7 countries (figure 3.20, panels a and b). Nevertheless, derivatives overall are relatively illiquid, with aggregate trading representing only a small fraction of trading in developed countries. Thus, turnover in exchange rate contracts stands at about 1.1 percent of GDP in LAC countries, compared with 7.3 percent of GDP in the G-7 countries. Moreover, trading on foreign exchange contracts is nearly exclusively (98 percent) in U.S. dollar contracts.

Factoring is another example of a rapidly expanding industry.[15] This expansion has taken place mostly in emerging economies, including in LAC-7 where factoring amounted to 2.6 percent of GDP in 2008–09 (figure 3.20, panel c). Chile and Mexico provide examples of particularly fast

FIGURE 3.16   **Equity market capitalization as a percentage of GDP, within LAC**

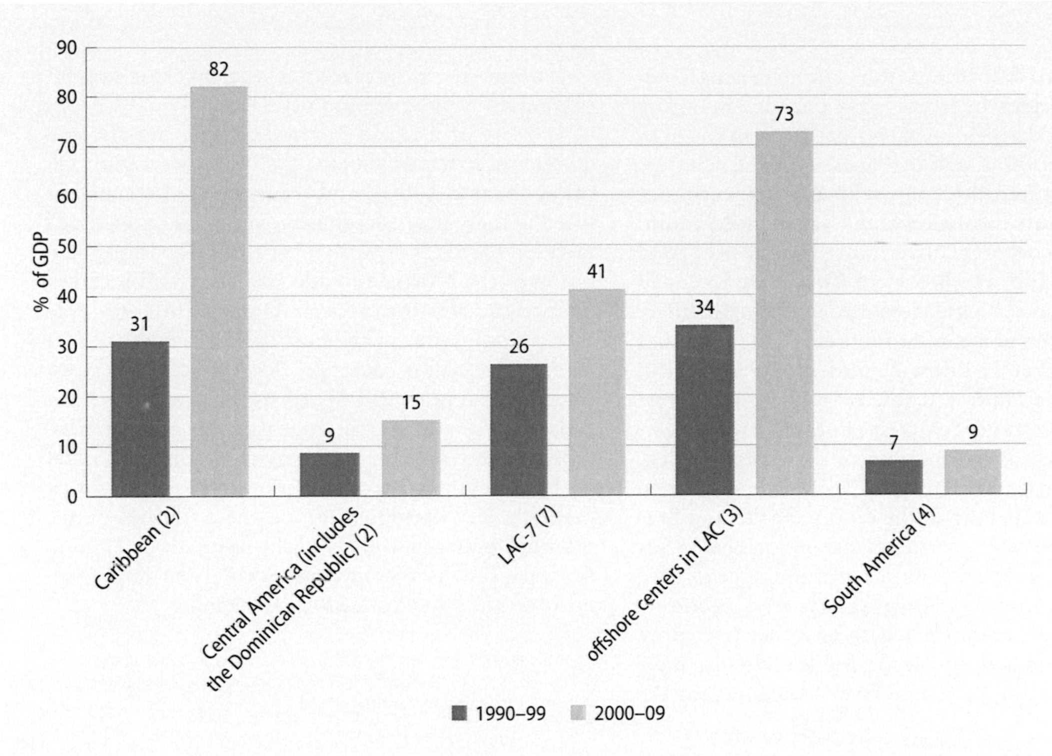

Source: Didier and Schmukler 2011a.
Note: This figure shows equity market capitalization as a percentage of GDP between 1990 and 2009 across LAC. Numbers in parentheses show the number of countries in each region.

development. In these countries, invoices can actually be traded on organized exchanges or online markets. Factoring in Chile is one of the largest among emerging economies, with an accumulated volume of 12 billion euros in 2009 (10.7 percent of GDP) and about 14,000 users.[16] Factoring in Mexico also represents an important market, with total industry turnover estimated at almost 11 billion euros in 2007 (almost 2 percent of GDP). In 2001, the Mexican development bank NAFIN (Nacional Financiera) created an online market for factoring services called Cadenas Productivas (productive chains), which is proving to be quite successful.[17] This reverse factoring program is relatively large, having extended US$11.8 billion in financing in 2008, which represents a significant share of the factoring market in Mexico.[18]

Credit by retailers (mainly department stores) is another interesting case of direct competition to banks. It is rising rapidly in LAC, with Chile as a particularly notable example. The largest department stores have become nontrivial providers of household credit in recent years. Although banks are still the main external financing source for Chilean households, representing 68 percent of the total household financial debt, household credit by retailers accounts for 11 percent of total household financial debt, 17 percent of total consumer debt, and 35 percent of nonbank debt (figure 3.21, panel b).[19] The model has been so successful that Chilean retailers are exporting it to other countries in LAC. Financial cooperatives and credit unions present another alternative to bank financing.[20] However, loans from these institutions generally account for only a small

---

BOX 3.2   The equity market in Brazil

The equity market in Brazil has gone through significant changes over the past decade, bringing clear improvements in corporate governance. In December 2000, the São Paulo Stock Exchange (Bovespa) created three new corporate governance listing segments through which issuers could voluntarily adopt corporate governance practices beyond those required by the Brazilian Corporate Law and by capital market regulation more generally. Bovespa listing segments now include the traditional Bovespa, Level 1, Level 2, and Novo Mercado. Each of these market segments requires progressively stricter standards of corporate governance.[a] The main goal of the creation of these distinct segments, and in particular of Novo Mercado, was to reverse the weakening of the equity markets in Brazil that had been occurring at the end of the 1990s by fostering good corporate governance practices, such as disclosure, transparency, and accountability. In fact, equity markets have become more liquid and less concentrated, and more firms have been issuing equities. These trends suggest that the

improvements in governance and investor protection might well have paid off.

In spite of a timid beginning, due mostly to a number of external shocks, the Novo Mercado took off by the mid-2000s, and the number of companies listed in these new corporate governance segments of Bovespa has risen steadily over time. The implementation of the Novo Mercado has been well received by foreign investors, as well. During 2004–06, foreign participation in the corporate governance segments captured, on average, 70 percent of the stock offerings. Santana (2008) argues that the Novo Mercado has allowed Brazilian companies and, particularly, new entrant companies to access foreign capital without having to cross-list on international stock markets. For example, among the 27 initial public offerings between 2004 and the first half of 2006 in Bovespa, only two companies were listed simultaneously on the New York Stock Exchange.

a. See Didier and Schmukler (2011a) for a more detailed analysis. A description of the rules governing these different segments is available at Bovespa's website (http://www.bmfbovespa.com.br).

---

fraction of the total. In the LAC-7 countries, they are even smaller than in other emerging economies, accounting for only 0.7 percent of GDP against 2.0 percent in Asia and 1.7 percent in India (figure 3.21, panel a).

Another product currently experiencing fast development is exchange-traded funds (ETFs). ETFs are traded portfolios composed of not only stocks, but also commodities and bonds. They facilitate portfolio diversification and possess stocklike features (such as transparency and frequent pricing as well as ease of trading), and they have low trading costs. ETFs have been growing considerably in developed and emerging countries alike over the past few years. In LAC, these products have been on the rise in countries like Mexico. ETFs are also gaining ground in secondary markets, with an increasing share of total trading in stock markets (figure 3.21, panel c).

Finally, securitization has been on the rise as well. Structured finance grew very fast in developed countries over the last decade, the United States being the leading market.[21] However, the global financial crisis in 2008 dealt a blow to structured finance, and worldwide net issuance fell from about US$2 trillion in 2007 to less than US$400 billion.[22] Since then, it has been slowly regaining ground, reaching almost US$750 billion in 2010 (still much below precrisis levels). Across LAC, primary market securitization activity has risen over the past decade. Thus, securitized instruments have shown signs of increasing depth on different asset classes, particularly in Brazil and Mexico. Gross issuance for LAC countries as a whole rose from US$2.0 billion in 2000 to US$24.4 billion in 2010, with Mexico and Brazil the largest issuers. Although some of these issues were cross-border—typically

FIGURE 3.17   Pension fund, mutual fund, and insurance company assets

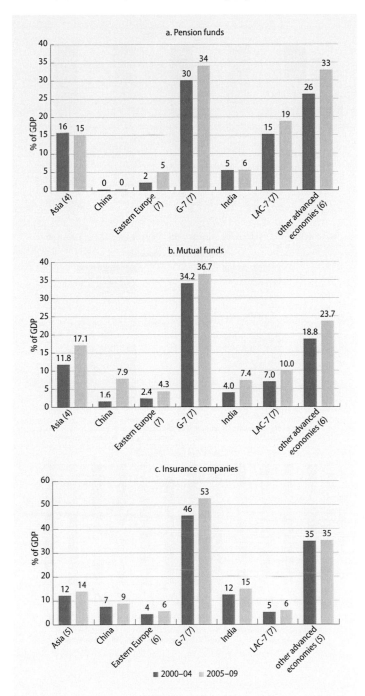

Source: Didier and Schmukler 2011a.
Note: This figure shows the total assets of domestic institutional investors—namely pension funds (panel a), mutual funds (panel b), and insurance companies (panel c). Panel a shows average pension fund assets as a percentage of GDP between 2000 and 2009. Panel b shows average mutual fund assets as a percentage of GDP between 2000 and 2009. Panel c shows average insurance companies assets as a percentage of GDP between 2000 and 2009. Numbers in parentheses show the number of countries in each region.

FIGURE 3.18   **Composition of pension fund portfolios**

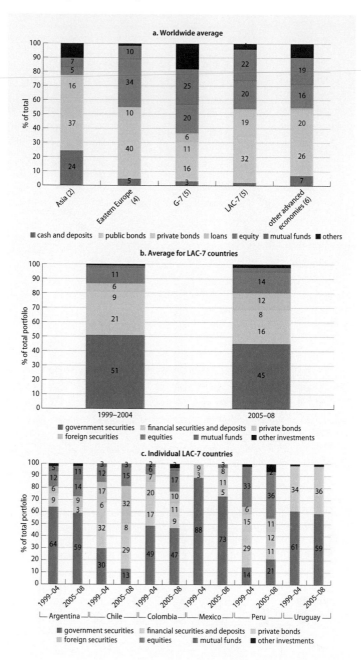

Source: Didier and Schmukler 2011a.
Note: This figure shows in panel a the most recent composition of pension funds portfolio holdings for the latest available information, 2009 mostly. Panel b shows the average composition of pension fund investments as share of the total portfolio between 1999 and 2008 for LAC-7 countries, excluding Brazil. Panel c shows the data for individual countries.

FIGURE 3.19   **Mutual fund portfolio holdings**

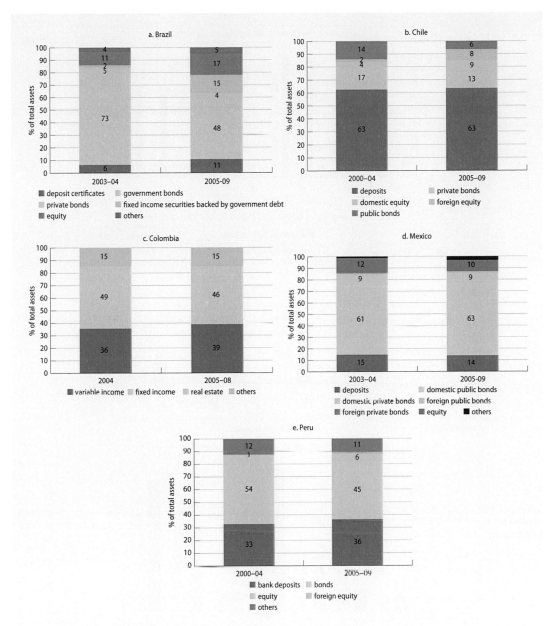

Source: Didier and Schmukler 2011a.
Note: This figure shows the composition of the mutual funds portfolios in LAC-5 countries. For Peru, *fondos mutuos* and *fondos de inversiones* are considered. Equity includes *acciones de capital* and *acciones de inversión* for *fondos mutuos.* In the case of investment funds, equities are composed of *acciones de capital, fondos de inversión,* and *otras participaciones* until 2002, and *derechos de participación patrimonial* from 2004 onward. In the case of Colombia, *fondos vigilados* and *fondos controlados* are reported in different tables for 2002. Period averages are calculated using simple averages.

FIGURE 3.20   **Derivative and factoring markets**

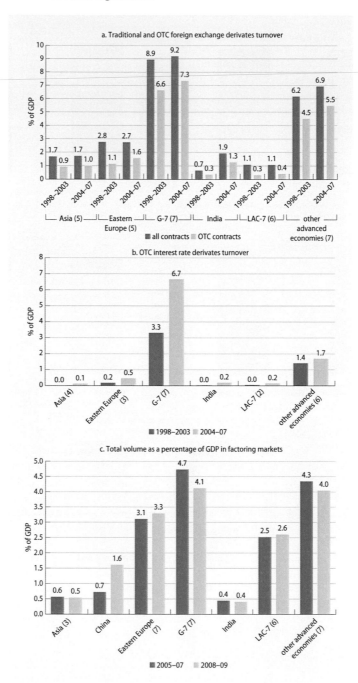

Source: Didier and Schmukler 2011a.
Note: Panel a shows the average annual foreign exchange derivates turnover as a percentage of GDP between 1998 and 2007. Panel b shows the average annual OTC interest rate derivates turnover as a percentage of GDP between 1998 and 2007. Panel c shows the average yearly turnover as a percentage of GDP in factoring markets between 2005 and 2009. Numbers in parentheses show the number of countries in each region.

FIGURE 3.21   Financial cooperatives, credit unions, and exchange-traded funds

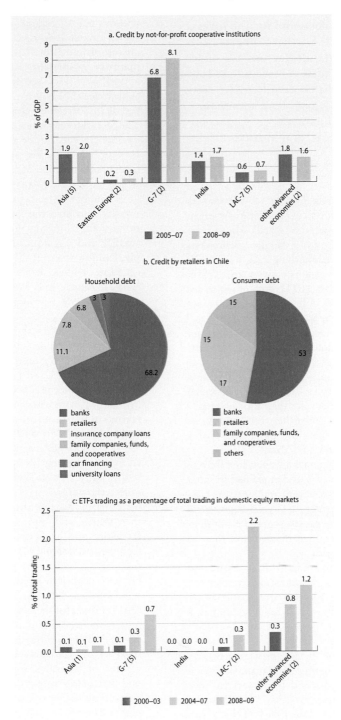

Source: Didier and Schmukler 2011a.
Note: Panel a shows the average amount of credit provided by not-for-profit cooperative institutions as a percentage of GDP between 2005 and 2009. Panel b shows credit by retailers in Chile in December 2008. Panel c shows the average ETF value trading per year as a share of total trading in domestic equity market between 2000 and 2009. The share in each country is also reported on top of the bars. Numbers in parentheses show the number of countries in each region.

between US$2 billion and US$4 billion over the past five years and mostly on futures—domestic issuance accounts for the largest share of the market. Furthermore, securitization has also expanded across a broader set of asset classes, such as new and used car loans, consumer loans, credit card receivables, equipment leases, and mortgages. This broadening of asset classes is particularly apparent in Brazil and Mexico.

Notes

1. This chapter draws heavily on the papers "Financial Development in Latin America: Stylized Facts and the Road Ahead" by Tatiana Didier and Sergio Schmukler (2011a) and "Benchmarking LAC's Financial Development" by Augusto de la Torre, Erik Feyen, and Alain Ize (2011), both of which are part of the Edited Volume that accompanies this LAC flagship report.

2. Throughout this report, the LAC-7 group comprises Argentina, Brazil, Chile, Colombia, Mexico, Peru, and Uruguay. We include Uruguay but exclude República Bolivariana de Venezuela, mainly because there is much more data for the former than for the latter.

3. However, results for other LAC countries should be taken with caution because of a general lack of data availability.

4. The statistical benchmarking analysis is the one presented in chapter 2 and explained in more detail in de la Torre, Feyen, and Ize (2011).

5. In fact, as documented in chapter 2, financial development in the most advanced economies has generally expanded much faster than in the rest of the world.

6. This simple addition of bank assets with bond and equity market capitalization entails some double counting; for example, bank assets likely include some bond holdings and perhaps even equities.

7. Such development likely comes from the improvement in monetary management and a shift toward floating rate regimes, which induced both banks and borrowers to limit their currency mismatches. See Ilyina, Guscina, and Kamil (2010) and the note by Levy-Yeyati (2011a) in the companion Edited Volume.

8. Market capitalization of corporate bonds in Brazil has grown from 12 percent of GDP in 2004 to almost 29 percent in 2009. See Didier and Schmukler (2011a) for a more detailed characterization of corporate bond markets within the LAC region.

9. As with bank debt, LAC countries have made an important effort to reduce currency and maturity mismatches so as to limit credit and rollover risks. See Broner, Lorenzoni, and Schmukler (2011).

10. See de la Torre and Schmukler (2004).

11. The fact that only a restricted set of firms uses capital markets can be at least in part driven by supply factors. For instance, the restricted investment practice of institutional investors is one possible explanation. As documented in a number of papers, institutional investors tend to invest in larger and more liquid firms, hence limiting the supply of funds to smaller and less liquid firms. See, for example, Dahlquist and Robertsson (2001); Didier (2011a); Didier, Rigobon, and Schmukler (2011); Edison and Warnock (2004); Kang and Stulz (1997); among many others.

12. La Porta et al. (1997) and Glaser, Johnson, and Shleifer (2001) show that protection of minority shareholders is fundamental to the development of a country's capital market. In addition, Klapper and Love (2004) show that good governance practices are more important in countries with weak investor protection and inefficient enforcement. According to Shleifer and Vishny (1997a) and Bhojraj and Sengupta (2003), good governance practices increase confidence among investors as they tend to reduce agency risks. Therefore, companies can access the capital market at lower costs and better terms, increase the value and liquidity of their shares, and improve their operating performance and profitability. Ashbaugh-Skaife, Collins, and LaFond (2006), for example, find that better corporate governance practices improve corporate credit ratings and reduce bond yields. De Carvalho and Pennacchi (2011) argue, for the case of Brazil, that migration from traditional markets to the Novo Mercado brings positive abnormal returns to shareholders and an increase in the trading volume of shares. Klapper and Love (2004) find that better corporate governance is associated with higher operating performance and higher Tobin's Q. Joh (2003) concludes that firms with higher control-ownership disparity exhibit lower profitability. Gozzi, Levine, and Schmukler (2010), however, argue that the causality might go both ways and that better

firms go to better corporate governance environments, not that better governance necessarily increases firm value.

13. The differences between panels a and b are due to three factors. First, the reporting periods are different. Second, the country groupings differ in that the Organisation for Economic Co-operation and Development (OECD) data in panel a exclude Argentina and Uruguay, and country data in panel b exclude Brazil because of a lack of disaggregation in its statistics. Third, the sources differ in their classification of foreign securities, which are not reported as a separate category in the OECD data.

14. These statistics are from Preqin, the industry's leading source of information where country-level information is not available. Note that Preqin's designations of countries within regions are different from those used in this chapter.

15. Factoring is a financial transaction where accounts receivables (that is, invoices) are sold at a discount to a third party. See Klapper (2006) and de la Torre, Gozzi, and Schmukler (2007b) for a detailed discussion of factoring per se as well as case studies.

16. Launched in 2005 as an alternative to bank factoring, the exchange Bolsa de Productos has been growing fast and might become an important source of SME financing in the near future. This exchange allows some form of reverse factoring, where invoices can be discounted and where the credit risk borne by the investor is that from the issuers of the invoice. Moreover, no collateral is needed from SMEs posting the invoice. Keys to the success of this initiative are that discounting invoices in Bolsa de Productos is cheaper than factoring through banks and that it provides investors with a higher yield than they can get in money markets.

17. See de la Torre, Gozzi, and Schmukler 2007a. This market "spearheaded" by NAFIN provides reverse factoring services to SMEs through the creation of chains between large buyers and their suppliers. All transactions are carried out on an electronic platform, which allows NAFIN to capture economies of scale, since most of the costs of the system are fixed and electronic access enables a large number of firms and financial institutions to participate.

18. The program has been so successful that NAFIN has entered into agreements with development banks in several Latin American countries, including Colombia, El Salvador, and República Bolivariano de Venezuela, to implement similar programs, while other development banks in the region are also considering replicating this model.

19. This high penetration of the retail sector in Chile has been related to the introduction of in-house credit cards. These credit cards issued by department stores became popular in Chile because they offered consumer credit, especially to the middle-income segment of the population, when the bank credit market to this segment was still incipient.

20. Financial cooperatives and credit unions are typically financial institutions owned and controlled by their members and operated with the purpose of providing credit and other financial services to them. Hence, they aim mostly at credit provision to households as well as micro-, small, and medium enterprises, either formal or informal. They vary significantly in size, ranging from small cooperatives with few members to others comparable in size to commercial banks.

21. Structured finance is, in its simplest form, a process where assets are pooled and transferred to a third party, commonly referred to as a special purpose vehicle (SPV), which in turn issues securities backed by this asset pool. In other words, structured finance transactions can help to convert illiquid assets into tradable securities. Typically, several classes of securities (called tranches) with distinct risk-return profiles are issued.

22. Net issuance includes issues sold into the market and excludes issues retained by issuing banks, while gross issuance includes those retained issues.

Financial Globalization: Where Does LAC Stand? 4

As countries become more integrated with one another (a trend that Latin America and the Caribbean (LAC) has embraced wholeheartedly), a comprehensive view of financial development requires looking not only at domestic financial activity but also at financial globalization.[1] This chapter explores two dimensions of financial globalization. The first is financial diversification, that is, diversifying portfolios by including foreign assets (or liabilities). The second is financial offshoring, that is, the use of more efficient foreign jurisdictions to conduct financial transactions. The chapter's main findings are as follows:

- While LAC's financial diversification has continued to rise, financial offshoring (which increased significantly in the 1990s) has not grown much over the past decade.
- However, valuation effects, in particular for equity investments, have been the main drivers of the increase in financial diversification.
- The growing international financial diversification has been accompanied by a changing portfolio composition (more reserve assets, less debt liabilities, and more equity liabilities), which has made globalization much safer.
- In contrast with other emerging economies, LAC's equity liabilities continue to be dominated by foreign direct investment (FDI) rather than by portfolio equity, which is consistent with the shortcomings of the local equity markets.
- The offshore issuance and trading of LAC-7 firms' equity has increased strongly, relative to onshore, which heightens concerns of market access for the smaller firms.
- Public sector bond financing has shifted toward domestic markets and away from foreign markets, reflecting countries' desire to reduce their dollar exposure and to develop their local currency public debt markets.
- While LAC countries have made significant progress toward issuing local currency bonds abroad, they still have a long way to go.
- Corporate bond financing abroad has experienced gains in maturity similar to bond financing at home, although only a few large firms have access to local bond markets, and even fewer have access to foreign bond markets.

The first section briefly describes the two dimensions of financial globalization. The second section analyzes the extent and implications of financial diversification. The third and last section explores financial offshoring, first of bonds and syndicated debt, then of equity.

The two dimensions of financial globalization

The financial diversification dimension of financial globalization is macroeconomic in essence. It relates to a country's capital flows and aggregate gross foreign positions in assets and liabilities. Domestic residents invest (or borrow) abroad, and foreigners invest locally, because this allows risk to be diversified more effectively (and returns to be equalized) across borders and instruments. In addition to enhancing the efficiency of resource allocation, the increased participation of foreign investors can also benefit local market development.[2] It can enhance liquidity, boost research, improve the quantity and quality of information available, and, more generally, increase transparency and promote the adoption of better corporate governance practices, thereby reducing agency problems.[3] This process can also have downsides, however. In particular, shocks that affect foreign investors (that is, changes in risk appetite that result in capital flow volatility) can also affect negatively the local economies through volatility and amplification effects.[4] Moreover, because foreigners tend to provide financing in foreign currency, this can lead to currency mismatches. Similarly, while domestic residents' investment abroad can help smooth their consumption and, hence, home outputs, such investments may also reflect capital flight caused by deteriorating conditions at home (risks of devaluation, default, and expropriation) that, other things being equal, can reduce the capital available for domestic financing.[5]

Instead, the offshoring dimension of financial globalization is mainly microeconomic in essence. It relates to the use of offshore (rather than onshore) markets or intermediaries by local residents for efficiency rather than for risk-diversification purposes. Thus, instead of listing a stock locally, a firm might prefer to list it on a foreign exchange, because the offshore market might be deeper and more liquid. Or, instead of opening a deposit account in a local bank, an individual might prefer to open it at an offshore bank, because it may provide better service for offshore payments. In either case, although the financial services provided offshore may be similar to those provided locally, they also may be cheaper or may have specific features that make them preferable for specific transactions. Clearly, when measuring the extent of local residents' financial activity, one needs to consider the activities conducted abroad to grasp the full extent of market depth.

However, one must also take into account the substitutability or complementarity of domestic and foreign activity.[6] For instance, when stock trading takes place in international markets, domestic activity might actually migrate abroad, with agents substituting foreign markets for domestic ones. This is not innocuous, because not all firms may have access to international markets. Thus, domestic exchanges might become illiquid after large firms go abroad.[7] As the smaller firms remain constrained to local financing sources, such a migration can reduce not only the liquidity of remaining firms in local markets, but also their ability to raise capital, jeopardizing the sustainability of domestic capital markets. At the same time, domestic and offshore markets may complement each other because, for example, they offer different financing choices; thus, foreign bond markets might be typically used for assets denominated in foreign currency, whereas domestic markets might be used for both domestic and foreign currency bonds.

Financial diversification

The financial diversification dimension of financial globalization was measured in this study based on the widely used de facto measures compiled by Lane and Milesi-Ferretti (2007), which are based on stocks (the stock of foreign assets and liabilities) as well as flows (gross capital flows by domestic and foreign residents).[8] The raw stock measures suggest increasing diversification, with LAC-7's integration comparable to that of other emerging economies (figure 4.1, panel a).

While Central and South America exhibit similar levels to LAC-7, the Caribbean countries are somewhat more integrated, largely reflecting their smaller size (figure 4.2, panel a). Controlling for GDP and

FIGURE 4.1   **Foreign assets and liabilities and gross capital flows**

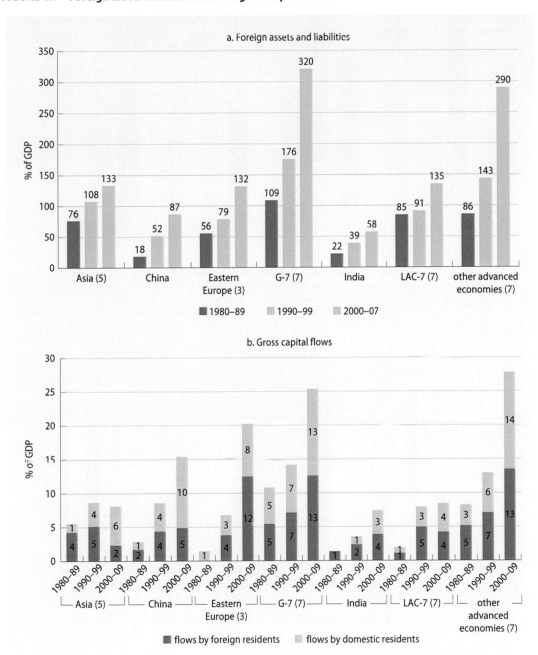

Sources: Authors' calculations based on Lane and Milesi-Ferretti 2007 and Didier and Schmukler 2011b.
Note: Panel a shows the foreign assets and liabilities as a percentage of GDP between 1980 and 2007. Panel b shows the flow by foreign and domestic residents as a percentage of GDP between 1980 and 2009. Numbers in parentheses show the number of countries in each region.

FIGURE 4.2   Within LAC: Foreign assets and liabilities and gross capital flows

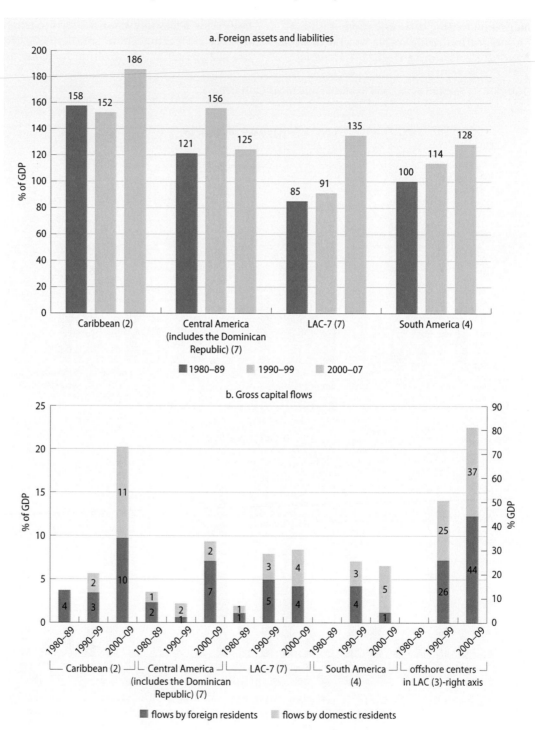

Sources: Authors' calculations based on Lane and Milesi-Ferretti 2007 and Didier and Schmukler 2011b.
Note: Panel a shows the foreign assets and liabilities as a percentage of GDP between 1980 and 2007 across LAC. Panel b shows the flow by foreign and domestic residents as a percentage of GDP between 1980 and 2009 across LAC. Numbers in parentheses show the number of countries in each region.

country structural characteristics using the same statistical benchmarking model as the one described in previous chapters, LAC-7's financial diversification (measured as gross equity and debt assets and liabilities) is close to benchmark (table 3.2).

However, as with market capitalization in chapter 3, the expansion of financial diversification also reflects large valuation effects.[9] When one incorporates these effects by scaling the foreign holdings of domestic equity by market capitalization (instead of by GDP), the change in cross-border holdings between 1999 and 2007 turns negative for LAC, in contrast with other emerging economies, where the change is positive (figure 4.3). This suggests that the often-cited increase in LAC cross-border equity liabilities, rather than a proactive relocation of international capital, has largely mirrored the growing depth of

local equity markets, which, in turn, have been boosted more by price increases prior to the crisis than by new (primary) issuance. The flow measures confirm that capital flows by domestic and foreign agents in the LAC-7 countries have remained relatively constant and moderate over the last decade (figure 4.1b). However, this pattern has not been uniform across LAC, as the Caribbean countries and offshore centers have experienced a strong increase in both inflows and outflows (figure 4.2b).

While de facto measures suggest that financial diversification across LAC-7 countries has been relatively stagnant over the past decade, a de jure index that measures the degree of capital account openness shows that financial globalization has been on the rise over the past 20 years, although it stabilized at a high level about 2004 (figure 4.4a).

FIGURE 4.3 **Valuation effects**

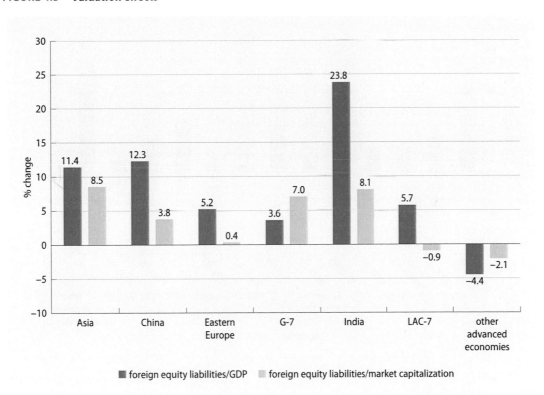

foreign equity liabilities/GDP   foreign equity liabilities/market capitalization

Source: Authors' calculations based on Lane and Milesi-Ferretti 2007.

FIGURE 4.4   De jure and de facto financial globalization measures

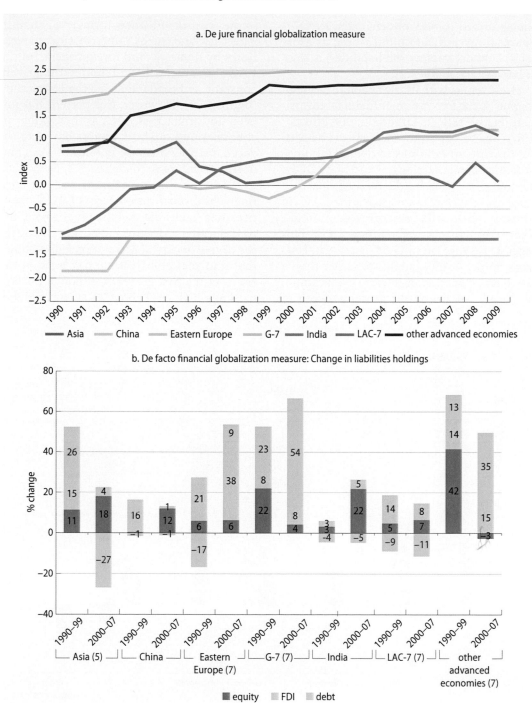

(continued next page)

FIGURE 4.4 **(continued)**

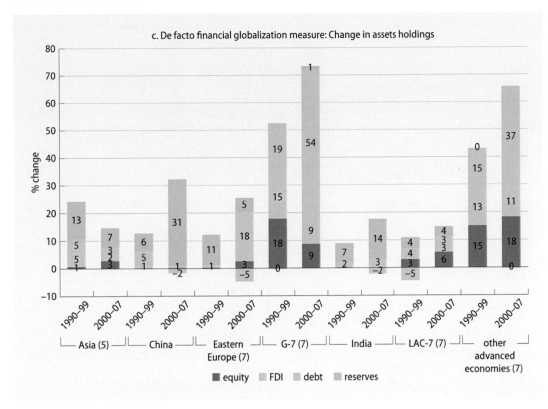

Sources: Authors' calculations based on Lane and Milesi-Ferretti 2007 and Chinn and Ito 2008.
Note: This figure shows in panel a the evolution of a de jure financial globalization measure. Panels b and c show the percentage change of de facto financial globalization measures for the 1990–99 and 2000–07 periods. Panel b shows changes in liabilities holdings over GDP. Panel c shows changes in assets holdings over GDP.

It also shows that, since the late 1990s, LAC countries are the most integrated emerging region, followed closely by Eastern European economies during most of the 2000s, and significantly ahead of Asian economies, including China and India.

When focusing on the change of external liabilities (measuring the investments of foreigners in domestic economies as a share of GDP), LAC-7 portfolio equity and debt positions have been on the rise. While FDI has declined, it still represents an important share of the liabilities (figure 4.4b). The fact that financial diversification in LAC-7 is still largely based on FDI, rather than on investment in portfolio equity, stands in sharp contrast with other emerging economies (except for Eastern Europe), where portfolio equity inflows have been much higher and often

have risen further during the past decade. This is consistent with LAC-7's less dynamic equity markets (see chapter 7).

On the asset side (measuring the investments of domestic agents abroad), bank and equity investments have been the fastest growing components of outflows when measured as a share of GDP (figure 4.4c). In net terms, LAC-7 countries have experienced declining debt liabilities and increasing equity liabilities. In fact, they have become net creditors with respect to the rest of the world as regards debt contracts and have acquired an increasing net debtor position as regards equity contracts, particularly through FDI (figure 4.5). These trends are matched across all subregions in LAC (figure 4.6).

These changes in portfolio composition—from a net debtor to a net creditor

FIGURE 4.5   Net foreign assets as percentage of GDP: Equity and bonds

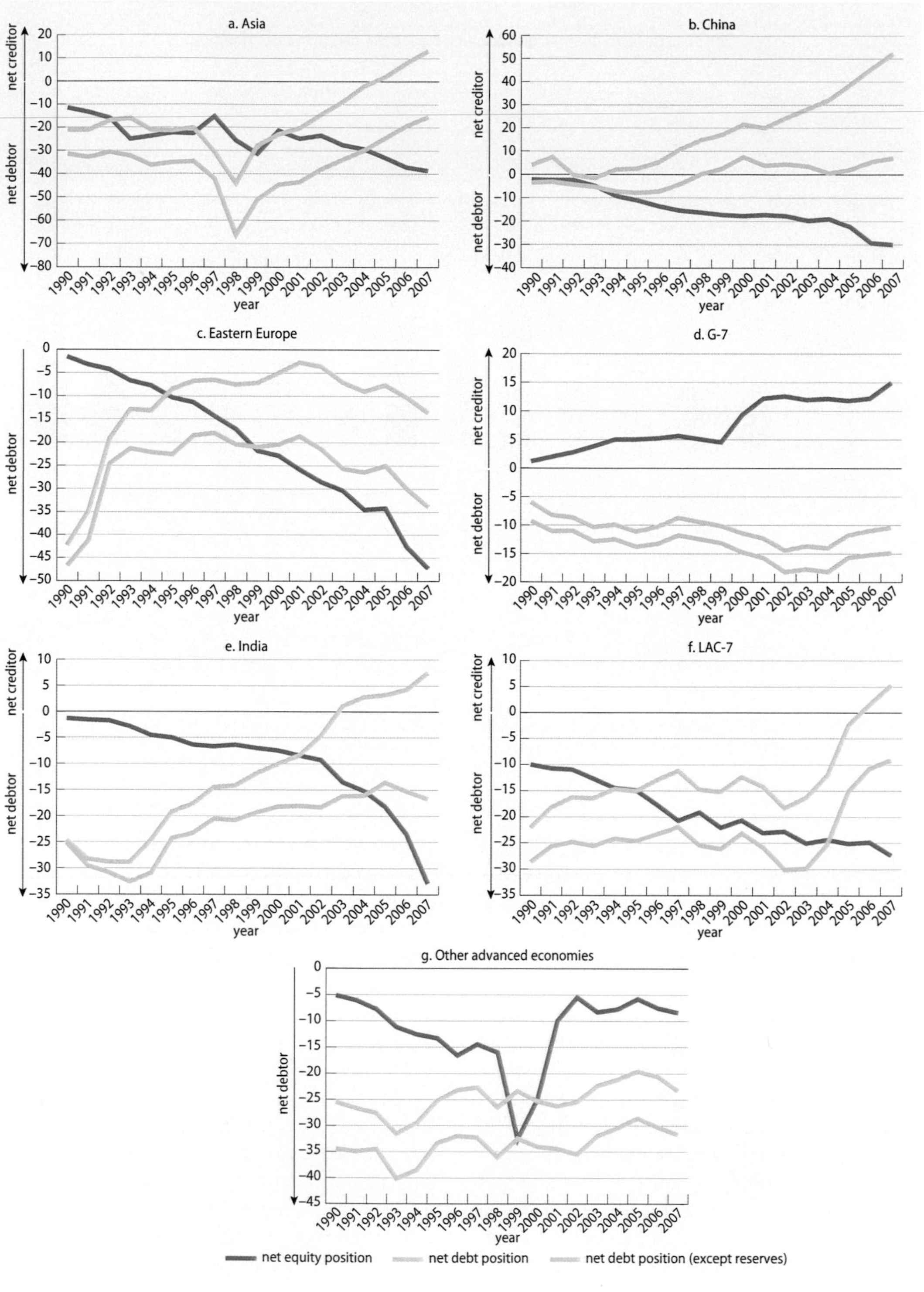

Source: Authors' calculations based on Lane and Milesi-Ferretti 2007.
Note: This figure shows the international net equity and net debt positions as a percentage of GDP between 1990 and 2007.

FIGURE 4.6   **Within LAC: Net foreign assets as percentage of GDP: Equity and bonds**

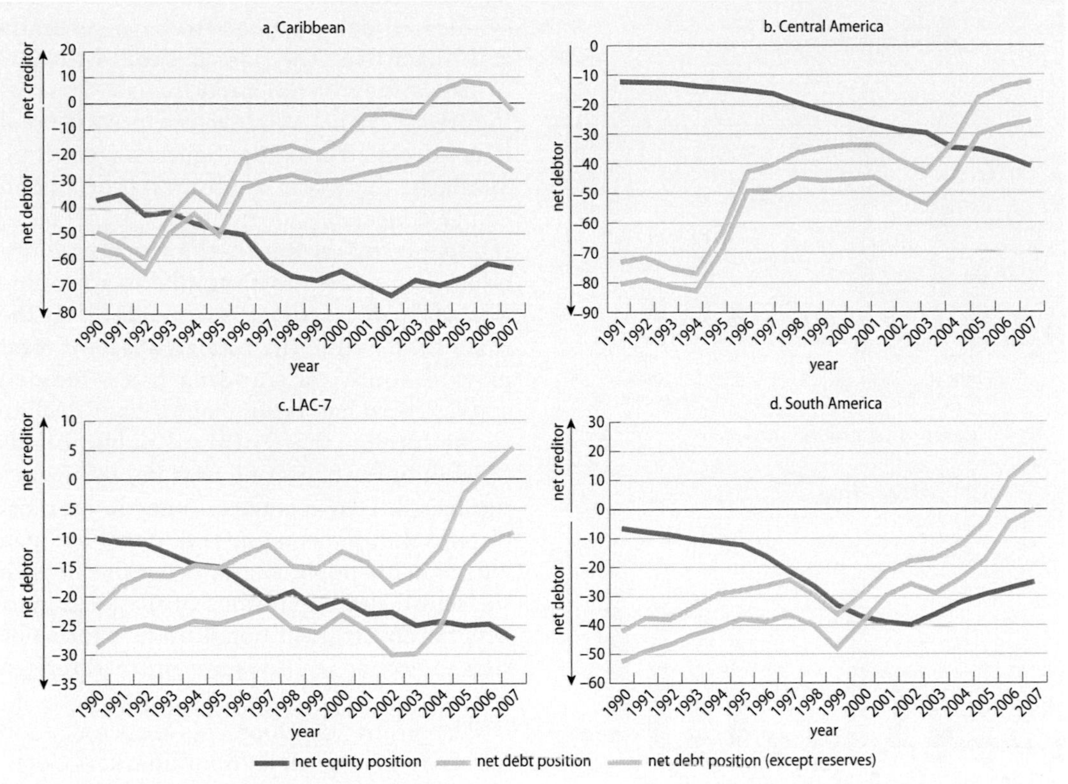

Source: Authors' calculations based on Lane and Milesi-Ferretti 2007.
Note: This figure shows the international net equity and net debt positions as a percentage of GDP between 1990 and 2007.

position—have resulted in a much safer form of financial integration, thus avoiding many of the downsides of financial global-ization.[10] In LAC's not-too-distant past, the devaluations that typically accompanied financial crises increased the burden of for-eign currency debt. On top of this, market shutdowns triggered rollover crises because of the high incidence of short-term debt. In contrast, during the recent global crisis, the devaluations have implied an improvement (when measured in local currency) in the external positions of LAC countries due to their net creditor stance. Moreover, external liabilities were reduced when equity prices plummeted, thereby shrinking net debtor equity positions. At the same time, the large pools of international reserves slowed down the appreciation of the domestic cur-rency during the precrisis expansionary period and then served as a self-insurance mechanism during the crisis, deterring cur-rency and banking panics. In fact, when the global crisis erupted, many countries held international reserves in excess of their stock of short-term foreign liabili-ties. This, in practice, eliminated concerns about debt rollover difficulties, limiting investors' incentives to attack the domestic currencies.[11]

Financial offshoring

During the 1990s, the LAC-7 countries spearheaded a strong process of financial

FIGURE 4.7   New capital-raising issues in foreign markets

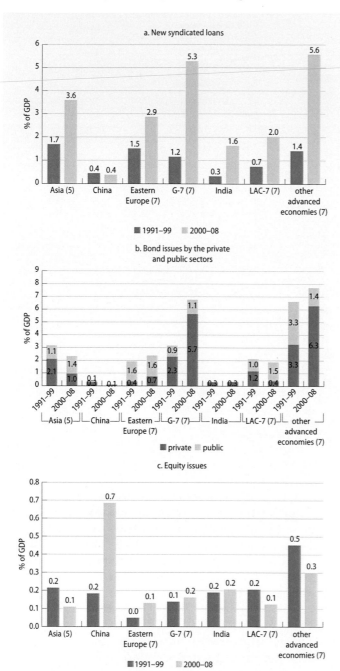

Source: Didier and Schmukler 2011b.
Note: This figure shows capital-raising activity in foreign markets. Panel a shows new syndicated loans abroad as a percentage of GDP between 1991 and 2008. Panel b shows bond issuance abroad by the private and public sectors as a percentage of GDP between 1991 and 2008. Panel c shows capital-raising equity issuance in foreign markets as a percentage of GDP between 1991 and 2008. Numbers in parentheses show the number of countries in each region.

offshoring. However, this expansion in the use of foreign markets, including bonds and syndicated debt, appears to have generally stabilized over the past decade. In terms of flows, new syndicated loans expanded (figure 4.7, panel a). However, private bond issues declined strongly (figure 4.7, panel b). Similarly, there was a substantial decline in equity issues abroad (figure 4.7, panel c). In relative terms however, the foreign equity issues increased substantially as a proportion of the total (figure 4.8, panel c). At the same time, while the foreign share of total private bonds outstanding has remained stable, there has been a significant decline in the foreign share of total public bonds outstanding, suggesting that public financing has shifted towards domestic markets (figures 4.8, panel a and 4.8, panel b). Such a decline for public bonds is consistent with the significant expansions of the local markets for government bonds and, at the same time, a decline in LAC governments' foreign indebtedness.

The positive developments in currency and maturity for domestic bond markets documented in chapter 3 were largely matched offshore. Thus, the maturity of LAC-7 private sector foreign bonds reached nearly 12 years in the past decade (up from about 7 years in the previous decade), whereas that for the public sector increased from 8 to 11 years (figure 4.9).[12] Similar increases in maturity were observed across all of LAC (figure 4.10). At the same time, both the public and private sectors were able to issue offshore bonds in local currencies. Thus, for the LAC-7 countries, 7 percent of private sector bonds and 9 percent of public sector bonds issued abroad in the past decade were denominated in local currency, against virtually zero during the 1990s (figure 4.11). While these amounts are small, especially when compared to the advanced economies, they signal the start of LAC's overcoming of original sin (that is, the inability to issue local currency long-term debt in foreign markets). Clearly, they also point to a long road toward full redemption.

The issuance and trading of equity abroad by LAC-7 countries (as well as many emerging economies) has usually taken the form of cross-listings through depository receipts. The offshore trading of LAC-7's depository receipts accounts for nearly two-thirds of total trade, compared to between 30 percent and 40 percent for other emerging economies (figure 4.12). Empirical work suggests that such offshoring of LAC equity markets has tended to limit the role of onshore markets, which, as flagged in chapter 3, have remained extremely illiquid.[13] The fact that access to the offshore equity market is even more limited than onshore—only a very small number of LAC firms have access to foreign bond and equity markets and, surprisingly, this number has declined further during the last decade (figure 4.13, panels a and b)—is an additional source of concern. This issue is explored in further detail in chapter 7.

Another important aspect of financial globalization (a sort of "offshoring in reverse") is the large physical presence of foreign-owned banks in LAC's domestic financial systems. The increased presence of foreign banks was largely a response to the financial crises of the 1990s and affected nearly all countries in LAC. Thus, between 1997 and 2001, the share of foreign-owned bank assets increased from 23 percent to 43 percent in the LAC-7 countries and from 26 percent to 38 percent in other South American countries (figure 4.14). In Central America and the Caribbean, the rise in foreign bank participation took place a little later (during the early 2000s), with the asset share of foreign banks growing from 20 percent to 31 percent and from 6 percent to 32 percent, respectively. As argued by Domanski (2005), letting the foreign bankers in would facilitate the recapitalization, consolidation, and strengthening of troubled banking systems. These objectives ended up trumping nationalistic concerns as well as concerns about the potentially adverse effects of foreign banks on access to financial services (see box 4.1).

FIGURE 4.8 **Relative size of foreign capital markets**

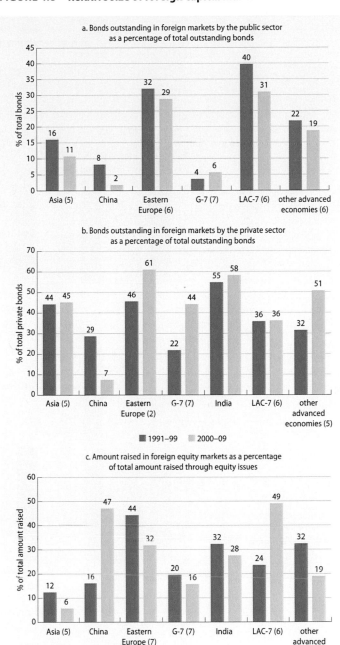

Source: Didier and Schmukler 2011b.
Note: This figure shows the size of foreign markets relative to total (domestic and foreign) markets. Panel a shows the ratio of outstanding public bonds in foreign markets to total public bonds between 1990 and 2009. Panel b shows the ratio of outstanding bonds by the private sector in foreign markets to total public bonds between 1990 and 2009. Panel c shows the amount raised in equity market abroad relative to total amount raised through equity issues in domestic and foreign markets between 1991 and 2008. Panels a and b are based on data from the Bank for International Settlements that defines international debt securities as those that have not been issued by residents in domestic currency and targeted at resident investors.

FIGURE 4.9   **Average maturity of bonds at issuance**

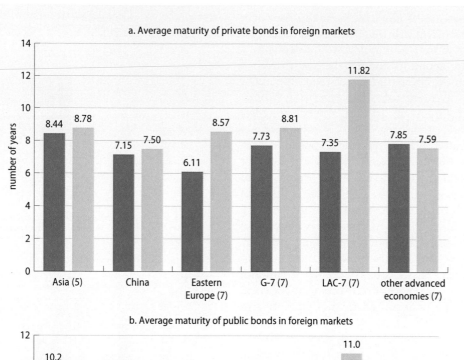

a. Average maturity of private bonds in foreign markets

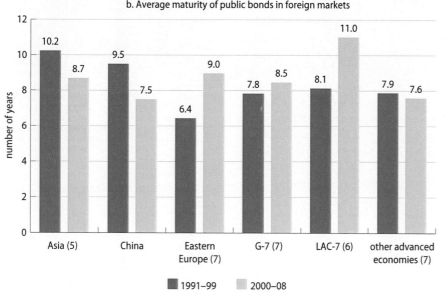

b. Average maturity of public bonds in foreign markets

■ 1991–99   □ 2000–08

Source: Didier and Schmukler 2011b.
Note: This figure shows the maturity (in years) of bonds issued by the private and public sectors in foreign markets between 1991 and 2008. Numbers in parentheses show the number of countries in each region.

FIGURE 4.10 **Within LAC: Average maturity of public and private bonds in foreign markets at issuance**

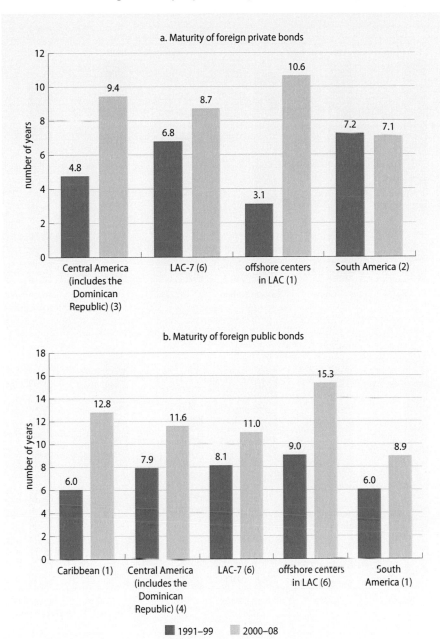

Source: Didier and Schmukler 2011b.
Note: This figure shows the maturity (in years) of bonds issued by the private and public sectors in foreign markets between 1991 and 2008 across LAC. Numbers in parentheses show the number of countries in each region.

FIGURE 4.11   **Ratio of foreign currency bonds to total bonds at issuance**

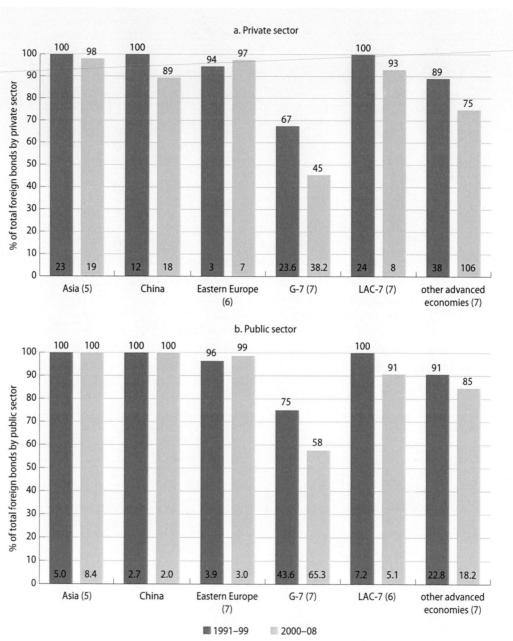

Source: Didier and Schmukler 2011b.
Note: This figure shows the ratio of foreign-currency-denominated bonds to total bonds issued by the private and public sectors in foreign markets between 1991 and 2008. Panel a shows data for the private sector. Panel b shows data for the public sector. Numbers in the base of the bars represent the average number of issues per year. Numbers in parentheses show the number of countries in each region.

FIGURE 4.12   Equity trading in domestic and foreign markets

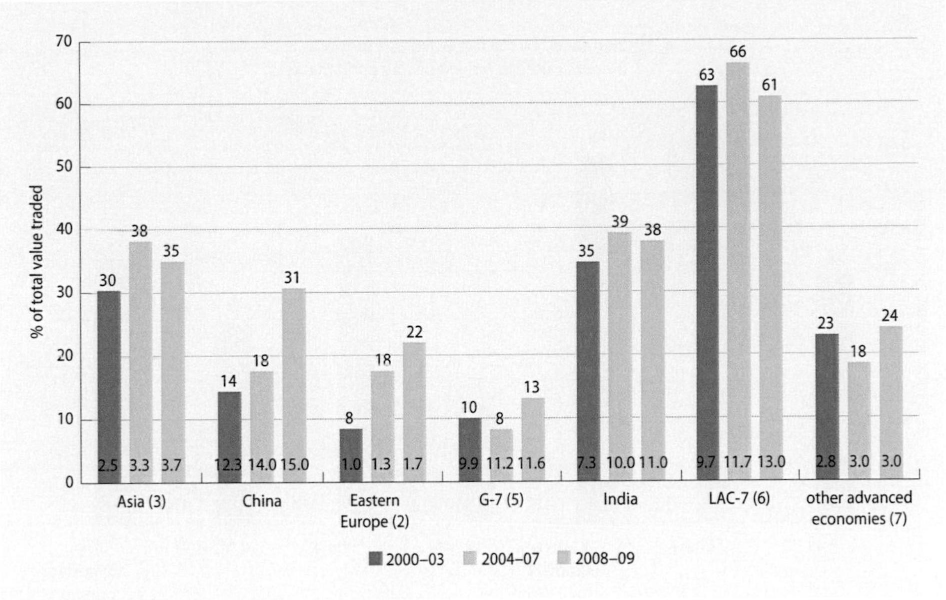

Source: Didier and Schmukler 2011b.
Note: This figure shows the cross-country averages of firm-level value traded in depository receipts over total value traded (in domestic markets and DRs). Only firms with DR programs identified in the DR Directory of the Bank of New York and with trading data reported in Bloomberg are considered in this figure. The average number of firms for countries within each region is also reported at the bottom of the bars. Numbers in parentheses show the number of countries considered in each region.

BOX 4.1   Costs and benefits of the participation of foreign banks in domestic financial systems

Numerous papers have analyzed the costs and benefits of the participation of foreign-owned banks in domestic financial systems (for example, Claessens and Van Horen 2008; Cull and Martínez Pería 2010). They generally find that foreign-owned banks tend to be more efficient than domestic banks in emerging economies. Foreign-owned banks may count on more diversified funding bases, including access to external liquidity from their parent banks even in times of crisis, which lowers their deposit costs. Foreign-owned banks can also better capture scale economies and bring technical skills, product innovation, and more sophisticated risk management practices. They can help boost competition in developing countries.

However, critics of foreign-owned bank entry argue that foreign banks can destabilize the local banking sector for a number of reasons. They can "import" shocks from their home countries and/or spread shocks from other developing countries in which they operate. Fierce competition with foreign-owned banks can threaten the survival of the local banks. In addition, foreign-owned banks can reduce

access to finance for a majority of domestic firms and consumers if they only concentrate on a selected segment of the market. In particular, the literature shows that foreign banks tend to have difficulties in lending to borrowers that lack the hard information to prove their creditworthiness (for example, Berger, Klapper, and Udell 2001; Mian 2003, 2006).

However, the evidence is mixed on the overall effect of foreign-owned banks on outreach. For example, competition from foreign banks could conceivably compel domestic banks to pursue new market niches (Jenkins 2000). Empirically, de la Torre, Martínez Pería, and Schmukler (2010) and Beck, Demirgüç-Kunt, and Martínez Pería (2011) show that there is no difference in the extent of foreign-owned banks' involvement with small and medium enterprises relative to large domestic and government-owned banks. Clarke, Cull, and Martínez Pería (2006) and Giannetti and Ongena (2009) find that foreign bank presence is associated with an improvement in firm indicators, particularly for young firms, though the effects are less pronounced for small firms.

FIGURE 4.13   **Concentration in foreign bond and equity markets**

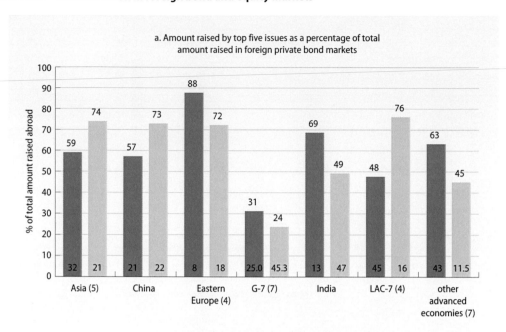

a. Amount raised by top five issues as a percentage of total
amount raised in foreign private bond markets

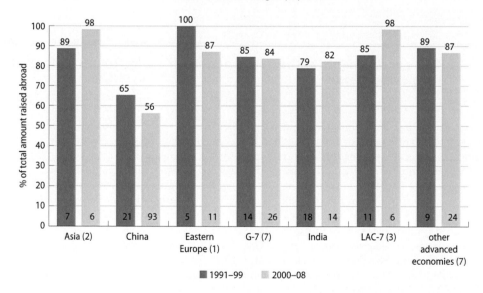

b. Amount raised by top five issues as a percentage of total
amount raised in foreign equity markets

■ 1991–99   ☐ 2000–08

Source: Didier and Schmukler 2011b.
Note: This figure shows the concentration in bond and equity markets. Panel a shows the amount raised by top five bond issues by corporations as a percentage of the total amount raised by the private sector in foreign private bond markets between 1991 and 2008. Only country-years with at least five issues were considered in this figure. Panel b shows the amount raised by top five equity issues as a percentage of the total amount raised by the private sector in foreign private equity markets during the same period. Panel c shows the cross-country average of firm-level value traded in DRs for the top five firms over total DR value traded in foreign equity markets between 2000 and 2008. Only countries with more than five firms with DRs programs were considered in this figure. All DRs identified in the DR Directory of the Bank of New York with trading data reported in Bloomberg are considered in this figure. Numbers in the base of the bars represent the yearly cross-country average number of issues. Numbers in parentheses show the number of countries considered in each region.

FIGURE 4.14   Foreign-owned bank assets as a percentage of total banks assets

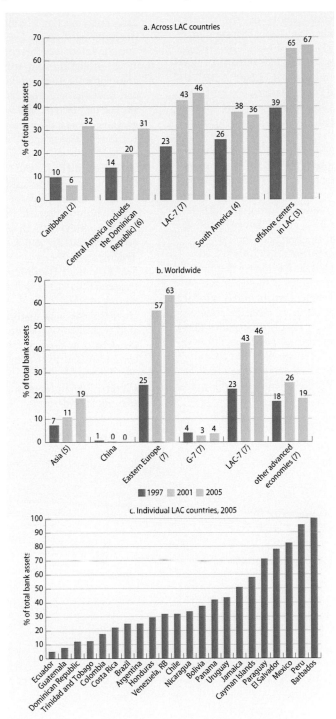

Source: Authors' calculations based on Claessens and van Horen (2008).
Note: This figure shows the average assets of foreign-owned banks as share of total bank assets in 1997, 2001, and 2005. Panel a compares the average ratio across regions within LAC, panel b compares the average ratio across LAC-7 against other emerging regions and developed economies, and panel c shows the ratio for every LAC country in 2005.

Notes

1. This chapter draws heavily on the papers "Benchmarking Financial Globalization in the Latin America and the Caribbean," by Tatiana Didier and Sergio Schmukler (2011b), and "Financial Globalization in Latin America: Myth, Reality and Policy Matters," by Eduardo Levy-Yeyati (2011b), which are part of the forthcoming Edited Volume that accompanies this LAC flagship report.
2. Foreign investors mostly invest in LAC markets but do not raise capital there. Local issues of equity or bonds by foreign firms accounted for less than 2 percent of the total capital raised in these markets during the 2000s. Yet foreign firms have generally been seeking more financing in emerging economies.
3. See Stulz (1999) and Errunza (2001).
4. Levy-Yeyati (2011b) finds evidence that financial globalization amplified the asset sell-off (particularly through benchmarked global equity funds) that occurred after the collapse of Lehman Brothers. He also concludes that the procyclical nature of portfolio inflows, which return to core markets in episodes of flight to quality, can amplify the effect of the global cycle on the emerging world in an undesirable way.
5. There is a large and rapidly growing literature analyzing cross-border capital flows and associated asset and liability positions from a portfolio perspective. See Broner et al. (2010) and the references therein.
6. When domestic and offshore activities are complements, the correlation between financial development and financial globalization should be positive, and when they are substitutes, the correlation should be negative.
7. See Levine and Schmukler (2006, 2007).
8. See also Lane and Milesi-Ferretti (2001).
9. See Gourinchas and Rey (2007) and Gourinchas, Govillot, and Rey (2010).
10. See de la Torre, Calderon et al. (2010a); de la Torre, Calderon et al. 2010b; Didier, Hevia, and Schmukler (2011); Gourinchas, Govillot, and Rey (2010); and Gourinchas, Rey, and Truempler (2011).
11. See Aizenman (forthoming), Aizenman and Pasricha (2010), Frankel and Saravelos (2010), among others.
12. However, the long maturities could be associated with relatively short durations if most of the debt is at floating rates. The data do not currently allow us to identify such effects.
13. See Levine and Schmukler (2006, 2007). Chapter 7 analyzes in more detail the possible reasons for this gap.

Financial Inclusion: Where Does LAC Stand? | 5

This chapter considers financial inclusion in Latin America and the Caribbean (LAC) countries, focusing on the typically underserved, particularly lower-income households and small entrepreneurs. Both theoretical and empirical studies have argued that financial inclusion matters.[1] Theory has shown that financial market frictions that prevent financial inclusion can lead to persistent inequality and poverty traps, and empirical work has confirmed the positive welfare effects that result from firms and individuals gaining access to financial services.[2] This chapter first measures financial inclusion in LAC and compares it to that in other regions using supply-side data obtained from bank regulators. Second, it analyzes barriers (pecuniary and nonpecuniary) to the use of banking services from a survey of banks and compares LAC to other regions. Third, it studies demand-side data from firm-level surveys and household-level surveys.[3] Finally, it analyzes the role of governments in the region in promoting financial inclusion. Main findings are as follows:

- Most available indicators of financial inclusion suggest that LAC-7 is not obviously underperforming compared to its peers; in fact, LAC-7 outperforms in a number of dimensions, including, surprisingly, the use of banking services by small and medium enterprises (SMEs).
- This relative success could reflect in part the fact that a majority of governments in LAC-7 have adopted comprehensive policies to promote financial inclusion.
- At the same time, lack of demand appears to be an important factor explaining the limited use of banking services by households.
- However, higher pecuniary fees on deposit and lending products could also be acting as barriers.
- In addition to such barriers, another potentially problematic area that requires governments' attention is the improvement of creditor rights, where LAC-7 lags significantly.
- By and large, non-LAC-7 lags LAC-7 in some indicators of financial outreach and in some government policies to promote inclusion; thus, there is scope for non-LAC-7 governments to play a more active role in fostering financial inclusion.

This chapter does not address the issue of financial sustainability, partly for lack of data. Nonetheless, it seems safe to say that the more governments promote (and succeed in enhancing) financial inclusion, the more attention they need to pay to the soundness and sustainability of such progress. As demonstrated by the recent global crisis, systemic fault lines are more likely to develop where borrowers' capacity to repay is stretched thinner.

The rest of this chapter is structured as follows. The first section presents the methodology used in the study. The second section presents the supply-side evidence. The third section reviews the demand-side evidence. The final section discusses the role of government.

Methodology

Financial inclusion is hard to measure in practice. A basic challenge is to distinguish access to financial services from the use of financial services. Access refers primarily to the supply of services whereas use (the observable outcome) is determined by demand as well as supply. Therefore, inferences about financial inclusion from measures of use of financial services do not necessarily imply the existence of market failures that warrant government intervention. Nonetheless, measuring the use of financial services is the first and most readily available way to assess financial inclusion. This analysis employs both types of data—supply-side data and demand-side (survey-based) data—to characterize financial inclusion. As in previous chapters, whenever there are sufficient data, both the raw data and the data controlled for gross domestic product (GDP) per capita and population density are presented.

The analysis concentrates on analyzing access to (and use of) banking services, because banks dominate the financial sector in Latin America, especially for households and SMEs, which are at the core of the financial inclusion concerns and agenda. Moreover, data for the banking sector are more readily available across countries, facilitating comparisons. However, wherever possible, data and initiatives that include nonbanks are presented and discussed.

Lack of access can reflect pecuniary barriers to the use of financial services, such as fees or minimum balances, as well as nonpecuniary barriers, such as documentation requirements, the number of locations where individuals can open accounts or apply for loans, the number of days to process a loan application, and so on. Thus, the chapter uses data from a survey of financial institutions conducted by the World Bank (see Beck, Demirgüç-Kunt, and Martínez Pería 2008) during 2004–05 to quantify barriers to the use of financial services. Because these data are available only for the largest countries within Latin America, it is not possible to compare LAC-7 countries to the other countries in the region.

There are a number of caveats and limitations to this analysis. First, as mentioned above, the analysis centers on banks and largely ignores nonbank institutions. Second, it focuses on payments, savings, and credit services. Because of a lack of data, it ignores insurance services. Third, indicators of financial inclusion, such as the number of deposits or loans per capita, may overestimate the extent of outreach, since some individuals and firms might have more than one account. Fourth, the supply-side data do not distinguish between individuals and firms in the use of banking services. Finally, in documenting the role of the government in promoting financial inclusion, this chapter is able to describe only efforts and policies, and it does not conduct a welfare analysis of the impact of these policies.

Supply-side evidence

Overall, the raw statistics on the number of branches, ATMs (automated teller machines), and deposits suggest that LAC countries are at par with economies in Asia but lag behind developed countries and Eastern Europe. The median numbers of branches and ATMs in LAC-7 are broadly similar to those in Asia but smaller than in Eastern Europe, the G-7 and other developed countries (figure 5.1, panel a). The LAC-7 countries also outperform other

FIGURE 5.1   Number of branches, ATMs, and deposit and loan accounts

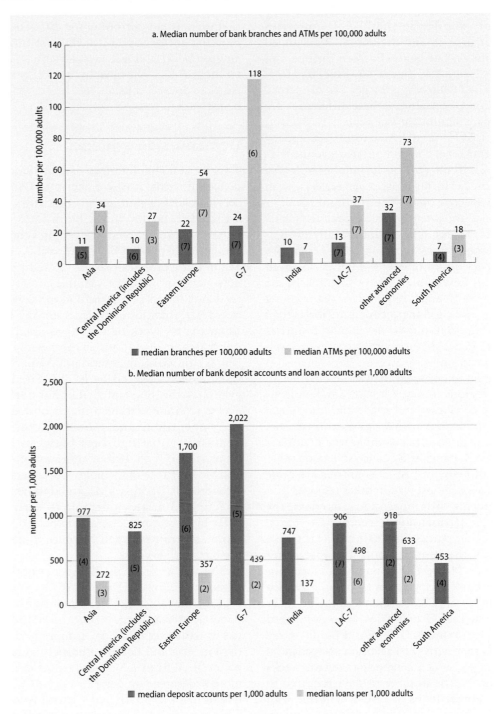

Source: Martínez Pería 2011.
Note: Panel a shows the median number of bank branches and ATMs per 100,000 adults in LAC-7 versus other regions and other countries in Latin America. Panel b shows the median number of bank deposit accounts and loan accounts per 1,000 adults in LAC-7 versus other regions and other countries in Latin America. The numbers in parentheses refer to the number of countries for which data are available.

LAC subregions. The median number of deposit accounts per 1,000 adults is also broadly similar in the LAC-7 countries to that in Asia and the non-G-7 advanced economies, but below Eastern Europe and the G-7 countries (figure 5.1, panel b). However, after controlling for per capita income and population density, these differences are no longer significant (see table 5.1). In fact, most LAC-7 (and LAC) countries appear to outperform the comparator groups (figure 5.2). In the case of the number of loans, LAC outperforms most other regions, even in the absence of any control (figure 5.3).[5]

There are several possible pecuniary barriers to access. The median minimum balances required by banks in LAC-7 countries are generally in line with what is observed for most developing countries. Similarly, the minimum balances required for maintaining savings and checking accounts are lower than those required in most developing countries and are in accordance with practices in developed economies. However, deposit fees in LAC tend to be higher than those observed in other regions (figure 5.4, panel a). Similarly, fees on consumer and residential (mortgage) loans in Latin America significantly exceed those in most other comparator countries (figure 5.4, panel b). By contrast, fees on other types of loans in LAC-7 countries are quite close to those observed in other regions.

In terms of nonpecuniary barriers, the number of documents required to open deposit accounts in Latin America also exceeds the requirements in most other countries. However, the number of locations where bank customers can open a deposit account or apply for a loan is comparable or larger in LAC-7 countries, even compared to G-7 economies. The World Bank survey reveals that with the exception of residential mortgages, which generally take two weeks to process, the number of days required to process other loans in LAC-7 is in line with what is observed in other developing regions.

Thus, the main barriers to the use of services in Latin America appear to be pecuniary costs or fees. Table 5.2, which shows regressions of deposit and residential mortgage loan fees against a number of possible determinants, including a LAC-7 dummy, confirms that even after controlling for differences in banking sector structure, the institutional environment, and per capita income across countries, fees charged by banks in Latin America are still considerably higher than the benchmark.

Demand-side evidence

This section characterizes demand-side evidence on firms' use and access to banking services with a number of indicators constructed from the World Bank Enterprise Surveys database. First, it examines the percentage of firms that have a deposit account. Second, it examines the use of credit products using an indicator variable constructed so that it equals one if the enterprise has an overdraft, loan, line of credit, or any bank financing for working capital or fixed asset purchases. It also looks at the median percentage of working capital and, separately, fixed assets financed by banks. Finally, it evaluates the share of firms that consider access to finance to be a major obstacle to their operations and growth. Across the analysis, it distinguishes between large firms (those with 100 or more employees) and SMEs (those that employ between 5 and 99 workers). Because SMEs tend to be more opaque and more vulnerable to economic volatility, they are generally expected to be more constrained when it comes to accessing banking services.

Not too surprisingly, the vast majority of firms (including SMEs) in LAC (as in other regions) have a bank account (figure 5.5, panel a). Across large firms and SMEs, the use of bank credit in LAC is more pervasive than in Asia and Eastern Europe (figure 5.5, panel b). Within LAC, the use of credit is more widespread among firms in LAC-7 relative to firms in South and Central America. There is, however, a noticeable difference (across all regions) between the share of large and small firms that use credit products.

While SMEs in the LAC-7 countries also appear to make the most extensive use of

TABLE 5.1 Regressions of indicators of financial inclusion on income, population density, and country-group dummies

	Log of branches per 100,000 adults		Log of ATMs per 100,000 adults		Log of number of deposits per 1,000 adults		Log of number of loans per 1,000 Adults	
	(1)	(2)	(3)	(4)	(5)	(6)	(7)	(8)
Log of GDP per capita, PPP	0.691 [17.98]***	0.713 [15.31]***	1.187 [15.95]***	1.189 [14.97]***	0.91 [14.38]***	0.931 [13.91]***	1.236 [14.93]***	1.254 [15.92]***
Log of population density	0.114 [2.65]***	0.115 [2.61]**	0.046 [0.81]	0.042 [0.72]	0.333 [5.17]***	0.345 [5.14]***	0.078 [1.19]	0.082 [1.23]
LAC	-0.082 [-0.43]		0.396 [2.27]**		0.226 [1.52]		0.648 [4.48]***	
LAC7		0.086 [0.61]		0.285 [1.21]		0.417 [1.68]*		0.716 [2.34]**
REST of LAC		0.012 [3.04]		0.486 [1.73]*		0.363 [1.42]		0.811 [2.50]**
Other countries		0.164 [1.03]		-0.001 [-0.01]		0.199 [0.99]		0.157 [0.54]
Constant	-4.229 [-10.32]***	-4.551 [-8.34]***	-7.735 [-10.44]***	-7.731 [-9.41]***	-3.007 [-4.55]***	-3.400 [-4.42]***	-6.1 [-7.48]***	-6.406 [-7.83]***
Observations	132	132	117	117	109	109	77	77
R-squared	0.667	0.67	0.796	0.796	0.765	0.767	0.833	0.834
F-test LAC7 = LAC_Rest		0.0578		0.405		0.0562		0.239
P-value LAC7 = LAC_Rest		0.81		0.526		0.813		0.626
F-test LAC7 = Other		0.477		1.769		1.429		14.10
P-value LAC7 = Other		0.491		0.186		0.235		0.000***
F-test LAC_Rest = Other		0.245		3.74C		0.724		12.89
P-value LAC_Rest = Other		0.621		0.056*		0.397		0.001***

Source: Martínez Pería 2011.
Note: PPP = purchasing power parity.
Significance level: * = 10 percent; ** = 5 percent; *** = 1 percent. Robust t-statistics are shown in brackets.

FIGURE 5.2 **Actual versus predicted number of deposits per 1,000 adults**

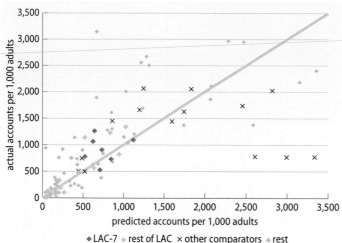

Source: Martínez Pería 2011.
Note: Predicted numbers were obtained regressing the log of ATMs per 100,000 adults on the log of GDP per capita in constant purchasing power parity terms and the log of population density.

FIGURE 5.3 **Actual versus predicted number of loans per 1,000 adults**

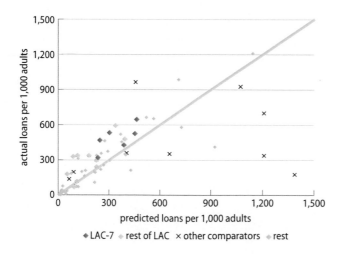

Source: Martínez Pería 2011.
Note: Predicted numbers were obtained regressing the log of loans per 100,000 adults on the log of GDP per capita in constant purchasing power parity terms and the log of population density.

bank loans to finance their purchases of fixed assets, the difference in the extent of use between large firms and SMEs is remarkably large compared to that in Asia or Eastern Europe (figure 5.6, panel a). Broadly similar results are found for the share of working capital financed by banks (figure 5.6, panel b). The final indicator of access to credit among firms is firms' responses to a survey question about their views on access to finance.[6] Again, there is not much difference between LAC-7, Asia, and Eastern Europe as regards the percentage of SMEs that declare lack of access to be a severe obstacle (figure 5.7). In sum, SMEs in LAC (and especially in LAC-7) do not appear to be lagging in absolute terms behind firms in other developing countries as regards their access and use of bank credit. That being said, the substantial difference in access between the larger and smaller firms in LAC is a potential matter for concern that deserves further exploration.

Demand-side information at the household level is very limited and hard to compare across countries, because the survey instruments and the samples vary from country to country. However, comparable household surveys were recently conducted by the Corporación Andina de Fomento (CAF) in Argentina, Brazil, Colombia, Peru, and Uruguay, which is referred to below as the LAC-5 group (see www.caf.com). The surveys revealed that 51 percent of households in LAC-5 have a bank account. Among households that do not have an account, the main reasons cited include lack of funds (61 percent) or absence of a job (19 percent). Only 11 percent of households cited "not trusting financial institutions" or "not being able to meet the requirements to open an account," and 7 percent complained about high fees. The statistics regarding the use of bank accounts among households in countries outside the LAC-5 are very similar. Approximately 52 percent of households have an account and, among those that do not, 72 percent mention lack of money as the main reason. Only 5 percent of households complain about high

FIGURE 5.4   **Annual fees**

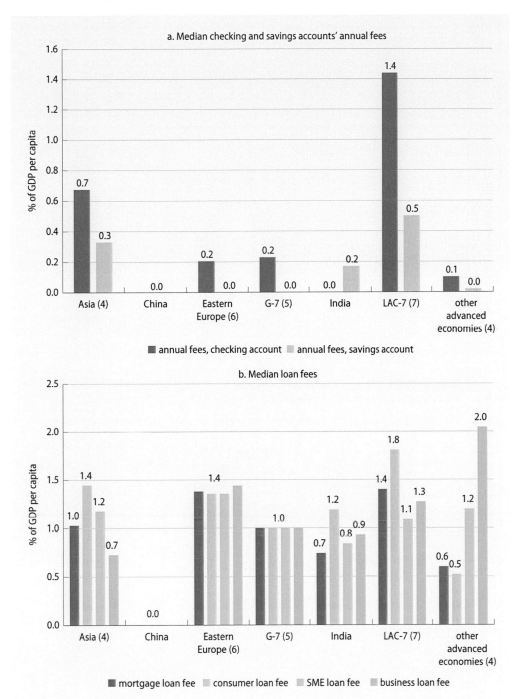

Source: Beck, Demirguc-Kunt, and Martínez Pería 2008.
Note: Panel a shows the median checking and savings accounts annual fees as percentage of GDP per capita. Panel b shows the median loan fees as percentage of GDP per capita. Numbers in parentheses show the number of countries in each region.

TABLE 5.2 Regressions for deposit and loan fees

Variables	Annual fees checking account (% of GDP per capita)				Annual fees savings account (% of GDP per capita)			Fee mortgage loan	
LAC-7	2.47 [3.30]***	3.014 [2.11]**	4.222 [2.16]**	2.153 [3.18]***	1.203 [2.62]**	1.132 [2.27]**	2.501 [1.88]*	2.348 [1.85]*	2.852 [1.81]*
Countries outside comparator group	4.141 [2.96]***	0.892 [1.01]	0.158 [0.13]	1.454 [1.95]*	0.431 [1.15]	-0.251 [-0.56]	4.608 [1.54]	1.311 [1.64]	0.729 [0.69]
Concentration (% of assets held by top 5 banks)		0.019 [0.72]	0.058 [1.62]		-0.009 [-0.90]	0.014 [1.62]		-0.021 [-0.80]	-0.013 [-0.36]
Legal rights index		0.242 [1.08]	0.307 [1.01]		0.014 [0.18]	-0.007 [-0.10]		-0.052 [-0.27]	-0.09 [-0.45]
Credit information index		-0.409 [-1.01]	-0.533 [-1.04]		0.137 [0.99]	0.203 [1.72]*		-0.049 [-0.16]	-0.053 [-0.20]
Cost of enforcing contracts		0.077 [3.11]***	0.068 [2.56]**		0.013 [1.46]	0.014 [2.61]**		0.029 [0.84]	0.048 [1.26]
Heritage index of financial freedom		0.089 [1.84]*	0.074 [1.14]		0.023 [1.59]	0.017 [0.93]		0.053 [2.12]**	0.064 [1.41]
Log of GDP per capita (PPP)			-1.51 [-1.97]*	-2.157 [-2.31]**	-0.549 [-2.05]**	-0.967 [-3.06]***		-0.665 [-1.36]	-1.053 [-1.92]*
Share of bank assets held by government banks			-0.027 [-0.57]			-0.011 [-1.03]			-0.003 [-0.12]
Share of bank assets held by foreign banks			0.030 [1.17]			-0.002 [-0.36]			0.001 [0.07]
Constant	-0.906 [-1.38]	5.809 [0.82]	9.756 [1.14]	-1.588 [-2.41]**	2.637 [1.21]	5.699 [2.15]**	0.607 [0.93]	5.182 [1.21]	7.384 [1.55]
Observations	69	59	45	69	59	45	66	58	44
Pseudo R-squared	0.0152	0.122	0.142	0.0265	0.166	0.296	0.00291	0.0552	0.0967

Source: Martínez Pería 2011.

Note: This table shows tobit estimations for deposit and mortgage loan fees against country dummies, along with a series of variables proxying for bank structure, institutional environment, and income per capita. In particular, LAC-7 is a dummy that equals 1 for Argentina, Brazil, Chile, Colombia, Mexico, Peru, and Uruguay. Countries outside comparator group is a dummy that takes the value of 1 for countries other than those in the comparator group, which includes G-7 countries (Canada, France, Germany, Italy, Japan, United Kingdom, and United States); other developed countries (Australia, Finland, Israel, New Zealand, Norway, Spain, and Sweden); comparable countries in Asia (China, India, Indonesia, Republic of Korea, Malaysia, Philippines, and Thailand); and Eastern Europe (Croatia, Czech Republic, Hungary, Lithuania, Poland, Russian Federation, and Turkey). Robust t-statistics are shown in brackets. Significance level: * = 10 percent, ** = 5 percent, *** = 1 percent.

FIGURE 5.5   Firms' use of bank accounts and credit products

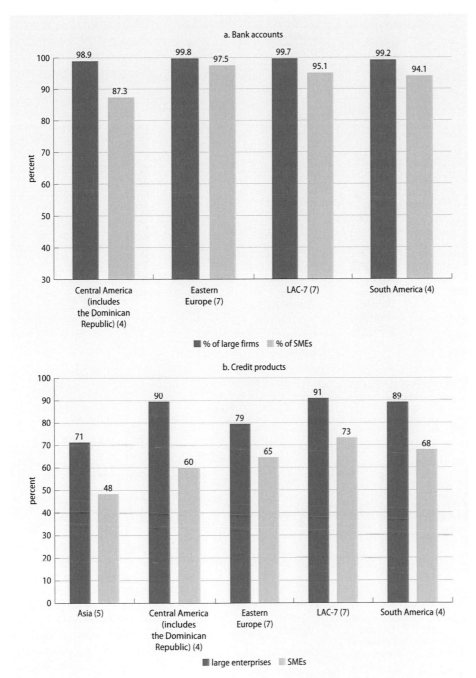

Source: Martínez Pería 2011.
Notes: Panel a shows the firms' use of bank accounts. Panel b shows firms' use of credit products. Numbers in parentheses show the number of countries in each region.

FIGURE 5.6   **Fixed assets and working capital financed by banks**

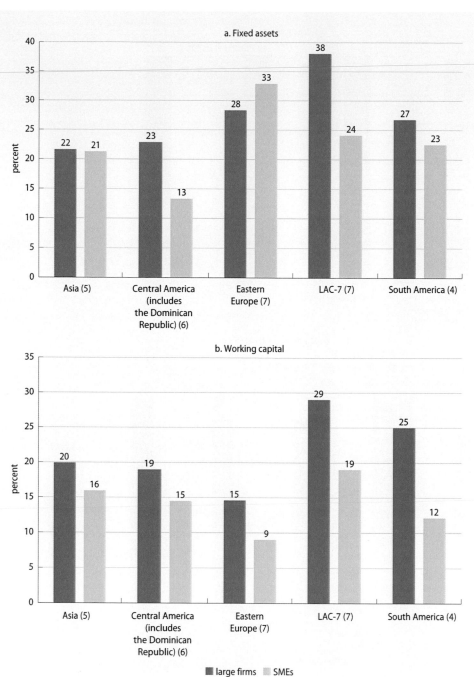

Source: Martínez Pería 2011.
Note: Panel a shows the percentage of fixed assets financed by banks. Panel b shows the percentage of working capital financed by banks. Numbers in parentheses show the number of countries in each region.

FIGURE 5.7   Percentage of firms that consider access to finance as a severe obstacle

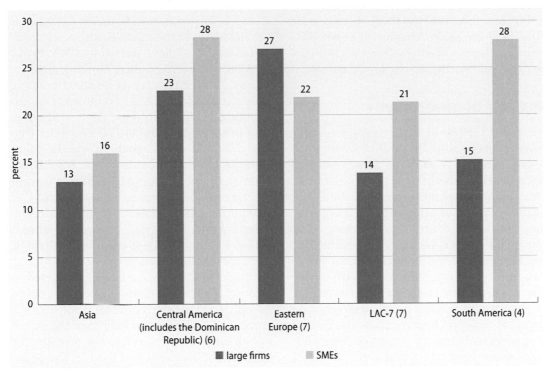

Source: Martínez Pería 2011.
Note: This figure shows the percentage of firms that consider access to finance as a severe obstacle. Numbers in parentheses show the number of countries in each region.

fees, and 13 percent mention not meeting the requirements to open an account. Overall, the fact that half of households do not use an account appears to be driven mainly by demand considerations, such as the lack of savings or income.

Loan use is even less typical than the use of bank accounts. Only about 21 percent of households in LAC-5 have a loan, and 62 percent have never applied for one. In the case of other LAC countries (Bolivia, Ecuador, Panama, and República Bolivariana de Venezuela), only 16 percent of households have a loan, and 66 percent never applied for one. A large proportion (70 percent in LAC-5 and 66 percent in other LAC countries) said they did not apply for a loan because they considered borrowing too risky and preferred not to be in debt. In LAC-5, only 24 percent did not apply because of

insufficient income or collateral. Among other countries in the region, 29 percent of households did not apply because of insufficient income or collateral. Hence, across Latin America, households that do not apply for loans appear to opt out of using credit services mainly because they have a strong aversion to being in debt.

Overall, the household data reveal that the use of banking services is rather limited in Latin America. Importantly, households' responses to questions about why they do not use services suggest that lack of income and self-exclusion play a more important role than supply-side considerations, like high fees and stringent documentation requirements. It is important to note, however, that these surveys are based on a small sample of households that reside only in urban areas. Nationally representative surveys that include rural areas might provide a different picture of the level of usage and the reasons behind it. Furthermore, because these surveys were done only for Latin America, it is not possible to compare their results to what might be observed in other developing countries.

The role of government

Analyzing the role of the government in promoting financial inclusion is difficult since it can encompass so many aspects—from documenting whether the government has an explicit mandate to promote financial inclusion, to examining specific government programs and/or interventions targeted to improve financial inclusion, to evaluating the adequacy of the financial sector infrastructure and the contractual environment. Furthermore, assessing the welfare impact of government policies designed to promote financial inclusion is particularly hard, since it requires isolating the impact of these policies from other factors that can also affect welfare. A full evaluation of government policies is beyond the scope of this chapter. Instead, this chapter focuses on documenting the efforts and policies in place to promote financial inclusion in LAC and on comparing them to those enacted by governments in other regions.[7]

As regards regulators' de jure mandate to increase financial inclusion (including having a document laying out its strategy), LAC-7 outperforms Eastern Europe but lags significantly behind Asia (figure 5.8, panel a). A rather similar picture appears for de facto commitments (figure 5.8, panel b). Across the LAC region, LAC-7 outperforms other subregions (figure 5.9).

Access to financial services in many developing countries is hampered by the lack of a widespread network of banking outlets, particularly in rural areas, which financial intermediaries generally do not find profitable. In this context, correspondent banks or mobile branches can play a significant role in expanding the access to financial services.[8] Over the past decade, bank regulators in LAC-7 have started to allow banks to enter into correspondent banking arrangements. Nevertheless, correspondent banking is less common in LAC-7 countries than it is among economies in Asia, Eastern Europe, and other advanced non-G-7 countries (figure 5.10). Mobile branching, on the other hand, is more common among LAC-7 countries than among countries in Asia (except China and India), Eastern Europe, and G-7 economies. Again, LAC-7 countries are way ahead of their neighbors in the region when it comes to correspondent banking and mobile branches (figure 5.11).

Aside from adopting policies targeted to promote outreach among specific groups (such as SMEs, the poor, or rural inhabitants), governments can influence the extent to which financial services are provided by financial institutions and used by the population at large by ensuring that the appropriate financial sector infrastructure and regulations are in place. In particular, the supply and the use of credit services will be influenced by the degree to which credit information is widely available to banks and the extent to which creditors feel that their rights are protected. On the basis of an index that measures rules and practices affecting the coverage, scope, and accessibility of credit information made available through either a public credit registry or a private credit bureau, LAC-7 countries come out ahead of any other comparator developing countries (figure 5.12). However, when it comes to the legal rights index, which measures the degree to which collateral and bankruptcy laws protect the rights of borrowers and lenders and thus facilitate lending, LAC-7 countries underperform most developed and developing countries. Clearly,

FIGURE 5.8   Governments' commitment to financial inclusion

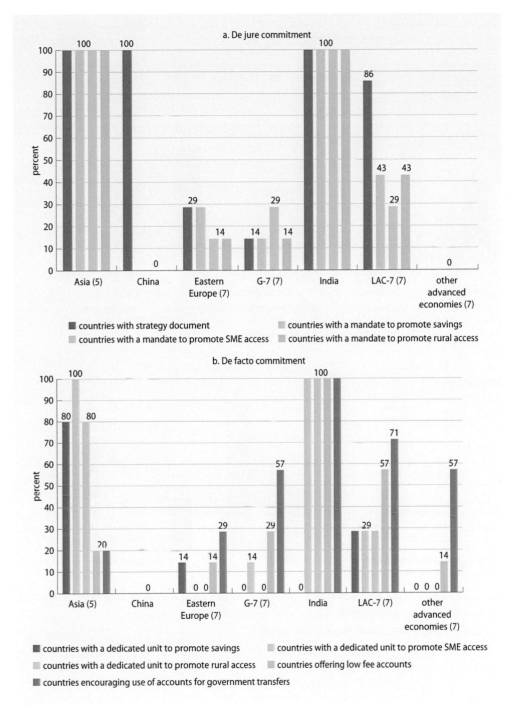

Source: Martínez Pería 2011.
Note: Panel a shows governments' de jure commitment to financial inclusion. Panel b shows governments' de facto commitment.

FIGURE 5.9 Governments' commitment to financial inclusion: LAC-7 versus other LAC comparators

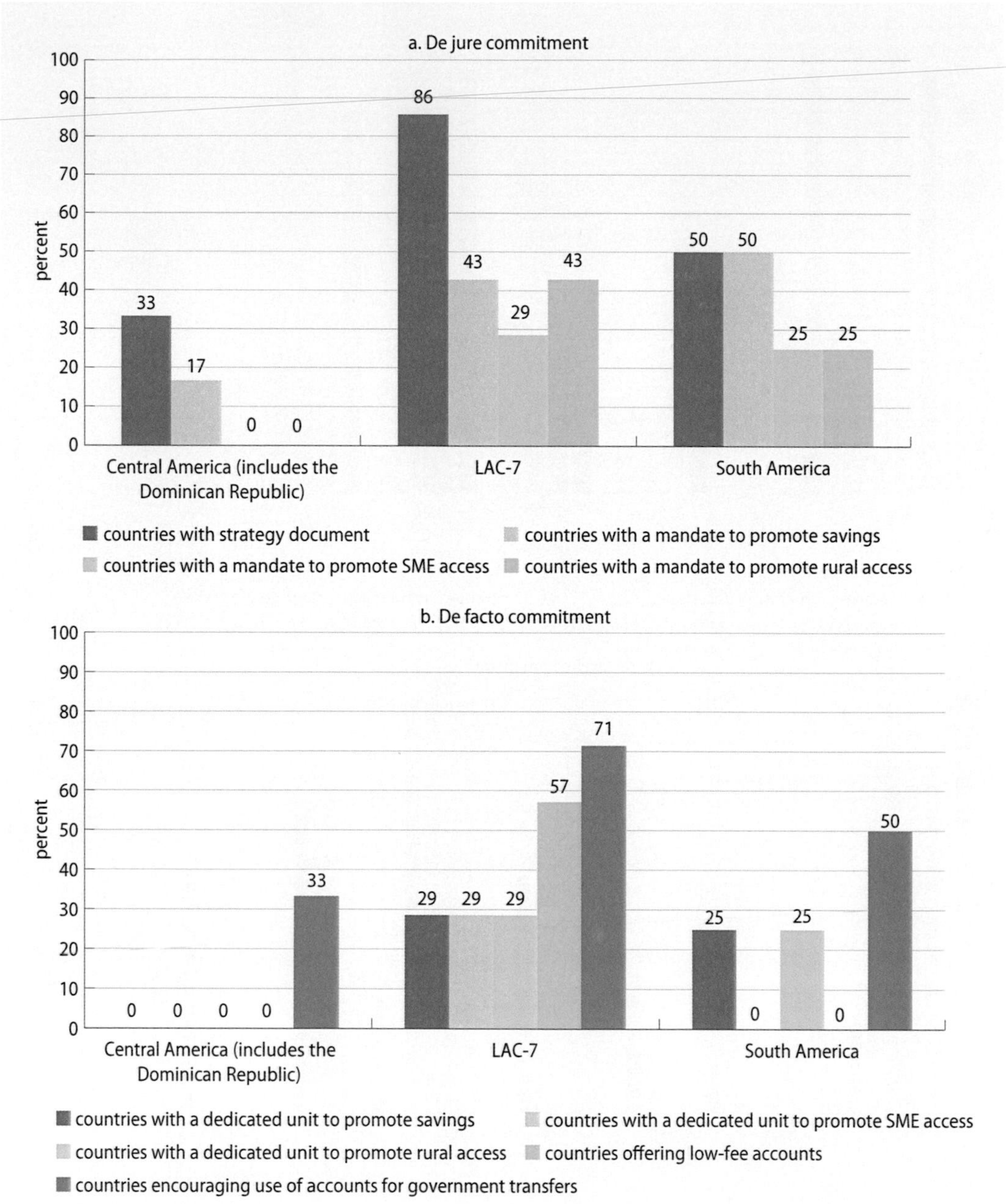
a. De jure commitment
percent
100
90
80
70
60
50
40
30
20
10
0
33
17
0
0
86
43
29
43
50
50
25
25
Central America (includes the Dominican Republic)
LAC-7
South America
countries with strategy document
countries with a mandate to promote savings
countries with a mandate to promote SME access
countries with a mandate to promote rural access
b. De facto commitment
percent
0
0
0
0
33
29
29
29
57
71
25
0
25
0
50
Central America (includes the Dominican Republic)
LAC-7
South America
countries with a dedicated unit to promote savings
countries with a dedicated unit to promote SME access
countries with a dedicated unit to promote rural access
countries offering low-fee accounts
countries encouraging use of accounts for government transfers

Source: Martínez Pería 2011.

FIGURE 5.10   **The adoption of correspondent banking and mobile branches**

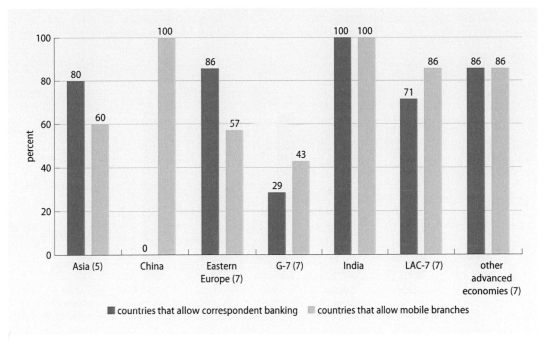

Source: Martínez Pería 2011.

FIGURE 5.11   **The adoption of correspondent banking and mobile branches: LAC-7 versus rest of LAC**

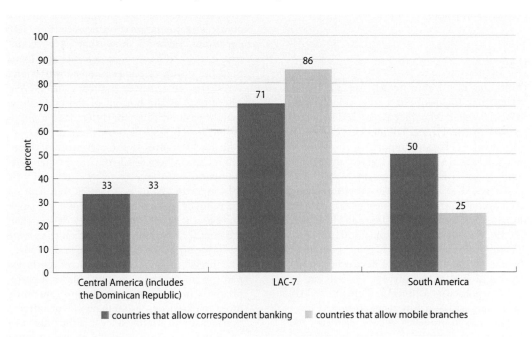

Source: Martínez Pería 2011.

FIGURE 5.12   **Index of credit information and legal rights**

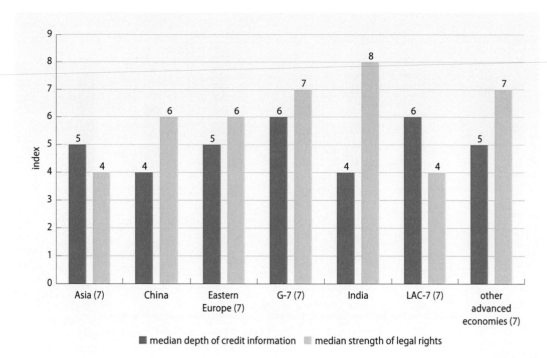

■ median depth of credit information   ■ median strength of legal rights

Source: Martínez Pería 2011.

legal rights reforms should be a priority for LAC-7 governments.

Notes

1. This chapter draws heavily on the paper "Financial Inclusion in Latin America" by María Soledad Martínez Pería (2011), which is part of the Edited Volume that accompanies this LAC flagship report.
2. For theoretical studies, see Aghion and Bolton (1997), Banerjee and Newman (1993), and Galor and Zeira (1993). For empirical work, see, among others, Banerjee et al. (2009), Burgess and Pande (2005), Dupas and Robinson (2009), and Karlan and Zinman (2010).
3. This chapter uses firm-level surveys conducted by the World Bank across developing countries and household surveys carried out by the Corporación Andina de Fomento (CAF) in the largest Latin American cities.
4. Differences in branches, ATMs, deposits, and loans across country groupings are explored by regressing these variables against separate dummies for LAC-7, for other LAC countries, and for other noncomparator countries, controlling for population density and GDP per capita. Table 5.1 shows that LAC-7 countries appear to have more deposits and loans than the group of comparator countries and are similar in terms of branches and ATMs. The F-tests at the bottom of the table show that, after controlling for differences in population density and income, there are no significant differences in the indicators of financial inclusion between LAC-7 and other LAC countries.
5. It is important to note, however, that data on the number of loans are available for a small number of countries—certainly fewer than the number of countries for which data were available on deposits, branches, and ATMs.
6. The firms' answers obviously reflect firms' perceptions, so there could be biases if entrepreneurs from certain regions are inherently more pessimistic. Nonetheless, considering this measure is useful, since it is the only variable that, to some extent, takes into account the cost of financing.

7. Some specific government initiatives adopted in the region include, among others, the development of correspondent banking in Brazil, government bank-sponsored microfinance programs in Brazil and Chile, and enhancements in conditional cash transfer programs in Argentina, Brazil, and Colombia. See boxes 1 through 5 in Martínez Pería (2011) for further information.

8. Correspondent banking arrangements are partnerships between banks and nonbanks with a significant network of outlets, such as convenience stores, post offices, drugstores, and supermarkets to distribute financial services. Mobile branches are offices where banking business is conducted, and they are moved to one or more predetermined locations according to a predetermined schedule.

9. A score of 1 is assigned for each of the following six features of the public credit registry or private credit bureau (or both): (1) Both positive credit information (for example, outstanding loan amounts and pattern of on-time repayments) and negative information (for example, late payments, number and amount of defaults and bankruptcies) are distributed. (2) Data on both firms and individuals are distributed. (3) Data from retailers and utility companies as well as financial institutions are distributed. (4) More than two years of historical data are distributed. Credit registries and bureaus that erase data on defaults as soon as they are repaid obtain a score of 0 for this indicator. (5) Data on loan amounts below 1 percent of income per capita are distributed. Note that a credit registry or bureau must have a minimum coverage of 1 percent of the adult population to score a 1 on this indicator. (6) By law, borrowers have the right to access their data in the largest credit registry or bureau in the economy.

The Banking Gap | 6

Chapter 3 showed that banks in Latin America and the Caribbean (LAC) (and LAC-7 banks even more so) lagged their benchmarks as regards the scale of intermediation and its cost (net interest margins). This apparent banking gap should matter, however, only if it translates into lower output growth or limits households' welfare. While a wealth of studies link private bank credit to output growth, poverty, and inequality, what holds across countries may not necessarily be as relevant for a specific country or even region.[1] The lack of domestic bank credit could be offset by a surplus of other forms of external funding, whether domestic or international, or it could reflect a lack of demand for lendable funds rather than a lack of supply. The policy implications of the banking gap clearly differ depending on its causes, such as whether it reflects weaknesses in the financial infrastructure and market environment or whether it is mainly the enduring legacy of a troubled past. Based on the available evidence, this chapter presents a brief discussion of the underlying issues and policy implications.[2] Main findings are as follows:

- Although partly offset through alternative channels of debt finance, particularly cross-border channels, LAC's banking gap

is real enough: LAC banks lend less and charge more than they should.
- While LAC's banking gap affects all forms of credit, it affects mortgages the most and consumer credit the least.
- In the case of commercial credit, while the gap primarily affects small and medium enterprises (SMEs), the severity of its impact is not clear and needs to be investigated in more depth.
- The largest fraction of the gap simply reflects LAC's turbulent macrofinancial history, which puts the spotlight on macroeconomic policy and good prudential oversight.
- Limited demand for credit, reflecting LAC's mediocre output growth in the past, explains another substantial chunk of the gap; while this link between output growth and credit goes in the opposite direction from the one generally emphasized in the recent finance literature, ultimately it also puts the spotlight on productivity-enhancing credit policies.
- A significant share of the gap reflects remaining weaknesses in the enabling environment that need to be addressed, particularly regarding the enforcement of contracts and the effectiveness of creditor rights.

- While there are some indications that LAC banking systems may also face efficiency issues due to insufficient competition, the evidence thus far is not conclusive.

The rest of this chapter is structured as follows. The first section breaks down the credit gap by type of credit and reviews the evidence regarding the possible substitution of domestic bank credit by other forms of lending. The second section sorts out supply from demand effects. The third section reviews the legacy of LAC's turbulent past, and the final section concludes.

Is the banking gap real?

Table 6.1 presents a decomposition of the credit gap by type of credit for 2007 and 1996, using as a benchmark the median credit structure for a sample of middle-income countries for which data are available. As a proportion of its expected (benchmark) level, total private bank credit is about half of what it should be and has widened substantially over the past decade. When different lending categories are considered, the gap is now greatest for mortgages and smallest (although still large) for consumer loans. As already noted in chapter 3, the gap has narrowed considerably for consumer credit

but opened for commercial credit, and it has opened even more for mortgage credit.

These gaps could just reflect measurement problems, if the lack of domestic bank finance were largely offset by foreign finance or by a surplus of domestic nonbank finance. Unfortunately, because of data limitations, it is not straightforward to test this possibility.[3] To gauge the role of foreign finance, one can turn to the International Monetary Fund (IMF) statistics on balance of payment accounts, which provide data on gross foreign debt liabilities that can be used as a point of reference, albeit private and public accounts cannot be separated. These data indicate that the fluctuations in domestic credit to the private sector for four of the LAC-7 countries were to a good extent matched by opposite (albeit much dampened) changes in gross debt liabilities abroad (figure 6.1). While the correlation is significantly negative (close to minus 40 percent), the two series are clearly orders of magnitude apart. Thus, while there is evidently some substitution, it is quite limited. At the same time, foreign private debt securities issued by LAC-7 corporations abroad (that is, nonbank credit to corporations) do not outperform relative to the benchmark. In fact, as shown in the summary benchmarks table shown in chapter 3, they slightly underperform (table 3.2). Therefore, one can safely conclude that, while cross-border credit (from markets or intermediaries) may have substituted for domestic bank credit *at the margin*, it clearly did not do so *on average*.

To understand the extent of domestic substitution of bank credit by domestic nonbank intermediaries (such as factoring and leasing companies, finance companies, credit cooperatives, microfinance corporations, and savings and loans), one can turn to the evidence presented in chapter 3 on factoring and lending by credit cooperatives. It suggests that such nonbank credit cannot be an important offset, both because it does not seem to be unusually large relative to peer regions and because it is too small, relative to bank credit. Moreover, the region slightly underperforms (rather than outperforms) the benchmark in terms of the issue of domestic corporate paper

TABLE 6.1 LAC-7 credit gap by type of credit, 1996 and 2007

	Expected	Actual	Gap	Gap/expected
Year: 1996				
Credit to the private sector as a percentage of GDP				
Commercial	24.7	19.4	5.2	21.1
Mortgage	8.4	5.4	3.0	35.7
Consumer	8.8	3.4	5.4	61.4
Total	41.8	28.2	13.6	32.5
Year: 2007				
Credit to the private sector as a percentage of GDP				
Commercial	22.9	14.5	8.4	36.7
Mortgage	12.6	3.1	9.5	75.4
Consumer	11.2	6.5	4.7	42.0
Total	46.7	24.2	22.5	48.2

Source: de la Torre, Feyen, and Ize 2011.
Note: This table estimates a breakdown by type of credit of the total credit gap identified in chapter 3 based on a comparison of predicted and actual values for four of the LAC-7 countries for which this information is available (Chile, Colombia, Mexico, and Peru).

FIGURE 6.1   Offshore versus onshore credit to the private sector, LAC-4

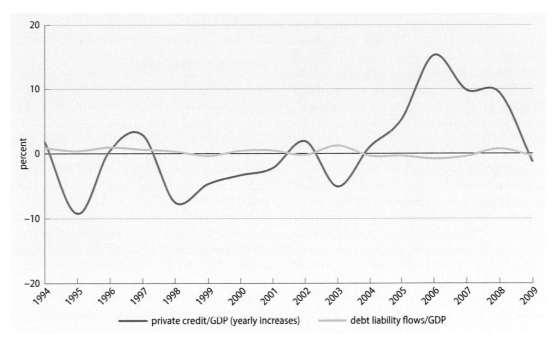

Source: Authors' calculations based on WDI data.
Note: LAC-4 includes Brazil, Chile, Colombia, and Mexico.

(table 3.2). Thus, the evidence again suggests that the average (that is, structural) lack of domestic commercial credit by banks has not been similarly offset by a surplus of domestic nonbank funding.

That being said, one can safely assume that any remaining gap should affect mostly SMEs rather than large corporations, since the latter are able to switch sources of finance (whether at home or abroad) rather easily, depending on cost and availability. Even there, however, the evidence as to whether LAC's SMEs have had a particularly hard time getting financing, as discussed in chapter 5, is not particularly conclusive. A World Bank survey of interest rates charged by banks to small and large firms does suggest that LAC's small firms may indeed pay more for their credit. However, the difference between LAC and other regions is not that large (table 6.2).[4] Conversely, one could view the rapid growth in SME credit during the past decade as indirect evidence of a credit gap, since it suggests the existence

TABLE 6.2   Real lending rates by type of firm, 2007
percentage points

	Asia	Eastern Europe	LAC-7	Other advanced economies
Real interest rates to low-risk customers				
Small enterprises	2.0	−2.3	5.5	−1.5
Medium enterprises	1.3	−2.7	3.9	−2.0
Large enterprises	2.4	−2.5	0.8	−2.2
Real interest rates to high-risk customers				
Small enterprises	6.3	−0.9	7.0	0.5
Medium enterprises	5.1	−0.9	6.0	0.0
Large enterprises	6.9	−1.4	1.9	−0.5

Source: Beck 2011.

of an ongoing process of catching up. LAC banks seem to have expanded their credit to SMEs quite rapidly and aggressively, particularly to those with supply links to the large corporations.[5] All in all, the only safe conclusion at this point is that economists just do not know enough about the size of (and fluctuations in) SME lending across banks and nonbanks to provide a clear answer about the severity of the impact of the credit gap on the productive sector. Clearly, this is an area for priority research.

This section concludes with a brief look at the other two types of credit. As regards personal (consumer) credit, one could also view its rapid expansion as an indirect indication of a possible catch-up on an initial gap (figure 6.2). If so, however, the gap has narrowed considerably. Indeed, there is a widespread perception among policy makers in the region that the banking system has been concentrating too much on financing consumption rather than production. In the case of mortgages, some substitution could come from the specialized institutions for housing finance that flourished in the past. However, these institutions have, for the most part, run into deep trouble and been discontinued (see box 6.1). There is also, in some cases, an important supply of mortgages coming from public provident funds (such as Infonavit and

Fovissste in Mexico).[6] However, even if one adds these funds to the total supply of mortgages, the gap remains large.[7]

Supply or demand?

Sorting out supply from demand effects in the market for lendable funds is tricky, since the equilibrium reflects both sides of the market simultaneously. Nonetheless, an argument based on differential elasticities of supply and demand can shed some light. This section considers prices first, then quantities.

If supply were much more elastic than demand, then one would expect real interest rates (that is, net of expected devaluation and expected inflation) to be close to world rates and, hence, rather low. If, instead, demand were much more elastic than supply, then interest rates would reflect local demand

FIGURE 6.2   **Evolution of private credit by type of credit across LAC-7 countries**

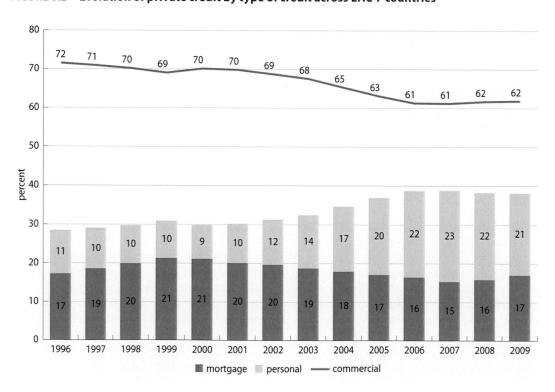

Source: Didier and Schmukler 2011a.
Note: This figure shows the average composition of private credit by type of credit for LAC-7 countries. LAC-7 comprises Chile, Colombia, Mexico, and Peru.

BOX 6.1   A brief history of housing finance in LAC

Housing finance grew fast in some LAC countries in the 1990s; in others, the growth has come in the 2000s. Outstanding housing loans grew from 12 percent to nearly 20 percent of GDP in Chile, from 2 percent to over 10 percent of GDP in Mexico, and from 1.5 percent to nearly 5 percent of GDP in Brazil. Still, except for Chile, housing finance relative to GDP remains, on average, underdeveloped relative to where it should be for countries with similar characteristics. LAC even experienced the rare phenomenon of regression in its development path: Colombia has still not returned to the level prevailing before the 1998 crisis, and the Argentine market continues to dwindle, having now reached only a fourth of the level that prevailed before the 2001–02 crisis.

The single most important reason for this underdevelopment is macroeconomic instability, to which long-term finance is highly sensitive, as evidenced by the disruptions of supply following episodes of deep turmoil. As a result, one feature that is strikingly common to many LAC countries is the pervasiveness of indexation, which is intended to protect long-term investors against the consequences of unexpected inflation (see chapter 8 for more on indexation).

Historically, the mobilization of savings for housing finance was done through specialized institu-

tions: savings and loans such as Sistema Nacional de Ahorro y Préstamo (SINAP) in Chile, Entidades de Ahorro y Préstamo in República Bolivariana de Venezuela, Sociedades de Ahorro y Préstamo (SAP) in Paraguay, and Corporativas de Ahorro y Préstamo in Colombia. In all cases, to help attract long-term capital, these institutions benefited from an exclusive right to offer indexed savings products. For example, in Colombia, the Corporaciones de Ahorro y Vivienda (CAVs) were created at the same time as a specific index, the UPAC, and, by regulation, CAVs denominated all their operations in this form of currency. But the index became problematic as it migrated from being based on the consumer price index (CPI) to being based on a nominal interest rate. Moreover, prosperity based on regulatory privileges proved once again to be fragile. SINAP collapsed in the 1970s, 10 years after the creation of the system, when the Chilean government opened the indexation option to all institutions. In Colombia, the CAVs collapsed following the 1998 crisis, which was triggered by a dramatic increase in defaults that resulted from retroactive changes in the indexation system (back to the CPI-based index). The SAP sector also collapsed in Paraguay in the wake of the late 1990s turmoil, again because of asset-liability mismatches linked to indexation.

conditions and, hence, probably would exceed world rates. In fact, real lending rates in LAC have exceeded U.S. rates by close to 800 basis points on average over the past decade (figure 6.3).

The first question to examine, then, is whether the high borrowing rates mainly reflect a banking intermediation problem or a high cost of bank funding. Real deposit rates, while also higher in LAC, have exceeded U.S. rates by only 100 to 200 basis points over the past decade. Moreover, the deposit rate differential has always been below the country risk differential, as measured by the Emerging Markets Bond Index (EMBI) premiums (figure 6.3). This suggests that funding rates

in LAC are not particularly high. Moreover, recent work on emerging sovereign bond rates (Broner, Lorenzoni, and Schmukler 2010) shows that in normal times the region faces a fairly elastic supply of foreign funds. Except at the longer end of the maturity range in times of world market turbulence, bond rates are basically determined by the world appetite for risk, with LAC behaving like other regions. The gradual shrinking of country premiums and their increased dependence on global fluctuations in risk appetite (rather than idiosyncratic factors) tell a similar story.

Hence, the bulk of the differential in funding costs to borrowers reflects much higher

FIGURE 6.3   **Real lending rate, real deposit rate, and EMBI: differentials between LAC-6 and the United States**

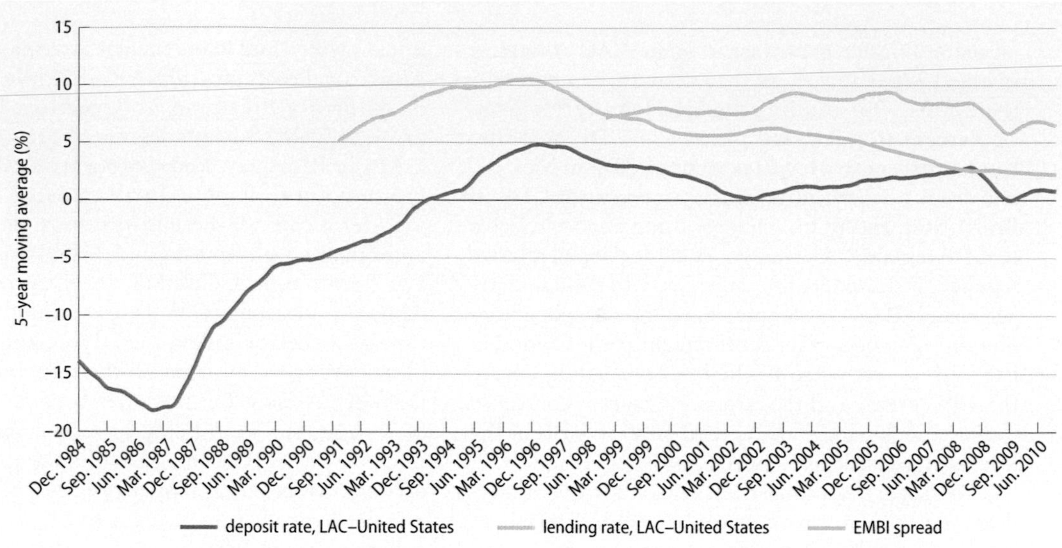

Source: Authors' calculations based on local sources.

bank interest margins, which is consistent with the benchmarking evidence presented in chapter 3. The obvious question, therefore, is: what is behind these fatter margins? Gelos (2009) breaks down bank intermediation spreads in LAC and concludes that higher overhead accounts for about two-thirds of the explained difference between LAC and other developing countries, with higher deposit rates (which translate into higher spreads) and higher reserve requirements accounting for most of the rest (figure 6.4). Gelos concludes that the higher overheads must reflect inefficiencies due to lack of competition. However, Gelos fails to detect supporting evidence based on either the H-statistic (Panzar and Rosse 1987) or bank concentration ratios. A more recent study (Anzoategui, Martínez Pería, and Rocha 2010) reaches a similar conclusion based on the Panzar-Rosse H-statistic as well as the Lerner index.[8] In fact, LAC outperforms (rather than underperforms) as regards either of these two indexes. Clearly, this is also an area that requires more research.

However, the high overheads could also reflect a problem of insufficient scale, which itself may reflect high costs of doing banking business due to a weak informational and enforcement environment. Given the limited intermediation (the bank credit gap relative to benchmark), LAC banks may have a harder time spreading the fixed costs. Using individual bank data, Gelos (2009) indeed finds that bank size is a key determinant of bank spreads. A similar result is obtained here using countrywide data. Including the ratio of private credit to GDP (a proxy for scale) as an additional control in the workhorse benchmark regressions presented in chapters 2 and 3 explains about two-thirds of the current excess margin (table 6.3). Hence, the evidence suggests, perhaps not too surprisingly, that the high margins and the limited scale of intermediation are largely mirror images of each other.

This, in turn, suggests exploring in more depth LAC's underperformance as regards the size of banking intermediation. Adding a basic set of enabling environment

FIGURE 6.4   Net interest margins: Contribution of different factors in explaining differences between Latin America's average and that for developing countries

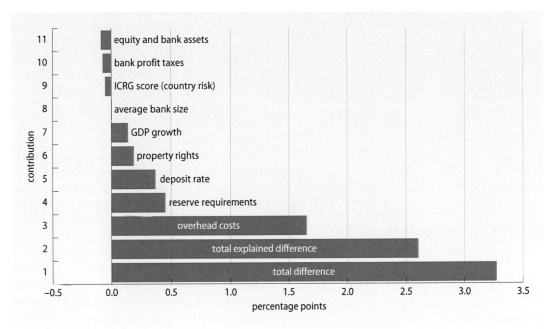

Source: Gelos 2009.

indicators—contract enforcement costs, creditor rights, property rights, and credit information—to the basic benchmark regressions for private bank credit shows that some of them (enforcement costs and creditor rights) have a significant impact. Since LAC significantly underperforms on both of these indicators, the two variables together explain about 2.6 percentage points of GDP of the credit gap (table 6.4). While this constitutes only a modest fraction (about 13 percent) of the total gap, measurement noise is likely to bias downward this result. Its share of the total explained component of the gap (nearly one-fourth) probably provides a more accurate sense of the magnitude of its importance.

Considering quantities now instead of prices: the low volume of commercial credit could be reflecting a lack of bankable projects and, hence, a low demand for credit. LAC's lackluster growth could, in turn, be a reflection of lack of investment rather than

TABLE 6.3   LAC bank net interest margins, bank overheads, and private credit

	Net interest margins	Net interest margins	Overheads	Overheads
Private credit (% of GDP)	−0.0261***	−0.0236***	−0.0247***	−0.0229***
	(−8.280)	(−6.314)	(−9.833)	(−8.390)
Contract enforcement index		−0.247*		−0.072
		(−2.224)		(−0.724)
Legal rights index		0.0538		0.0653
		(−0.976)		(−1.395)
Credit information index		−0.0161		−0.0153
		(−0.214)		(−0.276)
Property rights index		0.00697		−0.00324
		(−0.883)		(−0.467)
Constant	4.669	15.90**	5.172	17.92***
	(1.087)	(2.426)	(1.519)	(2.956)
Observations	1,280	459	1,280	459
R-squared	0.36	0.49	0.35	0.48

Source: de la Torre, Feyen, and Ize 2011.
Note: The contract enforcement index is the principal component of the following indicators from the World Bank's Doing Business: contract enforcement costs, number of days to enforce a contract (in logs), and number of procedures to enforce a contract. The legal rights index and the credit information index also are from Doing Business. The property rights index is from the Heritage Foundation. Robust *t*-statistics are shown in parentheses.
Significance level: * = 10 percent, ** = 5 percent, *** = 1 percent.

TABLE 6.4   LAC-7 Private credit gap: A decomposition by source

	Dependent variable: Bank private credit (% of GDP)			
	(1)	(2)	(3)	(4)
Enforcement contract index	−4.047*			−5.318**
	(−1.864)			(−2.358)
Legal rights index	1.662			1.671
	(−1.547)			(−1.385)
Credit information index	−0.526			
	(−0.379)			
Property rights index	0.235			0.069
	(−1.301)			(−0.335)
Annualized average sample GDP growth		7.450***		5.59**
		(2.935)		(−2.433)
Credit crash dummy (% of period)			−86.92***	−77.69**
			(−2.816)	(−2.042)
Workhorse controls	Yes	Yes	Yes	Yes
Explained credit gap based on LAC-7 median values:				
Contract enforcement index	1.51			1.98
Legal rights index	0.64			0.65
Credit information index	0.47			
Property rights index	1.15			0.34
Annualized average sample GDP growth			3.70	2.80
Credit crash dummy (% of time)			7.02	6.27
Total explained gap	3.77	3.70	7.02	12.04
Gap	20.9	20.1	18.9	15.7
Percent of total explained gap	18	18	37	77

Source: de la Torre, Feyen, and Ize 2011.
Note: The contract enforcement index is the principal component of the following indicators from Doing Business: contract enforcement costs, number of days to enforce a contract (in logs), and number of procedures to enforce a contract. The legal rights index and the credit information index are from Doing Business. The property rights index is from the Heritage Foundation. Robust *t*-statistics are shown in parentheses.
Significance level: * = 10 percent, ** = 5 percent, *** = 1 percent.

lack of savings. And lack of investment could, in turn, reflect low productivity rather than a high cost of funds. Indeed, a sizable literature emphasizes LAC's structural productivity and growth bottlenecks, which derive from institutional weaknesses as well as overvalued real exchange rates.[9]

However, directly ascertaining whether investment is driving savings or whether savings are driving investment is a perilous matter, given the obvious endogeneities. Should the supply of foreign savings be relatively elastic, this would, of course, tilt the balance toward investment driving savings. As discussed above, and with the proper caveats, this seems to be consistent with the relatively high elasticity of demand for LAC bonds. Another piece of evidence

going in the same direction, but admittedly also quite impressionistic, is that the recovery of credit in LAC has been mostly in consumer lending rather than in commercial loans, which may suggest that, as a whole (but possibly with the exception of credit to SMEs, as discussed above), firms are not starved for credit (figure 6.2). Finally, while LAC banks' high liquidity could just reflect caution, it could also be consistent with limited demand for credit.

A more direct test of possible demand effects is to check the extent to which output growth has affected finance. In the wake of the finance and growth literature, it has been customary to think in terms of current finance affecting future output growth. Here, the opposite test is carried out: has past output growth affected current finance? Should this be the case, it could mean that another causality link—going from low output growth to low investment, low demand for lendable funds, and hence a low stock of commercial credit—may also be at play. Indeed, this is the case. LAC's underperforming output growth over the past 30 years appears to explain a sizable part of its current banking underperformance (table 6.4).

Are these the ghosts of a turbulent past?

LAC's macrofinancial history of the past 30 years was turbulent, to say the least. A quick comparison with other regions is sufficient to prove the point. LAC was the region where crises were both the most frequent and the most encompassing, featuring the full range and mix of currency, banking, and debt crises (table 6.5). A bird's-eye view of events can be obtained by contrasting the dynamics of real interest rates in LAC with those of real bank credit since the late 1970s, based on medians for the LAC-6 countries (Argentina, Brazil, Chile, Colombia, Mexico, and Peru) and comparing real interest rates in LAC with those in the United States (figures 6.3 and 6.5).[10] There were three clear credit cycles:

THE BANKING GAP **103**

one during the early 1980s, one lasting most of the 1990s, with an interruption in 1995 due to Mexico's "tequila crisis," and one that is ongoing after a brief interruption due to the global financial crisis. The first cycle started with a period of easy money and low real U.S. rates. It ended brutally in 1982 with U.S. interest rates rising sharply in the wake of Federal Reserve Chairman Paul Volcker's stabilization efforts and LAC rates going in the opposite direction, as the region's inflation rates went through the roof. The second cycle started with LAC's mostly failed exchange-rate-based stabilizations that resulted in high real interest rates, strong currency appreciations, and large capital inflows; that cycle ended with twin crises in most countries. The third cycle started in the early years of the millennium under the twin impetuses of domestic macrostabilization and the strongly stimulative world environment resulting from China's accelerated growth and large U.S. deficits.

In view of this eventful background, a key question is whether the comparatively low levels of credit in the region today are a lasting reflection of the sharp collapses of credit during the 1980s and 1990s. To test this notion, one needs to differentiate between collapses due to genuine disintermediation (that is, banking crises) and

TABLE 6.5 Number of crises by type, 1970–2007

Country or region	External debt crisis	Domestic debt crisis	Banking crisis	Currency crisis	Any type of crisis
Asia (5)	5	0	14	17	27
China	0	0	3	2	5
Eastern Europe (7)	6	2	13	15	28
G-7 (7)	0	0	16	1	17
India	0	0	1	1	2
Other advanced economies (7)	0	0	9	10	18
LAC	47	13	53	72	149
Caribbean (2)	5	0	3	7	14
Central America (+ Dominican Republic) (6)	11	2	13	14	33
LAC-7 (7)	16	7	21	36	63
Offshore centers in LAC (3)	2	1	1	0	3
Other South America (4)	13	3	15	15	36

Source: Broner et al. 2010.

FIGURE 6.5 Real credit to the private sector and compounded real deposit rate index, LAC-6

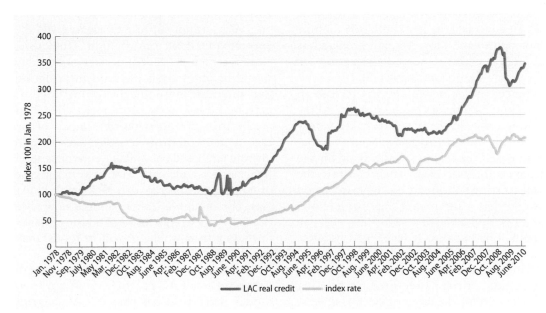

Source: Author's calculations based on WDI data.

collapses due to debt monetization (that is, inflationary outbursts resulting in strongly negative real interest rates). While the former are associated with a clear worsening of both banks' and borrowers' balance sheets, the latter are more likely to be associated with an improvement, so they could leave different imprints. At the same time, however, debt monetizations are likely to have undermined the credibility of local currencies, thereby boosting domestic financial dollarization. Hence, unless countries allowed dollarization to take hold—despite its drawbacks—one would also expect a lasting impact on banking systems' capacity to intermediate.

To test for these effects, a worldwide credit crash variable is constructed that reflects mild, strong, and severe annual drops in the ratio of private credit to GDP; the variable is included in the basic benchmark regressions of private bank credit, together with a dummy for countries that underwent episodes of extreme inflation during the past 30 years. To test for induced dollarization effects, a deposit dollarization variable is added as well as a variable representing the interaction of inflation and dollarization. The credit crash variable is indeed very significant, explaining as much as a third of the current credit gap in LAC (table 6.6). In contrast, the hyperinflation dummy is not significant. However, inflation and its interaction with financial dollarization are also jointly significant (table 6.7).

Hence, the evidence appears to lead to the following joint set of conclusions: (a) the banking crises of the past have taken a very significant toll on LAC's financial intermediation, and the region is still paying for the sins of its abrupt cycles;[11] (b) in contrast, the monetizations induced by hyperinflation have not left a significant imprint; (c) however, inflation has had a significant negative impact, not because it weakened balance sheets, but because it made financial contracting more difficult, particularly at the longer time horizons required for housing finance; and (d) the latter effect was at least partly offset, for the countries that allowed it, by financial dollarization.[12]

Remarkably, the credit crash variable also helps explain banks' high interest margins as well as their comfortable financial soundness indicators (profitability, capital, and liquidity) (table 6.6). This suggests that banks that underwent crises were able to raise their margins (thereby raising their profitability), reflecting a forward reassessment of risks as well as perhaps a need to recoup the losses incurred during the crisis. At the same time, they became more prudent in managing risk, which led to less lending and higher prudential buffers. While this is not too surprising, it is rather remarkable that these effects continue to be evident a decade or two after the crises.[13]

Where is LAC now?

Altogether, the evidence suggests that the domestic banking gap, although partly offset through alternative channels of debt finance, particularly cross-border channels, is nonetheless real enough. LAC banks lend less and charge more than they should. However, while there are good reasons to think that, in the case of commercial credit, this gap affects SMEs more than it does the large corporations, the size of the impact—even on SMEs—is not sufficiently clear, given the currently available information. Obviously, more research is needed; of particular value would be an analysis of credit information that provides more insight into lending to marginal borrowers. More research is also needed to ascertain the possible impact of the lack of credit on firms' leverage, activity, and investment, based on available enterprise-level financial accounts data. Similarly, in the case of mortgages, the gap also looks real. However, not enough is known about the precise extent to which other forms of housing finance (including from public provident funds) may be offsetting the lack of bank credit.

The largest fraction of the banking gap simply reflects LAC's turbulent history. Even though much time has passed, LAC has not yet fully recovered from the repeated credit crashes of its past. The main policy lesson here is that financial sustainability is the name of the game. The long-run costs of financial crashes are too large to be taken lightly. This puts the spotlight squarely on macroprudential policy and good systemic prudential oversight. These issues are addressed in chapters 10–13.

Historically low demand for credit, as proxied by LAC's mediocre output growth of the past, explains another substantial chunk of the gap. To the extent that output growth has to do with other (nonfinancial) policies, such as macroeconomic policy or supply-side structural policies to enhance productivity and competitiveness, the possible policy responses go beyond the financial sector. However, one can also argue that output growth (and, hence, ultimately financial depth) could have been boosted by financial policies focused on overcoming the limited marginal productivity of capital by lowering the cost of finance; that is, policy might have increased the number of bankable projects by increasing their profitability. A possible avenue for doing this is to stimulate demand for longer maturity loans by SMEs through public guarantees, an issue that is addressed in chapters 8 and 9.

A significant share of the banking gap also has to do with remaining weaknesses in the enabling environment. Much progress has been made in resolving informational frictions. Indeed, LAC is ahead of many emerging markets in the development of credit bureaus, for example. But LAC still has a long way to go in addressing contractual frictions, particularly as regards the enforcement of contracts and the preservation of creditor rights. While there are some indications that LAC banking systems may also face efficiency issues associated with insufficient competition, the available evidence is not conclusive. Should lack of competitiveness be confirmed through further research, a policy agenda to address it would need to be developed.

TABLE 6.6   LAC banks' interest margins, financial soundness, enabling environment indicators, and credit history—growth and crashes

	Net interest margin	Return on investment	Capital as % of total assets	Liquid assets as % of total assets	Regulatory capital
Enforcement contract index	−0.155	0.0438	0.353	2.366	0.247
	(−0.713)	(−0.42)	(−0.857)	(−0.726)	(−1.326)
Legal rights index	0.156	0.051	−0.192	0.787	0.312***
	(−1.318)	(−0.931)	(−0.903)	(−0.496)	(−3.131)
Property rights index	0.0246	0.00367	0.0659*	−0.0129	0.0347**
	(−1.192)	(−0.387)	(−1.769)	(−0.0502)	(−2.481)
Annualized average sample GDP growth	−0.0971	0.00887	−0.0202	0.156	−1.054***
	(−0.471)	(−0.108)	(−0.0642)	(−0.0504)	(−8.303)
Credit crash dummy (% of period)	20.83**	5.068**	17.52*	13.39	27.90***
	(−4.332)	(−2.266)	(−1.897)	(−0.183)	(−7.092)
Constant	7.914	9.730**	−19.96	187.9	12.26
	(−0.958)	(−2.504)	(−1.170)	(−1.408)	(−1.611)
Observations	88	88	98	98	78
Pseudo R-squared	0.48	0.32	0.21	0.19	0.27

Source: de la Torre, Feyen, and Ize 2011.
Note: The contract enforcement index is the principal component of the following indicators from Doing Business: contract enforcement costs, number of days to enforce a contract (in logs), and number of procedures to enforce a contract. The legal rights index and the credit information index are from Doing Business. The property rights index is from the Heritage Foundation. Robust *t*-statistics are shown in parentheses.
Significance level: * = 10 percent, ** = 5 percent, *** = 1 percent.

TABLE 6.7   LAC private credit, financial dollarization, and inflation, 2005–08

	Dependent variable: Average private credit to GDP				
	(1)	(2)	(3)	(4)	(5)
Dollarization – (period mean)	−17.73*		49.93*		
	(1.770)		(−1.851)		
Dollarization – (last)				55.77**	62.59*
				(−2.002)	(−1.774)
Log period inflation – (period mean)		−6.38***	−15.16***	−15.27***	−17.81***
		(−2.952)	(−3.572)	(−3.690)	(−2.988)
Dollarization (mean)* Log Inflation (mean)			23.23**		
			(−2.249)		
Dollarization (last)* Log Inflation (mean)				24.84**	29.45*
				(−2.261)	(−1.893)
Constant	176.6**	167.2***	118.4	103.1	133.6
	(−2.321)	(−2.653)	(−1.557)	(−1.347)	(−1.234)
Observations	128	162	128	128	86
R-squared	0.68	0.73	0.72	0.72	0.73

Source: de la Torre, Feyen, and Ize 2011.
Significance level: * = 10 percent, ** = 5 percent, *** = 1 percent.

Notes

1. On links between private credit and growth, see, for example, Beck, Levine, and Loayza (2000), and King and Levine (1993). A recent survey of the literature can be found in Arizala, Cavallo, and Galindo (2009), who analyze the impact of financial development on industry-level total factor productivity. On links between financial depth, poverty, and equal opportunity, see Beck, Demirgüç-Kunt, and Levine (2007) and Rajan and Zingales (2003).

2. This chapter draws heavily on the papers "Benchmarking Financial Development" by Augusto de la Torre, Erik Feyen, and Alain Ize (2011) and "Financial Globalization: Some Basic Indicators for Latin America and the Caribbean" by Tatiana Didier and Sergio Schmukler (2011b), which are part of the forthcoming Edited Volume that will accompany this LAC flagship report.

3. BIS reports the data only on syndicated loans reported in chapter 4.

4. Given the very limited coverage of the survey, this evidence is mostly indicative.

5. Beck, Demirgüç-Kunt, and Martínez Pería (2011) document some of the drivers underlying the rapidly expanding capacity of large banks to lend to SMEs based on public information rather than relationship lending. De la Torre, Martínez Pería, and Schmukler (2010) find that the involvement of LAC banks with SMEs appears to be increasing, particularly for the SMEs connected to the large corporations. Based on a background econometric study for the Financial Sector Assessment Program for Chile, Didier (2011b) confirms that the "connected SMEs" get better treatment in terms of access to bank credit.

6. Provident funds for housing, based on mandatory savings, are particularly notable in Mexico. According to the Asociación Hipotecaria Mexicana, they accounted for almost 85 percent of the number of new housing loans and more than 70 percent of the volume of new loans in 2010. They are also present in Brazil, Colombia, and República Bolivariana de Venezuela.

7. For Mexico, the supply of mortgages as a proportion of GDP increases from 3.0 percent to 5.3 percent in 2009 when credit by Infonavit, Fovissste, and Sociedad Hipotecaria Federal are considered, which is still significantly below the benchmark level of 12.6 percent for 2007 indicated in table 6.1.

8. The Panzar-Rosse H-statistic contrasts the elasticity of a firm's revenue with that of its input costs (under perfect competition, an increase in input prices should lead to a one-for-one increase in output prices and, hence, revenue). The Lerner index calculates the disparity between prices and marginal costs (that is, it is a measure of the markup).

9. See for example McMillan and Rodrik (2011) for a discussion emphasizing the low growth of output and employment in LAC's higher-productivity sectors.

10. The compounded real (deposit) interest rate is included in the figure because it provides some indication of "autonomous" changes in credit that are simply driven by the compounding of interest rates. Thus, the difference between the real credit and real interest rate lines is a measure of the truly exogenous component of the credit cycle.

11. Interestingly, when adding a simple credit volatility variable (the year-to-year variance of private to GDP credit) as an additional control in the benchmark regressions of credit, it is not statistically significant. Hence, it is credit crashes—but not volatility per se—that leave a substantial and lasting imprint on financial development.

12. These links between financial depth, inflation, and dollarization were first explored by de Nicolo, Honohan, and Ize (2005).

13. Evidence showing that LAC banks currently enjoy substantial prudential buffers (capital, liquidity, and profitability) is presented in chapter 10.

The Equity Gap | 7

As argued in chapter 3, domestic equity markets across Latin America and the Caribbean (LAC) remain illiquid and highly concentrated. This relative underdevelopment stands in contrast to the significant number of capital market reforms introduced over the last two decades and the improved macroeconomic stance (figure 7.1), which were expected to help LAC equity markets develop toward their benchmark. This chapter attempts to shed light on the possible causes for this underperformance. It first reviews some of the most common explanations put forth by practitioners, policy makers and academics, including the effects of globalization, free float, market concentration, institutional investor behavior, and corporate governance. The chapter then refers to additional possible causes. Main highlights are as follows:

- The offshoring of stock market turnover in LAC (the trading of equities abroad) has been particularly large.
- Such offshoring seems to significantly explain the domestic underperformance in the trading activity of the larger firms; however, it does not directly explain the low trading activity of the smaller firms, since the latter are not traded abroad.

Contributing factors to the low domestic trading of the smaller firms may include the negative spillover effects of the offshoring of the larger stocks; the dominance of buy-and-hold pension funds relative to more active institutional traders such as mutual funds; and weaknesses in corporate governance (particularly with respect to minority shareholder rights and protections) and the general enabling environment (particularly as regards property rights).

- For reasons that remain to be fully elucidated, the region's history of macroeconomic and financial turbulence may also be a potential culprit of the low domestic liquidity.
- Besides the obvious improvements in macrostability, stock market infrastructure, and the general enabling environment (which should all help, but at the margin), developing a proper policy agenda remains thorny, particularly for the smaller countries and the smaller firms, given the decisive importance of scale (size of markets and of issues) and network effects in stock market development.

The rest of this chapter is organized as follows. The first five sections review the impact

FIGURE 7.1 **Percentage of LACs that implemented capital market reforms, various years**

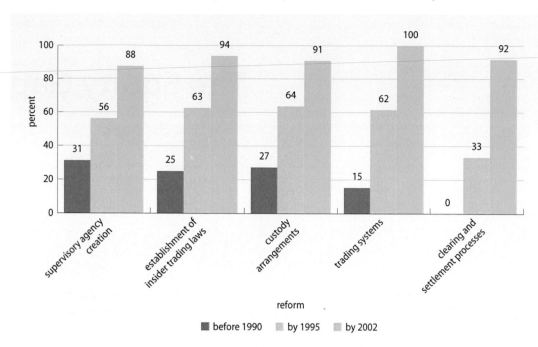

Source: de la Torre and Schmukler 2007.
Note: This figure shows the cumulative percentage of Latin American countries having implemented specfic capital markets reforms at different points in time.

of globalization, free float, market concentration, institutional investors, and corporate governance, respectively. The sixth section reviews additional factors, and the final section concludes.

Effects of globalization

Calculation of effects begins by analyzing whether the lack of liquidity (that is, the low turnovers) in the domestic equity markets can be due to the offshoring of stock market activity described in chapter 4 as part of financial globalization. As the offshoring of stocks does not engender balance sheet mismatches, it has no systemic vulnerability implications, even when the country that engages in offshoring has a weak currency. However, the offshoring of stock issuance and trading can have adverse effects on the liquidity of the domestic stock market. It can do so through various channels (Levine and Schmukler 2007). First, it can shift the trading of firms that issue abroad out of

the domestic market—the "liquidity migration" effect. Second, it can lead to a drop in the trading and liquidity of the stocks of the remaining domestic firms. This in turn can happen through two effects. The first effect ("negative spillovers") is linked with the increase in cost per trade at home due to fixed costs. The second effect ("domestic trade diversion") follows from the fact that the internationalization of stock issuance and trading induces improvements in reputation, disclosure standards, analyst coverage, and the shareholder base, all of which induce investors to shift their attention from firms trading onshore to firms trading offshore.[1]

Figure 7.2, panel a shows the "total turnover" for the stocks of (large) firms with depository receipts (DRs) in the New York Stock Exchange—obtained as the sum of onshore and offshore trading divided by their market capitalization reported for the onshore market.[2] It also shows the domestic turnover for these same (large) firms and the

FIGURE 7.2 Onshore and offshore equity markets

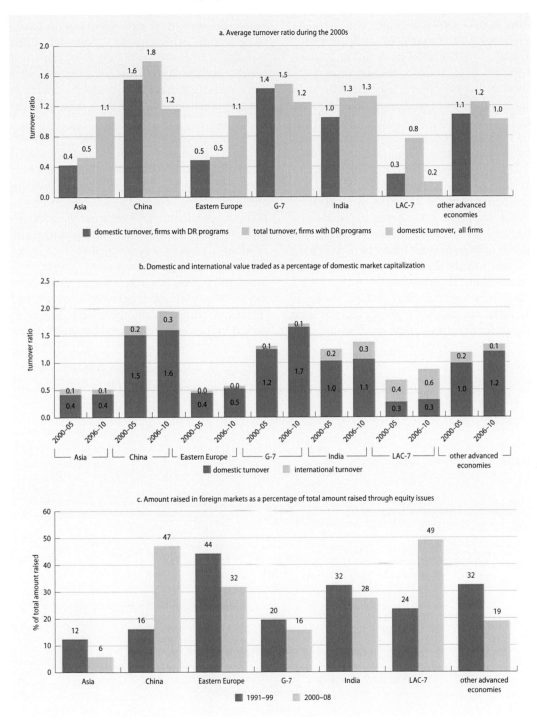

Source: Didier and Schmukler 2011b.
Note: This figure shows characterizes domestic and foreign equity markets. Panel a shows the average between 2000 and 2010 of the turnover ratios in domestic markets for firms with DR programs as well as the total turnover ratios, which consider domestic and foreign trading activity. It also shows the aggregate turnover ratio in domestic markets for all listed firms. Panel b shows, for firms with DR programs, the average ratio of domestic and foreign value traded as a share of their market capitalization (that is, domestic and foreign turnover ratios between 2000 and 2010). Panel c shows the amount raised in equity market abroad relative to total amount raised through equity issues in domestic and foreign markets between 1991 and 2008. All DRs identified in the DR Directory of the Bank of New York, with trading data reported in Bloomberg, are considered in this figure.

turnover for all firms in the domestic market. The striking result is that, once offshore trading is taken into account, the turnover of the large LAC firms nearly triples and is even higher than that of its Asian or Eastern European peers. Indeed, for the large LAC firms, turnover abroad dominates turnover at home, much more so than in other regions. The effect is so large that for the large LAC firms with DR programs there does not seem to be an equity gap. Thus, offshoring does appear to be largely responsible for the atypically low domestic trading for these LAC firms. Moreover, the increase in total turnover for the large LAC firms has occurred nearly entirely offshore (figure 7.2, panel b). And the new issues of equity by LAC firms have been mostly done offshore, rather than onshore (figure 7.2, panel c).

The story for the smaller LAC firms is quite different, as they typically do not have access to foreign stock markets. The very low total domestic equity turnover suggests that the liquidity for the smaller firms (that do not trade abroad) is extremely low in LAC, compared to other regions. Moreover, it has remained broadly stable even as the total turnover of the large firms has increased very substantially (figure 7.2, panel b), which is broadly consistent with the negative spillover view.

A further check on the impact of offshoring on the domestic turnover can be obtained by first controlling the cross-country data on domestic stock market turnover and foreign turnover for economic development (gross domestic product [GDP] per capita) and country size (population) and then plotting the residuals of the two series against each other and running a regression (figure 7.3). Interestingly, the regression line is negative, suggesting some substitution between onshore and offshore trading. At the same time, however, except for one country (República Bolivariana

FIGURE 7.3   Average of residuals of domestic and foreign turnover, 2005–09

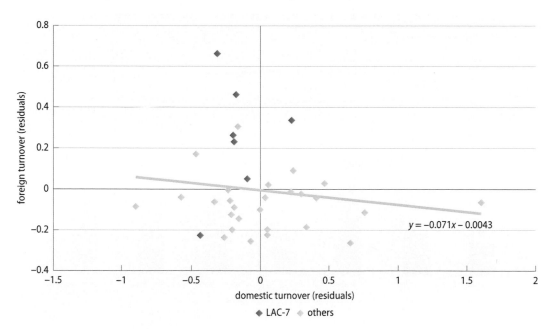

$$y = -0.071x - 0.0043$$

◆ LAC-7   ◆ others

Source: Authors' calculations based on Didier and Schmukler 2011b.
Note: This figure shows the scatterplot of domestic and foreign equity turnover, defined as the average total value traded per year in domestic and foreign markets over domestic market capitalization for those firms with DR programs. The 2005–09 average residuals of domestic and foreign turnover are reported. Residuals are obtained from ordinary least squares regressions of domestic or foreign turnover on GDP per capita and population. All DRs identified in the DR Directory of the Bank of New York, with trading data reported in Bloomberg, are considered in this figure.

de Venezuela), all other LAC countries are bunched up on the upward left of the scatter plot, suggesting that LAC countries are atypical in that they trade more than expected offshore, less than expected onshore. This supports the view that offshoring has displaced domestic stock trading much more in LAC than in other regions.

A final check is reported in table 7.1. It shows the results of a battery of regressions of domestic stock market turnover using the same workhorse benchmarking model used in chapters 2 and 3. While the limited data availability is a strongly limiting factor, a remarkable result is that once one introduces in the regressions the share of foreign trading, the LAC dummy ceases to be significant. This result provides additional support to the view that much of the apparent LAC equity gap can be explained by the region's extraordinary reliance on offshore trading.

Free float

Another argument often put forth as a possible reason for LAC's equity gap is the low level of freely tradable stocks (free float). That is, a substantial component of market capitalization in LAC corresponds to shares that are closely held and hence not available for trading in open exchanges. When firms are controlled by large shareholders (typically rich families), which is more likely to be the case in countries with poor investor protection and high concentration of wealth, secondary market liquidity might dry up.[3] In this case, the turnover figure is distorted, since trading captures only the free-floating shares while market capitalization aggregates all the shares.

This argument is assessed by adjusting the equity turnover ratio (value trade divided by market capitalization), that is, by considering in the denominator only the market capitalization of the free-floating shares.[4] Figure 7.4 shows that adjusting for free float increases LAC's domestic turnover significantly. However, it does the same in the case of other regions. In fact, in Eastern Europe and China, the correction is even stronger than it is in LAC. Hence, LAC's low free float does not appear to account for much, if any, of the region's abnormally low domestic stock market turnover.

Market concentration

The evidence presented in chapter 3 also indicated that access to equity markets in LAC remained limited and concentrated, with the bulk of equity market activity depending on a few issuers and issues. By limiting the options available to portfolio managers, the

TABLE 7.1   Benchmarking model

	Dependent variable: Value traded over GDP				
	(1)	(2)	(3)	(4)	(5)
LAC-7 dummy	−50.54***	−72.62*	−26.13	−101.4**	−75.71**
	(−2.756)	(−1.766)	(−0.559)	(−2.501)	(−2.458)
Foreign value traded as % of total value traded			−114.9*		
			(−1.827)		
Foreign market capitalization as % of total market capitalization				411.5**	
				(2.143)	
Amount raised by top 5 equity issues as % of total amount raised					−31.85
					(−0.604)
Constant	−40.89	194.5	54.84	−417.4	407.9
	(−0.186)	(0.181)	(0.0535)	(−0.402)	(0.557)
Workhorse controls	Yes	Yes	Yes	Yes	Yes
Number of observations	86	34	34	34	47
R-squared	0.613	0.435	0.509	0.532	0.444

Source: Authors' calculations based on Didier and Schmukler 2011b.
Note: Robust *t*-statistics are in shown parentheses.
Significance level: * = 10 percent, ** = 5 percent, *** = 1 percent.

FIGURE 7.4   **Trading activity in domestic equity markets during the 2000s**

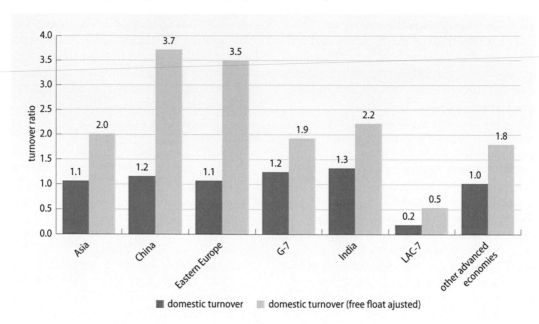

Source: Authors' calculations based on Dahlquist et al. 2003 and Didier and Schmukler 2011a.
Note: This figure shows the trading activity in domestic equity markets. It shows the average turnover ratios, defined as the total value traded per year in domestic markets over total market capitalization, between 1990 and 2009. It shows the same data but adjusted by the Dalhquist (2003) free float indicator for each country for 2003.

high concentration could limit trading, leading to the low turnover.

As a check of whether this is the case, a similar exercise to that described above is conducted for domestic and offshore turnover. That involves first running separate regressions of equity market turnover and concentration ratios on GDP per capita and population. The residuals for the two variables are then plotted and displayed along the fitted regression line (figure 7.5). The results are unimpressive. The regression line is flat—indicating that market concentration has little correlation with turnover—and LAC countries are distributed fairly evenly above and below the fitted line—suggesting that market concentration for the region as a whole is not particularly atypical. In fact, market concentration appears to be a feature of many countries, particularly developing ones.

Institutional investors

The predominance of pension funds among institutional investors could also contribute to LAC's equity gap, as pension funds do not engage in active trading but instead mostly buy-and-hold.[5] As discussed in more depth in chapter 8, current regulations tend to reinforce the preference for "buy-and-hold" investment strategies, which can be detrimental to market liquidity.[6] More generally, institutional investors tend to invest in larger and more liquid firms, hence limiting the supply of funds to smaller and less liquid ones.[7]

To check the impact of the pension-fund biased institutional investor universe in LAC capital markets on the domestic equity market turnover, the exercise again controls the data for GDP per capita and population. The residuals are again plotted, along with the fitter regression line (figure 7.6). Remarkably, the regression line is flat as regards pension funds but clearly upward sloping as regards mutual funds and insurance companies. This may be viewed as supporting the evidence presented in chapter 2, whereby the growth of pension funds has a strong policy

FIGURE 7.5   **Domestic turnover and concentration**

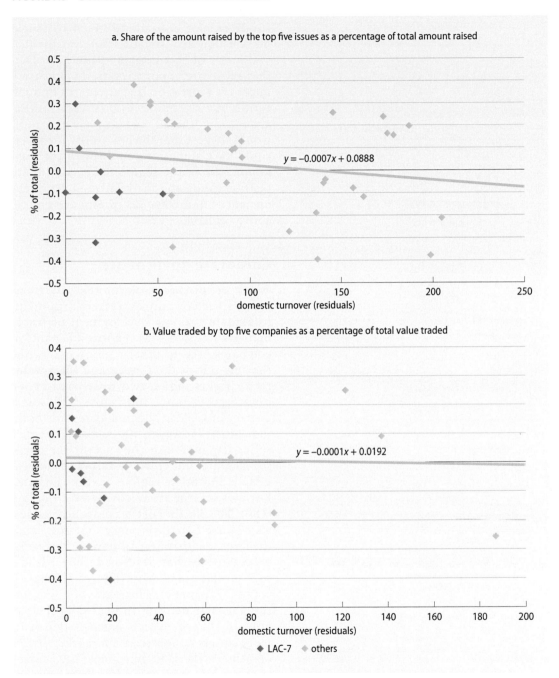

a. Share of the amount raised by the top five issues as a percentage of total amount raised

$y = -0.0007x + 0.0888$

b. Value traded by top five companies as a percentage of total value traded

$y = -0.0001x + 0.0192$

◆ LAC-7   ◆ others

Source: Authors' calculations based on Didier and Schmukler 2011b.
Note: This figure shows scatterplots of the 2005–09 average residuals of two measures of concentration in domestic equity markets against the average residuals of the domestic turnover ratio. Panel a shows the average amount raised per year by the top five issues as a share of total issues in domestic markets. Panel b shows the average share of value traded by the top five companies as share of the total value traded per year in domestic markets. The turnover ratio is defined as the total value traded per year in domestic markets over domestic market capitalization. Residuals are obtained from ordinary least squares regressions of the variables on GDP per capita and population. LAC countries are reported in darker colors.

FIGURE 7.6   Domestic turnover and institutional investors

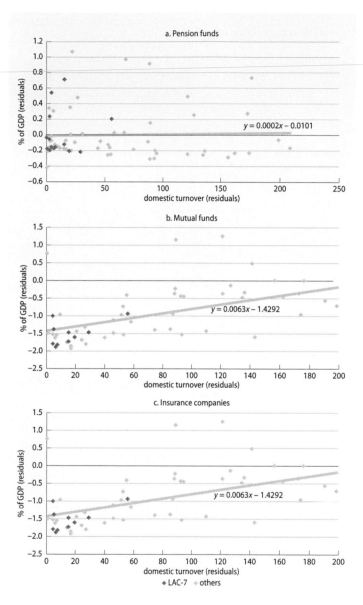

a. Pension funds

$y = 0.0002x - 0.0101$

b. Mutual funds

$y = 0.0063x - 1.4292$

c. Insurance companies

$y = 0.0063x - 1.4292$

◆ LAC-7   ◆ others

Source: Authors' calculations based on Didier and Schmukler (2011a, 2011b).
Note: This figure shows scatterplots of the 2005–09 average residuals of institutional investors' assets relative to GDP against the average residuals of the domestic turnover ratio. Panel a shows the assets of pension funds as a percentage of GDP. Panel b shows the assets of mutual funds as a percentage of GDP. Panel c shows the assets of insurance companies as a percentage of GDP. The *turnover ratio* is defined as the total value traded per year in domestic markets over domestic market capitalization. Residuals are obtained from ordinary least squares regressions of the variables on GDP per capita and population. LAC countries are reported in darker colors.

component, whereas that of other institutional investors tends to go hand in hand with economic and financial development. However, if one interprets the causality in the other direction, it could also suggest that, in contrast with other institutional investors such as mutual funds, pension funds do not contribute much to stock market liquidity because they mostly buy and hold. In this interpretation, the fact that most LAC countries are bunched up under the regression line as regards mutual funds but are more evenly distributed around the line as regards pension funds would suggest that the low equity turnover could have something to do with the predominance in the region of buy-and-hold pension funds and the relative underdevelopment of mutual funds (presumably more active traders).

Corporate governance

Weak corporate governance practices are also a commonly stated argument to explain the low development of stock markets (see box 7.1). Figure 7.7, panel a compares LAC to other regions as regards the anti-self-dealing index and the antidirector rights index, two widely used corporate governance indicators.[8] To some degree, LAC-7 lags behind as regards both indicators. However, the region fares significantly worse in the case of the anti-self-dealing index, where the gap between LAC-7 and other regions (except Eastern Europe) is large (0.39 compared to 0.55–0.80). The plotting of the controlled residuals of these two governance indicators and the domestic turnover (following the same procedure as that described above) leads to a similar conclusion (figures 7.7, panel b and 7.7, panel c). The regression line for the anti-self-dealing indicator is clearly upward-shaped, which suggests that it is more closely connected with market development. At the same time, most LAC countries are bunched up under the regression line, which confirms LAC's strong underperformance as regards this indicator and suggests that LAC's equity gap might have something to do with it.[9] Given the difficulties in measuring corporate governance and the multiple dimensionality of this concept, some caution is warranted, however.[10]

BOX 7.1 **Corporate governance and equity market development**

There is a large literature relating corporate governance practices and stock market development. According to Shleifer and Vishny (1997a) and Bhojraj and Sengupta (2003), good governance practices increase confidence among investors as they tend to reduce agency (information and enforcement) risks. Therefore, companies are likely to have access to capital at lower costs and better conditions, to increase the value and liquidity of their shares, and to improve their operating performance and profitability.

Ashbaugh-Skaife, Collins, and LaFond (2006), for example, find that better corporate governance practices improve corporate credit ratings and reduce bond yields. De Carvalho and Pennacchi (2011) argue, for the case of Brazil, that migration from traditional markets to the Novo Mercado brings positive abnormal returns to shareholders and an increase in the trading volume of shares. Klapper and Love (2004) find that better corporate governance is associated with higher operating performance and higher Tobin's Q. Joh (2003) concludes that firms with higher control-ownership disparity exhibit lower profitability.

The positive links between good corporate governance and stock market development are documented in many papers. For example, La Porta et al. (1997) and Glaser, Johnson, and Shleifer (2001) show that protection of minority shareholders is fundamental to the development of a country's capital market. In addition, Klapper and Love (2004) show that good governance practices are more important in countries with weak investor protection and inefficient enforcement.

However, using evidence from the stock market internationalization process, Gozzi, Levine, and Schmukler (2010) argue that the causality might go both ways and that better firms go offshore, to better corporate governance environments, not that better governance necessarily increases firm value.

Other factors

Finally, LAC's low growth, turbulent macrofinancial history, and remaining weaknesses in its enabling environment might also contribute to explaining its low domestic equity market turnover. Checking for such effects is done by adding to the econometric workhorse model presented in chapters 2 and 3 proxy measures of economic prospects (average GDP growth for the past three decades) and macrofinancial turbulence (credit crashes, as defined in previous chapters). The calculation also adds various indicators of the quality of the enabling environment (contract enforcement, property rights, credit information).

The results (table 7.2) are tentative as they do not fully survive robustness tests, but they do hint in some specific directions while underscoring the need for more research. In particular, financial crashes and low growth are significantly associated with the low domestic stock market turnover when introduced separately. Interestingly, however, they lose their significance when the LAC-7 dummy is added. This could suggest that, while financial crashes and low growth affect many other countries outside the LAC, they have had special consequences in the case of LAC, so much so that they have become tightly interwoven with LAC specificities (the LAC-7 dummy). Also, our econometric test for enabling environment indicators suggests that contract enforcement costs, property rights, and information are also part of the story of the low turnover in LAC's domestic stock markets (these variables retain statistical significance even when introduced together with the—also significant—financial crashes variable). However, like the financial crashes and growth variables, the enabling environment indicators also lose significance once the LAC-7 dummy is added. Again, this might suggest that the effects of a low growth, financial crashes, and enabling

FIGURE 7.7   Domestic turnover and corporate governance

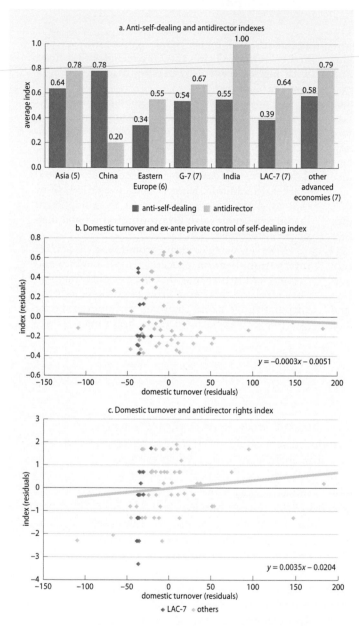

environment weaknesses are wrapped up tightly in the region's history and are crucial in making LAC what it is now as regards financial development.

Conclusions

A first clear conclusion in this chapter is that offshoring appears to account for much of LAC's domestic equity market turnover gap. This gap probably does not matter for the larger firms: whether their stock is traded in Mexico City or in New York is largely immaterial and the fact that it is traded mainly in New York may actually produce additional benefits for these firms. But the gap does matter for the smaller firms to the extent that they cannot rely on international markets and are thus constrained by the lack of access to equity finance at home. Even if these firms' access to debt finance at home was adequate (which does not seem to be the case, as discussed in chapter 6), that would not substitute for the lack of access to equity finance, as the latter plays a unique role in long-term business expansion.

Two interrelated but clearly distinct questions in this regard are first: Why is the offshoring of equity turnover so large in the case of LAC? And second: Why has offshoring seemingly had such a depressing impact on domestic equity market liquidity? Levine and Schmukler (2007) shed light on the second question, providing evidence that illustrates the channels through with the adverse effect appears to work, as noted above. Yet there are no solid answers as to why LAC has an abnormally large amount of stock traded abroad relative to what is traded at home in the first place, and why the equity markets for the remaining firms have lagged so much behind. The history of low economic growth (to the extent it is associated with uninspiring expected returns to investment) and, perhaps more importantly, LAC's history of financial crashes may have something to do with it. However, the empirical tests conducted above do not directly address the reasons underlying offshoring. Hence, the results speak more to the depressing effect of such factors on equity

Source: Authors' calculations based on Djankov et al. 2008.
Note: This figure characterizes the relation between corporate governance and liquidity in domestic equity market. Panel a shows the anti-self-dealing and antidirector indexes. The anti-self-dealing index intends to capture the strength of minority shareholder protection against practices where management or controlling shareholders use their power to divert corporate wealth to themselves. The antidirector index intends to capture the stance of corporate law toward shareholder protection. Higher levels of the indexes imply stronger shareholder protection. Panels b and c shows scatterplots of the residuals of two indexes of corporate governance against the residuals of the domestic turnover ratio for 2003. Panel b shows the ex-ante private control of the self-dealing index. Panel c shows the antidirector rights index. The *turnover ratio* is defined as the total value traded per year in domestic markets over domestic market capitalization. Residuals are obtained from ordinary least squares regressions of the variables on GDP per capita and population.

TABLE 7.2   Domestic equity turnover and enabling environment indicators

	Dependent variable: Stock market turnover					
	(1)	(2)	(3)	(4)	(5)	(6)
LAC-7 dummy	−35.83***			−27.02**		−32.12**
	(−4.837)			(−2.505)		(−2.635)
Credit crash dummy (% of period)		−134.00*		−109.20	−125.70***	−72.19
		(−1.902)		(−1.524)	(−3.049)	(−1.042)
Annualized average sample GDP growth			6.315**	3.164		0.440
			(2.424)	(1.385)		(0.225)
Contract enforcement index					−4.298*	−1.477
					(−1.970)	(−0.495)
Credit information index					4.452***	2.091
					(2.738)	(0.976)
Property rights index					0.592***	0.510**
					(3.211)	(2.153)
Constant	306.9***	359.3**	353.9***	296.0***	445.7***	319.3**
	(4.010)	(2.390)	(2.786)	(2.730)	(4.343)	(2.348)
Workhorse controls	Yes	Yes	Yes	Yes	Yes	Yes
Observations	107	107	86	86	103	84
Pseudo R-squared	0.46	0.44	0.49	0.54	0.47	0.55

Source: de la Torre, Feyen, and Ize 2011.
Significance level: * = 10 percent, ** = 5 percent, *** = 1 percent.

market development overall than to the offshoring per se.[11]

A second, more tentative conclusion is that the preponderance of pension funds over other institutional investors and the remaining weaknesses in corporate governance, contract enforcement, and property rights have also contributed to LAC's domestic equity market turnover gap. As regards the role played by institutional investors, to the extent that the (policy-driven) rapid development of pension funds has retarded the growth of other institutional investors such as mutual funds, one could conclude that such policy choices might have had a cost in terms of equity market development. But much caution is needed in interpreting the evidence. First, the impact of pension funds on the development of the mutual fund industry is not clear. While pension funds may substitute mutual funds by giving investors an alternative savings channel, pension funds may also help mutual funds develop by investing part of their portfolios in them. Moreover, as shown in chapter 8, the asset management behavior of LAC's mutual funds does not

seem to differ that much from that of pension funds.

As regards the possible impact of LAC's weaknesses in corporate governance on the equity market, one might take the view—considering the experience of Brazil's Novo Mercado, whose development appears to have been spurred by the tightening of governance norms—that such weaknesses are of first-order importance. Yet, much of the success of the Novo Mercado may have more to do with Brazil's comparative size advantage than with governance reforms. Indeed, an alternative for the smaller countries might be to follow a "lighter governance" path that is more suited to the smaller firms, while accepting the trade-off of having a reduced scope for minority shareholders (who would be less reluctant to own stock under lighter governance arrangements). Such a light version might be characterized by more benign accounting and public disclosure standards, more private equity placements and over-the-counter activity, less reliance on centralized local exchanges, and concentrated (rather than atomized) stock ownership. However, given the structural illiquidity and, hence, limited price revelation capacity of these markets, their ultimate economic benefits are unclear.

To overcome the constraints imposed by small size of markets, many have recommended the cross-border integration of LAC stock markets. Indeed, the past decades have seen several attempts toward regional integration of stock exchanges around the world.[12] Recently, Chile, Colombia, and Peru reached an agreement of this sort, which focuses on integrating such functions as listing, order routing, and execution. The agreement also fosters efforts aimed at regulatory convergence, but it so far does not envisage common clearing and settlement systems. Despite the potential benefits of securities market integration in terms of scale and network effects, these attempts have tended to fail (Lee 1999). Many reasons have been given for this lack of success, including legal and regulatory differences across countries, adverse effects of different national currencies in the absence of sufficiently developed currency derivatives markets, informational barriers across markets (including differences in accounting and disclosure standards), and larger than expected difficulties in integrating market infrastructures. However, as discussed in de la Torre, Gozzi, and Schmukler (2007a), even if these obstacles were appropriately overcome, there remain some fundamental reasons that cast doubt on the proposition that regional integration of stock exchanges would be superior to the alternative of a deeper and better integration with the developed stock markets, for example, the New York Stock Exchange, which are unrivalled in terms of the depth of their liquidity pools and quality of their contractual environment.[13]

In any event, ascertaining the policy path for stock market development in LAC, especially for the smaller countries, is fiendishly difficult, much more than is commonly recognized. Of course, there are enabling environment reforms (for example, in property rights and corporate governance frameworks) that everyone agrees should help. There are in addition, even for the small countries, many improvements in stock market infrastructure that can also help, including those aimed at reducing fragmentation in issuance and trading, enhancing securities clearance and settlement arrangements, organizing securities lending and borrowing facilities, improving valuation methods, promoting contract standardization, and upgrading financial reporting. However, what is also evident is that such reforms would at best only correct for a modest proportion of the domestic equity turnover gap and may, rather, continue to deepen the trend in favor of offshoring.

Thus, the larger questions remain. What is the proper level of governance standards one should shoot for? Should the smaller countries simply "throw in the towel," forget about developing a local stock market, and accept that equity funding is available mainly for their large resident corporations and mainly through the use of international stock markets? Or should they persevere for the sake of their smaller firms? Is there any significant advantage in pursuing regional stock market integration compared to simply promoting global integration? The only thing one can take for certain is that LAC will need to look beyond the simplest conventional wisdom: macrostability and compliance with international standards might help, but they won't suffice.

Notes

1. Levine and Schmukler (2007), for example, find empirical evidence of a significant negative effect of offshoring on domestic stock market liquidity, and their results are consistent with both views expressed above. Some theories, however, argue instead that offshoring may enhance integration and thereby stimulate domestic trading and boost the liquidity of domestic firms. See, for example, Alexander, Eun, and Janakiramanan (1987); Domowitz, Glen, and Madhavan (1998); and Hargis (2000).

2. The domestic market capitalization of these firms includes all the stocks issued at home even if they are completely traded abroad (via DRs).

3. See Dahlquist et al. (2003).

4. Free float data used in this assessment are provided by Dahlquist et al. (2003). While it is the only one available for a large sample of countries, it is unfortunately a bit outdated (it refers to 1997).

5. Raddatz and Schmukler (2011) show that Chilean pension fund administrators (PFAs) trade infrequently. On average, a PFA trades only 13 percent of its assets, and the monthly changes in asset positions correspond to just 4 percent of the initial total value of the assets. This result contrasts sharply with the 88 percent mean turnover ratio found in Kacperczyk, Sialm, and Zheng (2008) for a sample of 2,543 actively managed U.S. equity mutual funds between 1984 and 2003.

6. See Gill, Packard, and Yermo (2004).

7. See, for example, Kang and Stulz (1997); Dahlquist and Robertsson (2001); Edison and Warnock (2004); Didier, Rigobon, and Schmukler (2010); and Didier (2011a), among many others.

8. See Djankov et al. (2008). The anti-self-dealing index intends to capture the strength of minority shareholder protection against practices where management or controlling shareholders use their power to divert corporate wealth to themselves. The antidirector index, conversely, tries to capture the stance of corporate law toward shareholder protection. Higher levels of the index imply stronger shareholder protection. Djankov et al. (2008) finds the anti-self-dealing index to be a better predictor of a variety of measures of stock market development across countries.

9. In terms of individual countries, Argentina, Mexico, and Uruguay have the weakest corporate governance indicators. Brazil is an interesting case, as its antidirector index takes the maximum possible value while its anti-self-dealing index is one of the lowest in the region. This might be a result of the recent developments in the Brazilian stock market (discussed in chapter 3) whereby firms can adhere to stricter corporate governance rules by choosing where to list. While this might have boosted the value of the antidirector index, which measures the extent of legal protection, it might not have had an immediate effect on actual self-dealing practices.

10. In unreported results on two more corporate governance indicators (ex ante private control of self-dealing and public enforcement index), LAC-7 seems to be overperforming, to the point of being even slightly ahead of the G-7 countries.

11. Caution in interpreting the increase in off-shoring as caused by macroeconomic volatility is further warranted considering that Claessens, Klingebiel, and Schmukler (2006) find that improvements in macroeconomic (as well as institutional) fundamentals are associated with a proportionally greater expansion of turnover offshore than onshore.

12. This process has been particularly strong among European countries (Claessens, Lee, and Zechner 2003; Licht 1998; McAndrews and Stefanadis 2002).

13. While it is true that regional financial integration may reduce trading and issuance costs because of economies of scale, it seems doubtful that such cost reductions would be greater than those that could be achieved by global integration. Similarly, while it is true that neighboring investors may have informational advantages on regional firms compared to more remote foreign investors, it is not clear that such advantages would be better exercised by trading in a regional market than in a global one. Likewise, the conjecture that regional stock exchanges would facilitate access for medium-size enterprises needs to be reexamined, for these firms are segmented out of the international *and* local stock markets mainly because of the small size of their potential issues, not because of the size of the markets. The solution, therefore, is arguably not with bigger markets, regional or global, but with bigger issue sizes.

Going Long | 8

In the previous chapters, the Latin America and the Caribbean (LAC) region's financial development and main developmental gaps were discussed from a broad cross-country perspective. This chapter narrows the focus to explore an issue that is at the core of effective, sustainable financial development: the capability of "going long," that is, of sustainably generating sufficient long-term financial contracts—long maturity and long duration—for private agents and projects.[1] Chapter 6 identified the lack of mortgages as a central component of the banking gap in LAC. Chapter 7 discussed the possible reasons underlying the liquidity gap in the equity market. This chapter digs deeper into the credit gap by reviewing why LAC has had such a hard time providing long-term finance, particularly mortgages. The equity gap is also examined again, but from a different and complementary angle. In particular, the questions asked are: Why are investors so hesitant to become locked into less liquid equity securities or longer-term debt contracts? To what extent is this problem specific to LAC, and what can be done about it? Main policy conclusions are as follows:

- LAC countries will need to consolidate the gains made in the use of the local currency in long-term financial contracts; in addition to sound macroeconomic policies, this will require persistence in promoting the use of consumer price index (CPI)-indexed bonds for the long-maturity segments of public debt.
- LAC countries will also need to strengthen contract rights and their enforcement, two areas where LAC lags.
- As regards market discipline, LAC will need to promote standardization and benchmarking of funds (especially pension fund management) in terms of asset valuations and returns, in a way that focuses investors on long-term rather than short-term returns.
- At the same time, governments will need to find the proper balance between regulating the way investors invest (effectively playing "big brother"), on the one hand, and letting them assume the risk, on the other.
- LAC will also need to find the best mix of channels and instruments to help spread risk and reduce participation costs, including through securitization, covered bonds, mutualized second-tier finance facilities, and a general deepening of markets for insurance and hedging products aimed at reducing default risks over longer horizons

(such as rainfall-index-based insurance for farmers or home-equity insurance).

- LAC policy makers will need to be realistic about the feasibility (and desirability) of relying on liquid secondary markets to promote participation by aligning investors' desire for an exit option with borrowers' long-term funding needs. Where domestic markets are small, reforms aimed at promoting secondary market liquidity are likely to lead to only modest improvements; and where market arrangements succeed in deepening domestic liquidity, wedges between private and systemic interest can widen as private agents increasingly free ride on liquidity and relax their monitoring efforts.
- Hence, an alternative avenue for dealing with collective action frictions is to mandate participation, as in private pension funds, for example; when combined with policies to promote the development of a vibrant annuities industry, as in Chile, this approach has been one of the brightest and most promising in the region. Nonetheless, the design problems that stand in the way of developing the annuities market in many countries will need to be removed.

The rest of this chapter is organized as follows. The first section reviews the main issues faced in going long. The second section discusses the options. The third section takes stock of LAC's current situation. The final section concludes by briefly reviewing the main policy challenges going forward.

What are the issues?

The importance of long-term contracts for economic and social well-being is uncontested. On the borrowing side, limiting the cost of issuing long-term debt is central to viable housing, infrastructure, and long-term corporate finance. If long-term borrowing is too expensive, borrowers must limit their funding—thereby limiting investment and, in the end, economic growth—or they must keep it short term—thereby becoming exposed to rollover or price risk. On the savings side, investing long term is central to resolving the problems of retirement, education needs, health shocks, and premature death—key facets of life-cycle consumption smoothing. The capacity of investors to stay put—that is, to hold risk over long horizons and capture the risk premium—makes a huge difference in accumulated returns over a lifetime.[2] Thus, a financial system's capacity to spread long risk effectively is crucial to a viable private pension, education, or health system.

While the financial architecture in LAC has evolved in a variety of ways to facilitate the spreading of long risk, barriers and pitfalls remain. Overcoming them is key to a harmonious, sustainable financial development. However, this is a challenge that even the most developed financial systems have struggled to meet, as evidenced by the recent U.S. mortgage crisis. In fact, the *sustainable* production and use of long-term instruments—say, a 30-year fixed-rate mortgage or a lifelong annuity—are clear signs of a mature and socially useful financial system. In this sense, going long is a key point of intersection between financial development and financial stability.

The two sides of the market for going long typically have a hard time meeting, because long-term financing commitments face large aggregate risk (inflation, growth, political risk) as well as idiosyncratic risk (project risk on the one hand and agency risk—asymmetric information and/or enforcement costs—on the other). The longer one commits, the more exposed one becomes to these risks. Where will prices be 20 years from now? Where will society be? Will the project fail? What will the borrower do, and will he still be there? Hence, while borrowers would like to limit the risk of long-term investments by fixing the terms of finance, lenders may not be willing to assume the risk associated with going long and may thus prefer to lend at short durations. The problem is complicated further by the fact that making fully rational long-term investment decisions is beyond the capacity of the average investor.[3] The price at which lenders are willing to assume the long risk may exceed the price that borrowers are ready to pay.

What are the options?

As discussed in chapter 2, one of the main functions of financial intermediation is precisely to assist in closing the two key related mismatches that arise in the process of going long. There is first a mismatch between households' need to invest long term (for example, for old age or in education) and their natural preference for staying short so as to have ready access to their funds. And then there is a mismatch between lenders' preference for staying short and borrowers' need for going long. Thus, depending on the degree of risk and uncertainty aversion, the perceived risk-return trade-offs, and the constellation of relative risk premiums, investors can

- refuse to "bite the bullet" and remain in short-term positions;
- "bite the bullet" and go long even if this means becoming illiquid;
- go long, but only where they perceive that they can exit early if needed (that is, if they benefit from the liquidity provided by the market or an institution); or
- go long, but only if they can limit risk by purchasing insurance from other market participants or from the state.

Frictions (both agency and collective) will dictate which (or which combination) of these options is likely to dominate at a given stage of financial development. Thus, depending on how financial services shape up to circumvent or limit the frictions, investors *in practice* face the four following options:

- Invest indirectly in long-dated assets (via a fund), thereby remaining fully exposed to the risks, but rely on an asset manager for the day-to-day management of the risk and an early exit option when needed and if allowed by the fund (*the asset management option*).
- Invest in a leveraged intermediary, such as a commercial bank or an insurance

company, which may then engage in maturity transformation and absorb the risks while providing downside risk insurance to investors (*the asset-liability management option*).
- Invest directly in long-dated assets, but limit the risk by relying on secondary market liquidity and/or by purchasing market insurance (*the market insurance option*).[4]
- Invest directly in long-dated assets, but limit the risk through public guarantees (*the public insurance option*).

Clearly, these options are not mutually exclusive. In fact, the asset management option and the market option work largely together, as asset managers invest mostly in the market. However, these options bring up conceptually distinct issues and provide, therefore, a useful way to organize the discussion. All of them face problems.

In the *asset management option*, investors can choose between a variety of funds, from the most liquid—money market funds—to the least liquid—hedge funds, venture capital funds, private equity funds—with defined-contribution pension funds, other mutual funds, and personal brokers lying somewhere in between.[5] In all cases, investors are fully exposed to the risk of the fund investments and face a basic agency problem: Will the asset managers adequately fulfill their clients' interests?[6] If investors are proactive and switch funds in response to fund fees and short-term returns (as typically occurs in mature stages of financial development), asset managers may take too much risk and trade too much in order to attract customers by boosting short-term returns.[7] In that case, though they may appear to be "alpha traders" who beat the market by having superior skills, they actually are buying assets with substantial tail risk.[8] By contrast, if principals (investors) are passive (as is generally the case in the less developed systems), asset managers have little incentive to screen and monitor counterparty risk, may not optimize in terms of the risk-return trade-off, spend too much in marketing, trade too little, and still collect juicy fees. Except for the most illiquid and specialized funds, where investors know the manager sufficiently to entrust their funds for extended periods of time, liquidity (the ability to withdraw on short notice) is the name of the game. This can often lead asset managers to promise more liquidity than they can deliver.

In the *asset-liability management option*, investors again face a range of options, from the shortest and most liquid (commercial banks' checking account deposits) to the longest and least liquid (life insurance and annuities), with repurchase (repo) agreements and investment banks lying somewhere in between. Asset-liability managers (ALMs) fully benefit from the upside of their investments and provide insurance and liquidity to investors by interposing capital, provisions, or liquidity buffers between their assets and liabilities. ALMs, however, do not bear the full downside, reflecting limited liability as well as public policy (deposit insurance or bailouts). Hence, unless checked by market discipline or regulation, ALMs have an incentive to screen and monitor but may still take too much risk with someone else's money. ALMs will also naturally tend to engage in maturity transformation, acquiring interest rate risk but pocketing the maturity premium if things go well, and taking capital losses or going bust if things go badly. In both cases, ALMs raise the stakes through leveraging. ALMs focused on life insurance have their funding secured (for example, through the sale of long-term insurance policies) and are thus not exposed to the risk of runs. Such freedom from runs and the need to match assets to long-dated liabilities make life insurance companies the ideal dedicated long-term investor. ALMs focused on banking, by contrast, offer deposit redemption at par and on demand and, hence, can be subject to liquidity runs that induce them to engage in socially inefficient fire sales and deleveraging.[9] This limits the maturity transformation that banks can perform. Through runs or insolvency, both types of ALMs can ultimately fail, however, prompting public bailouts.

In the *market insurance option*, within sufficiently developed systems, investors may buy directly from a broad menu of debt and equity securities. Debt securities (bonds) range from those that mainly bear market risk (covered bonds[10]) to those that bear both market and default risk (asset-backed securities), with structured products (for example, with senior tranches or built-in guarantees) somewhere in between. To cope with the risks of such long-dated exposures, investors may rely on market liquidity (that is, count on being able to dispose of the security at little cost by selling it in the secondary market). Where available, investors may also use market insurance, hedges, or derivatives, such as credit default swaps, to hedge against credit risk, or swaps, futures, and options to hedge against market risk (interest rate risk, currency risk, and equity price risk). As illustrated by the recent global crisis, none of these instruments is problem free. For instance, asset-backed securities put all the risk squarely on investors (or the guarantors) but may expose them to originate-and-distribute incentive problems. Covered bonds may shift the credit risk to other bank claimants, including depositors, who become junior claimants; structured products create risks of excessive complexity and opacity; derivatives pose counterparty risk. In addition, insurance markets are quite incomplete, even in mature financial systems.[11]

In the *public insurance option*, governments can provide direct long-term finance through first-tier public banks or facilitate the acquisition of long-term finance from the private sector (in the form of commercial loans, infrastructure bonds, housing bonds, annuities, and even equity stakes). In the second case, the state can provide explicit guarantees aimed at limiting the risk of long-term instruments or implicit guarantees aimed at facilitating the early exit from long-term finance commitments by the private investors (liquidity lending of last resort or risk absorption of last resort). In all cases, the main problem is the inadequate pricing of risk that may undermine monitoring incentives and promote social moral hazard (that is, the incentive to take on excessive risk with the expectation of keeping the gains but passing on the losses to the state).

Thus, depending on whether and which (agency or collective) frictions are resolved through the above market arrangements or policy enhancements, there are four possible outcomes:

1. All frictions and incentive problems are satisfactorily resolved.
2. Agency frictions are not resolved.
3. Agency frictions are resolved, but collective (participation) frictions are not.
4. Whether agency frictions are resolved or not, the state assumes a dominant role in resolving collective frictions. (It can do so through guaranteeing private contracts or becoming a financial intermediary that issues long-term bonds and provides long-term finance directly through first-tier operations.)

Outcome 1 is, of course, the happy one, where full financial lengthening (investing in long and possibly illiquid instruments) takes place. Outcome 2 is the opposite case, where financial lengthening and deepening just does not happen (short-termism dominates). Outcome 3 is where investors invest long term but only if they can exit by resorting to secondary market liquidity. However, under systemic events, unless the state is there to provide liquidity of last resort (thereby effectively converting a type 3 outcome into a type 4 outcome), this raises an insoluble collective action problem. Moreover, as discussed in chapter 2, this can encourage free riding on market liquidity and weaken monitoring incentives, thereby also exacerbating agency problems. Hence, absent regulation that internalizes systemic risk, the financial system will develop, but in a brittle, crisis-prone way. Similarly, in outcome 4, the absorption of risk by the state may help deepen the availability of long-term contracts, but this is likely to be accompanied by social moral hazard (that is, the transfer of risk to the state), giving rise to fault lines that will ultimately rupture with devastating repercussions.

In sum, for financial development to be well anchored and sustainable, a solution needs to be found where investors invest with a long-term horizon (including in illiquid securities) but with only limited risk absorption by the state, or if with risk absorption by the state, with adequate pricing of the public guarantees.

Where is LAC?

LAC has made considerable progress over the past decade in addressing many of the issues raised above. In particular, it has achieved a remarkable lengthening of maturities in its public sector debt and has by and large restored the primacy of its local currencies with respect to the dollar, as documented in chapter 3. Yet challenges lie ahead. Among the many wonders expected from defined-contribution pension funds (several of which have indeed been realized, at least partially), many hoped that the funds would also contribute to lengthening the maturity of investments and overcome the lack of liquidity in capital markets. Yet, the reality in these particular aspects has been somewhat sobering, for, as shown in chapter 3, in much of the region these funds continue to concentrate their portfolios in public sector bonds or relatively short-term bank deposits or in private debt securities. In many LAC countries, the public sector remains the main or even the only entity able to provide, guarantee, or enhance long-term debt finance. And this is despite the fact that the region is nowadays awash with investible funds, which makes the situation all the more puzzling. Clearly, going long is harder than often believed.

Pension funds

Defined-contribution pension fund administrators (PFAs) have become the dominant asset managers in several financial systems throughout the region.[12] Because of imperfections on the demand side (that is, the contributing workers) and complex industrial organization issues,[13] they suffer from three interrelated problems: they are expensive for what they do; they invest for the most part in relatively safe, liquid, plain vanilla assets; and they tend to spend too much on marketing and collection. Although the share of government bonds and bank deposits has been declining, it still accounts, on average, for about 60 percent of PFAs' portfolios.[14] And where PFAs invest in market instruments, they mostly buy and hold, limiting their investments to the highest rated and most liquid instruments. The preference for investing short term and safe, rather than long term and risky, largely reflects the fact that defined-contribution pension funds are pure asset managers that do not have a formal liability, let alone a long-term liability. Pensioners, not PFAs, are the ones absorbing all the investment risks.[15] Finally, and most importantly, to take advantage of both the higher liquidity and the risk diversification benefits, PFAs increasingly invest offshore rather than onshore (figure 3.21b).

Management fees have been coming down but are still relatively high, resulting in generally very high rates of profitability for PFAs.[16] To the extent that fees are proportional to inflows and that fees collected for past contributions do not move with workers when they switch PFAs, a PFA that captures relatively younger workers (with fewer assets) will have higher earnings than one that serves mainly the oldest workers (with more assets).[17] Since net inflows to PFAs do not strongly respond to investment performance or management fees but tend to respond instead to the number of salespeople, PFAs have a built-in incentive to attract the youngest customers by spending heavily in marketing.[18] The available evidence also suggests that PFA managers face strong direct incentives toward conservatism. Compensation generally increases in relation to the ranking among peers in monthly or quarterly gross returns, which raises incentives to take risk. However, there are also tight controls and penalties for deviating from the industry benchmark or hitting the regulatory band, which limits risk taking and promotes herding.[19] On balance, the evidence suggests that, despite their presumed long-term investment mission, PFAs behave very much

as pure asset managers (rather than ALMs). Their incentives are tilted toward the short term and against risk taking.[20] Thus, initial hopes for a direct impact of pension funds on the development of long-term finance in a broad and sustainable manner have so far been fulfilled only to a limited extent.[21]

Mutual funds

In contrast with pension funds, much less is known about LAC's mutual funds. In principle, the high interest rate margins of commercial banks open much space for mutual funds to compete and to offer better returns compared to bank deposits. However, LAC's mutual funds appear to bask in the glow of these high margins more than compete. Reflecting the importance of financial conglomeration and name recognition, they are heavily concentrated and tightly related to banking groups. Their fees are substantially above the 1 percent to 2 percent range that prevails in most developed countries (table 8.1).[22] At the same time, the proceeds from the fees are mostly spent on advertising and distribution rather than on asset management.

In fact, mutual fund managers in LAC appear to have few internal or external incentives to engage in high-quality asset management. Performance bonuses are rarely used; when they are used, they are paid on gross returns, with no distinction between alpha and beta risk.[23] Moreover, the size of the bonus is small, managerial turnover is high, and portfolio management is usually an entry-level position.[24] Nor are there substantial performance incentives coming from the market. The systematic response of mutual funds' customers to short-run returns is limited in the region, and investor behavior is rather volatile.[25] In addition to a possible lack of investor sophistication, the latter is likely to reflect a lack of transparent and standardized information, which prevents meaningful and timely benchmarking between peers.

Altogether, the incentives faced by mutual fund managers overwhelmingly lead them to invest conservatively by buying short-term

TABLE 8.1   Mutual fund fees in selected Latin American countries
percent

	Annual fixed fee	Funds with performance fee	Entry fees (% amount deposited)	Exit fees	Exit fees (% funds with sliding scale)	Office expenses fees	Funds with minimum investment	Sample of funds
Balanced funds								
Argentina	2.6	0	0.5	0.50	0	0.0	50	2
Brazil	2.0	70	0.0	0.50	0	0.0	100	10
Chile	4.8	0	0.0	2.38	60	0.0	80	5
Colombia	1.9	0	0.0	0.00	20	0.0	100	5
Mexico	4.2	0	0.0	0.00	0	0.8	50	4
Peru	3.0	0	0.0	1.17	0	0.0	100	3
Average	3.1	12	0.1	0.76	13	0.1	80	
Bond funds								
Argentina	2.6	0	0.2	3.00	20	0.0	80	5
Brazil	2.4	0	0.0	0.00	0	0.0	100	10
Chile	1.5	0	0.0	0.00	40	0.0	100	5
Colombia	1.6	0	0.0	0.00	0	0.0	100	4
Mexico	3.2	0	0.0	0.00	0	0.0	60	5
Peru	2.5	0	0.0	1.92	0	0.0	100	3
Average	2.3	0	0.0	0.82	10	0.0	90	
Equity funds								
Argentina	3.9	0	0.2	0.40	20	0.0	80	5
Brazil	2.3	40	0.0	0.50	0	0.0	100	10
Chile	4.4	10	0.0	0.00	70	0.4	70	10
Colombia	0.6	0	0.0	0.00	0	0.0	100	1
Mexico	3.7	0	0.0	0.00	0	0.2	20	5
Peru	3.2	0	0.0	1.83	0	0.0	100	3
Average	3.0	8	0.0	0.46	15	0.1	78	
Money Market Funds								
Argentina	1.2	0	0.2	3.00	20	0.0	80	5
Brazil	2.1	0	0.0	0.00	0	0.0	100	10
Chile	1.3	0	0.0	0.00	0	0.0	80	5
Colombia	1.2	0	0.0	0.00	0	0.0	100	4
Mexico	4.0	0	0.0	0.00	0	0.0	80	5
Peru	2.2	0	0.0	0.08	0	0.0	100	3
Average	2.0	0	0.0	0.51	3	0.0	90	

Source: Raddatz 2011.

or liquid assets or buying and holding only the most highly rated assets, including a high proportion of government bonds and bank liabilities (table 8.2).[26] The relative importance of money market mutual funds that invest heavily in short-term, low-risk instruments leaves even less scope for searching for yield. At the same time, the strong emphasis on allowing investors to have immediate access to their money exposes mutual funds to significant redemption risk. This, together with mutual funds' strong links with banking groups and frequent mark-to-market weaknesses, reinforces mutual fund incentives to invest mainly in highly liquid assets while creating systemic vulnerabilities to runs.

Personal brokers

Mutual funds' weaknesses—together with the high wealth concentrations that are typical in the region—appear to open substantial room for personal brokerage and wealth management services for the more

TABLE 8.2   Share of deposits in portfolios of Chilean mutual funds

Type of mutual fund[a]	Mean	Minimum	Maximum	Cumulative share of total assets
Money market funds	78.0	8.2	98.0	40.0
Medium- and long-term funds	30.7	0.0	88.9	75.1
Short-term maturity	65.5	21.9	93.1	86.8
Capital market funds	0.7	0.0	2.8	92.3

Source: Raddatz 2011.
a. Types according to circular number 1578, Values and Securities Supervisor (SVS). http://www.svs.cl/normativa/cir_1578_2002.pdf.

sophisticated and wealthier investors. However, the industry is mostly unregulated, little is known about its operations (except that, as with mutual funds, a fixed fee is charged on assets under management), and there are very few directly available statistics on its importance.[27] The preference for personal brokers reflects a gradual, step-by-step switch from "related lending" to "related investing." The increasing availability of public information gradually reduces the importance of traditional banking intermediation. Yet, because of the lack of sufficient public information on asset managers, investors continue to rely on private information to pick and choose them. However, brokers also seem to be increasingly attracting smaller and less sophisticated investors, much as they do in U.S. investment banks. As a result, given the lack of regulation and transparency, some supervisory authorities in the region are starting to voice concerns about issues of investor protection. While the portfolios managed by personalized wealth management services are more likely to be invested with long horizons in mind, it appears that a large share is invested in international markets.

Hedge funds, venture capital funds, and private equity funds

High-risk, low-liquidity funds aim at the next stage of wealth and sophistication. They are starting to appear in the deepest markets of the region, particularly Brazil, with an often dominant participation of offshore funds.[28] Although in LAC, these types of funds are mostly unregulated and seem to have the capacity to leverage themselves, they do not seem to have done so yet to a substantial

extent. While, initially, regulation severely constrained the participation of institutional investors in such funds, ongoing reforms are increasingly opening the door for investment in these instruments by pension funds and mutual funds. How much they invest in long-term assets is, however, difficult to ascertain, given the dearth of data.

Commercial banks

Commercial banks for the most part stay short, largely matching the duration of their assets to those of their liabilities. This, in turn, reflects their own risk-management preferences—LAC banks are already highly profitable without taking too much risk, as shown in chapter 10—as well as prudential requirements, which generally penalize maturity and duration mismatches. Commercial banks limit the risks of going long by using floating-rate mortgages or by matching the long duration of their assets to that of their liabilities through covered bonds (as in Chile) or long-term public finance (as in Brazil or Mexico, where commercial banks channel second-tier long-term loans from development banks). Until the global crisis hit, commercial banks in the region were increasingly following the route taken in advanced economies, of passing their long-term exposures on to institutional investors and the capital markets while increasingly relying on fee income (rather than on intermediation margins) to boost profits.

Investment banks

In many LAC countries, commercial banks are not allowed to engage in capital market activities directly. Instead, financial groups can engage in capital market activities through an investment banking subsidiary with a separate license. In other countries, brokers and dealers effectively conduct the business of investment banking. Thus far, LAC investment banks (and broker-dealers) have mainly conducted brokerage and underwriting activities. While they have scope for engaging in large-scale maturity transformation, as in the United States, thus far they have not taken the opportunity, in large part because capital markets have not yet reached the stage where financing long-term securities with overnight repos might be viewed as a sustainable and profitable activity. In addition, LAC investment banks, where they formally exist, tend to be subject to the same capital and other prudential regulations as commercial banks. Hence, the type of leverage in investment banks that we saw in the United States is not feasible in LAC.

Life insurance companies

With the notable exception of Chile, life insurance products in LAC are underdeveloped, in part reflecting the remnants of the sour memories left by inflationary erosions of the not-too-distant past. In Chile, their success has hinged essentially on three factors: the establishment of the UF (*Unidad de Fomento*), a CPI-indexed unit of account that eases long-term investing by allowing investors to hedge against inflation at virtually no cost; the mandated nature of defined-contribution pension funds, which creates a captive demand for annuities upon retirement;[29] and the government guarantees on annuities, which limit the risks of going long. Thus, in sharp contrast with mutual funds and defined-contribution pension funds, life insurance companies, especially those that provide annuity products, invest a large fraction of their portfolio at long horizons.[30] They have to search for long-term assets to match their long-term liabilities and are not exposed to runs—that is, lack of liquidity is not a pressing issue.[31]

While competition can lead the life insurance companies to translate the higher returns from investing long into attractively priced policies, those companies become, in the process, exposed to nontrivial solvency risks. At the same time, the illiquidity of their liabilities, the complexity of their business activities, and the structure of their contracts—which are concerned with limiting moral hazard on the side of the insured rather than that of the insurance company—severely limit the scope for direct market discipline from policy holders.[32] Nonetheless, reinsurers (who understand the insurance business well) are likely to exert more effective market discipline on those insurance companies that choose to reinsure their residual exposures. In any event, insurance companies in general, and life insurance companies in particular, need to be heavily regulated and effectively supervised to ensure that their assets (including unpaid premiums) can cover their expected liabilities and that short-run profits are not overstated (or, equivalently, that expected losses are adequately and promptly provisioned). Substantial progress appears to have been made in this area in many countries where life insurance companies are significant, but much remains to be done.

An important related issue is that, while annuities-oriented life insurance is already a maturing industry in Chile and poised to thrive in LAC countries where Chile-style pension reforms were implemented, there is an insufficiently smooth connection between the accumulation phase (the period during which workers contribute to their pension funds) and the decumulation phase (the period after retirement, when workers withdraw their funds or receive a monthly pension from an annuity until death). Pensioners are subject to important risks at the juncture of the two phases (the so-called annuitization risks) that need to be addressed. In other countries where the systems of defined-benefit, mandatory, privately administered pension funds are maturing, much policy attention will need to be paid to ensure an adequate formation of a robust annuities industry.[33]

Housing finance

The limited development of mortgages in most of LAC (documented in chapter 6) is testimony to the difficulties of going long (box 8.1). In Chile, which has the deepest mortgage market of the region, mortgages have developed mostly around UF-denominated covered bonds issued by banks at terms that match the mortgage loans, with life insurance companies and pension funds being the largest buyers and holders of such bonds.

In Mexico, the private market for mortgage-backed securities (MBS) that was starting to mushroom under the nurturing care of state-related institutions—mainly, the Federal Mortgage Society (SHF—Sociedad Hipotecaria Federal), the National Housing Fund for Workers (Infonavit), and the Housing Fund of the Social Security and Services Institute for State Employees (Fovissste)—became mostly frozen in their tracks in the wake of the global financial crisis. Investors were spooked by the apparent similarities between the SHF-led mortgage development strategy and that of Fannie Mae and Freddie Mac in the United States. Contagion was exacerbated by the financial difficulties encountered by some newly unregulated but poorly monitored Sofoles, the special-purpose finance companies largely funded by SHF, and by the market's difficulty in sorting out the good Sofoles from the not so good. The insufficient standardization of securitization issues did not help. Thus, the market for MBS in Mexico has become mostly circumscribed to issues by the large public entities in charge of developing low-income housing (Infonavit and Fovissste). However, these public issues have tended to crowd out the private issues because they issue paper on terms that private issuers cannot match. A legal framework to introduce covered bonds is now being prepared as part of a reform of bankruptcy rules applicable to banks.[34]

In Colombia, better standardization, large tax breaks, and important regulatory advantages have kept the market for MBS more whole. Yet most of the issues remain in the possession of commercial banks, which therefore capture the tax breaks. Initially, commercial banks acquired the MBS to recompose their balance sheets in the wake of the 1998–99 housing finance crisis involving savings and mortgage corporations (Corporaciones de Ahorro y Vivienda). As in Chile, Mexico, and Uruguay, plans are under way to prepare new legislation that would facilitate the issue of covered bonds under a modern contractual and legal framework (see box 8.1).

In Brazil, the mortgage market remains largely under the direct control of large state institutions with tailor-made arrangements, including a government-owned commercial bank (Caixa Economica Federal) that is the main player of the housing finance system, SBPE.[35] The latter is underpinned by below-market cost of funding, mobilized through passbook savings accounts (Caderneta de Poupança) at semiadministered rates (taxa referencial), and a taxlike worker contribution (Fundo de Garantia do Tempo de Serviço, or FGTS). This system, which churns out long-term mortgages from short-term savings deposits and taxlike funds, results in a segmentation that hampers the development of market-based finance and hence the overall provision of housing loans, while generating some liquidity issues for the SBPE sector itself.[36]

Bonds

Progress in macroeconomic management, along with strong demand from institutional as well as foreign investors over the last decade, has contributed to considerable improvement in LAC in lengthening the maturity of both public and private bonds and in moving away from the perils of dollarization. As documented in chapter 3, yield curves have been extended and flattened, and the local currency has made substantial gains relative to the U.S. dollar. The development of longer-maturity, fixed-rate, local currency corporate bonds is particularly remarkable, especially in Chile, Colombia, and Mexico. In part, this success has reflected investors'

BOX 8.1   Covered bonds versus mortgage-backed securities: LAC's recent experience

LAC had a leg up on developing MBS. Many countries developed—or in some cases improved (Brazil, Chile)—their securitization frameworks in the 1990s, including legal structures, true sale criteria, accounting rules, and tax treatment. In fact, LAC pioneered the concept of trust in the civil law context that prevails in the subcontinent. Other technical innovations that laid the groundwork for securitization included: (a) the use of mortgage loans legally designed to be easily transferable and sold to institutional investors, such as Mutuos Hipotecarios Endosables in Chile and Letras Hipotecarias in Argentina; (b) the judicious use of the existing mutual fund legal structure as a basis to set up special purpose vehicles (SPVs) in Brazil; and (c) the securitization of future cash flows stemming from leasing of housing contracts in Chile. The market that grew the most in this initial period, thanks to this efficient legal background (and temporary monetary stability), was Argentina. However, the development of MBS has been far from linear and remains in question today. Colombia and Mexico, the two countries where active MBS exist, provide valuable development lessons.

In Mexico, MBS grew in parallel with nondepository mortgage lenders (Sofoles and Sofomes), the main drivers of the market bounce after the "tequila crisis." This development was supported by guarantees from the state-owned SHF and enhancements by U.S. monoline insurers. When commercial banks became active again in housing finance, their involvement helped diversify the source of MBS overseen by SHF. A dual oversight system developed, wherein the Comisión Nacional Bancaria y de Valores (CNBV) effectively delegated much of the oversight to the SHF, which refinanced or guaranteed the loans on a contractual basis. However, the scheme was severely jostled when the 2009 economic downturn affected the Mexican housing finance market. As Sofoles' portfolios—which were largely originated through developers and included a large portion of developer loans—incurred growing nonperforming loans, a confidence crisis developed that hindered the rollover of the short-term debt imprudently issued by some Sofoles. Gaps in

the regulation of fiduciary functions, the demise of the monoline insurers, and sheer contagion from the disturbingly similar U.S. debacle all contributed further to the severe downgrades imposed by the rating agencies. As a result, private MBS came to a halt. At the same time, however, Infonavit and Fovissste (whose activity grew partially in a countercyclical way) developed their own MBS programs. These programs were a big success, not only because of the low-risk profile of the portfolios, but also because of the attractive conditions the public provident funds were able to afford. Instead, the private sector was largely crowded out. Thus, Mexico's main challenge at this point is to reinstate the conditions for a viable private MBS market.

Colombia, on the other hand, has not been as adversely affected by the global financial crisis. One major reason, aside from the very strict lending norms set by the 1999 mortgage law, has been the crucial role of a private central structure, Titularizadora Colombiana (TC). Since 2002, TC has been providing comfort to investors by its diligence in arranging deals and organizing market transparency. The tax relief enjoyed by MBS investors until 2011 also contributed to investors' success.

Although several countries, including Argentina, Colombia, and Paraguay, have a framework for covered bonds, Chile is the only case where this instrument has been actively used. In fact, the Letras de Credito Hipotecario (LCH)—based on a pass-through mechanism guaranteed by the mortgage originators—had been in existence since 1855.[37] However, the issuer of LCH, a public specialized institution, sank with the financial crisis of the 1930s. When the savings and loan (Sistema Nacional de Ahorro y Préstamo, or SINAP) system collapsed, the LCH were revitalized and combined with the newly created private pension funds and the widely accepted UF, thereby triggering a remarkable development of housing finance. In fact, the very long maturities (20 years) and fixed (real) rates appeared in Chile much before such features became available in many more-advanced economies. LCH were improved by allowing commercial banks, and not only nondepository specialized lenders, to issue them and by designing a more precise process for

(continued next page)

enforcing the privileged status of bondholders in case of a bank's insolvency.

LCH have become much less pivotal, however, especially since 2004, progressively losing market share (11 percent of housing portfolios in 2010, down from 86 percent in 1995). Three main factors explain this disaffection: (a) a wave of prepayments in 2004–05 in a context in which the value of the prepayment option was not priced properly; (b) lack of flexibility—LCH can fund only new loans, cannot be restructured, and must comply

with strict regulatory norms; and (c) decreasing profitability of the LCH business—given the pass-through nature of the bonds, banks earn a fixed commission with no accessory incomes such as treasury reinvestment or active asset-liability managers.[38] Recently, LCH regulation was given more flexibility, allowing, in particular, 100 loan-to-value ratios for the highest rated borrowers and adjustable rates. At the same time, the regulation allowed the funding of housing loans through unsecured "bonos hipotecarios."

preference for debt over equity, arguably due to residual problems in corporate governance and other hindrances to the development of domestic equity markets, as discussed in chapter 7. Yet problems remain. For example, in countries such as Brazil, most local currency corporate bond issues continue to be short maturity or floating rate. Secondary market liquidity for corporate debt remains, by and large, a key hindrance to further market development. And issuing costs continue to be high, limiting access to all but the largest firms.[39]

Together with mortgage bonds, infrastructure bonds provide the other natural source of supply of longer-term financial assets. Public-private partnerships (PPPs) and the growth of institutional investors (pension funds and insurance companies) have both played a crucial role in closing the gap between demand and supply. In many LAC countries, however, development banks (for example, BNDES in Brazil, Banobras in Mexico) are the key players in providing long-term local currency finance for infrastructure projects. Syndicated bank loans and credit from multilateral agencies also play an important role, but more often than not in foreign-currency-denominated finance. Infrastructure finance

is, almost by definition, highly illiquid, not least because it typically requires complicated tailor-made structures. This tends to limit significantly the appetite for infrastructure bonds among mutual funds and defined-contribution pension funds. Moreover, a key piece of this equation went missing in the wake of the global crisis with the demise of the monoline insurers, which played a key role in ensuring the rating and enhancing the market attractiveness of the bonds.[40] Governments are thus now faced with the dilemma of whether and how they might need to step back in to fill the guarantee gap.

Long-term hedges

Except perhaps in Chile—which has patiently and persistently managed to develop a world-class CPI-indexation scheme with deep, liquid markets and a well-trusted indexation methodology—indexation remains a stumbling block to long-term finance in most of LAC (see box 8.2).[41] Finding a good point of intersection between what borrowers need (affordable fixed interest rates or effective protection against real wage fluctuations) and what investors want (credible, clean protection against consumer price fluctuations

BOX 8.2 LAC's indexation experiences in housing finance

LAC countries have struggled over the years with the inherent tension between indexes that accompany borrowers' capacity to pay (that is, that are linked to the real wage) and those that accompany investors' purchasing power (that is, that are linked to CPI inflation). While the former limit credit risk and are favored by borrowers, the latter are preferred by investors. Banks are torn between the two and can be faced with large asset-liability mismatches when they attempt to reconcile both sides of the market.

This was the case in Argentina in 2002. As an early response to the crisis, loans were indexed to the CPI to alleviate the impact of pesification on lenders. However, as inflation surged, indexation was switched to the wage index. But then, as wages increased dramatically, lawmakers reverted to CPI indexation. In Colombia, the definition of the UPAC (Unidad de Poder Adquisitivo Constante) index changed several times—from a CPI with a cap to a CPI–interest rate combination to an interest rate on short-term deposits. However, when short-term real rates rose in 1998, this triggered a surge of nonperforming loans and a fall in housing prices, eventually triggering a banking crisis. In Mexico, a double indexation scheme—indexing loan balances to the CPI, or using variable rates but limiting the increase of monthly installments to the increase of wages—was introduced. However, as the scheme resulted in large losses for banks, it was dropped in 1993 and replaced by variable rates linked to government bonds. Soon thereafter, however, as interest rates rose during the "tequila crisis," banks stopped extending housing loans.

Another approach has been to cover the mismatch between assets and liabilities with prudential buffers. For example, in Argentina in 2004, Banco Hipotecario started securitizing fixed-rate peso loans while offering investors variable rates. Similarly, the Mexican provident funds (Infonavit and Fovissste) have issued CPI-indexed MBS based on housing loans indexed to the minimum wage. In both countries, the credit enhancements needed to support such structures have been very high (25 percent or more). In Argentina, the widening asset-liability gap eventually deterred lenders from assuming the risk. In Mexico, the provident funds have been able to sustain this scheme only because they are not subject to the same capital charges as commercial lenders and because real wages have not fluctuated much over the past 10 years.

In a few cases, governments eventually took over the responsibility for narrowing the gap by designing government-backed hedging mechanisms. In Mexico, the government developed the "UDI [*Unidad de Inversión*] swap" to hedge the real wage index against the CPI. The UDI swap had good success until the correlation between minimum wages and inflation increased, making it less attractive. In Colombia, the government established the Fondo de Reserva para la Estabilizacion de la Cartera Hipotecaria (FRECH) through which mortgage lenders can buy protection against interest rate hikes (both arrangements are priced fairly). FRECH's actual usage has been limited, possibly for pricing reasons, but probably also because of the stabilized macroeconomic conditions.

---

with a deep secondary market) has proved to be difficult.

Derivative markets have developed substantially in the largest LAC countries over the past 10 to 15 years. Foreign exchange derivatives have become particularly deep in the wake of the free floating of the currencies and, as in Chile, of the regulatory requirements on the hedging of pension funds' dollar investments. However, interest rate swaps, the key piece underlying the development of

longer-term fixed-rate instruments, remain relatively undeveloped in most countries.[42]

What are the key policy challenges?

The road to developing markets for long-term financial contracts is a difficult one. This section stays away from policy details and focuses instead on broad directions, based on the general roadmap followed in this report. According to this roadmap, the role of policy is to help reduce the agency or collective frictions that hinder progress toward going long.

Concerning agency frictions, one finds four generic underlying policy issues. (a) How can the state continue to improve the enabling (macroeconomic and institutional) environment so as to facilitate long-term financial contracting? (b) How can the state encourage market discipline, and how far should it go in doing the monitoring itself on behalf of investors? (c) What market arrangements are more likely, at the current stage of financial development in LAC, to provide a successful mix of risk spreading and sound monitoring? (d) Finally, how far should regulators go in limiting the maturity transformation risk taken by financial intermediaries? The following considers each of these in turn.

As regards the institutional and macroeconomic environment, two issues seem to deserve special mention. First, countries will need to strengthen contract rights and their enforcement, two areas where (as noted in chapter 6) LAC lags. Second, countries will need to consolidate the gains made toward using the local currency in long-term contracts. In this regard, the main lessons from LAC's indexation experience can be summed up in three points. First, indexation cannot replace macroeconomic stability; when volatility becomes too high and relative prices fluctuate too much, it becomes very hard, if not impossible, to find indexes that meet all needs.[43] Second, good macroeconomic policies (including inflation targeting) can naturally limit the volatility of relative prices, to the point where a single CPI is probably sufficient. Third, even in well-stabilized countries such as Chile, a CPI can help boost the development of long-term finance, particularly in the annuities industry. Persistence will thus be needed in issuing and promoting the use of CPI-indexed bonds for the long-maturity segments of public debt.

As regards the promotion of market discipline, in addition to continuing to improve information to investors (such as increasing the transparency and disclosure of fees and returns),[44] the most promising route at this stage is to promote standardization and other ways of organizing information (including better benchmarks) that facilitate performance comparisons across asset managers or ALMs. The main pitfall to avoid, however, is to exacerbate investors' focus on short-term returns, which could in turn heighten asset managers' incentives to operate with short horizons. This caution is particularly important for pension funds. To prevent such problems, pension fund supervisors should help lengthen the benchmarks used to assess pension funds' performance.[45] A practical way to do so is to introduce a life-cycle fund in the context of a multifund scheme—a project Chile is now putting to the test.[46] As proposed by Blake, Cairns, and Dowd (2009), regulations that nudge defined-contribution pension funds into mimicking the investment behavior of a defined-benefit pension fund (which has a formal long-term liability that it must try to match with long assets) should also help.

In addition to encouraging market monitoring, governments must also decide the extent to which they are willing to play "big brother" to investors through public monitoring and regulation. This involvement may help solve problems of consumer protection and bounded investors' rationality. One aspect of this effort implies using regulation to encourage pension funds to lengthen their investments, including in socially beneficial ventures such as infrastructure bonds. The other aspect is to make greater use of smart default options that automatically channel investors into the portfolios that are most appropriate for them. However, the more governments take charge, the more they can undermine asset managers' screening and monitoring incentives (just following the regulations to the letter can become the name of the game). They can also undermine market monitoring by investors (who may think, "why bother?"). And they can generally promote moral hazard (if something goes wrong, it is the government's responsibility to fix it). In practice, therefore, a delicate balance between protecting investors and undermining monitoring has to be found.

Regarding the best market arrangements for combining market monitoring and risk spreading, a currently dominant theme for LAC is the choice between covered bonds and securitization. The former ensure "skin in the game" but fall somewhat short as regards risk spreading. As recently demonstrated, the latter can run into the opposite problem of risk spreading (originate-to-distribute) without sufficient "skin in the game." Although the global, postcrisis reevaluation of the benefits of covered bonds translated in the region into plans to develop frameworks in countries where the tool is not available (Brazil, Mexico), the question is whether further efforts should also be made at developing securitization.[47] In any event, the broadening of second-tier finance facilities that raise funds collectively should also be envisaged, especially in underdeveloped mortgage markets.[48] In addition to reducing participation costs—by spreading risk and achieving economies of scale—these facilities can also help promote competition and impose uniform lending and servicing standards to primary lenders. Whenever possible, however, such funding should be "mutualized" rather than "socialized"; that is, the second-tier finance facilities should be private rather than public.

Finally, regarding the regulation of maturity transformation, the use of risk-based capital requirements that penalize mismatches in duration can go a long way toward encouraging ALMs with long liabilities, such as life insurance companies, to invest long. In this case, the regulation is win-win since it has both stability benefits (reduces the risk to insurers) and developmental benefits (promotes long-term assets).[49]

Regarding collective frictions, a first avenue that governments can take to deal with them is to reduce participation costs. This can be done through continuing to improve the enabling environment and, where needed, promoting the availability of information as well as proper infrastructures for collecting and trading information. Because much of the information at issue is a public good,

governments can collect or subsidize the information needed to build indexes that can be used for trading and can facilitate long-term finance; such indexes might be housing prices by city, which can be used to generate futures contracts on housing prices or insurance products for home equity, or rainfall statistics, which can be used to generate rainfall-indexed insurance products and facilitate the lengthening of maturities in agricultural finance.

Where there are strong economies of scale in collecting information, as in the case of pension funds, unbundling the functions of collection and customer service from the portfolio management function (the so-called Swedish option) would enhance transparency and competition in the pension fund industry while also reducing costs (hence lowering fees).[50] Related policy actions to enhance market liquidity might include reducing fragmentation in securities issuance and trading, enhancing securities clearance and settlement arrangements, organizing securities lending and borrowing facilities, and promoting contract standardization. In addition, liquidity can be enhanced *along with* monitoring, by, for instance, (a) improving valuation methods and accounting and financial reporting standards for longer-horizon portfolios and (b) promoting (or even subsidizing) the production of publicly available analyses of asset managers' and ALMs' performance.

While such an agenda may well be warranted, LAC policy makers need to be realistic about the feasibility (and desirability) of adopting a U.S.-style solution that relies almost exclusively on liquid secondary markets to align investors' desire for an exit option with borrowers' long-term funding needs. This solution faces limitations because it hinges crucially on size (as discussed in chapter 7) and can lead to systemic fragility—the "dark side." The following discussion considers these two aspects in a bit more detail.

As regards the issue of size, as noted in chapters 2 and 7, in the absence of sufficient size—of markets and of issues—domestic capital markets can be easily caught in a low-liquidity trap. This constitutes sobering news for the small domestic capital markets in LAC and helps explain why the issuance and trading of Latin American stocks continue to move to the international financial centers where global market liquidity clusters. Thus, where domestic markets are small, reforms—even if desirable—are likely to lead to only modest improvements in secondary market liquidity.

As regards the dark side of market liquidity, if market arrangements succeed in deepening domestic liquidity (a big "if" for a small country), wedges between private and systemic interest can widen as private agents increasingly free ride on liquidity and relax their monitoring efforts. Alternatively, serious problems can be created if, frustrated with the illiquidity of the domestic market for long-term contracts, the government makes too expensive a commitment to providing backstop liquidity (via the central bank or development banks) at too low or no cost. This, in turn, connects with two key issues that will be discussed later in this report: revisiting the risk-bearing role of the government in financial development (chapter 9) and adjusting prudential oversight to deal with the dark side (chapters 10–13).

A second key avenue for dealing with collective action frictions is to mandate participation rather than just promote it. This approach includes, in particular, participation in privately administered defined-contribution pension funds. When combined with policies to promote the development of a vibrant annuities industry in the decumulation phase of life-cycle savings, as in Chile, it provides one of the most promising levers for the development of long-term finance. As the mandatory defined-contribution systems mature, retirees naturally and increasingly demand annuities from life insurance companies. In turn, the latter need to match those liabilities systematically by investing in long-term assets.

However, the design problems that may stand in the way of the development of the annuities market need to be removed (through legal reform, among other means).[51] For example, in Mexico, the demand for annuities from retirees is postponed for decades, until new entrants to the system retire.[52] In Colombia, the required years of contribution and the option for workers to move to the public pension system imply that a rather small proportion of the forthcoming waves of retirees will qualify for an annuity. Such flaws should be avoided whenever possible. To facilitate the link between pensions and insurance, governments may also introduce state guarantees on annuities, with strong capital buffers in life insurance companies acting as the first line of defense. In addition, the composition of asset holdings in the workers' pension fund as they approach retirement should be as similar as possible to the asset portfolio composition of the life insurance company from whom workers will buy their annuity. In addition to tilting a significant share of overall pension fund investments in favor of longer-term, illiquid assets as workers age, this should also help substantially to reduce annuitization risks.[53]

Notes

1. This chapter draws heavily on the papers "Institutional Investors and Agency Issues in Latin American Financial Markets: Issues and Policy Options," by Claudio Raddatz (2011), and "Mobilizing Long-Term Resources for Housing Finance: Trials, Errors, and Achievements in LAC" by Olivier Hassler, which are part of the forthcoming Edited Volume that will accompany this LAC flagship report.

   Duration is the weighted average maturity of a debt contract, where the weights arise from the contractual periodicity with which the interest rate adjusts. If the interest rate is fixed for the life of the contract, maturity and duration coincide. Duration is shorter than maturity if the interest rate is periodically adjusted within the life of the contract. The excess of maturity over duration is larger, with more frequent interest rate adjustments. This chapter uses the labels of "long-term" and "short-term" debt contracts to denote both long (short) maturity *and* duration.

2. Recent estimates of worldwide risks and returns, by Dimson, Marsh, and Staunton (2006), based on 19 (mostly high-income)

countries, indicate that the risk premium that may be captured by going long is about 450 basis points. In choosing a proper portfolio composition, there are, of course, risk-return trade-offs that need to be taken into account and that depend on the age and human capital characteristics of the investor. For theory and simulations along these lines, see Campbell and Viceira (2002) and Viceira (2010).

3. See Benartzi and Thaler (2007).

4. The securities themselves can, of course, be structured so as to offer hedging and insurance features by, for instance, incorporating put options, collars, indexation, and so on.

5. Hedge funds are something of a hybrid. Because the funds are leveraged, hedge fund managers need to hold capital. However, the risks of the investments are ultimately passed on fully to investors; that is, hedge funds do not engage in asset-liability management to provide downside risk insurance to investors.

6. Given that pure asset managers (that is, managers of unleveraged funds) have no "skin in the game" (the gains or losses of the investment are fully passed on to the investors), their incentives can be aligned with those of the investor only through the way in which they are compensated or through regulation. In turn, their compensation may be affected by the direct incentives provided to asset managers by the companies for which they work or by indirect incentives resulting from investors' decisions to shift their portfolios across competing funds. For an extensive discussion of incentives and compensation issues, with a focus on LAC, see Raddatz (2011).

7. Since portfolio selection should generally depend on the investment horizon, short-term return maximization is unlikely to be optimal from a longer-term perspective (see Samuelson 1969; Merton 1969).

8. Distinguishing the true alpha traders is hindered by the bounded rationality of investors. Consistent with the findings of behavioral finance, even financially literate investors are found not to monitor adequately the behavior of asset managers and may not react elastically to performance, measured in terms of fund fees and returns. See Impavido, Lasagabaster, and Garcia-Huitron (2010) for an analysis of the related policy implications for LAC's pension funds.

9. While the reliance on short-term funding is traditionally depicted in the finance literature as a necessary condition for market discipline (to solve agency frictions), it becomes problematic when investors react to noisy signals by running rather than monitoring. See Calomiris and Kahn (1991), Diamond and Rajan (2000), and Huang and Ratnovski (2011). On the social costs of fire sales and deleveraging, see Shleifer and Vishny (2011).

10. These are bonds issued by a leveraged intermediary and backed by its full balance sheet. Covered bonds have a priority claim on the assets of the intermediary in case of bankruptcy.

11. See Shiller (2008) and Kroszner and Shiller (2011) for a detailed discussion of the social benefits of completing certain insurance markets that currently are underdeveloped or do not exist, for example, the markets for house-price futures (which can allow investors to short sell real estate without having to sell the underlying asset, for example, the house); livelihood insurance (which can protect working people from economic shocks to their income); or home equity insurance (which can protect mortgage debtors from unexpected losses in the value of their houses).

12. Privately administered pension funds are important in Bolivia, Colombia, Costa Rica, El Salvador, Mexico, Peru, and Uruguay, which implemented Chile-style pension reforms (that is, they created a mandatory, privately administered system of defined-contribution pension funds as a pillar of the national social security system) over the past decades. Argentina had a system of that type until recently, when it reverted to a pay-as-you-go system. Privately administered but voluntary pension funds are also a prominent feature of Brazil's financial system, where a significant (yet declining) share of assets in this industry is held in defined-benefit occupational pension funds. The rapid growth of these open pension plans benefitting from tax advantages has in turn promoted the development of the life insurance industry.

13. See Impavido, Lasagabaster, and Garcia-Huitron (2010).

14. It appears unlikely that the bias toward short-term government bonds and deposits could result purely from a lack of other instruments. Raddatz and Schmukler (2008) show that pension funds do not invest in all assets in which they are allowed to invest,

even among equities. Opazo, Raddatz, and Schmukler (2009) show that Chilean pension funds bid less aggressively for central bank bonds with longer maturities than for those with shorter maturities.

15. Thus, PFAs that administer defined-benefit pensions appear to invest differently from those that administer defined-contribution pensions.

16. For example, in Chile, the return on equity of pension funds in 2009 was 24 percent, compared to 17 percent for banks and 4 percent for insurance companies.

17. Various LAC countries (including Costa Rica, the Dominican Republic, El Salvador, Mexico, and Peru) have changed (or are considering changing) the fee structure of their pension funds from a pure flow basis (contributions) to a pure stock basis (assets under management). However, as long as pension funds do both collections and portfolio management, neither extreme is likely to be optimal as neither fully matches the underlying cost structure of the funds.

18. Cerda (2006) shows that there is a positive but very small correlation between inflows and performance. Calderón-Colín, Domínguez, and Schwartz (2008) show that, for the Mexican PFAs, there is a substantial fraction of the population shifting to the PFAs with the lowest returns and highest fees. Berstein and Cabrita (2007) show that Chilean workers are not responsive to price and cost signals. Srinivas, Whitehouse, and Yermo (2000) argue that the compulsory nature of contributions and minimum state guarantees on returns limits workers' sense of ownership and reduces their incentives to exert market discipline. Instead, it may induce them (correctly or incorrectly) to assume that the government is implicitly accountable for securing their pension. Despite recent progress, assessing the performance of (and benchmarking) PFAs remains problematic.

19. Several studies have documented the presence of herding in trading among PFAs in Chile (Olivares 2005; Raddatz and Schmukler 2008). Strong herding is observed even where pension fund returns are not regulated, not least because compensation incentives are linked to performance vis-à-vis an industry benchmark.

20. Thus, pension funds tend to be very similar to mutual funds in their investment behavior: they are tactical, follow the pack, and focus on the short-term returns. See Didier, Rigobon, and Schmukler (2011).

21. This is certainly not meant to suggest that pension fund reforms were a failure. Indeed, the growth benefits of the system of individual pension fund accounts have been well recognized. For example, Corbo and Schmidt-Hebbel (2003) find that Chile's pension reform, partly through its positive impact on capital market development, raised GDP growth by an additional one-half percentage point per year, on average, between 1981 and 2001. Nor are the limitations of defined-benefit, mandatory pension funds meant to be LAC specific. Indeed, the tendency of pension funds to herd and to buy and hold is widely recognized the world over. See for example Blake, Lehmann, and Timmermann (2002).

22. The fee structure is relatively standard and consists mainly of a management fee proportional to assets under management, and, to a smaller extent, a combination of entry and exit fees. Explicit performance fees are uncommon.

23. *Alpha risk* refers to the risk-adjusted excess return for investing in wisely selected securities that perform better than the market. *Beta risk* refers to the volatility of a security relative to that of the market.

24. The simple bonus structure in part reflects the fact that LAC has few or no fat-tailed instruments in which mutual funds can (or are allowed to) invest, lacks any standardization of investment styles and segments, and typically has a limited number of funds, which makes benchmarking against a style difficult.

25. While there is a significant correlation between Chilean mutual funds' lagged short-run excess returns (relative to the industry average) and net inflows of assets, the slope of this relation is small, with a 10 percent excess return resulting in inflows equivalent to 2 percent of assets (Opazo, Raddatz, and Schmukler 2009).

26. At first glance, the fact that asset managers invest in liquid securities while tending mainly to hold rather than to trade may seem puzzling. However, it is fully consistent behavior for an asset manager who has no incentives to incur the higher screening costs of investing in illiquid instruments, combined with risk of early investor redemptions.

27. This form of intermediation is analogous to the *separately managed accounts* offered by financial companies in the United States, where, according to some estimates, its size is similar to that of the mutual fund industry. In LAC, the only way to gauge its imprint is through the unaccounted share of financial assets that is not held by domestic financial institutions or foreign investors. A rough calculation for Chile, based on background research for the latest FSAP (Financial Sector Assessment Program; under preparation), suggests that personal brokers and wealth managers might manage as much as 17 percent of total household wealth, substantially less than pension funds (47 percent) but more than banks and insurance companies (about 11 percent each).

28. As of 2004, there were hedge funds located in Argentina, Brazil, Mexico, and many offshore locations. In Brazil alone, assets under hedge fund management reached about US$200 billion by the end of 2010. Private investment funds have started to appear in countries like Brazil, Chile, and Colombia. In Chile and Colombia, they managed assets worth 0.1 and 0.2 percent of GDP, respectively. Venture capital activity is also restricted to a few countries of the region, including Chile, where assets in venture capital funds reach 2 percent of GDP (10 percent of the mutual fund industry).

29. Admittedly, the demand for annuities is not fully mandated in the Chilean pension system because pensioners have the option to use phased withdrawals. However, by making the pension available at the time of retirement, the system creates a natural induced demand for annuities. Shifting the disability and survivorship benefits to the second pillar further contributed to buildup of demand.

30. See Opazo, Raddatz, and Schmukler (2009) for the case of Chile.

31. Notice, however, that life insurance companies increasingly combine traditional insurance services with access to "savings accounts" whose amounts can be withdrawn on demand. Indeed, such features were, in part, responsible for the failure of the Clico group in the Caribbean. This blurring of the lines between insurance and banking is one to watch carefully going forward. It clearly calls for uniform risk-based regulation across all leveraged intermediaries (see chapter 12).

32. In fact, shifting insurance providers is likely to be counterproductive for the insured because of preexisting conditions that can imply significant switching costs.

33. The obstacles and policy issues involved in the development of annuities markets for various Latin American countries are documented in their respective FSAP documents (http://www.worldbank.org/fsap). For the case of Colombia, see also Cheikhrohou et al. (2006).

34. A securitization platform, Hipotecaria Total (Hito), has been developed to import a Danish-style mortgage bond structure.

35. The Sistema Brasileiro de Poupança e Empréstimo (SBPE), which encompasses the largely predominant Caixa Economica Federal and 40 other banks, accounts for about half of total housing finance.

36. The taxa referencial also raises issues of liquidity risk, as it complicates the covering of a possible liquidity shortage with capital market funding.

37. LCH were based on similar arrangements initiated in Denmark, France, and Germany. As in France, mortgage-covered bonds were introduced together with a public housing bank.

38. Moreover, commissions were cut, from 3.5 percent down to 1 percent, between 1984 and 2006.

39. See Zervos (2004).

40. For references on the role of U.S. monoliners and local pension funds in the funding and guaranteeing of infrastructure bonds in LAC, see Escriva, Fuentes, and Garcia-Herrero (2010).

41. For a recent review of debt indexation issues in emerging economies, see also Holland and Mulder (2006).

42. While foreign exchange derivatives are generally more liquid, their development is often constrained by market asymmetries. In the case of the major currencies, the demand for opposite hedges comes from similar agents (for example, exporters) located on each side of the border, but for LAC currencies, the demand for opposite hedges comes mainly from local agents acquiring opposite exposures (for example, exporters versus importers). Thus, the two sides of the market can have difficulty locating each other when they do not have similar levels of financial sophistication.

43. The integrity and credibility of the CPI is, of course, also essential.

44. Shiller's (2008) six-point reform agenda to strengthen the information infrastructure for mortgage finance provides a useful reference. The proposed reform areas are subsidizing comprehensive, independent financial advice; establishing a consumer-oriented government financial watchdog; adopting and adapting default conventions and standards that work well for most individuals; improving information disclosure on financial securities; promoting the creation of large databases of fine-grain data pertaining to individuals' economic situations; and creating appropriate systems of economic units of measurement to which financial contracts could be linked (such as CPI-indexed bonds).

45. Academic work on defining long-term investment benchmarks has made substantial progress but now needs to translate the research into concrete and achievable policy proposals. In particular, a workable and credible decision-making structure, probably based on a committee of independent sages, might provide a proper institutional channel to define and periodically review the composition of the life-cycle portfolio. See Antolin et al. (2010) and Castaneda and Rudolph (2011).

46. The life-cycle fund can become the default fund, that is, the fund to which workers who do not positively choose a fund are assigned. The asset composition of that fund would change automatically as the worker approaches retirement age.

47. While mortgage-backed securities provide higher yields, they are less easy to trade than covered bonds—at least in their most common form of bullet repayable debt—because of the valuation difficulties they raise.

48. Such refinancing structures have already been established in quite a few countries in Latin America, including Costa Rica, Ecuador, the Eastern Caribbean, Mexico, and Paraguay. In Brazil, the provident fund FGTS is mandated to play a similar role. However, the inherent conflicts of interest resulting from the fact that FGTS is managed by Caixa hinders its openness toward other lenders.

49. However, regulators need to take care not to treat all maturity mismatches equally and symmetrically. Penalizing the maturity mismatches of ALMs with mostly short-term liabilities, such as banks, could have undesirable systemic implications because, by encouraging intermediaries to lend short, it could shift liquidity risk on the rest of the system. As discussed in chapter 12, the solution in this case is to penalize short funding rather than rewarding short investing.

50. A challenge under this option could be to keep the quality of customer service from deteriorating, however.

51. To be sure, the biggest challenge for LAC's pension systems remains their low coverage, despite their mandatory nature (Gill, Packard, and Yermo 2004). With the exception of Chile, less than half of the economically active population participates in the mandatory pension system, and, in many countries, coverage is below 25 percent. There is also the growing challenge for defined-contribution pension funds to produce an acceptable "replacement rate" of income after retirement (see de la Torre, Gozzi, and Schmukler 2007a). These challenges, however, fall outside the scope of financial development policy and mainly concern social protection policy.

52. Workers that were already in the system at the time of the reform have a "put option"—at retirement, they can "put" their accumulated fund to the Social Security Institute (Instituto Mexicano del Seguro Social, or IMSS) and receive benefits under the old pay-as-you-go system. The development of the market for annuities was further stalled following legal changes in 2001–02 that resulted in most disabled individuals electing benefits under the old system, contrary to the original intention of the pension reform, which was aimed at ensuring that disability, death, and workers' compensation benefits would be provided by specialized private annuity companies. Ultimately, the "put option" in the Mexican pension system became almost inevitable because affiliates transitioning to the new pension system did not receive, as their Chilean counterparts did, the so-called "recognition bonds" in compensation of the benefits that they had accrued under the under the old pay-as-you-go pension system up to the date of the reform. Instead, recognition bonds in Chile created a clean separation between the old and new systems, making it possible for them to be complementary, rather than substitutes.

53. A well-designed default life-cycle pension fund—like the one Chile is now experimenting with—can also help eliminate that discontinuity. See Rocha and Thorburn (2006) and Rocha, Vittas, and Rudolph (2011).

Risk Bearing by the State: A Collective Action Perspective | 9

Chapter 2 hinted at important roles that the state can play in achieving sustainable financial development. This chapter explores one such role in particular, namely, that of absorbing financial risk by providing loans or guarantees. As in other chapters of this report, the analysis proceeds along the lines of the finance paradigms by systematically contrasting the impact and implications of agency (information asymmetry and enforcement) and collective (collective action and collective cognition) frictions.[1] The chapter makes the following five points:

- The state has a comparative advantage over the market in resolving collective frictions, while the market has a comparative advantage over the state in resolving agency frictions.
- These comparative advantages naturally suggest that states and markets should complement, rather than substitute for or compete with, each other.
- In practice, however, this neat separation of roles can become murky because the paradigms interact; thus, states may need to address agency failures that hinder markets from resolving collective frictions or, conversely, collective failures that

prevent markets from resolving agency frictions. The former may justify first-tier state banking, the latter, second-tier state banking and state guarantees.[2]
- Such interactions have obscured the relative roles to the point that the basic conceptual underpinnings of the role of the state have been too often lost from sight, triggering polemical, lengthy, and inconclusive debates. In Latin America and the Caribbean (LAC), this has given rise over the past few decades to wide, ideologically charged policy swings—a play in four acts that this chapter reviews in some detail.
- Going back to first principles should thus help in rethinking and reorganizing the role of the state in financial development.

The rest of this chapter is organized as follows. The first five sections present the conceptual underpinnings of the risk-bearing role of the state within the framework of the finance paradigms.[3] The next section revisits and interprets LAC's policy swings over the past three to four decades concerning the role of the state in light of this conceptual discussion. The final section discusses policy implications going forward.

The role of the state in the pure agency paradigms

This section first considers the case of pure agency frictions, assuming for now that lenders are not risk averse and that there are no collective action frictions (such as externalities or coordination problems). According to the literature (which is vast), asymmetric information in credit markets, even without risk aversion, can lead to socially inefficient outcomes of either underlending or overlending. For example, Jaffee and Russell (1976) and Stiglitz and Weiss (1981) demonstrate the case for underlending by showing that asymmetric information can lead to adverse selection as higher interest rates attract riskier borrowers; thus, lenders may be better off rationing credit below the level that would be socially desirable.[4]

The appropriate policy response to these agency-driven market failures is not obvious. Most of the literature that finds that asymmetric information can justify state credit guarantees is of a partial equilibrium nature; that is, it does not consider the welfare effects of the taxes needed to finance the guarantees. However, the general equilibrium literature, which uses an appropriately stringent welfare criterion (requiring revenue neutrality *and* taking into account the distributional implications of the taxes levied to finance the state guarantees), systematically concludes that, in the absence of risk aversion, state guarantees cannot improve the market outcome, except when the state has an informational or enforcement advantage over the private sector, which is, in general, hard to argue (box 9.1).

To understand what is at stake, one can consider the student loan model of Mankiw (1986). This model focuses on the information asymmetry problem of adverse selection and assumes that lenders are risk neutral. Students' honesty varies over the population. However, the lender knows less than the borrowing student; specifically, the lender knows the mean of the distribution but not each individual student's characteristics. Moreover, reflecting enforcement and informational frictions, the lender cannot force repayment. Hence, the lender must raise the interest rate on all loans to cover the losses on the unpaid loans. But, by raising the price of all loans, the dishonest (those who do not intend to repay) prevent the honest (those committed to repaying) from borrowing. Because it would have been socially desirable for the honest to borrow, society is worse off.

BOX 9.1 **Welfare criteria in the theoretical literature on state guarantees**

The partial equilibrium literature that does not require revenue neutrality finds that state guarantees can improve things by increasing prudent credit (for example, Mankiw 1986; Smith and Stutzer 1989; Innes 1991; Benavente, Galetovic, and Sanhueza 2006; Arping, Loranth, and Morrison 2010). The literature that takes a general equilibrium view (and hence imposes revenue neutrality) can be classified into two groups. The first group uses a Kaldor-Hicks welfare criterion that simply looks at the total size of the pie but not at its distribution across the population (that is, it assumes away the welfare implications of allocating taxes across the population). With such a criterion, some papers predict that state guarantees can lead to an improved equilibrium (for example, Ordover and Weiss 1981; Bernanke and Gertler 1990; Innes 1992; and Athreya, Tam, and Young 2010). However, others do not (for example, Li 1998; Gale 1991; Williamson 1994). The second group of papers incorporates the welfare impacts of tax redistribution. The papers in this latter group uniformly conclude that, without an informational advantage and the ability to cross-subsidize, state guarantees cannot produce a Pareto improvement (for instance, Greenwald and Stiglitz 1989; Lacker 1994).

What can policy do about this? To answer this question, one should first notice that, in the absence of risk aversion, an unsubsidized guarantee (that is, a guarantee priced to cover expected losses) has no impact. While it reduces risk, this is of no consequence to a risk-neutral lender. The price of the guarantee matches the cost of the loan loss provisions that the lender would have to incur in the absence of the guarantee. As a result, the fairly priced guarantee adds no value and, hence, will not affect the lender's behavior.

By contrast, if the state provides a fully subsidized credit guarantee (a 100 percent default guarantee with a price equal to zero), the risk-neutral lender saves the cost of loan loss provisions and is thereby induced to lend to all students at the risk-free interest rate. From a partial equilibrium viewpoint, absent a requirement of revenue neutrality, the subsidized guarantee would, therefore, allow the social optimum to be reached. However, from a more stringent (and generally warranted) welfare perspective, the financing of the guarantee and the distribution of tax payments across the student population also matter. Unless the students who default also pay the tax, taxing only the nondefaulting students would make them pay for the sins of the defaulting students. Thus, although a subsidized guarantee could be socially justified, the nondefaulting, tax-paying students (including those who would not borrow without the guarantee) would prefer to go without it.

Clearly, taxing only the defaulting students would lead to a Pareto improvement. But doing so amounts to assuming that one can enforce taxation where one cannot enforce a loan repayment. The optimality of the (subsidized) guarantee in a Mankiw-type student loan model of adverse selection hinges exclusively, therefore, on a *differential enforcement capacity*. This does not make sense in a political system where the rule of law applies to states as well as to citizens. Any preferential collection capacity states may have should be made readily available to everyone through improving the judiciary, as part of a more supportive enabling environment. For

similar reasons, a private agent might consider offering screening services to the lender if he or she was better informed (hence better able to discriminate between the good loans and the bad loans) or better able to collect (hence make the dishonest pay for their sins). However, an agent with such capabilities (for example, one able to benefit from economies of scale in putting together an effective sorting system for borrowers) would be in the business of selling services to banks, not in guaranteeing their loans.

Broadly similar arguments can be developed when, instead of adverse selection, the problem underlying the failure of risk-neutral creditors to lend to honest students is one of enforcement. Supposing, for example, that borrowers cannot obtain a loan because they lack good collateral; hence, they cannot credibly commit to repaying the loan. In that case, viable student borrowers without collateral would be excluded from the loan market, resulting again in a socially inefficient equilibrium. By replacing the missing collateral, it is often argued, a state guarantee could bring such borrowers back into the market. The problem with this argument is that, absent any change in the students' own "skin in the game," they would confront the same commitment-to-repay problem. Thus, unless the guarantee is fairly priced (so as to cover the expected loan losses and other costs), the loan default losses would simply be shifted to the state (the guarantor). But if the guarantee is fairly priced, risk-neutral lenders would not pay for it because, by definition, they care only about expected losses and not about the variance of such losses. Unless the state has an enforcement advantage vis-à-vis private lenders—which, as was already argued in this chapter, is hard to justify—there is no case for a state guarantee.

The discussion in this section can be summarized as follows. In a world devoid of risk aversion and collective action frictions, agency frictions alone do not in general justify guarantees under a general equilibrium viewpoint that uses an appropriately restrictive welfare criterion. While the market outcome would be inefficient, a state that does not know more than, or enforce better than, the private sector cannot improve the outcome via credit guarantees. Indeed, one would generally expect the state to have a comparative disadvantage in dealing with pure agency frictions, rather than an advantage. If the state had a comparative advantage in this regard, the right policy would be to have only state-owned and state-run banks, which patently makes no sense.[5] More generally, in a world where distortions arise only from agency frictions, while the market equilibrium is inefficient, the state cannot improve on it by assuming risk, because there is no wedge between private and social interests—principals and agents want the same thing that society wants, namely, to overcome agency frictions and engage in mutually beneficial financial contracts. The only legitimate role left for the state in such a world is to improve the informational and enforcement environment so that markets can operate better.

Adding collective action frictions

This section considers collective action frictions that manifest themselves in the form of *social* externalities—for example, positive externalities to lending that are not internalized by the private lender—and continues to assume that lenders are risk neutral. The literature generally concludes that, in the absence of information asymmetries, any credit policy, including guarantees, is ineffective in improving the equilibrium outcome unless subsidized.[6] Indeed, subsidies and taxes are generally shown to be the best policy responses to a market failure arising from uninternalized externalities. However, the literature concludes that it becomes significantly more difficult to design optimal subsidies where externalities and asymmetric information coexist.[7]

One can see what is at stake by noticing first that, in the Mankiw (1986) model of pure agency frictions, the dishonest inflict negative *informational* externalities on the honest. However, barring differential taxation or enforcement capacity, there is no way for the state to internalize such externalities.

There is no collective action failure. The dishonest are simply getting away with mischief. Even if bargaining were costless, it would not pay for the honest to buy out the dishonest. Indeed, using the same reasoning as in the previous section, the honest would have to make a transfer payment to the dishonest that exactly matches the tax payments that would be required to cover a subsidized state guarantee or an interest rate subsidy. Similarly, even though it seems obvious that one should lend to every student whose return exceeds the social cost of funds, a state banker without an informational or enforcement advantage should not lend and behave exactly like a private banker.

How would adding social externalities and collective action frictions change this conclusion? If one supposes that lending to some targeted students (say, the ones studying to become primary school teachers) has positive social externalities (for example, a good basic education enhances the earning potential from college education in all fields of study), the market outcome would be inefficient even if private lenders could solve agency problems and properly identify all the creditworthy students. Private lenders, by pricing all loans uniformly, would fail to lend sufficiently to students planning to be primary school teachers because their earnings prospects are mediocre, even though those students can contribute the most to other students' earnings. The private lender does not internalize the externality. There is now a clear case of a *collective action* failure. Should students of all generations and in all fields of study be able to get together and bargain at little or no cost, they would agree on setting aside part of the increase in their future earnings resulting from a better primary education in order to subsidize the interest rates on the loans to future primary school teachers.

As noted, an unsubsidized (fairly priced) state guarantee in these circumstances would have no value to a risk-neutral lender. Instead, the state can resolve this externalities-driven market failure by coordinating agents through an interest rate subsidy program favoring loans to the would-be teachers and paid for by all other students. Of course, a straightforward wage subsidy to primary school teachers funded by general taxation would be even cleaner than a subsidized loan. This illustrates that, as long as there is no risk aversion, collective action frictions alone establish the case for tax and subsidy policy but not for state credit guarantees.

Another example is the case in which collective action frictions coexist with agency frictions while lenders are still risk neutral. Where wage subsidies to school teachers are not an available option, an alternative could be a subsidized lending program run by private banks. Since informational frictions require that bankers screen potential borrowers and monitor their performance, and since such efforts are costly, targeted interest rate subsidies dominate targeted and subsidized guarantees (recalling that, if the guarantee is fairly priced instead of being subsidized, the risk-neutral lender would not pay for it). While both policy instruments can similarly expand the level of targeted lending, the interest rate subsidy is preferable because it does not distort the lender's screening and monitoring incentives (the lender retains full "skin in the game").

But there might also be cases where the state's cost of monitoring whether private lenders appropriately screen loan applicants according to social criteria is greater than the cost of simply setting up a first-tier state bank that directly provides the subsidized loans.[8] In such cases, the assumption by the state of the risks associated with financial activities can be justified on the basis of the state's capacity to address agency frictions (that is, ensuring that the loans are given to the most socially desirable borrowers). However, it is crucial to note that such agency frictions arise out of an underlying collective action failure that prevents markets from internalizing externalities.

The bottom line for this section is, therefore, as follows. When social externalities and collective action frictions are added to agency frictions in a world devoid of risk aversion, the case for state intervention becomes clear, but it is hardly in the form of

credit guarantees. When these frictions are relatively light, the state might limit its intervention to that of a catalyst that brings together all interested parties and facilitates the transfers across parties required for a mutually beneficial equilibrium. When the frictions are harder to overcome, the state can circumvent them through a targeted tax-subsidy program, which internalizes externalities. However, the implementation of this program may run into agency frictions. Thus, depending on whether the state or the markets can better address these latter frictions, it might be optimal for the state to subsidize the loans provided by private lenders or to provide the loans directly through a first-tier state bank. Remarkably, however, the basic motivation underlying the state's intervention is always the need to address collective frictions, which introduce a wedge between private and social interests that markets cannot resolve on their own.

Adding risk aversion

Risk aversion among private lenders can now be added to the brew. Arrow and Lind's (1970) article remains the most fundamental and enduring conceptual framing for state risk bearing. They show that, when risk is spread in small amounts over large numbers of investors, capital can be priced at risk-neutral prices. They argue that the state's intertemporal tax and borrowing capacity gives it a unique ability to spread risk across large populations. Thus, state guarantees (as opposed to subsidies or loans) are naturally called for to reduce the cost of risk bearing and to encourage private investment or lending in the face of high risk or high risk aversion.

Curiously, the literature on partial credit guarantees has mostly ignored the Arrow and Lind perspective. Moreover, in the scant literature on this subject, a dominant theme is a rebuttal of the proposition that there is anything unique in the state's capacity to spread risk. For example, Klein (1996) argues that if the state's advantage did not lie purely in its coercive taxation powers (that is, its capacity to oblige taxpayers to bear risk through the tax system), then markets would be able to spread risk just as efficiently. But as Arrow and Lind themselves suggest, it may not be possible for the private sector to be completely risk neutral, even when risk is spread through broad ownership. Since the controlling shareholders of a firm need to hold large blocks of stock, and since such holdings are likely to constitute a significant portion of their wealth, the costs of risk bearing are not negligible, and the firm should behave as a risk averter. Thus, although Arrow and Lind hint at the existence of a link between risk aversion and agency problems (adequate monitoring is induced by large stake exposures), they do not develop the theory, nor has the literature picked up on that theme.

Thus, to help analyze whether there is indeed something unique about the state's risk-bearing capacity, risk aversion can be introduced into the well-known monitoring model of Calomiris and Kahn (1989).[9] In this model, an entrepreneur funds a risky project through a mix of retail and wholesale funding. Projects that are doomed to fail can be liquidated—thereby salvaging some of their value—if they are so identified at an early stage through monitoring. Retail investors do not monitor because they have too small a stake in the project relative to the cost of monitoring. If wholesalers engage in monitoring, they can recoup their investments in failing projects. But wholesalers would do so only if they have a sufficiently large stake in the project (sufficient "skin in the game") to warrant incurring the monitoring costs. However, because wholesalers are risk averse, having "skin in the game" inefficiently raises the cost of funds. A guarantor buying the risk that is concentrated in wholesalers and spreading it by reselling it in small amounts to retailers can therefore improve the market equilibrium.

In doing so, however, the guarantor faces two interrelated problems. First, he or she undermines wholesalers' incentives to monitor the entrepreneur and the project. This is the standard moral hazard problem faced in insurance markets. To induce wholesale lenders to monitor the borrowers

appropriately, the guarantor can monitor wholesalers and adjust the premium of the guarantee according to how well the lenders perform their monitoring. Of course, monitoring the monitor has a cost. Second, the guarantor's capacity to resell the risk to retailers will itself depend on the guarantor's ability to convince them that he or she is doing a good job at monitoring wholesalers and, hence, is offering retailers a fairly priced risk-sharing deal.

This, in turn, will require resolving two problems. First, retailers need to be able to monitor the guarantor's own monitoring efforts to resolve the moral hazard problem. Therefore, the monitoring story repeats at this level. Second, even when this information friction has been resolved (because the information certifying the quality of the guarantor's monitoring is available to retailers at no cost), the guarantor also needs to convince retailers to underwrite the guarantee. This will require *solving market participation frictions*. In view of the atomicity of their investments, absent a market architecture that allows for pooling, retailers may not bother to participate. The remainder of this section focuses on the first problem—that is, the guarantor's cost of monitoring the wholesalers—and leaves aside the second problem—that is, it assumes that there is no cost to retailers either in monitoring the guarantor or in participating in underwriting the guarantee. These latter costs will be reincorporated in the next section.

In the absence of risk aversion, wholesalers do not need to be paid to bear risk, implying that it would not be socially costly for them to retain "skin in the game" and that entrepreneurs would contract enough wholesale funding to allow wholesalers to recoup fully the cost of the socially efficient level of monitoring. Monitoring costs can, therefore, be absorbed efficiently by risk-neutral wholesalers, and *risk would not need to be spread out*. By contrast, when there is risk aversion but no cost of monitoring the monitor, *the risk borne by wholesalers needs to be spread out among retailers*, but this can be done at no cost. Since the guarantor can monitor wholesalers at no cost, he or she can offer a full guarantee and monitor wholesalers sufficiently well to ensure that they continue to monitor the borrowers appropriately. At the same time, since, by assumption, retailers can also monitor the guarantor at no cost, the guarantor can fully pass on (spread) the risk to retailers. Hence, the fact that monitoring costs disappear at the retailer level of the monitoring pyramid allows the market equilibrium to replicate the socially optimal solution.

In general, however, taking risk away from wholesalers is not cost-free, because it undermines the quality of their monitoring. If such a cost is too high, a full guarantee is no longer socially optimal. Hence, where the cost of ensuring good monitoring by risk-averse wholesale lenders is high, these lenders would monitor borrowers appropriately only if the lenders retain a significant risk exposure, which implies that *risk is no longer fully spreadable*. There is, therefore, a fundamental correspondence between the market's capacity to spread risk and the decline of monitoring costs as one goes up the monitoring pyramid.

The argument in this section can thus be summarized as follows. Unless risk is properly spread out, risk aversion, combined with agency frictions, introduces a deadweight cost that constitutes a source of market inefficiency. A guarantee may, therefore, be justified as a means to lower the cost of capital by spreading risk more broadly. However, the benefits of expanded risk spreading should exceed the costs of the weaker screening, monitoring, and enforcement. For guarantees to be desirable, it is thus critically important that their adverse impact on incentives for monitoring be limited. The latter depends on the extent to which the price of the guarantee internalizes moral hazard, which is a function of the quality of monitoring by the guarantor and, hence, of the cost of monitoring the monitor. When this cost is low, the market solution approximates the optimal solution because it replaces a socially costly "skin-in-the-game" requirement for good

(cheap) monitoring by a more efficient, pyramidal market monitoring arrangement that allows for full risk spreading.

This section has not said anything, however, about the nature, state or private, of the guarantee. As will now be shown, the comparative advantage of state over private guarantees depends not on monitoring costs and agency frictions but, instead, on collective action frictions (*the traditional justification for state goods*) that may, under certain environments, give state guarantees a definite edge over private guarantees.

The question of private or state guarantees

In the previous setting, the absence of monitoring or participation costs allowed retailers both to ascertain that the risk-sharing deals they were offered by the guarantor were fairly priced and to participate in the risk market, all free of costs. Thus, although the returns they would get from buying were small, retailers were nonetheless willing to underwrite the guarantor. With these assumptions, private guarantors should naturally emerge, provided that they can mitigate at a reasonable cost the problem of monitoring the wholesale lender. Hence, there would be no role for state guarantees. The only role for the state would be to strengthen the enabling environment so as to help alleviate the informational (or enforcement) frictions that hinder risk spreading.

However, this conclusion changes once one relaxes the assumption that retailers can monitor the guarantor at no cost while still maintaining the assumption of zero participation costs. For retailers to ascertain whether guarantors are offering them a fair deal, they need to certify the quality of the guarantors' monitoring, a costly effort. Because it is in the guarantors' own interest to have their monitoring certified (they will not be able to sell risk otherwise), and because they can include the certification cost in the price of their guarantee, guarantors can pay someone (say, a rating agency) to do the certification. However, this pushes the monitoring pyramid up one more layer, as retailers, in turn, need to be convinced that the rating agency has done a good job certifying guarantors. If monitoring the rating agencies could be done without cost, this would solve the problem. However, this is unlikely to be the case. The potential conflicts of interest between bond issuers and rating agencies that have emerged at the heart of the postcrisis debate on regulatory reform are testimony of the difficulty of solving this problem. Such difficulties carry a crucial implication, namely, that market monitoring issues (that is, the completion of the monitoring pyramid) are in general unlikely to be solved without the provision of a public good in the form of official oversight over the market monitors. Official provision of information and official oversight thus act as the last lines of defense to help close the monitoring pyramid.

Be that as it may, the key point is that these monitoring problems do not depend on the nature, public or private, of the guarantees. Indeed, with one possible caveat (more on this below), even if retailers faced no costs in participating in underwriting a guarantee, a state guarantor will face exactly the same monitoring problems and constraints as a private guarantor in terms of convincing retailers that the wholesale lenders will be under adequate vigilance. Thus, a state guarantee continues to be unjustified.

Things change further once one relaxes the last simplifying assumption—the absence of participation costs. Although having retailers participate in the risk market to spread risk efficiently would be socially desirable, individual retailers may not internalize this positive participation externality. Instead, the participation disincentives faced by retailers may require the guarantor to incur costs (for example, in advertising) to attract investors. In a well-developed financial system, the guarantor would not have to deal directly with retailers. Instead, an additional layer of agents—the asset managers, such as mutual funds, pension funds, or hedge funds—could pool retail investors for the guarantor, thereby reducing the costs of participation. But in an undeveloped financial system, the

costs of mobilizing participation will be high, so that adding those costs to the guarantor's certification costs might well raise total costs to a point where the guarantee is no longer viable.

Thus, the bottom line is that the ability of the guarantor to unload risk will very much depend on how well-developed financial markets are. In mature financial systems, the market can resolve participation frictions through a deep network of asset managers. In an undeveloped system, such frictions remain unresolved. This is precisely the point at which the state can help to complete markets, at least temporarily. Because state guarantors do not have to market their risk (the distribution is taken care of through the tax system and state policy), they can effectively resolve the collective action failure.

State guarantees can spread the risk all the more finely because they can do so across currently living taxpayers and across generations within a given jurisdiction. However, even in the case of intergenerational risk spreading, the state's advantage derives again from its capacity to address a collective action (participation) friction, rather than an enforcement (agency) friction. Indeed, trying to depict the inability of markets to contract across generations from a pure enforcement perspective is rather futile. Since it is not possible to write bilateral contracts with someone unborn, "enforcing" such contracts is meaningless. Instead, the state has an edge because of the intergenerational burden sharing that the political system is naturally designed to do.[10]

Based on the above conceptual premises, the conditions can now be stated under which public guarantees will be needed either to replace or to complement private guarantees in the face of idiosyncratic risk. The main conclusion is that, where private lenders are risk averse, and even where risks are idiosyncratic and therefore diversifiable in principle, the state can spread the risk more broadly than the market by resolving participation externalities—that is, the state can pool atomistic investors (or taxpayers) that would otherwise not participate in underwriting the guarantee. However, for state guarantees to be desirable, it is critically important that their adverse impact on monitoring and enforcement incentives be limited.

There is a clear infant industry argument for public guarantees, in the sense that they can be justified on a *transitory* basis when financial systems are underdeveloped—and therefore suffer from high monitoring costs and low participation—but only so long as they aim at crowding in (rather than crowding out) the private sector. Moreover, if idiosyncratic risk is fat-tailed, public guarantees may be justified on a more *permanent* basis, because even the more developed financial markets may not be able to reach the scale of participation that would be needed to atomize and distribute the risk sufficiently.[11] While more mature systems should enhance the scope for private guarantees by smoothing out agency frictions (by helping to close the monitoring pyramid) and collective action frictions (by pooling risk through asset managers), the spreading of fat-tailed risk may exceed the capacity of private guarantees. Again, permanent public guarantees in mature financial systems may be justified so long as they do not unduly erode the monitoring incentives of those protected by the guarantees.

One should note that, in all cases, the risk-spreading ability of the state and, hence, the rationale for public guarantees ultimately rests on the comparative advantage of the state in resolving collective action frictions (*the traditional justification for public goods*).[12] Public guarantees may have an edge over private guarantees not because the state can better resolve agency frictions but, instead, because collective action frictions may disable the market's ability to resolve such agency frictions.

Systemic risk

Finally, this section considers the case in which the risks in question are systemic, that is, they are not diversifiable. As discussed in chapter 2, systemic risk can arise endogenously in the process of financial development. That is the case, for example, when the apparently successful market-led reduction of agency and participation frictions may itself introduce—as a result of, say, interconnectedness—widening wedges between private and social interests. The key point is that public guarantees can be justified on a permanent basis in the presence of systemic risk, including that which is endogenously brewed in the process of financial development itself. The rationale in this case, however, no longer derives from the need to spread risk as broadly as possible but rather from the state's capacity to help coordinate agents' actions around an efficient risk-sharing equilibrium.

The argument in support of public guarantees under systemic risk has two threads, depending on whether systemic risk is a manifestation of highly uncertain and endogenous risk or a manifestation of correlated risk. First, in the case of highly uncertain and endogenous risk, the public guarantee may induce agents to abandon altogether the expected utility-maximizing framework and choose instead a "min-max" criterion such that they minimize their exposure to the maximum possible loss. In such a case, Arrow and Lind's (1970) risk-spreading argument no longer holds, because the total cost of risk bearing remains the same as the population of taxpayers becomes large, making risk nondiversifiable. However, public guarantees are still useful because they help resolve collective action failures. When all agents minimize their exposure to a worst-case scenario, they can end up behaving in a collectively irrational way because each individual acts on the basis of being affected more than the average. By eliminating such a scenario, public guarantees effectively function as a coordination device, much as deposit guarantees and lender-of-last-resort facilities can eliminate self-fulfilling bank runs.[13]

Correlated risk leads to a further breakdown of the Arrow and Lind criterion. Even if risk exposure is atomized and shared across a large number of investors, these investors remain risk averse because the returns on their investment become negatively correlated with their income and consumption. Because correlated risk applies to an investor deciding whether to invest in a private guarantee scheme as much as to a taxpayer deciding whether to vote for a state guarantee scheme, the state has no natural risk aversion advantage in this case. Nonetheless, public guarantees can still improve things by helping avert the collective action failures that magnify the impact of a systemic event. By coordinating agents' behavior around a collectively desirable outcome, public guarantees help reduce the risk of catastrophic downturns, thereby smoothing out private consumption, which, in turn, helps reduce risk aversion.

The justification for the state to assume financial risk is always derived from its ability to resolve collective action frictions better than markets, which is, indeed, the usual justification for public goods. This suggests a natural division of tasks, whereby markets take the agency roles but are supported by states wherever markets are unable to correct the collective failures. States and markets should thus naturally complement each other. In practice, however, this neat division of labor is complicated by the fact that the state's role is often justified at the intersection between the agency and collective paradigms. State risk taking may be needed to address agency failures that prevent markets from resolving collective frictions, as in the case of first-tier state banking reviewed in the second section, or, conversely, to address collective failures that prevent markets from resolving agency frictions, as in the case of risk spreading surveyed in the previous section, which can justify second-tier state banking

and state guarantees. Because it is complex and potentially confusing, this interaction between collective and agency frictions may have helped generate the large policy swings observed in LAC's recent history.

LAC's policy swings—a play in four acts

Although the importance of state banks in LAC fell steeply over the past 40 years, they remain significant in the region, accounting for over 20 percent of banking system assets (see table 9.1). Moreover, development banks, a subset of state banks, continue to be the instrument of choice for states to pursue financial inclusion and countercyclical credit objectives.[14] LAC's recent history of wide swings in the perceived developmental role of the state in finance can be depicted as a play in four acts.[15]

Act I: The state can do it better

A highly interventionist role for the state emerged in LAC in the 1950s, dominating financial development policy until the mid- to late 1970s. The premise was that the market, left to its own devices, would be incapable of internalizing growth externalities. Thus, development banks became the key policy vehicle to mobilize and allocate financial resources where markets failed, particularly in long-term finance, credit to small and medium enterprises (SMEs), housing finance, and agricultural credit. While this rationale rightly put the emphasis on the state's comparative advantage in resolving

TABLE 9.1 **Development banks in Latin America and the Caribbean: Operative modality of development banks at the beginning of 2009**

Operative modality	Development banks			
	Number of	%	Assets (US$)	%
First-tier banks	66	65.3	376,365	43.5
Second-tier banks	23	22.8	237,762	27.5
Banks of 1st and 2nd tier	12	11.9	251,043	29.0
Total	**101**	**100.0**	**865,169**	**100.0**

Source: ALIDE database.
Note: The database identifies a total of 101 development-oriented banks in 21 countries in LAC.

collective action frictions, in practice, the state became directly involved in solving agency frictions and in this capacity became a substitute for (rather than a complement to) financial markets. Thus, it is no surprise that Act I ended badly, with deeply atrophied financial systems and mismanaged state banks that turned into instruments of political clientelism saddled with yawning losses.[16]

Act II. On second thought, markets can do it better

In reaction to these problems, the conventional wisdom on the developmental role of the state in finance took a 180-degree turn toward a frankly laissez-faire view. This shift—a reflection of shifting intellectual winds worldwide—was dramatically stimulated in LAC by the debt and fiscal crises of the 1980s.[17] The key contention was that, precisely due to agency problems, bureaucrats can never be good bankers and can in fact do more harm than good. Moreover, given well-defined property rights, good contractual institutions, and information availability, markets can take care of most agency failures by themselves.[18] Therefore, state efforts should be primarily deployed toward improving the enabling environment.[19] In response, many development banks redefined their mandates, shifting from first tier to second tier. At the same time, to level the playing field, states placed the remaining first-tier development banks under the same standards of prudential oversight and corporate governance that apply to private banks and made efforts to enhance the banks' managerial quality and independence. However, this action put the banks in a difficult bind, still at the heart of the challenges they face today. On the one hand, they are unavoidably compelled to fulfill an (explicit or implicit) policy mandate that, almost by definition, exposes them to high-risk clientele and often limits their capacity to diversify risks. On the other hand, the new and stricter requirements to avoid losses induces them to seek less risky

and more lucrative lines of business, thereby putting them on a potential collision course with private banks.[20]

Act III. Let markets and the state cooperate

In the past decade or so, many development banks in LAC have moved away from risk taking, into nontraditional catalytic activities aimed at resolving collective action failures. These efforts began to materialize in innovative interventions, where development banks increasingly combined activities aimed at solving coordination problems with activities entailing risk absorption (particularly via credit guarantees). Such "pro-market activism," analyzed in some detail for Chile and Mexico by de la Torre, Gozzi, and Schmukler (2007c), included (a) the creation of infrastructures to promote participation and to help financial intermediaries achieve economies of scale and reduce the costs of financial services;[21] (b) investment bank–type activities centered on coordinating various stakeholders around structured finance schemes, and on enhancing such structures with state guarantees;[22] and (c) partial credit guarantee schemes to promote private sector lending to priority sectors.[23]

Act IV. When the going gets tough

During the recent global financial crisis, the issue of risk absorption by development banks came forcibly back to the policy debate, because, in many LAC countries, development banks performed vigorous countercyclical credit activities aimed at sustaining the flow of credit in the face of rising risk aversion among private banks. There is by now a strong consensus that these countercyclical interventions—which involved first- and second-tier lending as well as credit guarantees—were successful overall.[24] However, this has reopened contentious issues that seemed to have been finally settled. Development banks are now asking themselves whether they should grow bigger even in the good times so as to play a more forceful role in the bad times. There is thus a risk of another swing in the pendulum.

Toward a rebalanced policy

The main message from the conceptual analysis in the first five sections of this chapter is that the state should play to its strengths—helping resolve collective action failures—rather than to its weaknesses—dealing with agency frictions. This message implies that the state should seek to complement (rather than substitute for) markets, crowding *in* the private sector and harnessing its comparative advantage in dealing with agency problems, rather than crowding it out.

This approach opens three avenues to explore. The first, the least controversial, comprises policy interventions exclusively geared to solving participation frictions—along both the intensive margin (the same players engaged in more transactions) and the extensive margin (the incorporation of new players)—without dealing directly with risk. Rising financial inclusion makes it easier for the financial services industry to lower costs, expand market liquidity, and diversify risk, as well as for society to share in the benefits that come from the positive spillovers associated with scale and network effects. This observation justifies the state's catalytic roles portrayed in the previous section. But it can also explain the establishment and operation by central banks of large-value payments systems; the promotion by the public sector of clearing, settlement, and trading infrastructures; or the standardization of contracts. It can also justify mandated—or gently coerced—participation, as in the case of contributions to privately administered pension funds or the payment of state employee wages through accounts in banks that participate in a shared, open-architecture platform for retail payments. Given the presence of positive externalities, the state can also use well-targeted subsidies as part of these interventions.

The second avenue is still catalytic in essence but deals directly with risk spreading.

States can promote private sector participation in guarantee schemes, such as mutual guarantee associations funded by small local entrepreneurs, or guarantee schemes structured as joint stock companies with private participation. The experience across the world with such schemes has been generally positive, partly because they promote peer pressure, a purely private form of resolving collective frictions. Indeed, there is some evidence that such associations work best when they remain purely private, as this fully preserves incentives for group monitoring and limits moral hazard.[25]

Peer pressure may not work in all cases and all environments, however. Thus, the third avenue, more controversial and thorny, involves risk absorption and risk spreading through second-tier state banks, whether through guarantees or long-term loans.[26] In either case, it is the interaction of risk aversion, agency (monitoring) frictions, and participation frictions that justifies state insurance, even where risk is idiosyncratic. As noted, state guarantees may be temporary—a strictly developmental tool aimed at facilitating risk discovery and circumventing transitional collective action frictions—or permanent (in the face of fat-tailed risk). However, state-sponsored credit guarantee programs do not seem to be typically, at first glance, fully consistent with such first principles. They seem to be permanent rather than transitory, and they tend to target well-defined, recurrent, limited risks instead of insufficiently understood risks or tail risks where the state's comparative advantage in risk bearing and spreading could be more fully exploited. Moreover, these guarantee programs are typically justified based on asymmetric information, lack of collateral, or externalities instead of risk aversion. What explains these apparent disconnects?

Political economy offers one explanation. Correcting agency problems that hinder, for instance, SME lending (presumably ripe with positive social externalities) and lending to the lower-income households (presumably ripe with equity benefits if not externalities) sells better in the polity than correcting problems of risk spreading and differential risk aversion. In addition, it is not popular for the state to take on risk from private banks, even when doing so is fairly priced, because it smacks of being a bailout. Moreover, if the problem is risk aversion among private lenders, where should a risk-neutral state draw the line? Should the state sector reinsure or guarantee all productive lending at the risk frontier, not just financing to SMEs? Should state guarantees apply to all long-maturity loans, irrespective of firm size? Expanding the risk frontier across the board is naturally unpalatable to politicians insofar as they are held accountable. Indeed, over the years, parliaments in LAC and many other regions have strictly limited risk taking by state banks. Moreover, state bank managers are naturally risk averse. They protect their capital because they know that they will live or die with it.[27] And as already noted, the constraints that development banks face in terms of avoiding losses often induce them to compete with commercial banks to reap high returns for low risks, rather than—as the risk aversion rationale would suggest—to complement private activity by insuring risk taking at the frontier.

Instead, public guarantees to SMEs or to target clienteles, such as those reached through low-income housing or student loan programs, look like safe bets when they are well within the risk frontier. They appear to pay for themselves (hence are fiscally safe) when well priced and designed.[28] Moreover, early research seems to indicate that partial credit guarantees supplied by states do provide at least some additionality.[29] Why, then, not safely collect the low-hanging fruit instead of shooting for the moon? This preference for seemingly low-risk–high-political-return programs has been accentuated over the past decade or two in LAC and other regions, especially in the context of mediocre growth, high structural unemployment, and tight fiscal constraints. Lending or credit guarantee programs directed to those most affected by economic hardship have provided a convenient safety valve to relieve some of the buildup in political pressure.[30]

But the tendency of development banks not to move too aggressively toward the risk frontier reflects not just the political economy. It also reflects legitimate difficulties, particularly with the accurate pricing of guarantees. As noted, public guarantees are welfare-enhancing only as long as and as far as all the risks and incentive distortions they cause have been properly recognized and priced in. But risks at the frontier are not well understood, and they may be abnormally distributed, with fatter tails. Under such circumstances, the pricing of guarantees becomes inherently difficult, as the estimation of expected losses and the decomposing of risk premiums are subject to much error. Indeed, there are chilling cases of major failures and losses in ambitious state insurance programs that have aggressively aimed at crowding in the private sector toward the risk frontier. In part, such failures have reflected a misjudgment of expected losses.

Where does all of this lead? First, it is time for state lending and insurance programs to come clean as regards their rationale and the minimal conditions for success. Instead of justifying state loan and guarantee programs based on goals, as is so often the case and with which it is so hard to disagree, policy makers need to focus instead on *alternative means of achieving these goals*. Thus, public risk-bearing programs should be justified by comparing their costs and benefits with those of alternative channels of state intervention that do not involve any state risk taking. Where guarantee programs are deemed appropriate, the programs' objectives, mandates, and reporting and disclosure requirements need to be refocused around a risk aversion rationale and more clearly linked to the agency or collective action frictions with which risk aversion interacts. Policy makers also need to explain why the state can achieve that which markets cannot. Either these programs are really self-sustaining and therefore should be eventually divested to the private sector, or there are hidden risks (fat-tailed or systemic) that free markets cannot handle well and that need to be explicitly recognized and accounted for. Unless this is done right, state guarantees will likely end up subsidizing risks, and this is bound to distort incentives and trigger unpleasant fiscal surprises (as well as political upheavals) once downsides materialize (the recent U.S. experience in the subprime crisis is, of course, the most obvious illustration).

It is thus not enough that public guarantee programs break even in good times. If priced right, they should accumulate reserves in the good times against potential losses in the bad times. For tail risk, this implies charging for the full expected value of the tail losses. One possible approach to facilitate risk discovery is to auction the guarantees according to their coverage or price.[31] By setting volumes rather than prices, guarantors can better protect themselves against the risk of major mispricing. At the same time, volumes may be adjusted to meet countercyclical objectives. They can be raised in systemic downturns, when upward jumps in private risk aversion are more likely to trigger coordination failures, and reduced in upturns, when risk appetite can swell, fueling excessive credit expansion. To avoid head-to-head competition with the private sector in providing primary insurance, the state should prefer to provide its support through well-targeted reinsurance against tail risks.

As financial systems mature—and hence more information exists to assess and price risk—public loan and guarantee programs can be better targeted. For example, when risk scoring methods are available, fairly priced public guarantees can be targeted to be at, or just outside, the risk frontier, so as to ensure that finance reaches clients and projects that are too risky for private institutions to lend to without guarantees. When loans are made directly by first-tier public banks, making sure the interest rates on the loans are above market rates can help ensure that public risk bearing does not crowd out private risk bearing.[32]

The further one seeks to move away from the private risk frontier, the more caution is of course called for. However, risk taking can be bounded and state governance protected in a variety of ways. For example, earmarked

capital for specific insurance or countercyclical risk absorption can help state banks assume more risk in a responsible, bounded manner while protecting their capital from depletion. Alternatively, to align incentives, state banks can assume a limited part of the risk, the rest being covered by the state through earmarked capital or other means. Private-state partnerships in which the state assumes most (but not all) of the risk at a fair price may help facilitate price and risk discovery. Enhanced transparency, better measurement of risk and returns, and more sophisticated checks and balances (for example, through recurrent assessments by independent evaluation units or through occasional, more-strategic reviews by blue-ribbon committees) also should all help strengthen the governance of state banks or other state entities engaging in higher-risk activities.

As already noted, there might also be cases where, to internalize externalities, states may be better off dealing directly with borrowers through a first-tier state bank (that is, becoming agents) than through guarantees provided by a second-tier state bank. In particular, it has been argued that, in downturns, partial guarantees may not be sufficient to overcome bankers' heightened risk aversion. Thus, unless states are willing to assume most or all of the risk, which could subject them to unacceptably high losses, guarantee programs may fail to provide an effective countercyclical tool. Instead, as the argument goes, first-tier state banking provides the only reliable channel to increase lending in a reasonably safe fashion, that is, "when the going gets tough, only state banks get going." As reasonable as this argument may sound, it can also be turned on its head. The more state banks compete with private banks, the less private lenders are likely to share information with a state guarantor. Hence, a noncompeting state sector, one that complements but does not substitute, may in fact be best able to maintain open access to the private information that it needs to monitor the banks and extend the coverage of the guarantees during downturns in a fiscally responsible way.

An important final question is whether state banks should be supervised as private banks. In the case of first-tier state banks, the answer is an unqualified yes. Since state and private banks compete for the same business (they are potential substitutes, at least to a degree), they should be regulated and supervised in exactly the same way as private banks. For second-tier state banks, the answer is not so clear, however. Because such banks are in the business of ensuring against tail risks, the tolerance range involved in calibrating their capital under a value-at-risk criterion will need, by construction, to use less strict criterion than that applied to private banks. At the same time, the emphasis on uncertain frontier risk requires a different type of supervision. It should rely on high-end, holistic assessments by panels of experts that balance the economywide costs and benefits of the programs that the state bank engages in rather than ready-made, one-size-fits-all rules aimed at ensuring financial stability.

Notes

1. This chapter draws heavily on the paper "Risk-Absorption by the State: When Is It Good Public Policy?" by Deniz Anginer, Augusto de la Torre, and Alain Ize (2011), which is part of the Edited Volume that accompanies this LAC flagship report.
2. First-tier public banks are those that conduct their operations directly with their final customers; instead, second-tier public banks conduct their operations through commercial banks.
3. This chapter presents the arguments informally. A more formal discussion can be found in Anginer, de la Torre, and Ize (2011).
4. Likewise, overlending can occur. For example, when projects that would be equally profitable if successful have different probabilities of success, low interest rates can induce borrowers with low success probabilities to borrow, even though their expected returns are below the social rate of return. See de Meza and Webb (1987, 1999) and Beck and de la Torre (2006).
5. Notice, however, that multilateral development banks (MDBs) that lend to public sectors to finance investment projects may enjoy informational advantages vis-à-vis private lenders, such as knowing more than private lenders about state processes and procedures. This may justify MDB guarantees even in a world characterized by pure agency failures with no risk aversion.
6. See, for example, Raith, Staak, and Starke (2006); Penner and Silber (1973); and Lombra and Wasylenko (1984).
7. See Stiglitz, Vallejo, and Park (1993); Calomiris and Himmelberg (1994); and Bhattacharya (1997).
8. The argument that the state may be able to provide incentives to public lenders more easily than to private ones is in line with Holmstrom and Milgrom's (1991) result that increasing the incentives along a measurable performance dimension (costs or profitability) reduces the incentives along nonmeasurable dimensions. For a fuller discussion along these lines of the role of first-tier public banks, see also IDB (2005).
9. See Huang and Ratnovsky (2011) for an interesting extension of the Calomiris-Kahn model challenging the proposition that wholesale investors efficiently discipline the bank (or entrepreneur) to whom they lend.
10. Enforcement frictions (the other important type of agency frictions) may also help justify the need for public guarantees but, as with informational frictions, not because the state has any natural advantage in enforcing contracts. As already noted in the previous section on collective action frictions, there is no credible reason why enforcement failures can be resolved through the state's uncontested ability to tax but not through well-formulated private contracts and a well-functioning judiciary. Instead, the state may have an edge because costly contract enforcement is likely to require cost sharing, which again faces a collective action problem. In turn, taxation should not be viewed (as in Klein 1996) as a mechanism to oblige unwilling taxpayers to share risks, but instead as a simple, built-in coordination mechanism that facilitates the participation of all.
11. In principle, the Arrow and Lind (1970) argument continues to apply: no matter how lumpy the risk, it can still be distributed atomistically, provided there are enough retailers over which the risk can be spread. In Arrow and Lind, the number of retailers can go all the way to infinity. In practice, however, there

is an important difference between a large number and an infinite number. Moreover, and perhaps more important, participation frictions limit market depth even in well-developed financial systems. Thus, the number of retailers over which risk can be spread, even if large, may not be sufficient. That is why there may be a point at which a permanent public guarantee may be needed, even in mature systems, to bound the risk associated with unpredictable returns or where there is some probability, even if very small, of very large losses. Knightian uncertainty—when decision makers cannot determine the probabilities of events (see Epstein 1999)—is likely to have an effect similar to fat tails. The more uncertain the risk, the more finely it needs to be distributed, which, in principle, makes more of a case for public guarantees.

12. There may be some exceptions in which the public sector may also have a genuine advantage in dealing with agency frictions. For example, lenders and entrepreneurs may deal with each other on the basis of proprietary information and relationship lending. Private guarantors need to access this information to understand the risks. Yet (at least one of) the parties involved in these private deals may be reluctant to share the information since they might lose proprietary rents when the information is leaked. In that case, the public guarantor with preferential access to private information may reduce its monitoring costs, giving it an edge. However, one would expect such advantages to vanish as financial systems mature and information becomes increasingly public.

13. See Diamond and Dybvig (1983) and the more novel contributions of Caballero and Krishnamurthy (2008) and Caballero and Kurlat (2009) on the role of public guarantees under uncertainty. More generally, one could also argue that the state could behave collectively in a more rational way than individuals when the latter are subjected to systematic behavioral biases.

14. The Latin American Association of Development Finance Institutions (ALIDE) identifies a total of 101 development-oriented banks in 21 countries in LAC in 2009 (see table 9.1).

15. For a more detailed discussion of the evolution of the views on the role of the state in financial development, see de la Torre, Gozzi,

and Schmukler (2006, 2007c). For the corresponding evolution of the broader economic development paradigms in LAC, see Birdsall, de la Torre, and Valencia (2010).

16. Empirical studies have tended to find that public banks have done more harm than good (see Barth, Caprio, and Levine 2001; Caprio and Honohan 2001; IDB 2005; La Porta, Lopez-de-Silanes, and Shleifer 2002). In particular, these studies find that greater state participation in bank ownership is associated with lower levels of financial development, less credit to the private sector, wider intermediation spreads, greater credit concentration, slower economic growth, and recurrent fiscal drains. However, IDB (2005) finds that public banks tend to play a countercyclical credit role. For evidence on the history of recurring losses of public banks in Brazil, see Micco and Panizza (2005), and for Mexico, see Brizzi (2001). Goldsmith (1969), McKinnon (1973), and Shaw (1973) led the charge in arguing that dirigisme in finance leads to "financial repression." A number of cross-country studies try to measure the impact of financial repression (as measured by real interest rates or a variant thereof) on growth (see, for example, Easterly 1993; Lanyi and Saracoglu 1983; Roubini and Sala-i-Martin 1992; and World Bank 1989).

17. The laissez-faire view was also consistent with the application in LAC of Washington consensus–style reforms during the 1990s (see Birdsall, de la Torre, and Valencia 2010).

18. See Caprio and Honohan (2001); Klapper and Zaidi (2005); Rajan and Zingales (2001); World Bank (2005).

19. This paradigmatic shift also put emphasis on financial liberalization as a way to achieve efficiency. Thus, by the late 1990s, Latin America reached levels of financial liberalization comparable to those in the developed world. See de la Torre and Schmukler (2007).

20. In many cases, the resulting tension was exacerbated by the erosion of the cost-of-funds advantage that state-owned banks used to enjoy, reflecting financial globalization and the rising availability of funds.

21. The interventions examined there include the following. First is the case of the Internet-based market platform for factoring services created by the Mexican development bank NAFIN. In this platform, SMEs are able to discount competitively the accounts receivable claims they

have on large buyers. Second is the electronic platform implemented by BANSEFI, another Mexican development bank, to help small savings and credit institutions (the so-called *cajas*) reduce their operating costs by centralizing back-office operations. Third is the experience with correspondent banking in Brazil, where a nonfinancial public infrastructure with a large geographic coverage, the post office, was made available to financial intermediaries for the distribution of certain financial services.

22. The specific interventions examined in this respect include structured finance products created by FIRA, a Mexican development bank oriented toward agriculture. In one such scheme, FIRA set up a structure that ensures the provision of adequate working capital financing for shrimp producers, which required the coordinated participation—via a trust fund—of, in addition to shrimp producers, the large (international) shrimp distributor, commercial banks, and shrimp feed suppliers. FIRA enhanced the structure by providing second-loss default guarantees to commercial banks.

23. The interventions analyzed in this regard include the FOGAPE guarantee system in Chile, which is funded by the state and administered by BancoEstado, a public bank, and supports lending to small enterprises.

24. See, for instance, ALIDE (2009).

25. On the experience of mutual guarantee associations in Europe, see Columba, Gambacorta, and Mistrulli (2009). Lebanon provides an interesting example of a seemingly successful and profitable guarantee scheme structured as a joint stock company.

26. A long-term finance commitment can be viewed as a funding (liability) guarantee that provides protection against liquidity risk and price volatility, instead of credit default. Thus, instead of the development bank actually funding the commercial bank, an equivalent arrangement would be for the development bank to provide swap and lender-of-last-resort facilities.

27. Development banks in Mexico, for instance, are regulated and supervised on par with commercial banks and are required by law to preserve the real value of their capital.

28. See Honohan (2008) and Beck, Klapper, and Mendoza (2010).

29. See Larraín and Quiroz (2006); Haines, Madill, and Riding (2007); and Arvai, Rocha, and Saadani (2011).

30. See Rajan (2010).

31. This is the approach followed in Chile by FOGAPE. See Benavente, Galetovic, and Sanhueza (2006) and de la Torre, Gozzi, and Schmukler (2007c).

32. Some lending and guarantee programs by development banks in high-income countries are structured in this way. The Business Development Bank Canada (BDC) small business loan guarantee program is perhaps a prime example. See Rudolph (2009).

Prudential Oversight: Where Does LAC Stand? | 10

The Latin America and Caribbean (LAC) region has weathered the global financial crisis fairly well, in part because of the progress achieved in prudential oversight over the past two decades. This progress came in the wake of LAC's turbulent macrofinancial history, which stimulated substantial efforts to overhaul and tighten its prudential oversight. Somewhat ironically, this progress was occurring just as financial regulators in many developed countries were bent on easing intermediation through more market-friendly regimes with less expensive buffers. LAC's efforts were often spearheaded by repeated assessments of international standards, particularly the Basel Core Principles for Effective Banking Supervision (BCP). This chapter first reviews the progress and identifies some of the remaining gaps.[1] It then sets the background for discussing (in the final three chapters of this report) the challenges of systemic oversight, issues that were mostly ignored in the regulatory standards written before the global financial crisis, but for which LAC needs to prepare. Main findings are as follows:

- Important progress has been achieved by LAC countries in all main areas of bank oversight as defined by the precrisis Basel standards, including the institutional and accounting and disclosure frameworks, various aspects of regulation (entry, capital adequacy, credit risk, and other risks), and the main components of supervision (methods, internal controls, and consolidated and cross-border oversight).

- However, progress has been uneven, and important gaps remain, both across subregions and across themes.

- The LAC-6 countries (the LAC-7 group minus Argentina, for which a BCP assessment was not yet finalized at the time of this writing) were found to outperform their peers generally; the smaller, lower–income LAC countries generally underperformed; the Caribbean countries lie somewhere in between.

- Two basic legal framework issues—the independence of bank supervisors and their legal protection—need special attention in many LAC countries.

- The regulation of capital adequacy is uneven, with over half of LAC countries not fully meeting Basel I standards and only limited progress being made toward meeting Basel II.

- Bank supervision lags outside the LAC-6 countries, which illustrates that good implementation is often the most elusive component of oversight.

- Issues of consolidated supervision (both across members of the same financial group and across borders) continue to loom large; although LAC does not lag its peers (these issue are truly complex and tough nuts to crack), the combination of concentrated domestic ownership and large foreign ownership of financial conglomerates makes this issue particularly critical for the region.
- While the progress made in traditional oversight will help set the bases for addressing the new challenges of systemic oversight, LAC (like everyone else, for that matter) faces a difficult and complex agenda of reforms, with little time to spare as the risks rapidly build up.
- That being said, LAC's turbulent past (which has led to prudential buffers that are relatively large by international comparison), an arguably greater willingness among institutions to listen to their supervisors, and some hands-on experience with simple macroprudential tools and the management of systemic risk have given LAC a leg up, which the region should exploit to the maximum.
- While this analysis is backed by a variety of sources and assessments (not just the BCPs), strong caveats are nonetheless clearly in order, particularly since many of the underlying BCP assessments are dated.

The rest of the chapter is structured as follows. The first section describes the battery of sources and methods used for this assessment. The second section reviews the progress and gaps in traditional (that is, before the global financial crisis) oversight. The final section briefly describes the challenges ahead and possible handicaps in developing a systemic oversight capacity.

Methodology

The analysis in this chapter is based on quantitative as well as qualitative evidence. On the quantitative side, the analysis proceeds along

two dimensions. On the one hand, the ratings obtained by LAC countries in their BCP assessments are compared.[2] LAC is divided into three subregions (LAC-6, Caribbean, and other countries) and the 29 BCP ratings in each BCP assessment are grouped along 10 basic areas of oversight. This provides a picture of the relative effectiveness of oversight when one simply compares *across areas*.

On the other hand, an econometric analysis is conduced to benchmark the three subregions *across the world*, using the full sample of 149 BCP assessments that have been conducted to date (results are synthesized by subregion in table 10.1 and figures 10.1, 10.2, and 10.3; the methodology is explained in annex 10.A). This analysis of BCP ratings is completed with an econometric analysis of responses to a 2007 World Bank survey of supervisors that covers a broad range of supervisory practices (annex 10.B). In both cases, controls for economic development (that is, for gross domestic product [GDP] per capita, a key underlying determinant of the quality of oversight) are introduced. Thus, the basic question this exercise attempts to answer is how the three LAC subregions have performed in relation to their peers at similar levels of economic development. That subregions may not be performing well in some areas in absolute terms is to be expected, as these are tough issues for everybody. In other areas, however, the LAC subregions not only may be performing poorly in absolute terms but also may be lagging their peers. These areas clearly require more attention.

The assessments reveal weaknesses that are (or were) common to many LAC countries. Wide disparities exist across both principles and countries, however. As regards principles, some are clearly easier to meet than others, with the trickiest principles being met (fully or largely) by only about 30 percent of countries (figure 10.4, panel a). As regards countries, the top three LAC countries are close to being fully compliant as regards their average rating, while the bottom three are close to being on average materially noncompliant (figure 10.4, panel b). Not surprisingly, there have been very substantial improvements in

TABLE 10.1 Econometric analysis of BCP ratings

	Institutional framework	Authorizations	Capital	Credit risk	Other risks	Internal control	Supervision	Market discipline	Corrective actions	Consolidated supervision
LAC-6	-0.397	-5.838***	1.702	-4.067*	-5.988*	-3.999	-1.781	0.523	1.339	-5.459**
	(0.814)	(0.000)	(0.431)	(0.081)	(0.085)	(0.376)	(0.426)	(0.762)	(0.546)	(0.020)
LAC-6 – Update	1.810	5.009***	-6.006	-1.619	-4.543	1.744	-3.396	-7.625***	0.198	0.303
	(0.662)	(0.001)	(0.112)	(0.530)	(0.222)	(0.749)	(0.173)	(0.006)	(0.940)	(0.915)
Caribbean	2.516	1.833	7.061**	3.450	3.627	-0.271	4.133**	1.208	-1.316	5.640
	(0.292)	(0.179)	(0.042)	(0.192)	(0.243)	(0.949)	(0.044)	(0.615)	(0.456)	(0.164)
Caribbean – Update	4.057	1.405	0.528	2.371	0.146	4.188	1.205	1.804	3.932	1.438
	(0.162)	(0.473)	(0.896)	(0.511)	(0.967)	(0.564)	(0.620)	(0.583)	(0.154)	(0.763)
Rest of LAC	3.911*	3.788*	3.778*	1.634	3.771*	3.200*	4.989***	2.006	3.168	4.665
	(0.099)	(0.084)	(0.060)	(0.406)	(0.085)	(0.052)	(0.005)	(0.309)	(0.171)	(0.108)
Rest of LAC – Update	-2.680	1.976	0.401	3.652	2.384	0.423	-0.940	5.084	-3.910	-4.138
	(0.325)	(0.591)	(0.905)	(0.205)	(0.448)	(0.891)	(0.739)	(0.138)	(0.139)	(0.297)
Observations	144	150	150	150	135	150	150	150	149	112

Source: Heysen and Auqui 2011.
Note: LAC-6 countries include Brazil, Chile, Colombia, Mexico, Peru, and Uruguay. Robust p-value in parentheses.
Significance: *** p < 0.01, ** p < 0.05, * p < 0.1.

FIGURE 10.1   BCP assessments, LAC-6

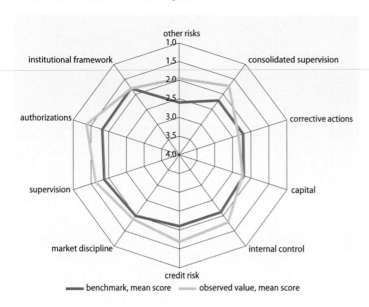

Source: Authors' calculations based on financial sector assessment program data from the World Bank and the IMF.

FIGURE 10.2   BCP assessments, Caribbean

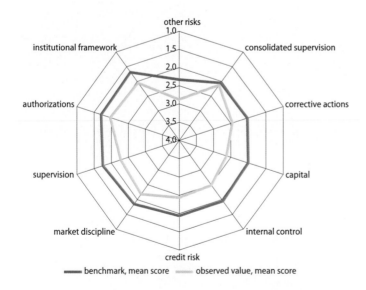

Source: Authors' calculations based on financial sector assessment program data from the World Bank and the IMF.

compliance over time in nearly all cases, as many LAC countries have used the results of these assessments to program and implement their reform agendas (figure 10.5).

At the same time, there is considerable variation across countries, depending on their level of economic development, both across the world and within the region. The coefficient of GDP per capita is always positive and significant, which shows that prudential oversight is a gradual, collective learning process that advances with overall economic development. In addition, the regressions also control for nonlinearities by introducing the square of GDP per capita. The coefficient in this case varies significantly in importance across principles. This variation reflects the fact that some principles are either less relevant to simpler financial systems (hence, not a real source of concern for those countries) or just tougher to fulfill (still a source of concern, but one that is relatively understandable). Thus, the corresponding regression coefficient can be used to score and rank the principles by order of complexity (figure 10.6).

Strong caveats are in order. As regards standards and codes, only the BCPs are reviewed and not the other reports of observance on standards and codes (ROSCs) reviewed by the World Bank and IMF (for example, the standards for insurance, capital markets, audit and accounting, creditor rights and insolvency systems, and so on, for which a meaningful cross-country comparison is more difficult due to the much more limited number of observations). Second, the BCP evidence is clearly limited in scope and needs to be interpreted with caution, as the styles and criteria of assessment were not necessarily fully uniform across regions. Third, many of the assessments date back a few years and hence do not reflect the most recent advances the assessed countries may have made. Many similar caveats also apply to the World Bank supervisory survey, which is also somewhat dated and where some questions can be misinterpreted; hence, the results may be open to question.

Be that as it may, the econometric evidence is valuable in that it picks up areas where a second look appears to be warranted. This quantitative evidence is complemented with a more qualitative, expert-based review of the main oversight reforms recently introduced, as well as with an assessment of the most important remaining issues.[3] In addition, the chapter uses the results of a recent survey on systemic oversight jointly conducted by the World Bank and the Association of Supervisors of Banks of the Americas (ASBA) (annex 10.C).[4]

The progress and the remaining gaps

At first glance, figures 10.1, 10.2, and 10.3 indicate very wide differences in overall compliance with the BCP principles across the three LAC subregions, even after controlling for different levels of economic development. LAC-6 countries generally outperform, while the other subregions underperform, the other LAC countries more strongly than the Caribbean. This suggests that much work may still lie ahead to improve bank oversight in the lower-income countries. Moreover, there are many areas where differences across countries are very large, resulting in low levels of significance for the underlying coefficients (table 10.1). A more detailed group-by-group analysis is thus warranted.

Three groups of principles (*institutional framework*, *authorizations*, and *market discipline*) show rather similar patterns. While the absolute scores are not perfect, they are relatively high, and except for the non–LAC-6 countries, the region is broadly on track with respect to its peers. This record suggests that the basic underlying conditions for a functioning oversight (clear objectives and responsibilities, independence, legal powers, effective entry and acquisition requirements, and basic transparency and disclosure—including good accounting and auditing practices) have been mostly put into place, albeit with some variation across subregions. Overall, this is good news. However, these are also areas where one would expect progress to be the easiest to achieve, both because it mostly requires hardwired legal and institutional reforms, rather than trickier and softer capacity buildups, and because such areas are truly minimum

FIGURE 10.3   BCP assessments, rest of LAC

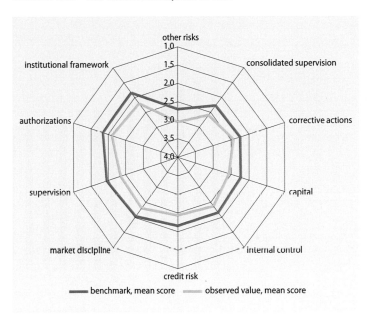

Source: Authors' calculations based on financial sector assessment program data from the World Bank and the IMF.

preconditions for an effective oversight—as, indeed, evidenced by their low complexity score (figure 10.6).

Although the BCPs do not show LAC's institutional framework as a whole to be worse than that of other regions, two basic legal framework issues—the *independence of bank supervisors* and *bank supervisors' legal protection*—are detected by the World Bank survey of supervisory practices to be worse in LAC than in other regions (even after controlling for differences in economic development). Indeed, these issues remain problematic beyond LAC. De jure independence includes such key components as budgetary independence and operational independence (for example, the capacity to issue or withdraw a license and the power to issue prudential regulations). De facto independence also requires freedom from political interference or industry capture. The region has weaknesses on both counts. The World Bank–ASBA survey reports that, while most supervisors have operational independence, fewer have budgetary and administrative independence to set salary scales (40 percent of

FIGURE 10.4 **Compliance with BCP principles by LAC countries**

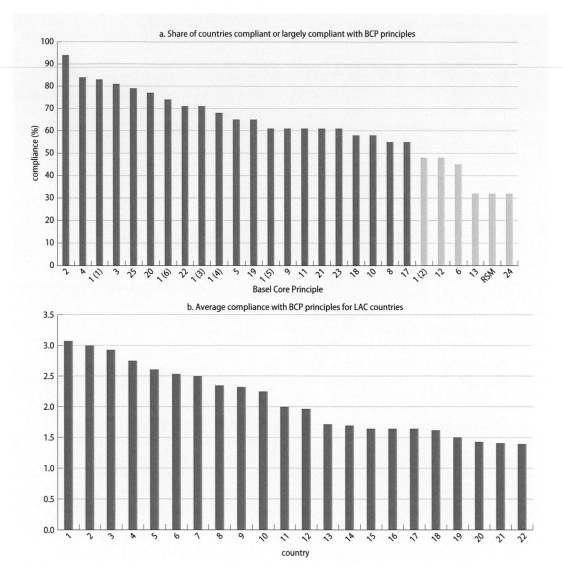

Source: Authors' calculations based on Financial Sector Assessment Program data from the World Bank and the IMF.
Note: This figure considers the last assessment of compliance with the BCP conducted for each country in the context of a Financial Sector Assessment Program. The list of core principles corresponds to the 2006 methodology. The assessments conducted under the original 1999 BCP methodology have been mapped into the revised 2006 methodology list of core principles. The term *bcpRMS* comprises four core principles associated with the supervision of risks that were part of one core principle in the 1997 BCP methodology: risk–management process (CP 7), liquidity risk (CP 14), operational risk (CP 15), and interest rate risk (CP 16). Panel a shows the average compliance across country for each principle. Panel b shows the average compliance for all countries with available information. In panel B, the ratings range from 1 (fully compliant) to 4 (noncompliant). Also for panel b, the number of principles in each country ranges from 23 to 28 depending on data availability.

respondents indicated the lack of such independence). Moreover, the World Bank survey of supervisory practices indicates that removing the head of supervision by executive decision without congressional approval is more likely in LAC than in the rest of the world. The de jure weaknesses are also corroborated by a recent survey on governance practices in regulatory agencies, which finds that LAC regulators lack sufficient independence to

FIGURE 10.5   Financial regulation and supervision progress in nine LAC countries

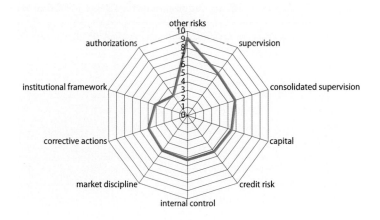

Source: Heysen and Auqui 2011.

issue regulations and, in some cases, to take certain severe, crucial actions, such as license revocation.[5] Nonetheless, significant progress in addressing these issues has been recently achieved in several countries, notably Chile, Colombia, and Mexico.

Insufficient legal protection for bank supervisors is also an important remaining issue in most of LAC (except, perhaps, for the Caribbean), with less than half of the countries providing adequate legal protection to supervisors.[6] The World Bank survey indicates that LAC supervisors are more likely to be personally liable for damages caused by their actions or omissions in the discharge of their official duties than are their peers elsewhere. Here again, however, many countries—including the Chile,

FIGURE 10.6   Complexity index

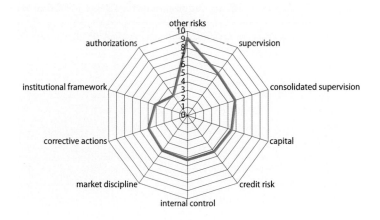

Source: Authors' calculations based on financial sector assessment program data from the World Bank and the IMF.

the Dominican Republic, and Peru—have recently taken important steps to upgrade their legal framework.

A second set of BCP principles (*capital adequacy*, and *oversight of credit risk and other risks*), which focuses on risk management, shows much unevenness across the subregions. For example, only one-third of LAC countries had an effective supervisory framework to determine whether banks have adequate risk-management policies, processes, and strategies for the size and nature of their activities. Both the Caribbean countries and the non–LAC-6 countries underperform on capital adequacy. More than half of LAC countries had capital requirements that did not meet the minimum Basel I international standards.[7] By contrast, LAC-6 countries are on track or even outperform on credit risk and other risks. As the latter are complex areas (figure 10.6), this suggests that the higher-income countries have worked hard and become proficient overall at addressing difficult risk-management issues.

However, much remains to be done. Most LAC-6 countries have implemented most of the legal or regulatory reforms required to conform to Basel I, including capital charges for market and operational risks (table 10.2). But the implementation of Basel II has been limited thus far.[8] Only a few countries have implemented the new capital requirements under Pillar 1.[9] Progress with the implementation of Pillars 2 and 3 has been similarly limited.[10] As regards credit risk, many countries have tightened their rules for loan classification and provisioning, but only the most advanced are moving toward a forward-looking, internal-model approach that focuses on expected (rather than incurred) losses. However, several countries have put in place comprehensive approaches that cover all stages of the credit process, thereby allowing supervisors to require improvements at an early stage. Some countries have also established global large-exposure limits by sector, region, or other highly correlated exposures, a measure that is particularly relevant in LAC in view of the relatively concentrated banking systems and income distributions. Finally, most partially dollarized countries in LAC have taken measures, including higher risk weights or provisions on dollar loans (especially those to debtors in the nontradable sector), to address the credit risks associated with borrowers' currency mismatches.

Next come two groups of principles with average to high complexity scores (*supervision* and *internal control*) in which Caribbean countries and, even more strongly, the other LAC countries also lag, particularly as regards supervision. Prima facie, this could indicate that much of the progress in

TABLE 10.2   **Capital adequacy requirements for selected LAC-6 countries**

	Argentina	Brazil	Chile	Colombia	Mexico	Peru
Capital adequacy ratio (% of risk-weighted assets)	8	11	8	9	8	10
Standard	Basel I	Basel II	Basel I	Basel I	Basel II	Basel II
Authorization for Basel II internal models	No	Yes	No	No	Yes	Yes
Power to require a higher capital adequacy ratio to individual banks based on the supervisory risk assessment	Yes	Yes	Yes	Yes	Yes	Yes
Capital charges for:						
Credit risk	Yes	Yes	Yes	Yes	Yes	Yes
Interest rate risk in the trading book	Yes	Yes	No	Yes	Yes	Yes
Foreign exchange risk	Yes	Yes	No	Yes	Yes	Yes
Other market risks (commodities, equity)	Yes	Yes	No	Yes	Yes	Yes
Operational risks	No	Yes	No	No	Yes	Yes
Basel II – Pillar 2	No	Yes	In progress	No	No	In progress
Basel II – Pillar 3	No	In progress	No	No	In progress	No

Source: Heysen and Auqui 2011.

prudential oversight in the lower-income countries may still be more on the books than in reality, with lack of effective implementation continuing to be a more severe problem.

Nonetheless, important progress in strengthening supervisory capacity has been made across the region. First, there has been a broad, but uneven and of recent vintage, shift from pure compliance-based supervision toward risk-based supervision.[11] Some countries now have well-defined and fully integrated risk-based systems and have substantially strengthened capacity by incorporating staff with the necessary skills, improving information systems, and upgrading supervisory processes. Others are still at the early stages, however, with change being hindered by a lack of human resources and a weak culture of prevention and enforcement. Important progress has also been achieved in many countries in relation to stress-testing capacity. In addition to developing their own capacity and models, many supervisors are now also requiring banks to conduct their own regular stress tests and to use the results to review their risk-management policies.

The weaknesses in the supervision of internal controls to a large extent reflect weaknesses in banks' own risk-management procedures. Here again, however, supervisors have made important progress. In line with international standards, most LAC countries have assigned to banks' boards of directors the primary responsibility for establishing and overseeing appropriate risk-management systems. Many countries have issued detailed and comprehensive norms or guidelines on banks' risk management. However, some countries have yet to develop the necessary supervisory capacity to assess their implementation. Others have used a less prescriptive, rating-based approach. In all cases, a key additional challenge for supervisors is to ensure that banks' board members have the experience and ability to carry out these new functions (especially in the local banks).

The final group (*consolidated and cross-border supervision*) includes all those principles related to the oversight of interconnections between financial institutions, whether domestic or cross-border. These are complex principles (figure 10.6) with which the whole world is having a hard time. Remarkably, however, the LAC-6 countries outperform their benchmark, which is indeed good news.

To some extent, this group of principles prefigures the challenges of systemic oversight, the main focus of this report. As regards consolidated supervision, only two of the 31 LAC countries were rated fully compliant, which is evidence of the complexities of the task. And only one-third of LAC countries effectively supervise the financial conglomerates that operate within their jurisdiction. The absence of legislation granting the powers to conduct consolidated supervision of conglomerates and the lack of a comprehensive regulation, including key prudential requirements on a consolidated basis, are not the only relevant problems. Opaque conglomerate structures and insufficient cooperation and coordination among supervisors are also widespread problems. As a result, there is substantial scope for regulatory arbitrage.[12] The high level of conglomeration and ownership concentration in the region is clearly an aggravating factor (annex 10.D).[13]

While LAC has made some progress toward establishing a proper legal and supervisory framework for consolidated supervision, most countries still have much work ahead of them to make that framework fully effective.[14] Regulation and supervision are, by and large, conducted according to license, even though many licenses can be part of a single financial conglomerate. The lack of control over holding companies domiciled abroad remains a widespread problem. Most countries face severe limitations in accessing information on parallel-owned banks set up in other jurisdictions. Many countries need to upgrade their capacity to access information and assess the risks posed by the nonbanking entities of a financial conglomerate, including through on-site examinations. Other common flaws include (a) the inadequate definition of a financial conglomerate (which leaves important sources of risk outside of the scope of supervision);[15] (b) the lack of a risk–management framework (including prudential requirements) and enforcement powers at the conglomerate level;[16] and (c) insufficient powers to control the establishment of potentially problematic cross-border operations, to require changes in the conglomerate structure when needed, and to mitigate local or cross-border regulatory arbitrage.

Both domestic and cross-border coordination among supervisors require further strengthening. As regards within-border coordination, while some countries still face legal restrictions, the most common problem is the lack of an effective operational framework for cooperation that goes beyond sharing information.[17] To address this problem, Colombia and Peru have established, or are in the process of establishing, a unified supervisory agency. However, coordination problems can continue to arise even within this unified body, especially where oversight is done by license. Thus, in Mexico and Uruguay, important organizational changes and a movement toward universal banking licenses have also been undertaken to address internal problems of coordination.

A fortiori, cross-border cooperation remains an even greater challenge, which is all the more crucial to the region in view of the importance of foreign banks.[18] No doubt, some significant improvements have taken place. Most countries have signed bilateral and multilateral memorandums of understanding (MOUs) as a framework for cooperation, and colleges of supervisors have been established to oversee the largest international conglomerates. However, many of the MOUs lack operational teeth, and important limitations remain, some of which are not adequately captured by the BCP assessments. First, the MOUs are often not effective in overseeing nonbanking groups or the nonbank entities of a banking group. Second, they do not include an adequate cooperation framework for troubled entities. Third, LAC countries that host subsidiaries or branches of large international banking institutions that are large for the host country yet small for the home country frequently see their concerns ignored or downplayed by the home

supervisors. Last but not least, many host (as well as home) supervisors of LAC conglomerates are unsatisfied with the scope, depth, and timeliness of the information shared by their counterparts across borders in the context of the MOUs.

The systemic oversight challenges ahead

Systemic oversight differs radically from traditional prudential oversight in that the whole is no longer simply the sum of the parts. Hence, the traditional institution-by-institution approach (making sure that each of the parts is sound and ready to go) is no longer sufficient, nor is the wider focus on individual financial conglomerates. It needs to be complemented in three fundamental ways: first, as financial systems become increasingly dense and interconnected, connecting the parts and understanding how the system is "wired" becomes the name of the game; second, as market failures (particularly collective failures) interact with macroeconomic conditions, endogenous unstable financial dynamics are generated that require a proactive dynamic response (prudential oversight turns time-dependent); and third, as financial development and financial stability become intertwined in increasingly complex ways, it becomes essential to get ahead of the curve and adjust developmental and prudential policies as a system of interconnected policies.

For all three reasons, the change in supervisory thinking needs to undergo a quantum leap. But, in addition, systemic supervisors need to improve the way they talk to each other (this is essential to connect the parts), to central bankers (this is essential to connect the dynamics, as well as to connect the parts with the whole), and to finance ministers and their staff (this is essential to connect stability and development). A tough and complex agenda indeed!

LAC clearly needs to get ready. Thus far, LAC has mostly escaped the dark side of financial development because the level of density and interconnectedness of its financial systems was still moderate. Yet LAC systems are rapidly evolving. Indeed, early signs of potential trouble ahead from heavily interconnected systems already showed up in the global financial crisis (for example, the problems of Sofoles financing in Mexico or corporate derivative options in Brazil and Mexico). Thus, in view of lead times and longer term dynamics, now is the time for thinking ahead. While banking crises caused by unsustainable macrodynamics may have become a thing of the past, "good" macromanagement can also set the stage for ultimately more lethal endogenous financial dynamics, as was recently the case in the United States and other developed economies. Last but not least, LAC's rising exposure to world turbulence—an inevitable side effect of financial globalization—is an increasing source of concern.

Thankfully, LAC has a leg up on the process. First, its prudential buffers are currently high. LAC banks largely exceed their benchmarks as regards key prudential buffers (solvency, liquidity, and profitability). Indeed, LAC currently has, on average, some of the highest reported prudential buffers in the world (figure 10.7). This consequence of LAC's turbulent past provides some breathing room to plan ahead. Second, as just

FIGURE 10.7   Selected soundness indicators
(yearly mediums)

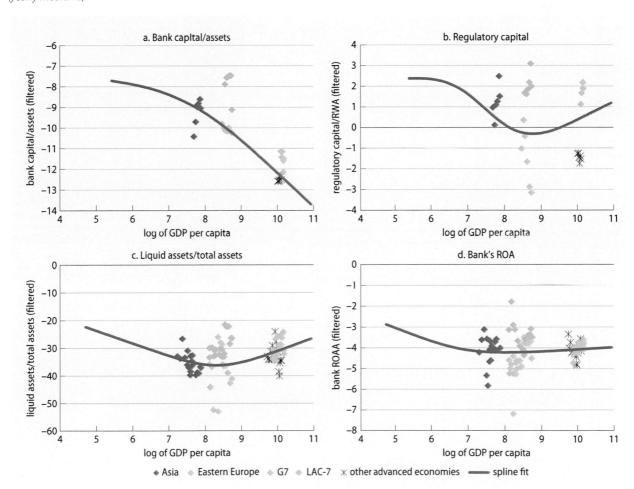

Source: de la Toree, Feyen, and Ize 2011.

emphasized, LAC supervisors have made important strides toward improving traditional oversight, thereby providing the essential foundation on which a sophisticated systemic oversight capability may be built. Third, LAC's numerous past crises have given its supervisors a definite learning advantage. While the roots and dynamics of the systemic crises of the past may differ from those of the future, in the end, both require supervisors to think and act systemically.

Last but not least, LAC's supervisors are well aware of the need for action. This comes out clearly from the World Bank–ASBA survey. There is a broad perception of an increasing likelihood that financial crises induced by systemic risk could erupt as systems develop and become more sophisticated.[19] Enhancing supervisory capacity to assess systemic risk is viewed as a top priority, closely followed by the need to adjust prudential norms to account for systemic risk, making prudential norms more countercyclical and enhancing supervisory powers to take discretionary actions. The majority of respondents also thought that there should be a fundamental redefinition of the roles and functions of supervisors toward making them more proactive (annex 10.C).

The reform agenda ahead can be broken down into three main pieces, each of which is discussed in the following three chapters of this report: macroprudential policy (chapter 11, focused on cyclical dynamics), microsystemic regulation (chapter 12, focused on interconnectedness), and systemic supervision (chapter 13). All three will involve a sea change in approaches and mind-sets.

Annex 10.A   Methodology for the econometric analysis of BCP Ratings

Regressions were run for 150 assessments of compliance with the Basel Core Principles for Effective Banking Supervision (BCP). The dependent variables take the following values: 1 (compliant), 2 (largely compliant), 3 (materially noncompliant), and 4 (noncompliant). Hence, lower coefficients are associated with better ratings (stronger supervision). Controls include GDP per capita, the square of GDP per capita, whether the ratings correspond to a first assessment or to an update, whether the assessment was conducted based on the initial or revised BCP methodology, a dummy for each of the three subregions, and, within each region, a separate dummy for the updates conducted

within the region (so as to detect regional progress). To improve the fit and simplify the analysis, the principles are aggregated into groups corresponding to 10 different dimensions of regulation and supervision (annex table 10.A.1). A principal component analysis was used to set the weights of each principle in the group. Benchmarked values for each group of principles in each region are calculated on the basis of workhorse regressions that do not include regional dummies. The benchmarked values are compared to the observed values for each group and region. To limit the impact of outliers, medians (rather than means) are used to calculate regional scores.

TABLE 10.A.1   **BCP consolidation into groups**

Group	1997	Core principles	2006
Institutional	1.1	Responsibilities and objectives	1.1
	1.2	Independence, accountability, transparency	1.2
	1.3	Legal framework	1.3
	1.4	Legal powers	1.4
	1.5	Legal protection	1.5
	1.6	Cooperation	1.6
Authorizations	2	Permissible activities	2
	3	Licensing criteria	3
	4	Transfer of significant ownership	4
	5	Major acquisitions	5
Capital	6	Capital adequacy	6
Credit risk	7	Credit risk	8
	8	Problem assets, provisions and reserves	9
	9	Large exposure limits	10
	10	Exposures to related parties	11
Other risks		Risk management process	7
	11	Country and transfer risks	12
	12	Market risks	13
	13	Liquidity risk	14
	13	Operational risk	15
	13	Interest rate risk in the banking book	16
Internal controls	14	Internal control and audit	17
Not included	15	Abuse of financial services	18
	16	Supervisory approach	19
	17	Supervisory techniques	20
Supervision	18, 19	Supervisory reporting	21
Market discipline	21	Accounting and disclosure	22
Corrective actions	22	Corrective and remedial powers of supervisors	23
	20, 23	Consolidated supervision	24
Consolidated supervision	24, 25	Home-host relationships	25

Source: Heysen and Auqui 2011.

Annex 10.B Highlights of the 2007 World Bank survey of supervisory practices

This analysis is based on the 2007 Survey of Bank Regulation and Supervision around the World (updated on June 2008), conducted by the World Bank.[20] The survey includes responses of 142 countries to more than 300 questions covering 12 broad topics: entry into banking, ownership, capital, bank activities, external audit, management, liquidity and diversification requirements, deposit protection schemes, provisioning requirements, accounting and disclosure, remedial actions, and supervision. Regressions, controlling for GDP per capita and including an overall LAC dummy (or alternatively just a LAC-7 dummy applying to the LAC-6 countries plus Argentina, which in this case is included in the survey), were run for 56 of the questions in the survey. Only specifications with at least one significant variable are presented (annex table 10.B.1). The main results are as follows:

- *Legal protection of bank supervisors (INDBANK).* Supervisors in both LAC and LAC–7 are more personally liable for damages caused by their actions or omissions as supervisors.
- *Independence of bank supervisors (INPOLI).* The removal of supervisors in LAC (but not LAC–7) is less subject to congressional approval and more subject to a simple decision by the president, prime minister, or minister of finance.
- *Restrictions on bank activities and investments (OVER3AR).* Banks in LAC (but not in LAC-7) face more restrictions in engaging in a variety of financial intermediation and investment banking activities, such as securities underwrit-

ing, brokering and dealing, mutual funds, insurance, and real estate investment.
- *Loan classification and provisioning (LOANC).* Loan classification practices are stricter in LAC (but not in LAC-7) than in the rest of the world.
- *Transparency and disclosure (ACCT-PRA):* Both LAC and LAC-7 lag in the adoption of internationally accepted accounting standards. However, LAC-7 outperforms in other transparency practices (FSTRANS). Also, LAC banks are more likely to be rated by external rating agencies than are their peers in the rest of the world (ERCMON).
- *Supervision resources* (PSUPPBNK). There are more professional bank supervisors per bank in LAC countries than in the rest of the world.
- *Frequency of on–site inspections* (ONSITEINS). The frequency of on–site inspections conducted in large or medium–size banks is lower in the LAC region.
- *Remedial powers of supervisors (OSPOWER).* LAC supervisors have greater powers to impose corrective actions on supervised institutions. They are also more likely to be able to declare a bank insolvent or to intervene in a bank's activities without court permission (DIPOWER). Moreover, LAC-7 countries' supervisors are also more likely to be able to appoint a liquidator or to supersede shareholders' rights without court permission (COURTINV).

Higher level of conglomeration (CONG10B). The percentage of capital in the largest 10 banks owned by financial conglomerates is higher than in the rest of the world.

TABLE 10.B.1   World Bank survey of supervisory practices

Variable	LGDPPC		LAC_DUMMY		Observations	R-squared
	a. BCL regressions with LAC_DUMMY (those that have at least one significant exogenous variable)					
SOR	−0.0612**	(−2.411)	−0.109	(−0.992)	133	0.05
CONG10B	1.329	(0.453)	31.82***	(3.776)	69	0.12
OVER3AR	−0.401***	(−4.474)	1.144**	(2.537)	130	0.19
BONF	−0.147***	(−4.447)	0.617***	(2.784)	131	0.18
NFOB	−0.134***	(−3.606)	−0.103	(−0.478)	132	0.07
OVERFCR	−0.361***	(−4.683)	0.712	(1.271)	129	0.15
OVERBNK	−0.549***	(−5.131)	1.591***	(2.730)	128	0.23
OVERAFC	−0.745***	(−5.387)	1.766**	(1.998)	127	0.22
LIMITFBEO	0.148***	(3.806)	0.0877	(0.656)	132	0.13
OSPOWER	−0.270*	(−1.869)	0.939**	(2.190)	103	0.06
PCPOWER	−0.407**	(−2.583)	0.629	(1.091)	107	0.08
DIPOWER	−0.00142	(−0.0273)	0.526***	(4.177)	130	0.04
COURTINV	0.105**	(2.369)	−0.195	(−1.351)	126	0.07
LOANCS	−23.32	(−1.503)	−112.4**	(−2.251)	79	0.06
PSTRING	−8.248**	(−2.088)	−4.547	(−0.411)	93	0.09
SUPTENURE	0.401*	(1.812)	3.103***	(2.659)	84	0.12
INDPOLI	0.0352	(1.428)	−0.205**	(−2.330)	129	0.04
INDBANK	−0.00405	(−0.235)	−0.459***	(−3.778)	129	0.15
INDSA	0.0106	(0.234)	−0.746***	(−4.336)	114	0.11
MULSUP	−0.00779	(−0.272)	−0.364***	(−3.283)	131	0.06
FUNDID	2.687**	(2.242)	10.77	(1.542)	101	0.06
GOVBANK	−4.175***	(−3.178)	0.826	(0.146)	102	0.08
FSTRANS	0.172***	(3.212)	0.110	(0.479)	123	0.07
ACCTPRA	−0.00109	(−0.0631)	−0.460***	(−3.867)	128	0.18
ERCMON	0.0803	(1.134)	0.695**	(2.140)	73	0.09
ONSITFINS	0.0160	(0.465)	−0.394***	(−2.661)	129	0.04
PSUPPBNK	0.0457	(0.189)	4.051***	(3.583)	90	0.10
BNKDEV	0.219***	(10.41)	−0.193**	(−2.282)	147	0.44

Variable	LGDPPC		LAC-7_DUMMY		Observations	R-Squared
	b. BCL regressions with LAC-7_DUMMY (those that have at least one significant exogenous variable)					
SOR	−0.0600**	(−2.357)	−0.0558	(−0.327)	133	0.04
CONG10B	−0.0381	(−0.0127)	30.87***	(2.814)	69	0.04
OVER3AR	−0.416***	(−4.536)	−0.0190	(−0.0251)	130	0.14
BONF	−0.154***	(−4.575)	0.399	(0.926)	131	0.11
NFOB	−0.132***	(−3.551)	−0.345	(−1.103)	132	0.08
NBFFOB	−0.0776	(−1.998)	−0.123	(−0.388)	131	0.03
OVERFCR	−0.369***	(−4.644)	−0.0856	(−0.0901)	129	0.13
OVERBNK	−0.570***	(−5.206)	0.405	(0.369)	128	0.17
OVERAFC	−0.769***	(−5.373)	−0.0630	(−0.0398)	127	0.18
LIMITFBEO	0.147***	(3.852)	−0.142	(−0.698)	132	0.13
OSPOWER	−0.298**	(−2.069)	1.353**	(2.115)	103	0.06
PCPOWER	−0.430***	(−2.763)	−0.197	(−0.244)	107	0.07
DIPOWER	−0.00867	(−0.164)	0.492***	(3.142)	130	0.01
COURTINV	0.108**	(2.448)	−0.297**	(−1.992)	126	0.07

(continued next page)

TABLE 10.B.1 (continued)

	b. BCL regressions with LAC-7_DUMMY (those that have at least one significant exogenous variable)					
Variables	**LGDPPC**		**LAC_DUMMY**		**Observations**	**R-squared**
PSTRING	−8.014**	(−2.022)	−28.05	(−1.053)	93	0.11
SUPTENURE	0.314	(1.430)	5.521***	(3.044)	84	0.15
INDBANK	0.00231	(0.129)	−0.526***	(−2.985)	129	0.08
INDSA	0.0285	(0.634)	−1.035***	(−3.525)	114	0.09
BACCT	−0.00721	(−0.222)	0.501***	(8.901)	125	0.04
FUNDID	2.481**	(2.079)	26.25**	(2.465)	101	0.10
GOVBANK	−4.166***	(−3.302)	16.71**	(2.035)	102	0.11
FSTRANS	0.170***	(3.189)	0.374**	(2.420)	123	0.08
ACCTPRA	0.00566	(0.315)	−0.558***	(−3.171)	128	0.11
ERCMON	0.0613	(0.854)	1.244***	(4.040)	73	0.15
PSUPPBNK	−0.0677	(−0.255)	2.543**	(2.291)	90	0.01
BNKDEV	0.220***	(10.32)	−0.302**	(−2.373)	147	0.44

Source: Heysen and Auqui 2011.
Note: Robust *t*-statistics are shown in parentheses;
Significance: *** $p < 0.01$, ** $p < 0.05$, * $p < 0.1$.

Annex 10.C   Joint World Bank–ASBA survey on systemic oversight

The joint World Bank–Association of Supervisors of Banks of the Americas (ASBA) survey was aimed at gauging the importance of systemic oversight issues in LAC, the status of practices in the region, and the main challenges going forward. Questions covered three broad topics: microprudential oversight, management of economic cycles, and macroprudential oversight. The survey was sent to all the LAC bank supervisory agencies that are members of ASBA. The head of banking supervision of the agency was asked to forward the survey to the financial stability or research department of the central bank, even if not an ASBA member. Of the 31 member countries of ASBA in the LAC region, 19 supervisors and 9 central banks responded to the survey. Responses indicated a broad consensus among regional financial authorities on the need to enhance the current systemic oversight framework. Financial authorities see an increasing likelihood that a financial crisis induced by systemic risk could occur as systems develop and become more sophisticated. Systemic risk monitoring needs strengthening, with smaller countries being less comfortable about their monitoring framework. Survey responses indicate the following:

- Enhancing supervisory capacity to assess systemic risks and to identify risks in sophisticated products is a top priority among supervisors.
- Regulatory perimeters in LAC are set quite wide, and resetting them does not appear to be a top priority at this time. Safety net perimeters, in contrast, are much narrower, mainly covering only commercial banks.
- The most pressing perimeter issues relate to risk shifting among conglomerates, but powers to regulate conglomerates do not appear comprehensive.

- Prudential regulations in LAC tend to be comprehensive, with the notable exception of regulations for cooperatives, although liquidity regulations are not widely applied.
- There is broad consensus on the need to adjust prudential norms to account for systemic risk. Regulation of the cross-sectional components of systemic risk is, as elsewhere, incipient. While LAC is ahead of other regions in the use of countercyclical provisions, the use of other countercyclical prudential regulations is limited.
- Supervisory authorities in LAC consider that there should be a fundamental redefinition of the role and functions of the supervisors, including making them more proactive.
- Supervisory powers to request additional buffers to account for the buildup of systemic risks appear limited in several jurisdictions. Agencies' legal mandates, political and industry pressures, and lack of adequate legal protection for supervisors hamper the exercise of supervisory discretion.
- In most LAC countries, the stability of the financial system is a collaborative effort among various regulatory bodies, albeit there appears to be scope for improving coordination between supervisors and the central bank as well as among different supervisors.
- Rethinking the organization of supervision is also considered an important factor in improving systemic oversight.
- There are important challenges on cross-border coordination dealing with systemic risk in the LAC region. Lack of effective arrangements for exchanging information across borders and for sharing the resolution costs of institutions operating cross-border are sources of concern among regional supervisors.

Annex 10.D   Financial concentration in LAC

In most of the largest LAC countries, financial institutions have been highly concentrated, and, as table 10.D.1 shows, they became more so between 1998 and 2008. The 10 largest banks have market shares of 75 to 90 percent. The situation is similar among life insurance companies and a little less concentrated among general insurance companies. The 10 largest mutual fund companies generally represent about 80 percent of the market. Among pension funds, the concentration is also extremely high. This suggests that competitive pressures may be less intense than in markets with larger numbers of participants and less concentrated distributions, such as the United States.

Moreover, the relative decline of banks and rise of nonbanks and capital markets intermediaries do not necessarily mean that the new players are becoming more predominant. Because of the prevalence of large business groups in Latin American countries, many of the important players among institutional investors have close ties to large banks. In some countries, they are actually part of the bank, while in others they belong to the same financial group. In addition, most countries permit nonbank financial firms to own banks. Thus, ownership concentration is high across all market segments (annex table 10.D.2).[21] It is particularly large in pensions, mutual funds, and investment banks. But it is also substantial in banks.[22]

TABLE 10.D.1   **Market share of largest companies and funds in selected LAC countries**

	Percentage of market share				
	Argentina	**Brazil**	**Chile**	**Colombia**	**Mexico**
A. Year 1998					
Banks					
Largest 5	48[a]	58[a]	59[a]	—	80[a]
All Insurance					
Largest 10	—	67[b]	—	—	100[b]
Pension Funds					
Largest 2	53[c]	—[c]	62[c]	77[c]	45[c]
B. Year 2008					
Banks					
Largest 5	51	67	73	64	77
Largest 10	74	76	94	86	92
Mutual Funds					
Largest 10	79	84	87	73	88
General Insurance					
Largest 10	54	—	—	78	—
Life Insurance					
Largest 10	82	62	73	61	88
Pension Funds					
Largest 10	—	60	100	100	92
Largest 2	—	—	55[c]	52[c]	33[c]

Sources: Raddatz 2011.
Note: a. Caprio and Honohan 2001.
b. Srinivas, Whitehouse, and Yermo 2000.
c. AIOS (Asociación international de organismos de supervisión de fondos de pensiones).

TABLE 10.D.2   Ownership concentration in selected Latin American countries

a. Percentage of largest 10 institutions related to largest 10 banks (%)				
	Argentina	**Brazil**	**Chile**	**Colombia**	**Mexico**
Insurance					
General	10	—	30	30	40
Life	10	50	40	30	50
Pension funds	—	10	40	33	50
Mutual funds	70	60	80	—	80
Investment banks and brokerages					
Investment banks	0	90	60	33	—
Brokerages	—	70	—	—	30

b. Share of assets of largest 10 institutions related to largest 10 banks (%)				
	Argentina	**Brazil**	**Chile**	**Colombia**	**Mexico**
Insurance					
General	6	—	34	21	23
Pension funds	—	2	53	53	64
Mutual funds	56	67	91	—	94
Invest. banks and brokerages					
Investment banks	0	98	52	83	—
Brokerages	—	87	—	—	30

Source: Raddatz 2011.
Note: Panel a shows the fraction of the largest 10 institutions in each segment (described in each row) that are related to the largest 10 banks in 2008. Panel b shows the share of assets in each segment that are in institutions that are related to the largest 10 banks.

Notes

1. This chapter draws heavily on the papers "Recent Trends in Banking Supervision in LAC," by Socorro Heysen and Martin Auqui (2011), and "Survey on Systemic Oversight Frameworks: Current Practices and Reform Agenda" by Eva Gutierrez and Patricia Caraballo, which are part of the Edited Volume that accompanies this LAC flagship report.

2. Thirty-one BCP assessments were conducted in the region in the context of the joint World Bank–IMF Reports on the Observance of Standards and Codes (ROSC) and Financial Sector Assessment Program (FSAP) since 1999—eight countries were assessed twice and one, Peru, was assessed three times.

3. See Heysen and Auqui (2011) for a more complete qualitative discussion of LAC's progress and current stand as regards bank oversight.

4. The survey helps identify the state of systemic oversight in the region and polls perceptions among regional supervisors about the key areas that will need development.

5. See Seelig and Novoa (2009).

6. It is often the case that supervisors' legal protection ends when they leave office. Such lack of continuity can have a seriously chilling effect on supervisors.

7. Lack of compliance is generally associated with the absence of capital charges to cover risks, such as market or operational risks, lower weights for some asset classes, or regulatory differences about what constitutes capital. In a few countries, regulatory forbearance has also been a problem.

8. The Basel II accord (introduced in 2004) has three pillars. Pillar 1 deals with capital requirements, Pillar 2 with supervisory review, and Pillar 3 with market discipline. Basel II is more comprehensive than Basel I and relies on more formal and systematic risk modeling.

9. While Brazil, Mexico, and Peru have implemented the capital requirements under Pillar 1, the use of internal models is still very limited. As of the end of 2010, only one such authorization has been issued by Mexico.

10. Only Brazil has established guidelines requiring banks to assess their capital adequacy under all risks contemplated in Pillars 1 and 2 and to have additional capital to cover losses generated during moments of stress.

And only Brazil and Mexico have initiated the implementation of Pillar 3.

11. Risk-based supervision calibrates the scope and intensity of supervision according to the level of risk individual institutions pose.

12. For example, to exploit supervisory gaps, a conglomerate that has its main business and ultimate shareholders in one country may choose a second country as its home supervisor.

13. The World Bank survey of supervisory practices confirms that ownership concentration is a particularly important issue in LAC. LAC countries exhibit a higher than average percentage of capital in the 10 largest banks owned by conglomerates (annex 10.B).

14. The World Bank–ASBA survey clearly confirms that the potential for risk shifting within members of a conglomerate, reflecting insufficient powers to regulate them, is viewed as a pressing issue. This is particularly the case for structures where financial (and real sector) companies that belong to the group are not owned by the bank but by an entity that owns the bank. Few countries require constituting a financial holding company to control the conglomeration of financial sector activities, and in the majority of cases the holding company can be created abroad. Capital requirements over holding companies are rare.

15. The World Bank–ASBA survey reports that in seven LAC countries the definition of banking groups or financial conglomerates in the law does not include nonfinancial group entities. In four countries, supervisors do not have the capacity to presume (based on objective criteria) which companies form part of the financial conglomerate. In some cases, parent companies or holding companies may also not be included in the definition of a financial group.

16. The World Bank–ASBA survey reports that only eight countries have the power to impose a special capital requirement for a financial group taken as a whole. While related-party limits appear to be in place in most cases, ownership limits exist for only half of the respondents.

17. The World Bank–ASBA survey reports that formal arrangements were in place to discuss and resolve potential issues of regulatory arbitrage across financial institutions with different licenses in only half of the countries. About 40 percent of respondents indicated that they conduct interagency crisis simulation exercises, but not on a regular basis.

18. The World Bank–ASBA survey reports the lack of effective arrangements for cross-border information exchange and discussion of common issues to be a very important concern for 75 percent of the respondents. The lack of effective arrangements to deal with cross–border crisis was noted by 63 percent of respondents; the lack of effective arrangements to discuss common issues between home and host supervisors was noted by 61 percent; the lack of effective cross-border inspections was noted by 57 percent; and the lack of effective arrangements for sharing the resolution costs of institutions operating cross-border was noted by 50 percent.

19. Most Latin American supervisors and monetary authorities think it unlikely that a financial crisis similar to the one recently experienced in the United States could happen in their countries under the current stage of financial development. However, as the system evolves in sophistication, over 50 percent of the respondents consider it somewhat likely that a U.S.-type crisis could materialize.

20. The survey results are discussed in Barth, Caprio, and Levine (2008).

21. The complexity of ownership structures in Latin America, which include control pyramids and cross-holdings, suggests that there is likely to be a downward bias in these estimates. For additional analysis and information on financial concentration in LAC, see Srinivas, Whitehouse, and Yermo (2000) and Impavido, Lasagabaster, and Garcia-Huitron (2010).

22. Caprio et al. (2007) report that, among LAC-7 countries, only 10 percent of the banks are widely held, and in 70 percent of the cases with concentrated ownership, the controller is a family. In the rest of the world, the share of widely held banks is 27 percent, and only 33 percent of the banks are family owned.

Macroprudential Policies over the Cycle in LAC | 11

The global financial crisis underscored the need for a new prudential oversight policy framework to curb and manage systemic risk and reduce the cost of boom-bust financial cycles. Systemic regulation has two main dimensions: one stresses the links through time (that is, time dependencies), which is the focus of what is defined here as macroprudential policy; and the other stresses the links across the financial system (that is, interconnectedness), which is the focus of "microsystemic" prudential policy.[1] Thus, the discussion of systemically oriented prudential oversight in this report is broken down into three tightly connected chapters. This chapter reviews macroprudential regulation as it applies to Latin America and the Caribbean (LAC); chapter 12 reviews LAC-relevant issues in microsystemic regulation; and chapter 13 looks at both dimensions but from a supervisory (rather than regulatory) perspective that stresses implementation.[2]

The literature on macroprudential regulation and policy has literally exploded over the past two years.[3] Thus, rather than trying to duplicate that material, much of which is highly specific and technical, this chapter, as the rest of this report, provides a more holistic and conceptual perspective that tries to link root causes to policy responses while remaining as LAC specific as possible. Key messages are as follows:

- The design of a proper macroprudential policy framework for LAC needs to be based on clear choices across a menu of progressively more ambitious goals. Those goals range from the most modest aim of correcting the distortions brought about by traditional prudential norms and other macroeconomic and financial policies, to the most ambitious objective of dampening "excessive" fluctuations in asset *and* business cycles (by inducing agents to fully internalize externalities). Between those choices is the intermediate (and currently more popular) goal of simply making financial systems more resilient to fluctuations (that is, taking the cycle as given).
- The framework also needs to reflect LAC's peculiarities as regards the risks and vulnerabilities the region has faced in the past; in particular, LAC's financial cycles have been more frequent and pronounced and have ended badly more often than in other regions.
- At the same time, the region is currently facing a particularly perilous mix of external pressures (capital inflow surge, commodity price boom) that raise the

premium for quickly establishing or consolidating the region's macroprudential capacity.

- In addition to clearly setting the goals of macroprudential instruments, other key design issues include the proper mix of rules and discretion, the choice between more specific or more broad-based instruments, and the choice between price-based versus quantity-based regulations.
- Other basic lines of action will include putting in place a proper institutional framework and a consistent policy mix; monetary, fiscal, capital controls, and exchange rate policies all need to complement and reinforce macroprudential policy.

The rest of this chapter is organized as follows. Following up on the main threads laid out in chapter 2, the first section briefly reviews the implications for macroprudential policy of the dynamics of the dark side in financial development. The second section explores how these dynamics may apply to LAC, first by reviewing the financial cycles of the past, and then by taking stock of the systemic risks that are building up and may continue to gather importance. The third section briefly discusses some key issues as regards the design of macroprudential policy. The chapter concludes by summarizing the main priorities and linkages in LAC's macroprudential policy agenda.

Macroprudential policy and the dynamics of the dark side

As in the case of monetary policy, the justification for macroprudential policy derives from the fact that economies go through socially inefficient cycles that call for policy action. Macroprudential policy focuses on achieving *sustainable financial system dynamics*, an objective that is not reducible to those of other macro (fiscal and monetary) policies. In particular, monetary policy alone—focused as it is on inflation and its volatility—is insufficient to manage these cycles because real and financial

transactions interact with the forces of the dark side (as surveyed in chapter 2), creating a class of social inefficiencies that are neither necessarily nor systematically associated with short- or long-term inflation dynamics. The aims of macroprudential policy are thus not perfectly correlated with those of monetary policy and go beyond the latter's main objective of coordinating and anchoring agents' expectations around a low and stable inflation target. In sum, the macrofinancial imperfections in the economy cannot be solved by a single instrument.

Inefficient financial system dynamics can be explained in two fundamental ways: (a) exogenous shocks that get amplified by various financial frictions and (b) dynamics that are endogenous to the financial development process itself (mood swings) and get amplified by heuristically adjusted expectations and the psychology of the masses, often generated and boosted by financial innovations. In the academic literature, the first type of dynamics is typically developed in models of rational expectations but mixed with agency or collective action frictions (that is, frictions associated with the costly enforcement, asymmetric information, and collective action paradigms). The second type is associated with Knightian uncertainty and bounded rationality (that is, the collective cognition paradigm).

In the first type, an exogenous shock that "comes out of the blue" sharply tightens a financial constraint typically derived from the need for "skin in the game," or collateral (because of asymmetric information or contract enforcement frictions). The financial constraint in turn activates massive asset purchases or fire sales that result in large changes in asset prices. In turn, the change in asset prices further tightens (or relaxes) the financial constraint by reducing (or raising) the value of the underlying collateral. Finally, the change in asset prices becomes consistent with fundamentals because it is validated by changes in productivity as assets change hands—between the more informed and the less informed (from the specialist arbitrageurs to the general market participants), as in Shleifer and Vishny (1997b); between the ones with better technologies and the ones with worse technologies, as in Kiyotaki and Moore (1997); or between the optimists and the pessimists, as in Geanakoplos (2009). Because individuals (or individual financial institutions) do not internalize these feedback effects, the upswing is characterized by a socially excessive expansion of credit and leverage.[4] Credit, asset prices, and real activity all rise in a self-reinforcing loop, and lending standards weaken as credit is extended to marginal borrowers.[5] These systemic fragilities that were built up in the boom deepen in the downturn, when feedback effects go in reverse, and a vicious circle develops between deleveraging, asset sales, weakening loan portfolios, and deteriorating real activity.

By contrast, in the mood swings story of adverse financial system dynamics, the inefficient amplification effects are endogenously gestated. Faced with the world of the new and unknown (that is, a range of nonreducible uncertainty about the future), market participants no longer have a steady frame of reference. As a result, as Keynes (1936) put it, "the market will be subject to waves of optimistic and pessimistic sentiment, which are unreasoned, yet in a sense legitimate . . . [Because of uncertainty] . . . no solid basis exists for a reasonable calculation." Up the cycle, financial innovations and the continuously improving economy fuel optimism and exuberance. At some point, however, a significant dissonance suffices to initiate a mood swing, fueled on the way down by acute uncertainty aversion.[6] In both cases, the adverse dynamics are amplified by flights to liquidity—that are individually protective but collectively self-destructive—and financial failures—that exacerbate the crisis through capacity losses, contagion, and interconnectedness.

The two types of market failures described above provide a clear rationale for macroprudential policy as an independent policy arena, different from that of monetary policy. It is not always easy, however, to neatly discern between the objectives and the use or misuse of monetary and macroprudential policy instruments in practice. For starters,

monetary policy can indeed be deployed to achieve macroprudential policy objectives— for instance, raising interest rates to tame an asset price bubble and avoid a deterioration of lending standards motivated by a search for yield—although not always without costs. Indeed, monetary policy not only may be a suboptimal policy to pursue macroprudential policy objectives but also may, by pursuing that policy, end up deviating from its main goal. The use of monetary policy to achieve macroprudential policy objectives can, furthermore, have adverse side effects— for example, a higher interest rate aimed at deflating an asset bubble can further stimulate "frothy" capital inflows, which in turn can increase financial system excesses. Conversely, macroprudential policy can overreach when, under the guise of pursuing its objectives, it is really used for other objectives for which it is not the best tool. This can be the case, for instance, when the real intention of deploying macroprudential policy is to cope with "impossible trinity" tensions arising from misguided exchange rate policy. Finally, there is a fuzzy area where macroprudential policy and other macro objectives overlap; hence, identifying the best policy tool is not always easy.[7]

In pursuing its ultimate objective of achieving sustainable financial system dynamics, macroprudential policy may be calibrated to pursue four progressively more ambitious lines of attack. For a modest first line of attack, macroprudential policy can simply concentrate on correcting those macroeconomic and regulatory policies that unnecessarily contribute to the adverse financial dynamics (that is, if one cannot help, one should at least do no harm). For a second line of attack, macroprudential policy could seek to limit the vulnerability of the financial system to adverse dynamics (that is, if one cannot control the dynamics, one may at least be able to make the financial system more resilient to those dynamics). For a third line of attack, macroprudential policy could aim at limiting the buildup of risks by controlling amplification effects (that is, if one is unable to prevent inefficient cycles, one may at least be able to limit their amplitude). For a fourth and most ambitious line of attack, macroprudential policy may try to maintain the economy on the right course at all times (that is, one can dispel the gestation of adverse dynamics in the first place by nipping them right in the bud).

The first line of attack may be built by maintaining sound fiscal and monetary policies (including avoiding unsustainable currency pegs), removing the inherent procyclicality of traditional (Basel I or II) prudential norms, and curbing other financial factors that fuel procyclicality, such as currency mismatches and social moral hazard (expectation of bailouts or a "Greenspan put" on monetary policy). Crucial to this first line of attack is to ensure that prudential buffers are really used as buffers (instead of being untouchable) when bad times hit, as argued for instance by Goodhart (2010b) and Hellwig (2010). The second line of attack requires building up stronger prudential buffers (whether solvency or liquidity); the third requires using macroprudential instruments as cycle dampeners; and the fourth requires introducing (possibly time-dependent) Pigouvian taxes (that help internalize externalities), monitoring and regulating financial innovation, and judiciously tightening or relaxing prudential limits along the path (to help coordinate or guide the behavior of market participants toward socially desirable outcomes). In all cases, policy actions take into account that the whole is more than the sum of the parts. Reflecting the interconnectedness, spillovers and externalities, and mood swings, what matters from the macroprudential perspective is not the riskiness of particular financial instruments or financial institutions—the realm of microprudential regulation—but rather their correlation with systemic risk.

While the literature on macroprudential policies is already vast, one seldom finds a clear and comprehensive characterization of goals and objectives along the above lines. Macroprudential tools and policies may affect several of these (increasingly ambitious) objectives, but they do it in different ways and to a different extent. At the same

time, the order of difficulty associated with each is clearly of a different magnitude. Thus, a properly thought-out reform agenda should carefully adjust the tools and policies to the objectives that can be realistically pursued at any point in time, taking into account the risks and vulnerabilities a financial system may face as well as the response capacity supervisors may have. The last two sections of this chapter explore these issues. However, the next section first reviews the stylized features of LAC's past cycles, to ground the subsequent discussion of macroprudential policy issues in LAC-specific realities.

LAC's cycles and vulnerabilities: Lessons from the past?

This section characterizes financial cycles in Latin America, drawing from a sample of 79 countries with quarterly information over the period 1970–2010.[8] Using time series techniques to date peaks and troughs and identify booms and busts, this section benchmarks cycles of credit, bank leverage (defined as the deposit-to-credit ratio), stock and housing prices, the real exchange rate, and capital flows by comparing LAC to industrial countries and non-LAC emerging countries.[9] Cycles that did not end with a banking crisis are also compared with those that did, and the last credit cycle (that is, the boom that preceded the global financial crisis) is compared with the previous cycles.[10]

LAC's financial cycles have been both quite frequent and more pronounced

Based on LAC's recent history, the unconditional probability (that is, the frequency over the sample period) of a credit boom in LAC is similar to that in other emerging economies but higher than in the industrial countries (figure 11.1). Similarly, the unconditional probability of an equity price boom is higher in LAC than in the industrial countries. Remarkably, however, housing price booms are substantially less frequent in LAC, which is consistent with the sharp underdevelopment of the mortgage market

FIGURE 11.1   Unconditional probability of booms and crises

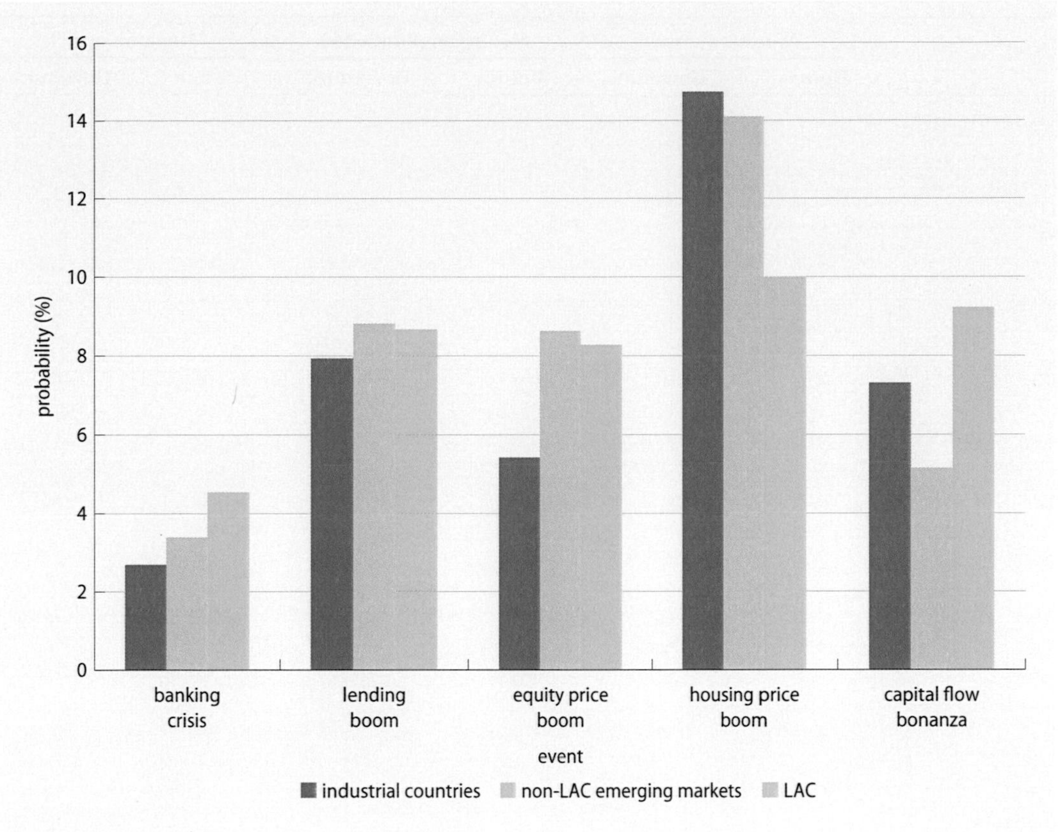

Source: Calderón and Servén 2011.
Note: This figure presents the frequency of banking crisis episodes in the sample of countries. It computes the unconditional probability of banking crisis as the number of years where a banking crisis takes place divided by the number of years in the entire sample of the country. Banking crisis episodes are identified as in Laeven and Valencia (2008). An analogous calculation is made for the frequency of lending booms, equity price and housing price booms, and capital flow bonanzas. Following Claessens et al. (2011a, forthcoming), these financial booms are defined as the top quartile of the upturn in credit, stock prices, housing prices, and gross capital inflows in the world sample.

identified and discussed in chapter 6. However, cycles (particularly credit) have been more protracted and abrupt, especially during downturns (table 11.1). For instance, the median drop in credit per capita in LAC during peak-to-trough phases is approximately 18 percent, four times larger than observed in industrial countries (4.4 percent) and over twice the magnitude seen in other emerging markets. Likewise, cyclical fluctuations in bank leverage, housing prices, and the real exchange rates exhibit greater amplitude in LAC, especially in cyclical downturns. These facts echo the history of macroeconomic instability of the region, as reflected by unsustainable fiscal and external positions, high inflation episodes, and recurring banking and currency crises.

Credit cycles in LAC have tended to precede output cycles and follow asset cycles

All macro variables are highly correlated with credit cycles but more particularly with output (more than 70 percent concordance) (figure 11.2).[11] However, real credit tends to precede output at turning points, particularly at the beginning of the downswing.[12] This pattern of precedence is even more pronounced in output downturns that coincide with a banking crisis (figure 11.3). At the

TABLE 11.1 Main features of real and financial cycles
Sample: 79 countries, 1970q1–2010q4

	Average duration		Median amplitude (%)		Median slope (%)	
	Upturn	Downturn	Upturn	Downturn	Upturn	Downturn
Real GDP						
Industrial countries	3.17	3.98	2.9	−2.4	0.6	−0.6
Latin America	3.36	3.76	5.6	−5.5	1.3	−1.4
Non-LAC emerging markets	3.34	3.61	7.5	−5.1	1.8	−1.6
Real credit per capita						
Industrial countries (IND)	5.08	6.12	3.9	−4.4	0.9	−0.9
Latin America	4.40	7.10	9.9	−17.7	2.4	−2.8
Non-LAC emerging markets	4.39	5.31	7.4	−7.1	2.2	−1.8
Credit-GDP ratio						
Industrial countries (IND)	4.56	7.15	3.5	−5.5	0.9	−1.0
Latin America	4.94	8.31	7.6	−15.9	2.0	−2.5
Non-LAC emerging markets	4.03	6.53	5.2	−7.4	1.2	−1.3
Bank leverage						
Industrial countries (IND)	4.31	10.33	3.3	−11.3	0.9	−1.5
Latin America	3.42	14.64	4.9	−31.4	1.9	−3.3
Non-LAC emerging markets	3.29	13.13	3.7	−20.4	1.3	−2.6
Stock prices						
Industrial countries (IND)	3.99	6.23	19.3	−35.9	5.3	−7.0
Latin America	4.09	6.42	36.3	−56.7	8.9	−11.2
Non-LAC emerging markets	4.08	6.21	33.4	−55.4	7.2	−8.9
Housing prices						
Industrial countries (IND)	3.94	7.06	2.9	−4.5	0.9	−0.9
Latin America	4.50	8.33	6.8	−19.7	2.4	−2.7
Non-LAC emerging markets	3.91	7.89	3.5	−8.1	1.0	−1.4
Real effective exchange rate						
Industrial countries (IND)	4.05	5.45	3.5	−6.7	1.0	−1.3
Latin America	3.94	6.01	6.4	−12.3	2.1	−2.3
Non-LAC emerging markets	3.72	5.89	5.4	−9.8	1.5	−2.0
Gross capital inflows (ratio to GDP)						
Industrial countries (IND)	3.29	5.17	3.7	−5.3	0.9	−1.1
Latin America	3.45	5.20	3.0	−4.2	0.6	−1.0
Non-LAC emerging markets	3.23	4.98	3.0	−4.4	0.8	−1.0

Source: Calderón and Servén 2011.
Note: The table reports the average duration (in quarters) of the different cyclical phases (downturns and upturns) for real and financial variables. The statistics for amplitude and slope refer to sample median across episodes (averages for those statistics are not reported but are available from the authors upon request). The duration of downturns (recessions or contractions) is the number of quarters between peak and trough. Upturns (or recoveries), on the other hand, are defined as the early stage of the expansion that takes place when either the real or financial indicator rebounds from the trough to its previous peak. The amplitude of the downturn is the distance between the peak in real output and its subsequent trough, while that of the upturn is computed as the four-quarter cumulative variation in real output following the trough. The slope of the downturn is the ratio of the peak-to-trough (trough-to-peak) phase of the cycle to its duration.

same time, lending booms are more likely to be preceded by booms in asset prices.[13] Not surprisingly, in the case of equity prices, this result suggests that the latter are early predictors of improving economic conditions. It is somewhat remarkable, however, that housing prices in LAC tend to precede (rather than follow) credit booms. This order

reversal is a reminder of the limited role played so far in LAC by the availability of mortgage credit in affecting housing prices. But this is likely to change in the future as mortgage markets develop, and is something for which the authorities already need to be preparing. Also somewhat surprisingly, LAC's capital flow bonanzas are less

FIGURE 11.2   **Synchronization between real output and financial cycles**

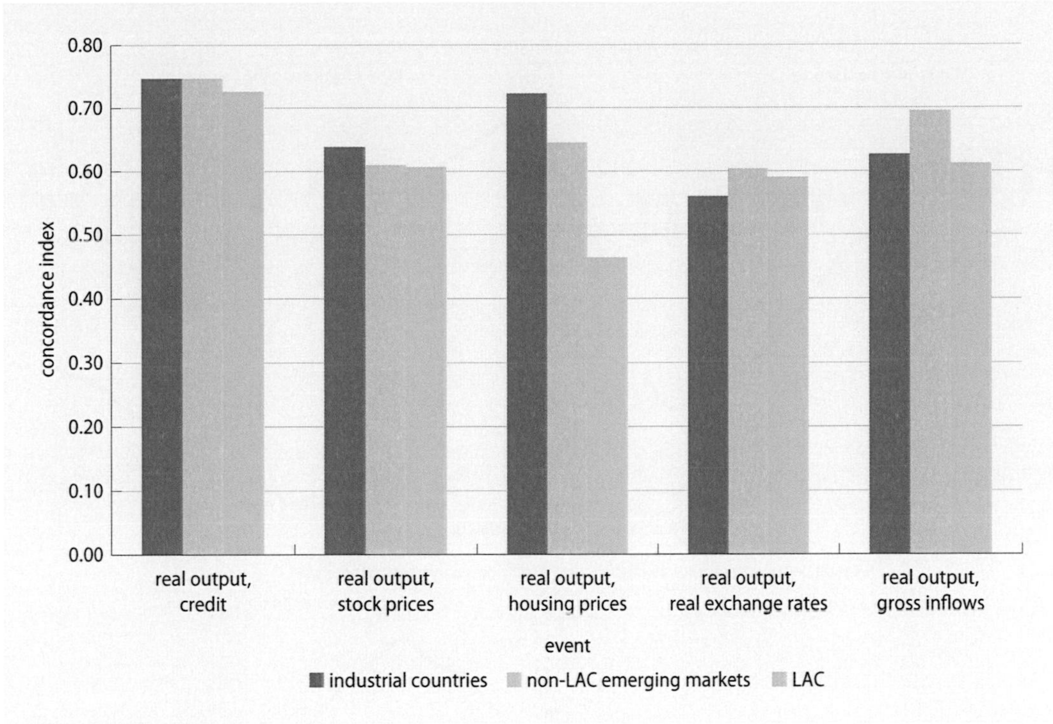

Source: Calderón and Servén 2011.
Note: The figures presented here represent the concordance statistics for the cycles of the corresponding pair of variables (Harding and Pagan 2002a). The concordance index takes values between 0 and 1 and measures the fraction of time that the two cycles are in the same cyclical phase. The concordance figures presented are computed over the period 1970q1–2010q4.

likely to be followed by lending booms than in other regions (figure 11.4), which may reflect the greater buffering role of exchange rates. Indeed, real exchange rates move more strongly with the credit cycle than capital inflows, a trend that has sharpened during the latest cycle (figures 11.5 and 11.6).

LAC's financial cycles have more often ended in crises

Financial crashes have occurred more frequently in LAC than in other regions (figure 11.1). For starters, the unconditional probability of a banking crisis is higher in Latin America (4.6 percent) than in industrial countries or other emerging markets (2.7 percent and 3.4 percent, respectively). The frequency of banking crises following lending booms is also higher in LAC than in

other regions. Nearly half of LAC's banking crisis episodes followed lending booms, and more than half of these crashes were preceded by either equity price booms or capital inflow bonanzas. Moreover, when crises have taken place, their costs have been very high, whichever way one wants to measure them.[14] In addition, the scale of the boom is a significant predictor of the occurrence of crises: bigger booms are more likely to end badly. In particular, the likelihood that an upturn in real credit per capita will end up in a financial crash is positively associated with the length and the size of the credit upswing (table 11.2).[15] Furthermore, the size of the credit boom remains a good predictor of financial crashes even after controlling for the size of the upswing in asset prices (stock prices and real exchange rates) and capital flows. Indeed, the magnitude of the

FIGURE 11.3   **Behavior of credit during downturns in real economic activity: Are financial cycles leading real cycles?**

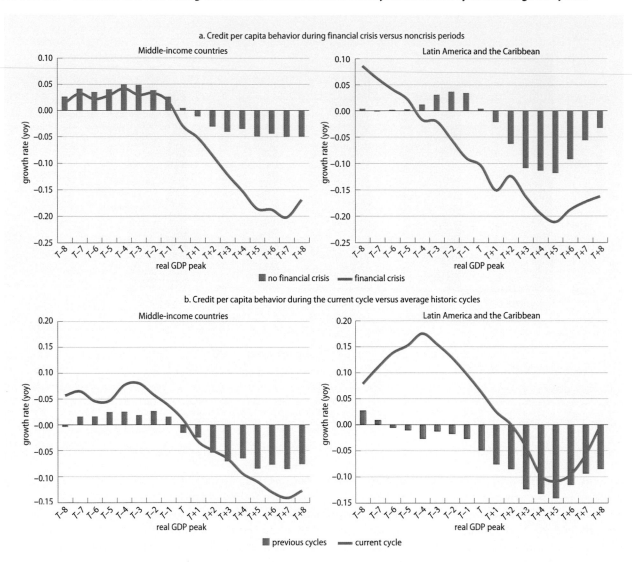

Source: Calderón and Servén 2011.
Note: This figure depicts the year-on-year growth rate (or variation) in credit and asset prices around 17 quarter windows centered around peaks in real GDP (*T*). The period *T* when the peak in real GDP takes place is identified using the Bry-Boschan quarterly algorithm (Harding and Pagan 2002b). Panel a shows the evolution of credit during peaks in real output associated to episodes of banking crisis (as defined in Laeven and Valencia 2008). Panel b distinguishes peaks in real GDP during the current cycle (2006–10) and the average of previous output cycles.

credit boom is the dominant crisis predictor; once it is considered, the occurrence (or the magnitude) of booms in other financial variables does not significantly increase predictive power.[16]

How much of a guide for macroprudential policy design are LAC's historical patterns of financial cycles? The answer is not simple. On the one hand, the duration, amplitude, and intensity of credit cycles in the world, and particularly in Latin America, have declined over time, especially during the past decade (figure 11.7). This worldwide dampening might be attributed to what has become known as the Great Moderation. But it was accentuated in LAC by the much

FIGURE 11.4   Unconditional and conditional probability of lending booms

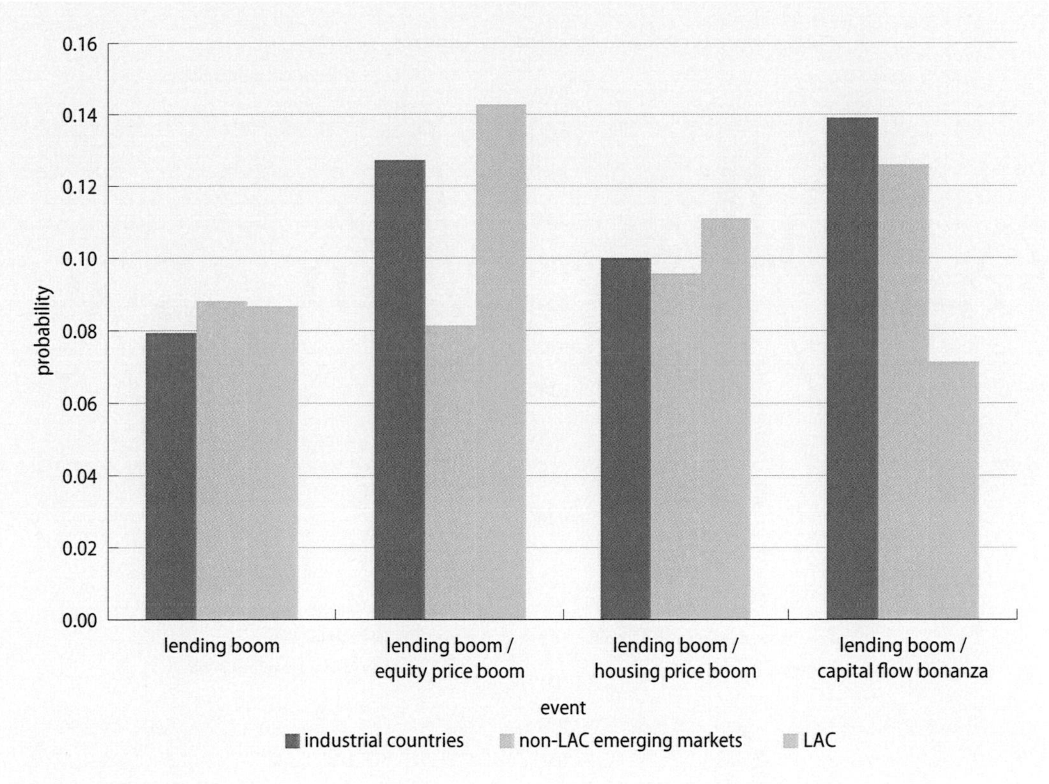

Source: Calderón and Servén 2011.
Note: Unconditional probabilities are computed as the frequency of lending booms over the sample. The conditional probability of lending booms reports the frequency of booms in asset prices or capital flows occurring in *t*, *t*–1 or *t*–2 that end up in a banking crisis in period *t*. Finally, note that financial booms and capital flow bonanzas are defined as cyclical components of the corresponding financial variables exceeding 1.75 times their standard deviation.

improved macroeconomic policy frameworks, lower debt burdens, and reduced currency mismatches. This improvement in LAC's macrofinancial "immune system" not only reduced the volatility of output over time but also made the region more resilient to global shocks.[17] Given this significant change, a simple extrapolation of frequencies and magnitudes of past cycles would not be a sound basis for macroprudential policy going forward. On the other hand, however, the importance of credit cycles relative to other cycles, as well as some of the sequencing results, are likely to survive as long as the basic financial structure does not change too much.

Be that as it may, the backward-looking analysis of cycles needs to be complemented by a more forward-looking survey of risks

and vulnerabilities.[18] Much of the region is currently experiencing a double tailspin push coming from outside and resulting from sharp worldwide cycle asynchronicity. On the one hand, there are large increases in commodity prices, associated with high Asian growth, that are resulting in a *terms of trade bonanza*. On the other hand, the continuously depressed economic conditions in industrial countries are producing very low world interest rates, which are in turn resulting in a *global liquidity flood*. Such outside pressures are combining with the inside pressures resulting from still stimulative home policies (both fiscal and financial). As a result, several countries in LAC are experiencing unusually strong capital inflows. Partly as a result, some are in the midst of sustained credit booms (for example, Brazil and Peru),

FIGURE 11.5   Real exchange rate behavior during downturns in real credit

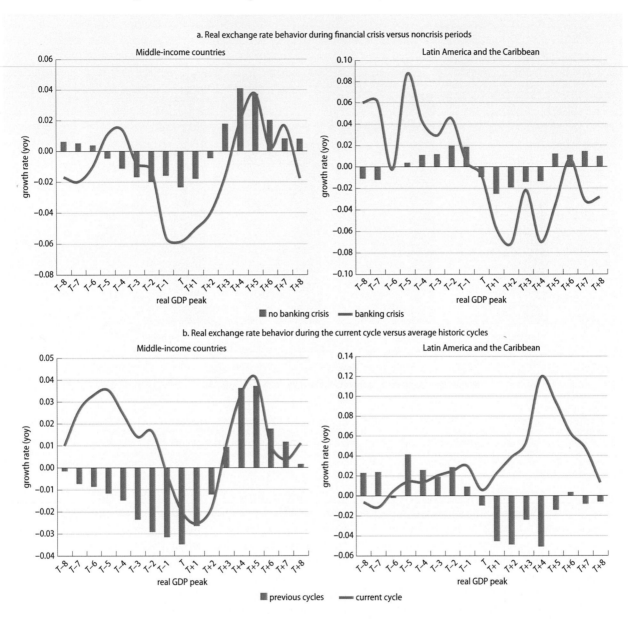

Source: Calderón and Servén 2011.
Note: This figure depicts the year-on-year growth rate (or variation) in the real exchange rate around 17 quarter windows centered around peaks in real credit per capita (*T*). The period *T* when the peak in real credit per capita takes place is identified using the Bry-Boschan quarterly algorithm (Harding and Pagan 2002a). Panel a shows the evolution of the real exchange rate during peaks in real credit associated to episodes of banking crisis (as defined in Laeven and Valencia 2008). Panel b distinguishes peaks in real credit during the current cycle (2006–10) and the average of previous credit cycles.

others in the midst of incipient credit booms (for example, Colombia).

As explained in chapter 6, the region's policy response has been much complicated by the world cycle asynchronisms. The strong Asian economic pull calls for raising interest rates, yet this conflicts head-on with the low world rates imposed by the depressed high-income countries. Managing this conflict has been further hindered by

FIGURE 11.6   Foreign capital and credit downturns

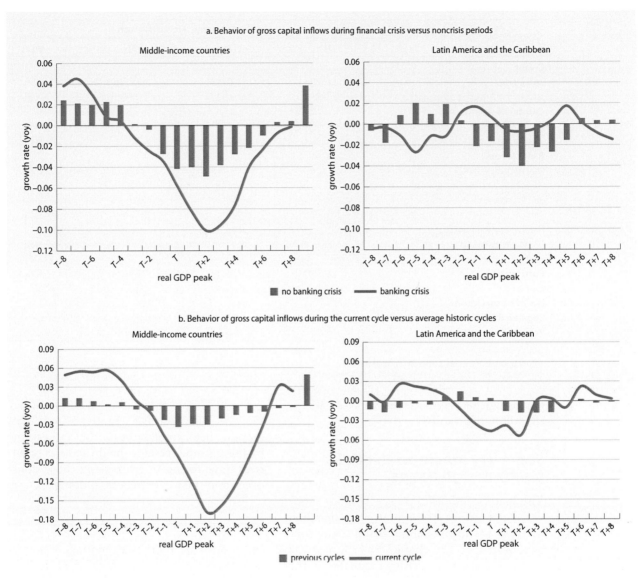

Source: Calderón and Servén 2011.
Note: This figure depicts the year-on-year growth rate (or variation) in the ratio of gross inflows to GDP around 17 quarter windows centered around peaks in real credit per capita (*T*). The period *T* when the peak in real credit per capita takes place is identified using the Bry-Boschan quarterly algorithm (Harding and Pagan 2002b). Panel a shows the evolution of the ratio of gross inflows to GDP during peaks in real credit associated to episodes of banking crisis (as defined in Laeven and Valencia 2008). Panel b distinguishes peaks in real credit during the current cycle (2006–10) and the average of previous credit cycles.

the region's relatively high interest rates—the lasting legacy of its turbulent past—and (as shown in chapter 4) by its relatively more open capital account compared to other emerging economies (particularly the Asian economies). Thus, monetary policy has struggled more than in other regions with the large and mounting real exchange rate appreciations. Altogether, the rising financial vulnerabilities and constraints faced by monetary policy make a very strong case for quickly establishing or strengthening the region's macroprudential policy capacity. In turn, the latter will need to address several

TABLE 11.2 **Size of financial booms and the probability of crisis: Probit analysis**
Sample: 79 countries, 1970q1–2010q4

	Dependent variable: Financial crash			
	[1]	**[2]**	**[3]**	**[4]**
Credit				
Real credit	1.1555**	1.3246	2.5876*	2.6228*
(amplitude of preceding upturn)	(0.518)	(1.027)	(1.364)	(1.405)
Capital flows				
Ratio of non-FDI inflows to GDP	..	−0.1269	−1.2177	−1.3084
(amplitude of preceding upturn)		(1.844)	(2.306)	(2.308)
Asset prices				
Real exchange rate	..	..	2.1246	2.2336
(amplitude of preceding upturn)			(2.208)	(2.291)
Stock prices (*real*)	..	..	0.1658	0.0984
(amplitude of preceding upturn)			(0.523)	(0.560)
Leverage of the banking system				
Credit-deposit ratio	..	..	..	−0.3075
(T-P amplitude)				(0.528)
Constant	−1.4536**	−1.3826**	−1.8141**	−1.7686**
	(0.163)	(0.256)	(0.345)	(0.366)
No. of observations	298	144	116	110
Log likelihood	−108.4	−58.0	−38.3	−36.8
Pseudo *R*-squared	0.0623	0.0581	0.2084	0.193

Source: Calderón and Servén 2011.
Note: Robust standard errors are shown in parentheses.
Significance level: * = 10 percent; ** = 5 percent; *** = 1 percent.

key design or policy issues, as discussed in the following section.

Some key macroprudential policy design issues

The macroprudential perspective has motivated a number of regulatory proposals. Most of them involve adjusting regulatory instruments to the changes in risk over the cycle, essentially tightening regulation in the upswing and relaxing it in the downswing. This approach raises a number of key questions that affect virtually all proposals. How ambitious should policy makers be? Should macroprudential regulations seek to protect the financial system only by adjusting prudential buffers over the cycle in the most efficient way? Or should macroprudential regulations go beyond, and also seek to dampen the cycle itself? Should the adjustment be based on rules, or left at the regulator's discretion? Should the trigger for macroprudential adjustments be aggregate, or institution-

specific? Should the macroprudential policy tools be price based or quantity based? This section sheds some light on these questions by taking into account the difficulties countries have found in addressing these questions, and their experiences in doing so.

Sweet spot versus overactivism

In considering policies to manage systemic risk over the cycle, one must first keep in mind that the financial cycle in part reflects fundamentals that are themselves procyclical. Investment opportunities and credit demand rise in the upswing, while the riskiness of prospective borrowers declines. Indeed, the Schumpeterian "creative destruction" that characterizes market economies itself introduces a real cyclicality that is intertwined with financial fluctuations. Thus, part of the financial cycle may reflect efficient adjustments to changes in the underlying real fundamentals (that is, real business cycle effects). Or it may reflect excess fluctuations that are best taken care of through traditional monetary policy. Moreover, distinguishing between financial cycles and trends is difficult, particularly in emerging economies with lagging financial depth (LAC's case), as rapid financial expansion may just reflect sustainable catch-up growth. Clearly, therefore, there is a risk of macroprudential policy overkill. Macroprudential policy should not seek to flatten the cycle altogether. It should focus, rather, on finding the "sweet spot"— that is, containing only the "excess" volatility caused by socially undesirable financial activity (calming the excessively stormy seas) and enhancing the resilience and stability of the financial system (protecting the boat from the rough seas). Identifying this type of financial excesses is a tricky task. The fact that only a small fraction of credit booms (about 1 in 10) end up in crashes is a further warning against the dangers of overactivism.[19]

Buffers or dampeners?

As noted, prudential buffers (capital, generic provisions, and liquidity) need to become available to financial institutions in the downturn, when funding costs rise and their lending portfolio and profitability deteriorate. Fixed minimum requirements (on capital, loan loss provisions, and so on), however high, are not helpful in this regard, since they have to be met continuously throughout the cycle.[20] Instead, the ability to draw down without penalty during downswings the buffers that were built in the upswing should help both better shield the financial system and dampen the amplitude of the cycle. At the same time, by giving institutions self-protection (capacity to absorb losses), the ability to use the buffers in bad times weakens the fire sale externalities (by reducing the need to sell assets). Moreover, countercyclical buffers that are usable by the institution can also help in bad times by offsetting the procyclical deleveraging effect of risk-weighted, Basel II–type, minimum capital requirements.[21]

Countercyclical capital buffers have been amply advocated in both the academic and

FIGURE 11.7 Main features of the credit cycle over time

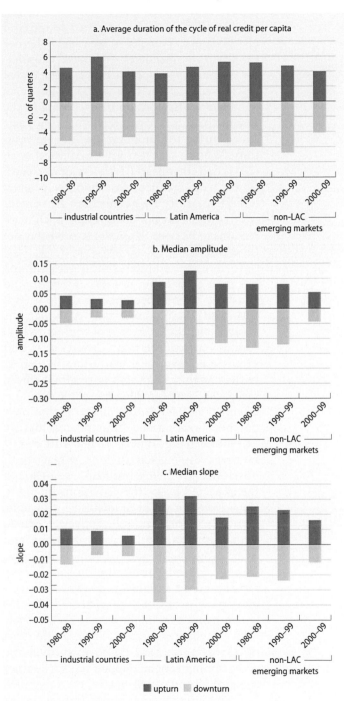

Source: Calderón and Servén 2011.
Note: This figure reports the average duration of the different cyclical phases (downturns and upturns) for real credit indicators per region and per period. The statistics for amplitude and slope refer to sample median across episodes.

the policy literatures.[22] However, there is at present only limited analytical research, and no actual experience, on their design and effectiveness. Thus, it is not clear whether the size recommended by the Basel Committee on Banking Supervision (2.5 percent of assets, see BCBS 2010a) would be adequate to substantially contain deleveraging in the downturn. Even less is known about their contribution to dampening aggregate volatility. While a recent study by Angelini et al. (2011) finds that Basel III–style countercyclical capital would reduce gross domestic product (GDP) volatility by as much as 20 percent relative to the no-buffer scenario, much work remains to be done to assess the robustness of these results.

In contrast, countercyclical provisioning has seen actual use, notably in Spain, and has more recently become popular in several LAC and Asian countries.[23] Although the objective is similar to that of countercyclical capital buffers, the main difference is that provisions have been traditionally seen as buffers against risks that have already been recognized (expected losses), while capital is intended as a buffer against risks that have not been recognized (unexpected losses). The underlying logic is that credit risk is incurred during expansions, when credit portfolios are being built up, even though the expected losses the provisions intend to cover have not yet been identified in specific loans. By giving banks incentives to extend loans more carefully in the upswing and by limiting the growth in bank profits and capital, dynamic provisioning should help restrain credit expansion. However, its primary purpose is not to prevent credit booms per se, a task that might require prohibitively high provisioning rates. Thus, while most observers agree that the Spanish dynamic provisioning scheme helped banks weather the global downturn better, there is much less agreement as regards its impact on the cycle.[24] In retrospect, it was clearly insufficient to tame the lending cycle or to prevent the boom in real estate prices. Nonetheless, it may also be argued that, without it, the credit boom and real estate bubble would have been even bigger.

Another option is to contain the risk buildup itself and address the risk spillovers by constraining financial institutions' leverage or short-term financing; or by directly targeting credit growth over the cycle through liquidity or reserve requirements. Thus, some have suggested introducing a maximum, adjustable leverage ratio.[25] Likewise, different schemes have been suggested to penalize short-term wholesale funding (noncore liabilities) and encourage the holding of systemically liquid assets.[26] In recent years, many emerging countries (included several LAC countries with inflation-targeting regimes, such as Brazil, Colombia, and Peru) have resorted to discretionary changes in banks' reserve requirements to moderate credit cycles (figure 11.8).[27] Their primary impact on credit derives from the fact that reserve requirements are unremunerated; hence, they introduce an implicit tax that widens the loan-deposit interest rate differential.[28] In practice, however, the cost effectiveness of reserve requirements in dampening the amplitude of the lending cycle (relative to other potential macroprudential instruments such as countercyclical capital requirements) remains to be fully demonstrated.[29]

Rules or discretion?

The limited experience with most proposals on countercyclical regulation, the fact that many of them remain untested, and the role of mood swings in financial dynamics all suggest the need for regulatory discretion. Indeed, rules are more congenial to a world of rational expectations than to one of uncertainty and bounded rationality. However, the more discretion the regulatory authorities exercise, the higher the political hurdles. Thus, the cooling down of the boom might be too little and come too late. Indeed, it is important to recall that countercyclical regulation would have been possible in many countries in the run-up to the global financial crisis, yet very few made use of them. Hence, all things considered, a "set it and forget it" countercyclical regulation based on well-defined rules is more likely to help deflect pressures on the regulator. But it is doubtful that rules-based countercyclical prudential norms would suffice, and a significant scope for discretion would likely need to be built into any robust macroprudential policy framework, an issue to which chapter 13 returns.

Regardless of whether rules or discretion predominate, matters are complicated by the lack of well-defined, easy-to-agree-on macroprudential policy levers as well as indicators to which the changes in that policy can be automatically tied. In contrast to monetary policy whose objective (price stability) can be represented by a well-measured summary index, financial stability is an elusive and multidimensional concept that is much harder to measure and monitor. Moreover, the trigger signal should be timely (ahead of the buildup of financial imbalances), should become available quickly, and should offer an early indication of cyclical turning points, particularly at the beginning of the downturn. A variety of indicators have been suggested for this purpose, ranging from GDP growth to the rate of growth of overall credit, the rate of growth of institution-specific credit, the credit-to-GDP ratio, or asset prices (particularly housing).[30] While they all show a considerable degree of comovement over the cycle, blindly following one or the other can result in very different paths of regulatory tightness.[31] Unavoidably, a variety of financial and real indicators thus would have to be used, as in the case of monetary policy, to get a more nuanced perspective and reduce the risk of doing more harm than good.

A further difficulty, as noted, concerns the distinction between trends and cycles. Sustained increases in credit might reflect healthy financial development (the bright side), rather than an unsustainable cyclical boom (the dark side). Thus, mechanically gearing regulatory stance to changes in these variables could have the unintended result of retarding financial deepening. This problem is even trickier in LAC because the region still has quite a way to go before it catches up with its benchmark.

FIGURE 11.8   Reserve requirements and reference rates

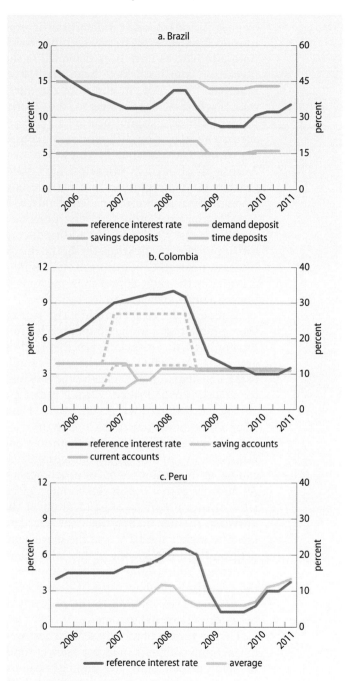

Source: Calderón and Servén 2011.

Specific or broad?

The question of whether macroprudential instruments should be specific or broad-based has multiple facets. A first facet is whether the changes in regulatory stance over the cycle should be top-down (guided by institution-specific indicators) or bottom-up (guided by systemwide indicators). Both alternatives have been defended in the literature, and both have been applied in practice.[32] There is, in addition, the question of whether, once triggered, the macroprudential norm should be applied equally across the board or differentiated according to institutions' specific characteristics. Across-the-board application may have greater dampening effect on the cycle but, by punishing the more prudent lenders, it could undermine individual discipline and encourage risky behavior. In addition, conditioning the application of the norm on institution-specific indicators of risk buildup is arguably the right approach if one aims at internalizing externalities.

A second facet is whether the norms should aim at containing all types of lending or should focus on specific types of lending and risks. A particularly relevant example is the housing sector. Concern with this sector is well justified since housing prices are closely synchronized with credit cycles. Thus, a fixed ratio of the size of the loan to the market value of the real estate (the loan-to-value ratio, or LTV) in mortgage lending standards can be an important source of procyclicality. As housing prices rise in the boom, a given LTV allows credit to expand more in the upswing, further fueling the asset price spiral. The higher the LTV and the more competition there is between lenders, the bigger this effect.[33] A similar reasoning applies to the cycle-independent ratio of debt service to income (DTI), owing to the procyclical behavior of personal income.

Thus, a variety of tools have been deployed in emerging countries in recent years at times of rapidly growing property lending and housing prices. Among those tools, caps on LTV ratios have seen considerable use, especially in Asia.[34] Limits on DTI ratios have likewise been applied in several countries to help contain lending to lower-quality borrowers.[35] In many cases, these adjustments have been only loosely related to quantitative indicators of risk, and in virtually all cases they have relied on judgment. On the whole, there is little systematic evidence on the extent to which they have been effective at restraining housing booms, although there is some anecdotal evidence that they may have increased banks' resilience to falling property prices. Beyond questions on their effectiveness, such sector-specific interventions are not devoid of other problems. First, they are hard to calibrate.[36] Second, their practical effectiveness may be limited because the more selective the intervention is, the more vulnerable it is to circumvention.[37] Third, the more selective the measures, the larger the risk of straying into the type of distortionary credit allocation policies that characterized the financial repression epoch a few decades ago.

Price based or quantity based?

A last but not less important issue is whether the countercyclical prudential norms should be price based or quantity based. Liquidity regulations, for example, can take the form of quantity constraints, such as minimum liquidity requirements, or price-based norms, such as Pigouvian taxes that discourage short-term (noncore deposit) funding. The more price based the norm, the easier it is to apply across the board—and the broader its application, the lower the risk of distortions and regulatory arbitrage; however, the harder it also becomes to properly calibrate it. Indeed, a case can be made that the higher the uncertainty about the impact of taxes and the more pressing the need for immediate results, the stronger the comparative advantage of quantity-based regulation.[38] In less mature financial systems, the relative advantage of quantity-based regulation is arguably stronger because it would carry a lower risk of distortion and the impact of price-based regulation would be more uncertain.

The path ahead

In defining the path ahead, the region will need to keep in mind three basic points:

(a) there is a particularly strong (and, in several countries, urgent) case for macroprudential policy in the region, (b) yet there is much uncertainty as to the effectiveness of macroprudential policy tools (which puts a premium on research), and (c) the deployment of macroprudential regulatory norms is not devoid of costs. In the end, it will all boil down to finding the sweet spot at which the gains are clear and the norms address the areas where the bright side of financial development begins to interface with the dark side. This is even harder because some of the costs of macroprudential policy may be visible and materialize immediately (for example, the immediate reduction in the credit available to the marginal but viable borrowers), whereas others (the distortions, regulatory arbitrage, and overall possible slowdown in the pace of sustainable financial development) may only become evident in the longer run. Nor will the benefits of macroprudential policy, in the form of reduced incidence of crises, become immediately obvious.[39]

In this context, three important criteria for macroprudential policy design and implementation come to mind: (a) the overall strategy needs to be organized in accordance with the four lines of attack identified earlier; (b) the institutional framework that is put in place should promote good judgment, transparency and accountability, and organized decision making; and (c) all the eggs should not be put in the same basket (macroprudential policy is not a magic bullet) and the strategy should emphasize complementarities with other policies. The second of these items (which lies at the interface between regulation and supervision) is dealt with in chapter 13. The other two are discussed next.

The lines of attack

The uncertainties described above militate in favor of a gradualist approach linked to the mentioned lines of attack. Thus, eliminating as much as possible the procyclicality and inconsistencies inherent in the precrisis Basel-style prudential norms would seem to

be the first order of business no matter what. If that approach does not help, at least it won't hurt. In fact, it is likely to help achieve the higher-order goals—certainly the buffering goal but also the dampening goal. The second order of business should be to enhance the stability of the financial system through better and stronger (liquidity and solvency) buffers. This does not mean, however, that one should give up altogether at this stage on the objective of dampening the cycle. As demonstrated by the use of reserve requirements, loan-to-value ratio, and debt-service-to-income ratio, a case can also be made for cautious yet firm experimentation of instruments aimed at this latter goal.

However, the goals should generally interact with the means. Thus, because a judgment is likely to be necessary when assessing financial stability and the need for intervention, a purely rules-based scheme of the type proposed by Basel III might be more feasible if used strictly as a buffer rather than a dampener. Instead, if one really wishes to affect the cycle, doing it through a purely rules-based scheme is most likely a pie in the sky. If it cannot be done for monetary policy (no central bank in the world has ever been able to blindly follow a Taylor rule based on output gaps, or the Friedman rule of a constant rate of money supply growth), the odds against doing it for macroprudential policy seem overwhelming. The scheme would survive only if it were bland enough, hence unlikely to have much impact one way or the other. In practice, one is thus probably left with a mix of rules and discretion, the former aimed at buffering the system, the latter at affecting its path over the cycle.

Another example of interaction between ends and means can be applied to the choice of specific versus broad-based instruments. As noted above, if one mainly aims (at least in a first phase) at dampening the cycle rather than internalizing externalities, a better case might be made for a simpler instrument that applies uniformly across financial intermediaries. The objective of inducing the internalization of externalities could then be pursued through Pigouvian taxes that aim to address systemic risk. They will do so by focusing on the wedges between private and social interests behind both excessive cyclical fluctuations and on the dark side of interconnectedness, as discussed in chapter 12.

The macro policy mix

Macroprudential policy tools are not the only ones available to policy makers for managing systemic risk. Monetary and fiscal policies (and possibly capital controls) also have a potentially important impact on the financial cycle and the buildup of aggregate financial risk. Indeed, the global crisis has revived interest in the powers of monetary policy to aid financial stability. In addition to restraining credit through higher interest rates, monetary policy can also affect the quality of lending through the so-called risk-taking channel.[40] Unduly low monetary policy rates lead banks to expand their lending to higher-risk borrowers. Empirical evidence tends to support this view.[41]

Before the global crisis, a consensus view seemed to have emerged in favor of "the Tinbergen principle" of separating monetary stability from financial stability. Targeting asset prices (beyond what was needed to target inflation) was viewed as impossible or, if possible, counterproductive.[42] However, an alternative view is now emerging in which monetary policy can dampen boom-bust episodes if it reacts to credit growth, asset prices, leverage, or other indicators of financial risk.[43] This means that monetary policy should become more restrictive during a credit and asset price boom and more responsive to indicators of financial stability. However, how to manage in practice the possible conflicts between price stability and financial stability without undermining the credibility of central banks is at this point a largely unresolved issue. What is clear, however, is that monetary and macroprudential policies should be viewed as complements, not substitutes. This view has prompted calls for central banks to assume both tasks in a fully integrated manner and using more than one instrument.[44]

Fiscal policy also has a key role to play, however. It can help mitigate the amplitude of the financial cycle and align the private and social incentives for risk taking. Indeed, the stabilizing potential of countercyclical fiscal policy has been underscored by the global crisis. The accumulation of fiscal buffers during the good times allowed a number of emerging countries, notably in Latin America, to adopt an expansionary stance when the crisis hit.[45] Yet, discretionary fiscal policy often faces considerable delays, which underscores the need to build up self-deploying automatic stabilizers, particularly in LAC.[46] In addition, fiscal policy can play a key role in internalizing externalities through Pigouvian taxes (thereby putting into place the last and more ambitious perimeter of defense).[47] However, in spite of the solid theoretical justification of this kind of taxes, little is known about their likely effectiveness in practice, how tax rates should be set, and to what extent they should be varied over the cycle. Thus, a simpler and more immediate step in the same direction would be the removal of fiscal incentives that favor debt financing over equity financing. Limiting the incentives for leveraging could have a major effect on the resilience of the financial system.[48]

Another policy area where some action might be needed to complement macroprudential policy is capital controls. As shown in the above section ("LAC's cycles and vulnerabilities"), capital flows and credit growth show a significant degree of comovement over the cycle, and financial crises in emerging markets have been frequently preceded by capital inflow booms. In particular, capital controls may be used to change at least the composition, if not volume, of inflows toward less risky forms.[49] However, though there is a massive literature on capital controls, there are few robust findings as regards their effectiveness, largely owing to the almost insurmountable difficulty of establishing the proper counterfactual scenario.[50] Perhaps one of the few conclusions on which everyone agrees is that capital controls quickly develop leakages, all the more so in the more advanced and globally integrated financial markets. Finally, it is important to stress that the aggregate vulnerability of most emerging economies to sudden capital flow reversals has declined substantially in recent years, owing in particular to the attainments of net creditor positions in debt contracts as well as to reduced financial dollarization.[51]

A last area where good coordination with macroprudential policy is also required is as regards the exchange rate regime. The region's transition to floating-rate regimes has enhanced its macroprudential policy independence at the same time as its monetary policy independence. A floating-rate regime naturally creates a wedge between the foreign and the local currency. The more volatile the exchange rate, the higher the risk of investing or borrowing in foreign exchange for local residents. Hence, floating-rate regimes not only should (and indeed have, as shown in chapter 3) reduce the dollarization of local financial intermediation, but also, by the same token, should limit the scope for offshoring by reducing the substitutability of local and foreign currency loans. The lower substitutability should reduce the scope for regulatory arbitrage across borders, thereby enhancing the scope for a more active macroprudential home policy, even when the latter is asynchronous with that of rest of the world. However, to the extent that macroprudential policy can help limit exchange rate volatility by assisting monetary policy (for example, by limiting the need for monetary tightening, hence, exchange rate appreciations during the booms), some underlying tensions will need to be managed. A well-integrated macroeconomic policy is therefore again of the essence.

Notes

1. The postcrisis discussion of the required reforms to systemic oversight generally includes microsystemic aspects within the broader category of macroprudential reforms. However, a terminological distinction is made in this flagship report because it helps organize the discussion more neatly.
2. This chapter draws heavily on the paper "Macro-Prudential Policies over the Cycle in

Latin America" by César Calderón and Luis Servén (2011), which is part of the Edited Volume that accompanies this LAC flagship report.
3. For a recent excellent general review of the literature on macroprudential policy, see Galati and Moessner (2011). Ostry et al. (2011) review the closely related issue of managing capital inflows. Terrier et al. (2011) offer a very detailed analysis of macroprudential policies and instruments in the Latin American context.
4. See Lorenzoni (2008) and Jeanne and Korinek (2011). An excessive expansion of credit and leverage can also be fueled by moral hazard. For instance, when an innovation opens new opportunities (the upside widens) or a macrosystemic shock wipes out a large part of the financial intermediaries' capital (the downside shrinks), agents may take increasing risk because they have increasingly little to lose relative to what they can gain.
5. See Dell'Ariccia and Marquez (2008) and Adrian and Shin (2010).
6. All in all, the mood swings story is more rounded and self-contained than the financial amplification story. However, it is also more ad hoc. It finds its roots in Keynes and Minsky and is generally consistent (albeit somewhat loosely) with the behavioral finance literature. Recent formalization attempts can be found, for example, in de Grauwe (2009) and Lo (2009).
7. As an illustration, one can consider a surge in capital inflows that are not driven by fundamentals. They can lead to an "excessive" appreciation of the currency (unnecessary loss of competitiveness), which is a relevant macroeconomic policy concern, as well as lead to the buildup of systemic risk in the financial sector, which is a relevant macroprudential policy concern.
8. The sample consists of 23 industrial countries and 56 developing countries, of which 15 belong to LAC.
9. The reader should be cautious with the interpretation of the housing price dynamics in LAC because the information is sparser than for industrial and other emerging-market economies. The lack of availability of a housing price index for the countries in the region restricts the LAC sample to Chile, Colombia, Mexico, and Uruguay.
10. Cycles ending up in a banking crisis are defined as those whose peak-to-trough phase coincide

or are followed by a banking crisis within two years. Episodes of banking crisis are defined as in Laeven and Valencia (2008), that is, as a situation in which the following four conditions are met: (a) rising nonperforming loans exhaust banks' capital, (b) asset prices collapse on the heels of run-ups before the crisis, (c) real interest rates are sharply raised, and (d) there is a large reversal or slowdown in capital flows.

11. The concordance indexes reported in figure 11.2 measure the proportion of time that two series share the same cyclical phase (that is, it measures the strength of the contemporaneous comovement). However, they do not provide information on whether financial cycles tend to precede real cycles. An event study analysis was used to evaluate statistical precedence.

12. Whether peaks in real credit or asset prices precede peaks in real output are detected based on regressions of (year-on-year) growth in credit on a 17-quarter window centered on the peak in real GDP (T). The period from $T-8$ to T represents the run-up to the downturn in real economic activity. On average, the period from T to $T+4$ may capture the downturn in real output whereas that after $T+4$ may capture the start of the recovery period. Figure 11.3 plots the estimated coefficients of these regressions.

13. An analogous regression analysis is conducted just as the one described above but with T representing the peak in real credit per capita.

14. Chapter 6 provides estimates of the long-run costs of crises in terms of financial disintermediation. As regards the fiscal cost of resolving banking crises, the estimate provided for LAC by Laeven and Valencia (2008) is an average of 16 percent of GDP.

15. Similar results are found by Barajas, Dell'Ariccia, and Levchenko (2009).

16. Similar results are found by Schularick and Taylor (2009) and Jorda, Schularick, and Taylor (2010).

17. The arguably *structural* improvement in LAC's macrofinancial policy frameworks over the past decades has been amply discussed in policy and academic circles, particularly in view of LAC's strong performance during the recent global crisis. See, for example, de la Torre et al. (2010a, 2010b, 2011).

18. More detailed and recently updated accounts of LAC's macrofinancial risks and vulnerabilities can be found in regional reports by the multilateral institutions and think tanks. See, for instance, Eyzaguirre et al. (2011), de La Torre et al. (2011), Izquierdo and Talvi (2011), and Cardenas and Levy-Yeyati (2011).

19. This leaves open the question, however, as to whether it is socially desirable to moderate cycles even when they do not end up in crashes. This question probably has two answers. First, from an ex ante perspective, what matters is to contain the risk of an eventual crash down the road. If one cannot a priori tell which cycles will end badly, then all cycles should call for a precautionary response, which puts more weight on the downside. Second, financial cycles may have social costs (for example, an over- or under-extension of credit) even when they do not threaten financial stability.

20. See Goodhart (2010b) and Hellwig (2010).

21. See Gordy and Howells (2006); Repullo and Suárez (2009); and Repullo, Saurina, and Trucharte (2010).

22. See Kashyap and Stein (2004); Hanson, Kashyap, and Stein (2010); Shleifer and Vishny (2011), Brunnermeier et al. (2009), and Goodhart (2011).

23. Countercyclical provisioning schemes have been introduced under various forms in Bolivia, Colombia, Peru, and Uruguay. The systems vary considerably in terms of design. See Fernández de Lis and García-Herrero (2010) for a comparative analysis of the cases of Colombia and Peru. Wezel (2010) provides a detailed description of the Uruguayan system. Galindo and Rojas-Suarez (2011) and Terrier et al. (2011) offer broad overviews of these systems.

24. See Saurina (2011).

25. See Goodhart (2010a).

26. See Brunnermeier et al. (2009) and Shin and Shin (2011).

27. Compared to (interest earning) liquidity requirements, reserve requirements are an inefficient prudential way to buffer banks' balance sheets against liquidity shocks. Reserve requirements can also be used as a monetary policy instrument (to mop up money supply), although less efficiently than open market operations. Reserve requirements can more rightfully claim to be a macroprudential tool when their monetary impact is fully offset by open market operations. Even then, however, it is often not clear if the countercyclical use of the reserve requirements reflects macroprudential concerns or is rather a cheaper way of

financing the accumulation of international reserves resulting from foreign exchange intervention. In this latter case, reserve requirements can be seen as an attempt by the monetary authorities to defeat the "impossible trinity"— that is, to pursue an independent monetary policy, along with exchange rate targets, in a context of open capital accounts. On this latter point, see Montoro and Moreno (2011).

28. If market financing or central bank loans are not perfect substitutes for deposit financing, the introduction of reserve requirements can also reduce the supply of loans by subjecting banks to liquidity and interest rate risk. Vargas et al. (2010) claim some empirical support for this mechanism in the case of Colombia.

29. Montoro and Tovar (2010) present a general equilibrium model in which reserve requirements help stabilize the business cycle in the face of demand shocks but not supply shocks. The Peruvian authorities report that a 1 percentage point increase in reserve requirements affects the output gap as much as a 25 basis points increase in interest rates. In Brazil, Carvalho and Azevedo (2008) find that reserve requirements affected banks' shareholders by affecting bank profits.

30. See Drehmann et al. (2010).

31. For example, using data for industrial countries, Repullo and Saurina (2011) find that the credit-to-GDP ratio often behaves countercyclically, and that in some countries it lags the cycle rather than leading it. Also, as noted by Goodhart (2011), it is not clear if the empirical regularities that favor one trigger over another would survive once regulation is allowed to change over the cycle, as this might induce behavioral changes on the part of financial intermediaries.

32. See for example Goodhart and Persaud (2008) and Drehmann et al. (2010).

33. See Borio, Furfine, and Lowe (2001).

34. Two examples are Hong Kong SAR, China, and, more recently, China.

35. These adjustments have sometimes been accompanied by other ad hoc measures, such as increases in risk weights applied to property lending for the calculation of regulatory capital (a step taken, for example, in India in 2005), as well as by direct controls such as credit ceilings, actively employed in some countries (notably China) to restrict bank lending to housing.

36. Thus, the Republic of Korea has seen a sharp reversal in its housing market following a recent tightening in LTV policy.

37. See Park (2011).

38. Weitzman (1974) provides an early version of this argument, which has been recently applied to the case of prudential regulation by Haldane (2010b), among others. The relative merits of prices versus quantities for the case of liquidity norms have been recently analyzed by Perotti and Suárez (2011).

39. See Viñals (2011).

40. The term was coined by Borio and Zhu (2008). It was more recently analyzed by Adrian and Shin (2011).

41. See Jiménez et al. (2008) for the case of Spain; Ioannidou, Ongena, and Peydró (2009) for Bolivia; and Delis and Kouretas (2011) for the euro zone.

42. See Bernanke and Gertler (1995) and Svensson (2010).

43. See Bordo and Jeanne (2002a, 2002b), Christiano et al. (2010), and Woodford (2011) for a dissenting view.

44. See for example Mishkin (2011) and Claessens et al. (2010).

45. The empirical evidence shows that this stance helped reduce considerably the real cost of the crash. See Didier, Hevia, and Schmukler (2011) and Corbo and Schmidt-Hebbel (2010).

46. See Debrun and Kapoor (2010) and Claessens et al. (2010).

47. The literature in this respect is in full bloom and includes models that connect Pigouvian taxation to credit booms (Jeanne and Korinek 2011), maturity mismatches (Perotti and Suárez 2011) or noncore liabilities (Shin and Shin 2011). Angeletos, Lorenzoni, and Pavan (2010) develop a model of asset price booms under information externalities in which procyclical asset taxes can improve welfare by narrowing the gap between market-determined prices of assets and their fundamental values.

48. See Hellwig (2010) and Goodhart (2011).

49. Capital controls may also be of use when capital inflows bypass regulated financial institutions and directly accrue to the nonfinancial private sector, thereby indirectly putting the local financial system at risk.

50. See Demirgüç-Kunt and Servén (2010) and Ostry et al. (2011) for references.

51. Calvo, Izquierdo, and Talvi (2003) find empirical evidence supporting the hypothesis that liability dollarization raises vulnerability to sudden stops and reversals in capital flows.

Microsystemic Regulation | 12

The previous chapter dealt with the dynamic dimensions of systemic oversight—that is, how to control the evolution of the system through time. This chapter focuses on the cross-sectional dimension of systemic oversight—that is, how to use microsystemic policies to address the spillovers and externalities inflicted by individual agents and institutions on the rest of the system—as that dimension relates to Latin America and the Caribbean (LAC).[1] The chapter first looks into the issue of how far the (prudential) regulatory net should extend and how uniform it should be. It then explores three key facets of cross-sectional systemic regulation, namely, systemically important financial institutions (SIFIs), systemic liquidity, and financial innovation. Key highlights of the chapter are as follows:

- While LAC's current approach of pushing the outside perimeter of prudential regulation as far away as possible has served the region well thus far, it is likely to face increasing challenges (including high demands on the already stretched human and financial resources of regulatory agencies) as financial systems mature.
- Thus, carefully designed policies that reduce the oversight load—possibly by delegating the oversight of the unregulated to the regulated or to auxiliary institutions—might become desirable in the future.
- LAC's current silo-based approach to setting the regulatory perimeter—where regulation is linked to the license, that is, to the type of institution, such as commercial banking, insurance, investment banking, or asset management—which also has served the region well thus far, will also need some revisions to limit regulatory arbitrage as well as to achieve better economies of scope.
- At the same time, the oversight of financial conglomerates—an inherent challenge for silo-based regulation—will need to be strengthened considerably, both across domestic silos and across borders.
- These improvements will need to be matched with the establishment of effective frameworks to deal with the failure of financial conglomerates and individual SIFIs.
- As with other regions around the world, the region will need to review its strictly prudential liquidity norms—many of which are currently set from a purely idiosyncratic (maturity mismatch) perspective—to make them consistent with a systemic perspective.

- The region will need to revamp its liquidity regulations to include a more systemic perspective and review its systemic liquidity access policies to better meet the challenges of the future. This aim will most likely require a revision of the criteria for access to the central bank liquidity facilities, as well as of the terms.
- Finally, while the region's current hands-on approach to the regulation of financial innovation has also served it well thus far, that approach may need to be revisited to allow the forces of innovation to more fully join the bright side of financial development.

The rest of this chapter is organized as follows. The first section briefly reviews the rationale for regulation and the flaws of the approach that prevailed prior to the global financial crisis. The second and third sections discuss the outer and inner boundaries of regulation, respectively. The next three sections discuss the regulation of SIFIs, systemic liquidity, and innovation, respectively. The final section concludes.

The rationale for prudential regulation

The case for financial sector regulation can be readily connected to the finance paradigms depicted in chapter 2. The "asymmetric information" paradigm justifies the need for prudential regulation aimed at protecting the uniformed (or unsophisticated).[2] Collective action failures (the collective action paradigm) justify the need for prudential regulation aimed at protecting the interests of the community (or, equivalently, of the financial system taken as a whole). Public policy can take two forms, one aimed at facilitating financial participation (inclusion along the intensive and extensive margins) through uniform rules of transparency and disclosure (a public good), and the other aimed at internalizing spillovers and externalities inflicted by individual participants on the system. The former underlies what is generally known as "market

conduct" regulation; the latter underlies the bulk of prudential regulation, a distinction on which the "twin peak" approach to regulation is typically based.[3] Market conduct regulation focuses on market integrity and consumer or investor protection issues and comes primarily in the form of disclosure requirements, accounting standards, conduct-of-business rules (including anti-money-laundering regulation), and governance and fiduciary responsibilities. Prudential regulation, by contrast, focuses on the safety and soundness of individual financial institutions and the stability of the financial system.

To the first two justifications for prudential regulation—asymmetric information and collective action—one must add the possible need for regulation aimed at addressing potential market failures under the collective cognition paradigm or curbing market power (a potential fifth finance paradigm). The former may justify the (arguably polemical) regulation of financial innovation.[4] The latter can justify the regulation of anticompetitive behavior. Traditionally, competition-oriented regulation was not seen as connected to, or as a part of, prudential regulation. Indeed, less competition was generally viewed by prudential regulators as promoting financial stability, rather than undermining it. However, the global crisis has brought a new twist to this debate, in the form of the possible need to regulate SIFIs differently. Hence, in addition to the traditional antitrust policy goals of curbing market power, excess pricing, and monopoly rents, a prudential regulation rationale emerges—to control the negative spillover effects and moral hazard associated with broad interconnectedness and the too-big-to-fail (TBTF) syndrome.

The benefits of regulation need to be balanced with its costs, however. Besides the cost of official oversight itself, there is the opportunity cost of the financial activity that may not take place because of regulation, the distortions of regulatory arbitrage, and the risk that official oversight may be perceived as a seal of approval promoting moral hazard and leading to the socialization of risks.

These costs of regulation have traditionally led to drawing a line in the sand, a regulatory perimeter that separates the fully regulated deposit-taking banks from the unregulated (or lightly regulated) other financial entities (including investment banks). This line-in-the-sand approach rested on two premises that have been deeply questioned by the recent subprime crisis: first, that the well-informed investors would exert effective market discipline on the market-funded financial institutions, and second, that buffering and ring-fencing of the deposit-taking institutions through prudential oversight would protect the "core" from systemic risk.

Consistent with this traditional line-in-the-sand approach, there was a general trend toward less intrusive supervision or outright deregulation (at least the absence of new regulation) for the unregulated financial entities, instruments, and markets that were rapidly growing at the outer edges of the commercial banking core. However, as the subprime-induced global financial crisis amply demonstrated, this approach was frankly inconsistent with the control of systemic risk (de la Torre and Ize 2010). The line in the sand promoted massive regulatory arbitrage, as differential returns encouraged investors (informed or not) to leave the world of the regulated and join that of less regulated, highly leveraged, and short-term-funded intermediaries where systemic risk was totally uninternalized. The exponential growth of shadow banking and rapidly rising interconnectedness of financial entities, regulated or not, spread systemic risk, putting in place the conditions for the global crisis.

While these developments were especially evident in the United States, the underlying issues are universal. For example, in LAC they came to light in full bloom in the case of the Mexican Sofoles (box 12.1). At the same time, as noted in chapter 3, LAC's financial deepening is taking place to an extent outside the domain of deposit-taking institutions. While much of this expansion thus far appears to have accompanied a gradual broadening of the demand for financial services, as opposed to regulatory arbitrage,

boundary effects are nonetheless already apparent. They are expected to become gradually more intense as financial systems continue to evolve. Hence, the question of where to set the outer boundary of prudential regulation applies to LAC as much as to other regions of the world.

The outer boundaries: Illuminating the shadows

There are many options as to where to set the perimeter of prudential regulation. Some of these, ranked by descending order of comprehensiveness, include regulating (a) all leveraged financial intermediaries (except the very small); (b) all leveraged financial intermediaries except those that borrow only from regulated institutions; and (c) all commercial banks plus any other leveraged financial intermediary that is considered to be a SIFI.[5] The third option is the one implicitly embedded in the U.S. financial reform law (box 12.2). It would involve setting the severity of regulation and intensity of supervision based on an assessment of the risk that a particular institution poses to overall financial stability. To limit exacerbating regulatory arbitrage (the so-called boundary effects), the norms could in principle be based on a continuous risk scalar that avoids any major jump at the border between the SIFIs and the other institutions. However, implementing such a smooth transition is likely to be quite difficult in practice, because openly naming some institutions SIFIs gives rise anyway to an abrupt border line, with institutions on one side of the border (the SIFIs) implicitly benefitting from a publicly recognized TBTF advantage. While one could try to eliminate this advantage by imposing a prudential surcharge for crossing the border (that is, for becoming a SIFI), getting it right could be devilishly hard. The problem may be compounded by the fact that this is a dynamically evolving problem and that moving institutions across borders is bound to have important, possibly destabilizing, signaling effects. Hence, there is a risk that the two groups—SIFIs and

BOX 12.1   The Mexican Sofoles

The Sofoles (Sociedades Financieras de Objeto Limitado) are limited-purpose, non-deposit-taking institutions with activities in a variety of sectors, including mortgages (and the associated financing of construction), consumer and small and medium enterprise (SME) lending, microcredits, and loans to the agriculture and education sectors. In some sectors (particularly mortgages), a large part of their funding is through public development banks. In others (such as the automotive sector), their financing is fully private. The Sofoles were created in the context of the North American Free Trade Agreement (NAFTA) to allow the similarly unregulated U.S. finance institutions to operate freely in Mexico. They grew rapidly after the 1995 Tequila crisis, when banks stopped lending altogether, reflecting public development policies as well as the banks' capacity to rapidly detect and exploit profitable market niches thanks to a close-to-the-field, savvy approach to lending. The Mexican banking law established that the Secretaría de Hacienda y Crédito Publico (SHCP) was in charge of authorizing and regulating the Sofoles. And while the charter of the Comisión Nacional Bancaria y de Valores (CNBV) included them within the list of institutions under its oversight, there was a lack of clarity as to the exact mandate of the CNBV. The concerns about the discrepancy between Sofoles' de facto light regulation and the perception by the public that they were fully regulated and supervised eventually led to an explicit and complete prudential deregulation of the Sofomes (Sociedades Financieras de Objeto Múltiple), a newly created multipurpose and more flexible license meant to replace that of the Sofoles. The Sofomes were subject only to licensing requirements, not to prudential regulation.

However, the Sofomes were hard hit by the global financial crisis. Some of them had started to depend heavily on the issue of short-term commercial papers, with much of the proceeds invested in risky and illiquid real estate investments. Under the favorable assessments of local rating agencies, the papers were gobbled up by a variety of investors, local and foreign. However, the subprime crisis brought the system to an abrupt halt and triggered a run of Sofoles debt. A relatively large mortgage provider, Sofol (Hipotecaria Crédito y Casa SA) collapsed owing to soaring bad loans and mounting refinancing difficulties, while Metrofinanciera SA, a major lender to builders, restructured under prepackaged bankruptcy protection after defaulting. In turn, Sofoles' financing problems immobilized the commercial paper market. Further contagion was avoided thanks only to the timely intervention of Sociedad Hipotecaria Federal (SHF), the development bank that had initially nurtured the growth of the mortgage Sofoles. Once the market abruptly shut its doors, SHF brought the Sofomes back in its fold through emergency credit lines.

non-SIFIS—may become fossilized. If so, the scheme would effectively end up having some of the same flaws as the ill-fated, line-in-the-sand approach that led to the crisis.

An arguably preferable option would be to avoid making any open distinction between the SIFIs and the other institutions and to go for an ample perimeter, that is, choose option a, to regulate all leveraged financial intermediaries (except, perhaps, for the very small). While a boundary effect always exists, under option a, it would be simply illegal to set up leveraged financial intermediation activities without a license and being subject to prudential oversight. Although the intensity of oversight (including the severity of regulation) could (and probably should) vary depending on the systemic importance of each institution, these variations would be strictly formula based and apply across the whole population of institutions within the perimeter, without any a priori distinction. However, a major drawback of this approach is that ensuring that even the small institutions are effectively supervised puts a very high burden on official oversight, thereby raising the cost of supervision across the board. Supervisors may soon realize that, though all leveraged intermediaries are made subject to prudential oversight by force of law, there may not

---

BOX 12.2   Reforming the regulatory perimeter: United States versus the European Union

Under the Dodd-Frank Act, the newly created Financial Stability Oversight Council (FSOC) responsible for macroprudential surveillance is entrusted with discretionary powers to submit non-commercial bank financial companies to supervision by the U.S. Federal Reserve (that is, to become a SIFI) if the council assesses that the bank's failure or its activities pose a serious risk for financial stability. The council may require any bank or nonbank financial institution with assets over US$50 billion to submit certified reports as to the company's financial condition, risk management systems, and transactions with subsidiaries that are regulated banks, plus the extent to which any of the company's activities could have a potential disruptive effect on financial markets or the overall financial stability of the country. To strengthen supervision of holding company subsidiaries, the Federal Reserve is authorized to examine nonbank subsidiaries that are engaged in banking activities. The proposals also aim to fill regulatory gaps by requiring that hedge funds and private equity advisers register with the Securities and Exchange Commission (SEC), and providing the SEC and Commodity Futures Trading Commission with regulatory powers on over-the-counter derivatives. At the same time, Title II of the Dodd-Frank Act empowers the Federal Deposit Insurance Corporation with an orderly liquidation authority for noncommercial bank SIFIs, aimed at reducing the TBTF moral hazard associated with them.

By contrast, the redefinition of the regulatory perimeter has received comparatively little attention in Europe, probably reflecting in large part its predominant universal banking model, which has limited regulatory arbitrage and the concomitant growth of shadow banking (nonetheless, regulatory arbitrage also occurred through the buildup of off-balance-sheet exposures with less stringent prudential requirements). Instead, efforts are currently concentrated on adding a supranational layer to existing supervisory arrangements, as exemplified in the creation of a European Systemic Risk Board responsible for the monitoring, identification, and prioritization of systemic risk. At the same time, the reform proposals aim at developing a single set of fully harmonized rules across Europe, thereby limiting cross-border regulatory arbitrage.

---

be enough human and financial resources to perform that job adequately across the entire universe of leveraged intermediaries (commercial banks, investment banks, insurance companies, cooperatives, credit unions, and so forth). Supervision on the cheap, moreover, can easily backfire, leading to a false sense of security and moral hazard among depositors and investors.

Option b would address in large part this latter problem. Like option a, option b would prudentially regulate the institutions that borrow from the public or in the market.[6] Unlike option a, however, it would *not* regulate the financial intermediaries that borrow only from the regulated ones. Thus, option b would reduce the cost of supervision (both the oversight cost and moral hazard cost) by effectively creating a two-tiered structure.

Because the regulated institutions would be subjected to full prudential oversight, including a possible systemic surcharge, they would pass on (through their lending rate) this surcharge to the unregulated institutions that borrow from them. At the same time, the supervisor could adjust the intensity of oversight (and the prudential surcharges) of the regulated intermediaries, taking into full account the risks that regulated institutions would be assuming in their lending to the unregulated. In this way, the regulator would effectively delegate the oversight of the unregulated to their regulated creditors, in a typical principal-agent relationship. This scheme would avoid regulatory arbitrage *and* limit the cost of oversight. At the same time, by opening the field to the new, smaller (prudentially unregulated) entrants, it would enhance competition and promote innovation in niche markets. Thus the small, unregulated intermediaries could develop on the fringes of the larger, regulated intermediaries. When successful, they could become fully regulated or be purchased by regulated intermediaries, much as happened in Mexico with the most successful Sofoles.

This approach would be somewhat similar to the manner in which the oversight of hedge funds was structured after the Long-Term Capital Management failure, with prime brokers exercising control of hedge funds through appropriate counterparty risk management, and regulators concentrating on the close supervision of the prime brokers. It may be argued that this approach failed to prevent hedge funds from building up highly leveraged positions, with the subsequent increase in systemic risk once the funds sold their positions. The counterargument is that—provided the hedge funds were subject to minimum transparency (auditing) requirements—the regulators could have raised the risk weights of the loans by the regulated intermediaries to the hedge funds, based on the leverage and systemic implications of the latter. The failure of oversight, if there was one, was not a failure of the scheme under which the agent was operating but one of misunderstanding as to what systemic risk was all about.

Except for the finance companies, which are unregulated in several countries (for example, El Salvador, Mexico, Peru, and Panama), financial regulation in LAC has thus far basically followed option a. Most supervisors have cast their net very broadly, while making efforts (often not very successful) to apply regulations uniformly within the perimeter. This approach has thus far functioned relatively well inasmuch as it has limited regulatory arbitrage at the edges of the perimeter. However, it has not fully eliminated arbitrage, neither inside the perimeter (see below) nor at the outer edge.[7] Indeed, even when all leveraged financial institutions are prudentially regulated, boundary effects (hence regulatory arbitrage opportunities) at the outer edge of the regulatory perimeter can take the form of outright illegal financial activities or financial activities conducted by nonfinancial entities that do not neatly fall under the definition of "intermediation" established in the financial legislation. Indeed, illegal intermediation has happened recently, for example, in Colombia, one of the LAC countries with the widest regulatory perimeter, as some illegal pyramid schemes mushroomed and eventually collapsed. The case of intermediation by nonfinancial companies seems to be spreading fast in LAC countries, especially through department stores that provide consumer loans, typically via credit cards, and fund them by, say, issuing commercial paper. In the case of Chile, for instance, regulatory perimeter issues have been recently brought to the forefront as a result of an alleged fraud, where a (prudentially unregulated) nonfinancial company that issued credit cards was automatically (and without the consent of the debtor) rolling over the nonperforming credit card debt to avoid raising loan-loss provisions.

Perimeter issues in LAC are likely to become increasingly complex and difficult to control as financial systems mature. Many countries in LAC already have an unresolved problem of how to adequately oversee the numerous smaller institutions, such as credit co-ops and microfinance institutions, where prudential oversight is required by law. In view of capacity and resource constraints, the challenges of expanding regulation into the outer edges of the system are daunting. In many LAC countries, full uniform oversight would add hundreds of institutions to the load carried out by supervisors. Resource considerations have already led a number of LAC countries to set up auxiliary models wherein regulatory responsibilities are delegated to nonsupervisory agencies, including industry associations.[8] While these and other models of auxiliary supervision usually entail incentives for these entities to cooperate with their regulators, the risk of a lack of regulatory independence and effectiveness looms large.[9] Restricted legal mandates and capacity to exert supervisory discretion are further complicating factors. A possible alternative to such a model, more along the lines of the two-tiered regulatory scheme suggested above, could be to allow the small credit co-ops to remain prudentially unregulated as long as they only fund themselves with their members under a clearly mutualized loss-sharing arrangement that makes them rather similar to mutual funds.

Another complicating factor is that only a few LAC countries are endowed with the statutory discretion to extend the perimeter as needed, particularly to any financial entity whose possible failure could threaten financial stability. In most countries (Uruguay being the only exception in the region), this prevents the authorities from flexibly redrawing the "line in the sand" in the face of a rapidly changing financial landscape. Even if laws were to be amended, empowering regulators to extend the perimeter as needed, in doing so the regulator may be confronted with powerful pressures.[10]

Last but not least, systemic risk may also emerge outside the financial sector. This may happen when the failures of large nonfinancial entities affect the financial intermediaries that lent to them or undermine the markets in which they (or their borrowers) operate.[11] Of course, if extending the perimeter to all financial institutions is already challenging enough, extending it to nonfinancial corporations is outright unfeasible. This can be viewed as further pushing the case in favor of an option b solution, in which supervisors engage in some form of delegated supervision. Through adjustments of risk weights, supervisors can induce the regulated institutions to internalize the risks they are taking (and contributing to spread to the rest of the system) by lending to borrowers (including the large, unregulated corporations) that engage in socially risky activities.[12]

The inner boundaries: Silos versus universal licensing

The global crisis also highlighted regulatory arbitrage within the perimeter, including between investment and commercial banking books, between on- and off-balance sheets, and across licenses (particularly between banking and insurance). The

importance of differential regulation for similar financial activities performed under different licenses has been well recognized by standard setters and supervisors, including in LAC.[13] The failure of the Caribbean CL group, where the line between insurance and banking-type operations became blurred, provides a particularly vivid illustration of the potential severity of these problems (annex 12.A). However, the pace of reform (in LAC as much as in the rest of the world) has thus far been slow, in part reflecting the complex trade-offs involved. There are two basic issues. First, although a functional focus—whereby the same risk-based regulation is applied based on the type of financial activity and across all leveraged financial intermediaries—may be ideal in principle, it can be difficult to implement in practice. Second, even when the same regulatory framework applies across the board, the question remains as to whether the same institution should be allowed to conduct all financial activities or whether the latter should be compartmentalized across separate silos.

As regards risk-based regulation, the calculation of value at risk (that is, the amount of capital that the firm needs to ensure its solvency with a certain probability over a certain period) should in principle be identical across licenses. Basel II provides a general model to follow, and the insurance regulation in the European Union is already moving in that direction, although implementation has proved to be technically demanding and data intensive. In the region, very few countries have implemented Basel II in full, and only Chile thus far is in the process of introducing a risk-sensitive solvency capital requirement for insurance companies.

As regards universal licensing versus silos, the debate is more conceptual than technical. The proponents of universal licensing argue that it not only eliminates the "inner" regulatory arbitrage (that is, the arbitrage between differently regulated activities) but also improves efficiency by allowing universal intermediaries (that combine credit, investment, securities, and insurance) to fully diversify their risk and exploit economies of scale and scope. This has benefits at the micro level (intermediaries can better hedge and diversify their exposures) as well as at the systemic level (participation costs are reduced and risk is more efficiently allocated across the population).[14] However, following the global crisis, an alternative view has emerged in favor of silos.[15] The argument is that universal licensing can result in a loss of institutional diversity, as all institutions end up behaving similarly and accumulating the same risks. Instead of limiting the exposure of individual institutions through diversification, such uniformity increases systemic risk (if one institution goes, everybody goes). It is also argued that economies of scale taper off past US$100 billion in assets, a size well below that of the larger international banks (Haldane 2009a). Moreover, the diseconomies of resolving the failure of large institutions tend to offset the economies of scale that they may achieve in their operations. Others have advocated a silo-type public utility approach that ring-fences retail banking from the rest of a financial conglomerate when the latter fails.[16]

Overall, this debate is far from being settled. As discussed in chapter 2, one may take the view that the more a financial system matures, the more interconnected it is likely to become, independent of the financial structure the regulator seeks to impose. At the same time, the financial structure itself is likely to evolve endogenously, irrespective of the regulation. As amply demonstrated by the global financial crisis, investors will leave in troves the presumed islands of safety to migrate where the returns (hence the risks) are located. Hence, systemic problems are likely to arise no matter what. At the same time, the more barriers one builds, the more opportunities one provides for regulatory arbitrage. Thus, a silo approach may provide some measure of systemic safety in the shorter run, but also create a false sense of comfort leading to an ultimately less-safe system. Instead, an approach that removes artificial barriers altogether but internalizes systemic risks uniformly through microsystemic regulation is

probably more challenging in the short run but may also have better chances of long-term success.

In LAC, the prevailing silo-based regulatory culture appears thus far to have served the region relatively well, particularly as it has been paired with a generally more hands-on and prescriptive approach to regulation. However, as financial systems mature, the approach is showing increasing strains. In some cases, it has led to artificial barriers between activities or to possible duplications, with the same activity being conducted under different regulations in different silos—as is the case, for instance, for deposit-like instruments issued by insurance companies. More generally, it has promoted the growth of large and complex conglomerates. On the bright side, these conglomerates can be viewed as a desirable hybrid between silos and universal banks that allows for effective economies of scope and scale (the conglomerates can—and increasingly do—operate as integrated institutions that share information systems and central services), as well as risk diversification at the conglomerate level. Moreover, by altering the regulatory limits on cross-silo claims and liabilities, the supervisor can in principle control the extent of risk exposure and diversification even at the level of the individual silos. On the darker side, however, the conglomerates are difficult to effectively regulate and supervise, even more so as the scope for interconnectedness increases, the identification of related parties becomes more complicated, and reputational effects provide new avenues for contagion.

The region's weaknesses in consolidated regulation identified in chapter 10, particularly the lack of comprehensive supervisory powers to conduct consolidated regulation and supervision, compound this problem. Most countries do not require conglomerates to formally establish themselves as a financial holding company (FHC), and even when they do, many countries lack the power to impose capital requirements on the FHC.[17] FHCs can often be created abroad and fall under foreign (rather than domestic) supervision, which exacerbates the cross-border supervisory coordination weaknesses also identified in chapter 10. These gaps leave open the possibility of multiple gearing (capital insufficiency disguised by the use of the same capital by more than one of the members of the conglomerate or by a member and the holding), a problem that is exacerbated when the conglomerate includes unregulated financial entities domiciled abroad. In these cases, judging the adequacy of capital commensurate with the risks being borne by the group as a whole is a difficult undertaking and an important source of systemic risk, given the interconnectedness and size of some of these financial groups.

In parallel with these inner perimeter issues, there are also lively discussions across the region on what the most appropriate supervisory architecture is. The two constructs are of course not independent. A universal license can be naturally paired with a single supervisor. Multiple supervisors (each administering a different license) naturally go together with a silo-based system. But different institutional arrangements can be found to address the challenges posed by cross-license regulatory arbitrage and the control of financial conglomerates, from line supervisors with explicit coordinating mechanisms (such as Chile), to unified supervision under a single agency different from the central bank (such as Colombia), and unified supervision housed within the central bank (such as Uruguay). While all alternatives have pros and cons, a single supervisor should in principle have some natural advantages in unifying the prudential treatment across different business lines, regardless of whether the business lines stem from the same or separate licenses. Ultimately, however, different organizational architectures can all work, provided there are effective coordination arrangements.

The SIFI problem

The SIFI problem looms large in LAC. In addition to the presence of large and complex financial conglomerates, many institutions can on their own be considered SIFIs. The single largest bank in Argentina,

Brazil, Chile, Colombia, and Mexico each holds about 20 percent of total banking sector assets (and 30 percent in Peru). Thus, if one defines as a SIFI any institution holding more that 10 percent of banking sector assets, LAC countries have the second highest number of SIFIs in the emerging world (figure 12.1).[18]

There is a consensus on the need to adjust the regulation of SIFIs to take into account the contribution that these institutions pose to systemic risk, including as regards the TBTF syndrome.[19] However, as already noted, calculating ex ante the systemic risk contribution of each SIFI is quite a challenging exercise, even more so when the markets for the equity and debt securities issued by the SIFIs are relatively underdeveloped and illiquid, as is the case for most LAC countries.

Moreover, larger buffers are unlikely to totally eliminate risks of default and the associated TBTF problem. Restricting the size of institutions (a solution envisaged by some) could hamper efficiency and is politically difficult, all the more so when the institutions are foreign owned. Even if financial institutions' internal growth were not limited in LAC, external growth could be limited by prohibiting mergers and acquisitions among the large institutions.[20] However, exceptional mergers and acquisitions would probably be needed to preserve financial stability in times of severe systemic distress, which further underlines the complexities and inherent tensions associated with this issue.

Thus, as in the rest of the world, the best defense against TBTF is probably to put in place suitable legal and procedural arrangements to resolve in a non-destabilizing manner the failure of SIFIs. Following the financial crises of the 1990s and early 2000s, bank resolution frameworks in many LAC countries were reformed.[21] To be sure, several of these frameworks remain untested, and implementation remains an issue since the reforms have mostly focused more on the legal than on the operational aspects.[22] Even where suitable bank failure resolution frameworks exist, however, arrangements to resolve the failure of financial conglomerates

FIGURE 12.1   **Average number of banks with more than 10 percent of total banking assets, 2006–09**

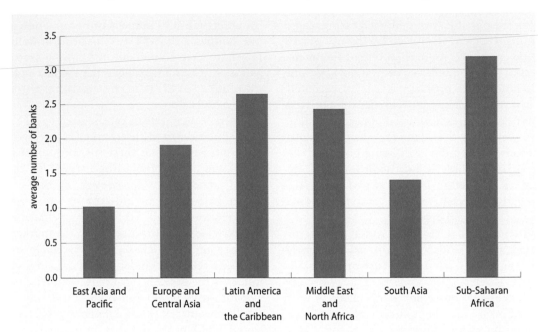

Source: Cortes, Dijkman, and Gutierrez 2011.

are generally not in place throughout LAC. In effect, in most of LAC, the resolution of financial institutions other than banks is still subject to the general bankruptcy code.

As in the rest of the world, LAC will need to introduce legal reforms that grant authorities the necessary powers to conduct an orderly resolution of large, complex financial conglomerates and nonbank SIFIs.[23] The use of contingent capital and bail-in debt as well as statutory bail-ins may also be appropriate.[24] Another tool that could be attractive for many LAC countries is the constitution of prefunded resolution funds with charge-to-bank levies.[25] "Living wills" can also play a useful role, though they can hardly be considered an alternative to integral resolution reform.

The resolution of complex financial conglomerates poses certain technical, legal, and political challenges specific to LAC. For starters, the civil law does not make things easy, as the room for flexibility in the resolution process tends to be curtailed by administrative

law. Then, being able to treat a group as a group "in death" requires being able to also treat it as a group in life. Thus, supervisors need to have the powers to conduct effective consolidated supervision and regulation, which, as already noted, is a substantial challenge in the region. Finally, the resolution of cross-border financial conglomerates will require enhanced cross-border harmonization of procedures. The fact that regional and global conglomerates usually operate in LAC through cross-border subsidiaries (rather than branches) should facilitate the task. Nevertheless, the lack of harmonized failure-resolution procedures and of burden-sharing agreements could prompt local authorities to block flows among group entities in order to ring-fence assets. As illustrated by the failure of CL Financial (annex 12.A), this issue looms particularly large in the Central America and Caribbean subregions. Difficult as it would be to set up, a prefunded resolution fund in these subregions would help, but regional coordination would be needed to avoid distortions and double taxation in setting such a fund.

Systemic liquidity: Norms and access

As demonstrated by the global financial crisis, the growing interconnectedness of financial institutions and markets as financial systems mature is increasingly likely to give rise to systemic liquidity disruptions. The latter can affect both funding liquidity (the ability to raise cash through borrowing or selling of assets) and market liquidity (the ability to trade an asset at short notice without affecting its price; see Adrian and Shin 2010; Brunnermeier and Pedersen 2009). As noted in the chapter 11, the liquidation of financial assets at fire sale prices under funding liquidity constraints is a major channel of amplification of systemic shocks in downturns. But interdependencies may also build up at the interface between financial institutions and financial markets and infrastructures.[26]

Not surprisingly, the reform of liquidity regulation has been the subject of lively discussions. It has become broadly accepted that the traditional prudential framework based on maturity mismatches—that allows intermediaries to borrow short if they lend equally short—is inadequate for systemic purposes.[27] Indeed, the new Basel III framework—which introduces a liquidity coverage ratio (LCR) and a net stable funding ratio (NSFR)—focuses instead on securing stable funding sources. And as regards the asset side, the framework differentiates between the truly systemically liquid assets and the other assets, including those that, while being short term, are not liquid in times of systemic stress.

Under current conditions, LAC banks should be able to meet these new liquidity requirements with relative ease, given the relatively modest share of nondeposit market funding and the relatively high share of public sector securities in their balance sheets. Moreover, LAC's previous experience with systemically oriented regulation—such as reserve or liquidity requirements on foreign currency deposits—should give its regulators

and central bankers a hedge in implementing a new framework for systemic liquidity. However, as systems mature and interbank markets continue to deepen, pressures toward holding higher-yield assets and exploiting market funding more fully will no doubt also continue to build up. In this context, the breadth of access to liquidity support facilities (lender of last resort, or LLR) is likely to become an increasingly key component of policy. The key questions in this regard are how far to extend the LLR perimeter in terms of institutions (that is, which institutions should have access in addition to banks) and instruments (that is, which instruments may be used as collateral, in addition to public securities). The systemic linkages increasingly taking place through funding markets also highlight the possible need for LLR facilities to support critically important markets, and not just individual liquidity-distressed financial institutions.

In LAC, the discussion on the scope of central bank liquidity support is particularly relevant but also particularly complex given the region's history. Reflecting the region's history of macroeconomic volatility and high inflation, most central banks operate under very restrictive LLR frameworks. Liquidity facilities are usually available only for a narrow range of financial intermediaries, chiefly deposit-taking banks, which constitute the backbone of LAC financial systems to date. Nonetheless, the increasing importance of nonbank financial intermediaries and broad funding markets described in chapter 3 will probably warrant a broader definition.[28] Collateral eligibility (which also tends to be on the conservative side, that is, typically restricted to public sector debt securities) and pricing arrangements (for example, deep haircuts and high margin calls) may also need to be reviewed. Understandably, many central banks in the region are reluctant to move toward more flexible arrangements out of concern for the possible impact on their hard-fought gains in credibility. Possible avenues to manage these inherent conflicts might include temporary relaxations of counterparty and collateral eligibility requirements under circumstances of systemic distress, the introduction of stronger analytical and governance LLR frameworks, and the creation of private liquidity pools and insurance arrangements.[29]

Financial innovation: Did LAC have it right?

As noted in chapter 2, financial innovation is an essential component of both the bright and dark sides of financial development. While it plays a fundamental role in expanding the quality and reach of financial services, the global financial crisis gave a disturbing glimpse of a world in which financial innovation could spin largely out of control.[30] The innovators did not care about the possible systemic perils of their creations (that is, the collective action paradigm at work), and much of the investing public did not understand the risks associated with them (that is, the collective cognition at work). To make matters worse, innovations were favorably sanctioned by the rating agencies and largely ignored by the regulators.

While one should thus think that regulation should have a potentially important role to play in controlling financial innovation, regulatory intervention faces the same cognitive problem that all investors face. Distinguishing between "good" and "bad" innovations is no trivial matter and depends in part on whether end users fully understand the risks associated with the innovations' use and, when they do not, whether they should be protected from their own mistakes. Faced with such uncertainties, regulators may be easily pulled in opposite, equally inappropriate directions, either rubber-stamping innovations under pressure from the industry, or putting a freeze on innovations under the pull of risk aversion.[31] Thus, the pitfalls associated with giving regulators the powers and mandate to regulate innovation may end up either contributing to moral hazard by sanctioning risky regulations or stifling financial development through excessive conservatism.

In LAC, most countries have followed thus far a relatively conservative approach to financial innovation whereby new financial products need to undergo regulatory preapproval before they become part of banks' permissible activities.[32] By and large, such a policy has resulted in regulators approving only plain vanilla products that they "understood" well. With the benefit of hindsight, one could say that this approach has worked relatively well, with banks and other financial institutions staying mostly clear of complex derivatives with a potentially high degree of toxicity. The extent to which such conservative behavior was induced by regulation or simply resulted from more limited market opportunities and/or more limited risk taking, or from a more traditional risk management culture among bankers, is not always clear, however.

Be that as it may, as financial systems mature, such a tight regulation of innovation (as noted above) is likely to show increasing strains. In this context, LAC regulators' limited independence might become more problematic, and regulators' need for staying ahead of industry practices might become increasingly taxing, given resource constraints. A more flexible approach that matches instruments to risk management needs and capacities across industry licenses is likely to be needed. Yet, doing this effectively without promoting regulatory arbitrage will not be an easy task. At the same time, and perhaps more important, it may be difficult to reconcile a tight control of innovation with the growing need for more sophisticated market instruments (such as credit swaps) that can help supervisors assess risk by putting a price on it (more on this in chapter 13). Hence, some system for "piloting" financial innovation before it is mainstreamed would be worth considering. Involving credible private sector representatives in the process of approving innovations would also help dampen the tendency of official regulators to be unduly risk averse.

All in all, a revision of LAC's approach to the regulation of financial innovation is probably an important but quite complex task lying ahead. There is little doubt that such a review will be required. However, unlike in other areas, there is perhaps less urgency here in changing what has so far worked relatively well. Hence, there should be enough time for well-pondered reforms.

The regulatory agenda ahead

Financial systems in LAC, aside from some Caribbean countries, have weathered the global financial crisis largely unscathed. The region's wide outer perimeter of prudential regulation; its closely circumscribed, silo-based inner regulatory perimeter; and its relatively hands-on approach to regulation (including that of financial innovation) have all contributed to this outcome, in part by keeping the emergence of a "shadow" banking system at bay. However, the few localized episodes of severe stress in the recent global crisis are probably early manifestations of a world yet to come, with ever-rising exposure to systemic risk through increasing interconnectedness and complexity. Already, the provision of financial services through conglomerates—a potential fulcrum for the buildup of systemic risk—is raising difficult issues in the inner perimeter. And the current policy of pushing the outer perimeter of regulation as far as the eye can see is likely to face increasing challenges. If one adds the difficulties of resolving SIFIs, managing systemic liquidity, and putting financial innovation to work on the bright—rather than dark—side, one gets a complex yet essential agenda for reform.

Tackling both micro- and macrosystemic risk calls for an eclectic approach that builds on ex ante prudential regulation as well as ex post safety net and resolution frameworks. As regards the perimeter of regulation, the region will need to find its own preferred road, building on its strengths but aware of the challenges posed by regulatory costs and the rising threat of finance in the shadows. On resolution issues, the region will need to address the current weaknesses as regards the bankruptcy framework for nonbank financial intermediaries. It will also need to face its demons in rethinking the financial system's safety net. It is simply not an option for central banks to let the problem pass. On financial innovation, a new balance between prudence and boldness will need to be found. Now is the time to push through the needed reforms, both to help deal more efficiently with the emerging challenges and to be better prepared to deal with an eventual fallout. The evolving international financial standards should provide a useful guide that is likely to be more evolutionary than revolutionary. However, countries will need to refine and adapt regulation and institutional setups to their particular circumstances.

Annex 12.A   Challenges posed by large, complex financial conglomerates: The case of CL Financial in the Caribbean

CL Financial is one of the largest conglomerates in the Caribbean, with interests in insurance, banking, energy, agriculture, and real estate, and operations in several countries (annex figure 12.A.1). The holding is incorporated in Trinidad and Tobago, with assets estimated at about 75 percent of the country's GDP in 2006. In recent years, life insurance subsidiaries expanded aggressively by selling deposit-like products to the public, promising a high rate of return, and invested the proceeds into U.S. real estate and other ventures whose values sharply declined during the global credit crisis.

As a result of the global credit crisis, CL Financial started experiencing liquidity pressures. Its investment bank subsidiary, CIB, faced a high level of withdrawal requests, and its insurance subsidiaries, Colonial Life Insurance Company (CLICO) and British American Trinidad (BAT), had trouble meeting statutory fund requirements. British American Insurance Company (BAICO) incorporated in the Bahamas and CLICO International Life incorporated in Barbados (CLICO Barbados) also entered into difficulties.

The collapse of CL Financial and its insurance subsidiaries represented a major challenge for the financial stability of the Eastern Caribbean Currency Union (ECCU; composed of Antigua and Barbuda, Dominica, Grenada, St. Kitts and Nevis, St. Lucia, and St. Vincent and the Grenadines). The exposure of ECCU policyholders and depositors to CLICO and BAICO is estimated at about 17 percent of ECCU GDP. The ECCU insurance and banking sectors are closely interconnected since (a) many financial institutions invested directly in annuity products from CLICO and BAICO, and (b) the companies provided insurance as collateral on banking assets such as mortgages.

In February 2009, Trinidad and Tobago authorities issued a rescue package to CL Financial. This included the provision of US$800 million (4 percent of GDP) to replenish CLICO's assets. CLICO and BAT were intervened and their management replaced. The new government that took office after the 2010 elections announced that the short-term investment business of CLICO would be separated from its traditional business, and the latter would merge with BAT. Insurance policies would be honored, backed by the statutory fund, but annuity and short-term investment holders would only be partially compensated. The plan was challenged by investors but upheld by the courts. A special fund was established for the credit unions.

The ECCU governments stressed that the collapse of CLICO and BAICO was a regional problem requiring a regional solution. In April 2009, the Caribbean Community (CARICOM) governments established a liquidity support fund for the policyholders of CLICO and BAICO to which Trinidad and Tobago contributed US$50 million. As of June 2009, BAICO was insolvent, with a deficit of US$287 million. BAICO was put under judicial management in September 2009, and the ECCU governments developed a resolution strategy in November 2009 to prevent the systemic consequences of liquidation. It is expected that BAICO will ultimately be liquidated and the annuity policyholders will be creditors in the estate. CLICO Barbados still operates independently. The governments of the ECCU resumed talks with the new government of Trinidad and Tobago to investigate how the country could support the resolution process further. Trinidad and Tobago has agreed to explore the creation of a CARICOM Fund with the support of the ECCU and Barbados to provide relief to policyholders of CLICO and BAICO.

FIGURE 12.A.1   CL Financial annual report, 2007

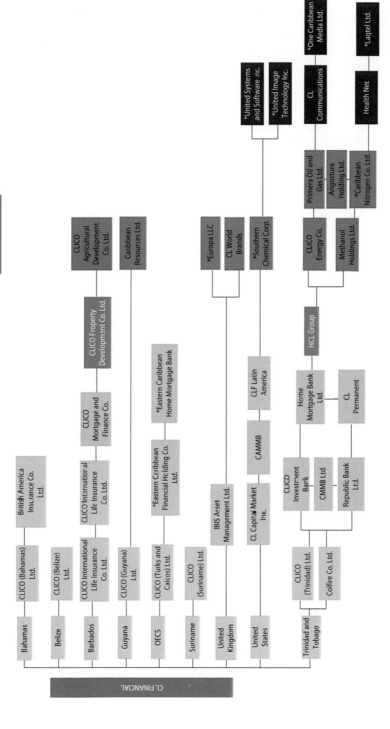

Source: CL Financial Annual Report 2007 (http://www.clfinancial.com)
Note: * = associate or joint venture company; OECS = Organisation of Eastern Caribbean States.

Notes

1. This chapter draws heavily on the paper "Micro-systemic Regulation: A LAC Perspective" by Mariano Cortes, Miquel Dijkman, and Eva Gutierrez (2011), which is part of the Edited Volume that accompanies this LAC Flagship Study.

2. In the words of Dewatripont and Tirole (1994), the state (the regulator) "represents" the interests of the small investor against those of the more informed (or more sophisticated) market participants who could be taking advantage of the little guys, eventually limiting their access to financial services.

3. On the "twin peak" approach to regulation see Taylor (1995, 2009).

4. Notice that the fourth paradigm, costly enforcement, does not justify prudential regulation. It does justify, however, the role of the state in facilitating contract enforcement (hence commitments) through improving the enabling environment, notably the collateral regime and the judiciary.

5. Any form of borrowing constitutes leverage in this definition, whether borrowing from retail depositors, from large depositors, from other financial institutions, or through the capital markets. Unleveraged institutions that engage in pure asset management, such as mutual funds, would be subject to market conduct regulation but not to prudential regulation.

6. Option b would require all leveraged financial intermediaries to have a license but, unlike in option a, not all would be prudentially regulated.

7. As revealed by the World Bank–ASBA survey, the global crisis appears to have heightened the awareness among LAC supervisors of the importance of regulatory arbitrage. Indeed, all the supervisory agencies that responded to the survey indicated that they are considering extending the perimeter to the hitherto unregulated, unsupervised intermediaries.

8. This model is especially popular for dealing with the cooperatives and small savings and loans, whose supervision is particularly labor-intensive given the small scale and geographical dispersion of the institutions (for example, El Salvador, Mexico, and Peru).

9. This is the case at present in Paraguay regarding the supervision of cooperatives—a systemically important segment of the financial system—where the board of the supervisory agency is selected by the industry. It is also the case of the *cajas* (savings and loan institutions) in Mexico, where oversight functions are delegated by the CNBV to the federations of *cajas*. By law, however, the CNBV retains ultimate responsibility for oversight of the *cajas* and its outcomes.

10. According to the results of the joint World Bank–ASBA survey, about 60 percent of respondents viewed limited legal mandates as hindering effective systemic oversight and the use of discretion; at the same time, 40 percent of respondents indicated that political and industry pressures were also an important hindrance in the use of discretion.

11. One such illustrative example is that of the difficulties encountered by Comercial Méxicana, a Mexican hypermarket group, which at the height of the financial crisis suffered sharp derivative losses in toxic foreign exchange (FX) derivatives. Its subsequent default in the autumn of 2008 contributed (together with the Sofoles) to the breakdown of the Mexican commercial paper market.

12. In any event, it is of course essential that supervisors carefully monitor (and assess the systemic implications of) the risks accumulating outside the financial sector.

13. For example, a capital charge on a credit risk held by a bank becomes a technical provision when transferred to an insurance company. See Joint Forum (2010). The World Bank–ASBA survey of LAC supervisors indicates that the perimeter issue that is perceived to be the most pressing is that of potential risk shifting between the entities of financial conglomerates, both cross-border and domestic.

14. Several high-income countries have continued to express a clear preference for universal licensing, even after the global crisis. Thus, the Hong Kong Monetary Authority continues "to see merit in the model of universal banking" (see Chan 2011). Similarly, while recognizing the need for stricter regulation of the largest banks because of their massive relative size, the Swiss Central Bank has recently noted the advantages of universal banking for diversifying and attracting high-net-worth individuals.

15. See, for example, Haldane (2009a) for the United Kingdom. Similar views in the United States have led to pressures toward fully reinstating the Glass-Steagall Act, eventually giving way to the "Volcker Rule," whereby "banking entities, which benefit from federal insurance on customer deposits or access to the discount

window, are prohibited from engaging in proprietary trading and from investing in or sponsoring hedge funds and private equity funds, subject to certain exceptions."

16. See, for example, Kay (2010). This is the approach proposed in the United Kingdom by the Independent Commission on Banking, the so-called Sir Vikers Commission (see Morrison & Foerster 2011).

17. As noted in Joint Forum (2010), definitional differences as to what constitutes a group and how entities enter for the purpose of calculating group capital also create problems for the assessment of risk and capital adequacy.

18. This is the definition proposed by Thompson (2009).

19. The Financial Stability Board (FSB) and the Basel Committee on Bank Supervision (BCBS) have stated that SIFIs, particularly the global ones, should have higher loss-absorbing capacities. See BCBS (2010b) and FSB (2010).

20. The U.S. reform, for example, prohibits mergers or acquisitions if the resulting company's market share (in terms of liabilities) would exceed 10 percent.

21. Legal reforms to the bank failure resolution regimes took place in the 1990s and early 2000s in Argentina, Bolivia, Colombia, Dominican Republic, El Salvador, Guatemala, Mexico, and Peru, among others. The reforms provide better resolution tools, including the transfer of assets and liabilities to an existing bank (purchase and assumption) or to a bridge bank.

22. Starting in 2008, financial crisis simulation exercises were conducted in several LAC countries with the support of the World Bank and the Financial Sector Reform and Strengthening Initiative (FIRST). In most cases, the exercises underlined the need to (a) develop a framework to assess the potential systemic impact of failing institutions; (b) improve operational readiness to resolve an institution through purchase and assumption or bridge bank tools; and (c) improve coordination between the different financial authorities and formulate a communication strategy to calm and reassure investors and the public.

23. See, for example, Squam Lake Working Group on Financial Regulation (2009).

24. Contingent capital and bail-in debt are securities (subordinated in the first case and senior unsecured in the latter) that contain contractual clauses prompting conversion to common equity when the institution is no longer viable, diluting existing shareholders' equity and applying a haircut on debt holders. Contingent capital conversion could also be triggered when the prudential ratios of the institution begin to deteriorate in the form of an automatic prompt corrective action. Statutory bail-in provisions empower liquidating authorities to write-down or convert debt into equity as part of the resolution procedure outside normal bankruptcy procedures. See FSB (2010) and BCBS (2010c, 2010d).

25. The purpose of such funds is to enhance the effectiveness of the resolution framework by ensuring that funds are readily available (its rationale is akin to that of deposit insurance funds with resolution powers).

26. In Brazil, for example, a drastic increase in market volatility boosted margin requirements at the stock and futures exchange, calling for a large posting of liquid collateral at a time of severe liquidity stress. See Mesquita and Torós (2010).

27. See, for example, de la Torre and Ize (2011).

28. Such a broadening of the LLR perimeter has already taken place on occasions of high financial sector stress. For example, in the mid 2000s, an emergency decree allowed securities brokers in Colombia to repossess their government securities directly at the central bank to address market disturbances.

29. Private liquidity pools and insurance arrangements are particularly attractive in the case of highly dollarized countries.

30. Haldane (2010b) finds that the real economic benefits of the precrisis surge in financial innovation have been unimpressive once corrected for the risks that were incurred.

31. The global financial crisis has spurred academic interest in the merits and perils associated with financial innovation and the implications for regulatory policy. See, for example, Gennaioli, Shleifer, and Vishny (2010) and Lerner and Tufano (2011).

32. This approach is reflected in the relatively high scores of LAC countries as regards the second Basel Core Principle, which deals with the permissible activities of banks. More than 90 percent of countries have been graded at least largely compliant.

Systemic Supervision | 13

Traditional prudential supervision starts from the view that strong individual banks lead to strong banking systems. Hence, it monitors the behavior of individual financial institutions. The global crisis exposed the fallacy of composition embedded in this view by showing that the risk to the system is greater than the sum of the risks faced by individual institutions. To some degree, the Latin America and Caribbean (LAC) region has grown quite familiar with systemic events, whether homegrown or imported.[1] While LAC supervisors have learned from these events and, partly as a result, have put in place a stronger supervisory framework, there is no room for complacency. So much is new in systemic supervision that sustained efforts by LAC supervisors to learn and adapt will be needed.[2] Main highlights in this chapter are as follows:

- Systemic supervision is all about making the connections through time, between the parts and the whole, and between stability and development.
- Systemic supervision should symbiotically complement systemic regulation by testing the rules and, where needed, fusing them seamlessly with the exercise of good judgment.
- Systemic supervision will require not only developing new analytical capabilities but also taking a different approach to gathering, analyzing, and circulating information, including a better use of market signals and more effective communication.
- Implementing this ambitious agenda will require new tools and, perhaps more important, new powers and a new organizational arrangement.
- LAC's experience with systemic events and generally more hands-on oversight culture (including as regards financial innovation) should provide a good basis to build on.
- However, LAC also faces special challenges, including high concentration in financial ownership (that promote interconnectedness and too-big-to-fail) and some shortcomings in independence, legal protection, and legal philosophy that weaken the grounds for supervisory discretion.
- While the region is already well on its way toward establishing financial stability committees, difficult issues of functionality, transparency, and accountability still need to be addressed.

The rest of this chapter is organized as follows. The first section deals with the new connections, the next section with the new approach, the third section with the new tools, and the fourth section with implementation. The final section concludes by mapping the agenda ahead.

The new connections

Systemic supervision is all about making the right connections. These include connecting the parts and the whole, connecting the parts through time, and connecting development with stability.

Connecting the parts and the whole

A tendency among supervisors is to equate good systemic supervision with good consolidated supervision. Clearly, the latter helps the former, as it connects the activities of the members of a financial group, thus helping identify potential channels of systemic contagion. Given that many financial firms are parts of conglomerates, a narrow stand-alone view of individual regulated entities is obviously insufficient to obtain a full picture of the conglomerate's risks. Thus, the gaps in consolidated supervision that were identified and discussed in chapters 10 and 12 clearly will need fixing. However, systemic supervision goes much beyond consolidated supervision. While focusing on a broader entity (the financial group), consolidated supervision still follows an idiosyncratically oriented approach. Systemic supervision, instead, looks at the financial system as a whole, recognizing and addressing the interconnectedness of all financial sector players, whether they belong to the same group or not, and seeking to understand how the system is wired, including the nature of the interactions between the parts and between the parts and the whole. Although the actions of each institution or financial conglomerate may be individually optimal and seem acceptable to a traditional supervisor, they may contribute to driving the system along a socially inappropriate and risky path that inflicts negative externalities on the rest of the system.

Connecting through time

Traditional prudential regulation, of the type prevailing before the global crisis, was mostly time invariant and, hence, mostly procyclical (that is, worsening inefficient systemic dynamics rather than leaning against the wind). Instead, to the extent that it extends beyond simple compliance and into the realm of true risk-based supervision, systemic supervision must become dynamic and forward looking, as both risks and risk exposures vary over time in an endogenous way. Hence, the supervisor's task must start where the regulator's ends. Even when regulation has been dynamically adjusted along macroprudential lines to correct for procyclicality, gaps are likely to be left between regulation—which, by construction, is a given—and the risks and exposures—which vary over time, often in unexpected ways. As discussed in chapter 11, the uncertainty as regards the risks faced by the financial system and its vulnerabilities (which limit the scope for rule-based regulation) further enhance the need for such state-contingent supervisory discretion. Thus, the supervisor's task is to complement the regulator's, filling up the gaps that a set rule unavoidably leaves in an uncertain and rapidly changing environment.

Connecting stability with development

Another key issue in formulating a new vision for supervision is striking the right balance between financial stability and financial development. If supervisory responsibilities are to be broadened to include systemic risks, there will be a need to find the appropriate trade-off between the necessary restrictiveness of the supervisory stance and the possible stifling of financial development. This is particularly important in LAC, because many countries, in part in response to their prior experience with crises, are perceived to have a more hands-on, less permissive supervision (including as regards the control of financial innovation) than is (or was) the case in most developed countries. Some argue, based on the experience of developing financial systems, that a relatively rigid framework may be needed initially but that greater supervisory flexibility may be appropriate once markets have developed.[3] Others argue that strict supervision can be consistent with further financial deepening, even in already well-developed systems (a view that the recent global crisis seems largely to have vindicated).[4] In any event, a right balance needs to be found because the modalities of supervision (that is, how, when, and where supervision is made more stringent) are likely to have an important impact on financial development.

A new approach

The new approach will need to deviate from the traditional one in a number of ways, including as regards the boundary between supervision and regulation, the intermingling of top-down and bottom-up approaches, the roles of off-site versus on-site supervision, the use of markets, and the provision of public analysis and information.

Regulating versus supervising

Systemic regulation implies rules that apply to all institutions. Moreover, as discussed in chapter 11, these rules may be based on aggregate, rather than institution-specific, parameters. For example, while a systemic regulation might establish a uniform maximum loan-to-value ratio, systemic supervision may need both to deviate uniformly from the rule (by changing this ratio) and to give supervisors the discretion to apply stricter standards to an individual institution because its actions pose a greater risk to the system. Thus, the inherent tensions and complementarities between regulation and supervision are an essential part of the "rules versus discretion" debate.[5] The challenge is to build sufficient discretion into the supervisory process but without relaxing

regulations so much that prudential oversight ends up losing its teeth. Granting supervisors discretion requires confidence that they are sufficiently independent of political pressures, have the expertise and technical capacity to make sensible judgments, and have the legal powers to enforce those judgments. The latter is an even greater challenge in civil law countries, such as in Latin America, where administrative law restricts supervisors' actions only to those actions that are specified in the law and accompanying regulations.[6] Nonetheless, as discussed below, setting up the right institutional arrangements (including, of course, adequate transparency and accountability) for a decision-making framework should go a long way toward meeting this challenge.

Top-down versus bottom-up

Systemic supervision examines risks from a top-down perspective and blends this analysis with a bottom-up analysis. The intermingling of bottom-up microsupervision with top-down systemic supervision provides an information feedback loop that allows for an enhanced assessment of systemic risks. Indeed, for systemic supervision to be truly effective, understanding the actions of individual institutions and their tolerance to various types of risks is necessary. One of the weaknesses in the financial stability analysis published thus far by central banks has often been the absence of the supervisors' perspective on what is happening at individual institutions. Combining bottom-up traditional supervision with top-down systemic supervision provides key synergies. Top-down supervision gains from the insights and information gathered by bottom-up supervision, and both add to and gain from new perspectives on systemic risks, thereby refining their assessments. However, the skill sets for top-down systemic analysis are very different from those needed for traditional bottom-up idiosyncratic supervision. At the same time, coordination between the two approaches is very important, particularly in countries where bottom-up supervision is outside the central bank (more on this below).

Off-site versus on-site

A closely related (but conceptually distinct) issue is the relative emphasis on off-site versus on-site supervision. At first sight, one might think that, because it involves the forest more than the trees (with a greater focus on systemwide analysis and research), systemic supervision is more about off-site than on-site. Hence, supervisory agencies might need to refocus to some extent and primarily concentrate on strengthening their off-site analysis. Indeed, if on-site supervision is limited to checking compliance with regulations, it will have nothing much to add to the identification of systemic risks.[7] However, the adoption of systemic supervision calls for a redefinition of the role of on-site supervision, rather than a downgrading. Although much of the work of mapping interconnectedness and monitoring links between the balance sheets of important institutions can be done off-site, it can best be verified by on-site inspectors. At the same time, on-site inspections are the best place to understand in full depth the evolving business models, the links with other parts of the financial system, and the risks associated with them. The insufficient communion of on-site and off-site supervision can thus lead to poor, or outright flawed, analysis. This is in fact not an uncommon result of institutional barriers between the central bank's financial stability staff and the supervisors, even where both staffs are located in the same institution.

Use of markets

A long-standing debate is carried on within the supervisory community regarding the efficacy of market-based financial indicators and the reliance on market discipline.[8] Traditionally, supervisors have, for the most part, paid scant attention to financial markets, except when market perceptions trigger liquidity problems.[9] At the same time, however, a good argument can be made that gaps in market discipline result, in part, from the insufficient exploitation of market signals, as well as the incompleteness of those signals. Hence, the question is not so much whether market discipline is good or bad, but rather how supervisors can make better use of market signals. Where the latter are weak, the issue is how to strengthen them. In recent years, various market instruments, such as credit default swap spreads, have emerged and can help detect something that supervisors may not have been aware of; or instruments may matter simply because they—as well as the prices of financial institutions' debt and equity securities, where available—gauge the state of expectations, which in turn helps predict pricing and the availability and cost of funding.[10] In LAC, more and better use of such signals, when available, is clearly desirable. Indeed, several central banks, for example, in Brazil, Chile, and Mexico, have been already doing work along these lines. But there is clearly ample scope for furthering such types of analysis.[11]

But limited capital market development in LAC, resulting in weak market signals, constitutes a severe limitation. Hence, a key question for the region is whether policy makers can help develop market instruments that promote risk discovery. The latter generally requires costly monitoring. Hence, for market participants to invest sufficiently in monitoring, they need to have sufficient "skin in the game." But, in view of risk aversion, large risk exposures can mean a high risk premium (see chapter 9). Thus, unless supported in some fashion by the state (and perhaps even subsidized), market instruments that aim at risk discovery may simply be too expensive to see the light of day, all the more so in shallower financial systems. An important research agenda for the region, therefore, is to help design, introduce, and support such instruments. Mandatory issue by financial institutions of subordinated debt or purchase of market-based insurance might be one such avenue to explore.[12]

Analysis and information

In addition to "skin in the game," another key requirement for proper market discipline is analysis and information. Private market participants (rating agencies, auditors, financial advisers, and so forth) can naturally provide much information on individual financial firms. However, the quality and depth of these assessments is limited by costs, conflicts of interest, and confidentiality. Thus, some of the required information is in the nature of a public good that supervisors must foster or provide. While total openness can be problematic (examination report data are generally kept confidential), a good argument can be made that more information, provided it is presented in a way that protects basic confidentiality regarding customers and business models, can only be for the better.[13] Indeed, this is already happening in LAC.[14]

But supervisors also need to provide analysis and information on the system, how it is wired and interconnected, and what risks may be brewing. This analysis and information sharing is something that only supervisors can do. Markets will most certainly not do it on their own because it is too complex, hence too costly and, given its public good nature, subject to too many collective action frictions (free riding). As financial systems mature and become increasingly complex and interconnected, such systemic analyses become increasingly valuable yet also increasingly costly. Supervisors need to scout ahead and search for upcoming icebergs. When risks are detected, supervisors may need both to inform (so that market participants can correct the course) and to act (thereby helping resolve coordination failures).[15] Generally, the former should facilitate the latter.

Financial stability reports, in LAC as in other regions, have become the main vehicle for regular reporting of the results of such exercises.[16] However, they have run into some practical difficulties. In particular, there is a question as to whether they provide meaningful and authentically transparent and candid diagnostics of systemic risk. The fact that these reports are published may induce supervisors to exercise self-restraint for fear of igniting a self-fulfilling run. Also, in some countries central banks lack access to detailed supervisory data on financial institutions and thus are constrained to an overly macro view.

New tools

Systemic supervision also will require developing new tools to map the risk boundaries and the interconnectedness between financial institutions and between markets and institutions.

Mapping the boundaries

Having a better feel for the location of the (systemic) cliffs is central to systemic supervision. Since one wants to focus on tail risk, and tail events may not have occurred, market data are unlikely to be sufficient.[17] One alternative is stress testing, a technique first widely disseminated through the Financial Sector Assessment Programs (FSAPs).[18] In LAC, many countries already conduct such exercises on a regular basis.[19] There are many difficulties inherent to systemic stress testing, however.[20] First, financial firms' natural incentive is to construct their own tests so that the tests result in a need for less equity capital rather than more. Second, models need to incorporate shocks, correlations, and joint default probabilities that are nowhere to be found in the data. Third, stress tests must expand beyond capital adequacy, into liquidity, which is generally where crises start. However, liquidity modeling is notoriously difficult. Fourth, "connecting the dots," identifying the potential fault lines, and looking both outside the box and beyond the horizon are the most difficult, yet most crucial, elements of good stress testing. Indeed, failure to identify the channels and links through which a crisis could emerge and spread (rather than simple compliance failures) was arguably the most severe supervisory failure in the United States.

Therefore, before proper models or crisis scenarios can be designed, understanding how the system is wired, and where the weakest connections are, is of utmost importance. Failing to do that results in a real risk of embarking on sophisticated but ultimately sterile number crunching. Supervisors need to discuss the simulations with financial institutions and impose uniform stress parameters derived from well-formulated, macro-based scenarios. In some cases, the latter may need to include such specifics as losses given default and declines in collateral values. Although these discussions are likely to be difficult, they constitute a prime opportunity for collective learning, not unlike those between the International Monetary Fund (IMF), the World Bank, and national authorities during FSAPs. Indeed, many LAC countries have already embarked on this route.[21] Much more work clearly lies ahead.

Mapping interconnectedness

One of the key lessons from the global crisis and the Lehman Brothers debacle is the extent and implications of financial institutions and markets' interconnectedness. The latter can take place through balance sheets, market prices and market sentiment, or ownership. The last channel is particularly relevant in LAC in view of the prevalence of large, opaque financial groups with highly concentrated ownership. It is often unclear how the real and financial components of the group relate to each other, how reputational effects may transmit across the group, and how a crisis will affect the parts and the whole, domestically as well as across borders.[22] In LAC, the prevalence of foreign banks and their subsidiaries brings about another crucial source of cross-border interconnectedness. Notwithstanding ring-fencing capital through capital requirements on branches, there is always the risk of a loss in confidence in the host bank if the parent experiences difficulties. Also, the parent's ability to support its affiliate and sustain its lending may become constrained. Understanding the full dimensions of the parent's

organization (which requires full cooperation with home supervisors) is therefore vital. Unfortunately, during the crisis some home supervisors were unwilling to share any information with host supervisors.

But balance sheet interconnectedness across institutions with different ownership also clearly matters. For example, given the high economic concentration of the real sector in many LAC countries, financial firms often become heavily interconnected through their borrowers. While market interconnectedness is less extensive in LAC than it was in the United States, it is no less crucial, as illustrated in Mexico by the spillovers on the whole commercial paper market of the financial difficulties incurred by a couple of small Sofoles. How financial institutions fund themselves is particularly critical. Financial firms that fund themselves mainly through wholesale markets or their offshore parents are of course much more vulnerable. Understanding cross-country contagion is also critical. Indeed, empirical work has shown how closely connected some Latin American countries' economies are to their neighbors (Sosa 2010). Thus, mapping of interconnectedness can be as much a statistical exercise based on analyzing price correlations as pure detective work aimed at dissecting each of the links described above.[23] In LAC, several countries have started to work on both sides of this problem. Again, however, there is much more to be done.[24]

Getting there

Implementing such changes will in turn require shaping up the necessary skills, making sure supervisors have the necessary powers, and putting in place proper organizational arrangements. Continued peer reviews may also help.

Skills

Boosting the skills required to address systemic risks involves a quantum leap, not a marginal improvement. It will likely require an altogether different skill set from that traditionally required for checking compliance. The supervisors engaging in systemic supervision will need to become fluent in economics, statistics, and finance and must venture into largely unmarked territory. Indeed, by some measure, they will need to engage in more research-like activities than in sheer day-to-day operations. To avoid a repeat of the ultimately fruitless (or even downright deceptive) fixation on quantitative modeling that prevailed among many financial institutions in the United States prior to the crisis, supervisory agencies will need to ensure a proper balance between quantitative and qualitative approaches.

Whether qualitatively or quantitatively oriented, attracting, forming, and retaining the qualified staff to conduct such analyses could be a severe problem, particularly where private sector demand for similar skills is intense and public sector pay is limited by cross-government scales. Where supervisory agencies are unable to attract the staff, they may need to form cooperative arrangements with central banks. Greater cooperation between the supervisory and financial stability staffs may be required even when they are both housed in the central bank. In all cases, traditional supervisor-economist rivalries will need to be put aside. That said, one finds some degree of comfort that supervisors across the regions are well aware of the challenges awaiting them.[25] Some countries are already on their way in using advanced analytical tools, particularly where the supervisory function is part of the central bank (such as Brazil) or where the supervisory agency has recruited economists to staff a macroprudential unit (such as Mexico). Many of the smaller countries have been slower to move.

Powers

Systemic supervisors will need sufficient powers to enforce systemic regulations, including the ability to order an institution to cease and desist from activities that pose a systemic risk. Of course the more supervisors rely on discretion, rather than rules, the more their powers will need to be balanced by adequate accountability. In this context, it is worrisome that the use of automatic corrective action triggers in LAC appears to be in need of significant strengthening.[26] LAC's remaining problems of insufficient independence and legal protection for supervisors (discussed in chapter 10) seem to add to the challenge. So does civil (Roman) law, which is the norm in most of the region, as it puts the burden of proof on supervisors rather than on the institutions they supervise.[27] The fact that systemic risks cannot always be anticipated and are hard to catalogue ex ante in legislation (to date, unlike with Basel II, no international standards or lists of systemic risks exist) raises the bar even further. Many LAC countries might have constitutional constraints to enacting legislation that facilitates true supervisory discretion. However, in civil law frameworks, all the relevant conditions and criteria (the so-called *casuística*) need to be spelled out ex ante, so that creative legal drafting will be needed to give supervisors sufficient scope for discretion in determining the systemic risks to address and actions to take.

Interestingly, most supervisors believe that the powers they currently have are adequate to request that a financial institution increase its capital, provisions, or liquidity based on a supervisory assessment of its exposure to systemic risks.[28] Even more surprisingly, a majority of respondents to the World Bank–Association of Supervisors of Banks of the Americas (ASBA) survey do not see the civil code as an important hindrance to the use of supervisory discretion. Rather, the agency's legal mandate and the weak legal protection are considered to be the main obstacles. Be that as it may, a strengthening of supervisory powers appears to be needed in many countries of the region. The institutional and legal frameworks in place are not likely to make this any easier.

Organizational arrangements

An overbearing issue in implementing systemic supervision is how to organize it. Because systemic supervision, by its construction, involves bringing together, from a holistic perspective, all parts of the financial system, one can take the view that all supervision should be consolidated into a single agency. If so, the need for better coordination between monetary and prudential management, as discussed in chapter 11, naturally points toward the central bank. Thus, after the crisis, some European countries have leaned toward bringing supervision back within the central bank's fold.[29] Indeed, many central banks in the world, including in most South American countries facing the Atlantic Ocean, already house monetary and prudential oversight policies in the central bank. However, where this is not the case, central bankers are often reticent to assume a full-blown supervisory task that—at least at its micro level—is highly resource-intensive and may be viewed as deviating from the pure macro-oriented analytical tasks associated with monetary management. The rise of an extremely powerful centralized agency that blends monetary, regulatory, and supervisory policies could also create a political backlash, feeding pressures for limiting the central bank's independence, thereby undermining monetary policy. Thus, many countries are leaning toward a Financial Sector Authority (FSA)-type consolidation of all supervisory activities outside the central bank.[30]

In many LAC countries, as suggested by the World Bank–ASBA survey of supervisors, interagency cooperation seems to require strengthening (see chapter 10). In some countries, a further potential problem is the lack of well-defined mandates. In some cases, countries had formalized arrangements that had grown out of previous experience with financial crises.[31] Other countries are contemplating the creation of a unified financial supervisor, separate from the central bank, following Colombia's lead. Even when the different parts of the financial sector are supervised within the same entity, internal coordination problems may arise, however. Thus, both Mexico and Uruguay have recently reviewed the organizational structure of their main supervisory agency to facilitate the

supervision of multiproduct financial firms. However, coordination arrangements for consolidated supervision of financial groups, important as they are, do not necessarily take care of systemic supervision.

The challenge, therefore, is to set up a suitable systemic oversight function endowed with appropriate governance arrangements for coordination and decision making. Where financial oversight and monetary policy are distributed among different institutions, an alternative to placing the systemic oversight responsibility with the central bank is to make it reside with a committee or council made up of the relevant authorities.[32] Many LAC countries are well on their way to establishing (or have already established), in line with international experience, such financial stability committees to monitor and address systemic risk. The region's experience with inflation targeting, which rests on effective monetary policy governance arrangements (that is, independent central bank boards, clear protocols for decision making and communication with the public, and strong accountability standards), should provide a valuable guide toward setting up appropriate governance arrangements for systemic oversight committees. To ensure the committees' effectiveness, transparency and accountability will be of the essence, including a proper framework and protocols for analysis, decision making, and reporting. The need for strong legal grounds and governance arrangements for the systemic and macroprudential oversight functions is even more crucial, considering the potential costs of the associated decisions on financial intermediaries (for example, spoiling the party. Regardless of the exact features of the organizational arrangement chosen, information needs to flow,[33] and staff must be encouraged to work together across agencies.[34] Given the natural tendencies of bureaucracies, this is easier said than done.

It is important to stress that the coordination function of a financial stability committee, focused as it is on macroprudential and systemic oversight (and where the central bank governor should be primus inter pares among committee members), is of a different nature than other coordination functions pertaining to financial oversight. An example of the latter is the coordination among those regulatory agencies needed to perform consolidated supervision of financial conglomerates, where the primus inter pares should arguably be the head of the supervisory agency that oversees the largest member of the conglomerate and where central banks that do not house regulatory functions need not even be a member. The failure to adequately separate different financial oversight coordination functions can end up overburdening the financial stability committees with extraneous responsibilities, thereby undermining their effectiveness.

In addition to home coordination, supervisors also need to coordinate across borders. In LAC, the importance of foreign banks makes this even more of a priority. As discussed in chapter 10, significant improvements had already taken place before the global crisis. However, the crisis has shown that the arrangements of the past were generally not sufficient to deal with the crisis. While there is no simple solution to this coordination challenge in a globalized world, LAC might be better off seeking a regional approach. This approach would help to ensure information sharing and coordination among regional systemic supervisors and would provide a unified front in dealing with the large developed countries with significant presence in Latin America. Alternative structures might include a college of supervisors, a formal regional body (possibly under the auspices of an international financial institution), or an association of systemic supervisors similar to the International Association of Deposit Insurers. Wherever needed, laws that limit information sharing across borders would need to be amended.

Peers

The April 2009 G-20 "Declaration on Strengthening the Financial System" tasked the IMF, the Financial Stability Board, and the Bank for International Settlements to develop guidelines on how countries can assess the systemic importance of financial institutions, markets, and instruments. Eventually, the international financial institutions and the Financial Stability Board are likely to develop standards of good practice in systemic oversight, in much the same way such standards already exist for other aspects of financial oversight. Given the many difficult issues outlined in this chapter, peer reviews based on such reports on the observance of standards and codes (ROSCs) should be helpful, once they become available. But given the experimental features of much that needs to be done regarding systemic supervision, countries may not necessarily want to wait until formal ROSCs have been established. Whether through formal ROSC assessments or just exploratory consultative missions, the region should benefit from such peer reviews. In addition to contributing to the analytical process, ROSCs can provide the authorities with some of the ammunition they may need to strengthen their powers and independence.

The agenda ahead

Like the rest of the world, LAC needs to tackle a work agenda for strengthening the supervision of systemic risks that is as rich as it is complex. It will need to do so taking into account the region's specific features, relative weaknesses, and relative strengths. Some of the region's specific features that will probably color the way this agenda is implemented include the high concentration of ownership, substantial conglomeration of financial sector services, and strong presence of foreign banks. In addition, the region continues to be exposed to large swings in capital flows, partly the result of remaining interest rate differentials with respect to world rates; it is still—albeit decreasingly—dollarized; its oversight has been strengthened substantially and can now be viewed as generally hands-on and rather restrictive; many of its policy makers and supervisors are familiar with dealing with systemic crises; and its financial institutions are, by and large, cautious and well protected.

Indeed, the last three of the above features can generally be put on the "comparative strengths" side of the ledger. These strengths and the fact that the region has passed the test of the recent global crisis with mostly flying colors should not be viewed as a reason for complacency, however. As with other regions, LAC needs to prepare itself to address the challenges of systemic supervision. In doing so, it will need to address some institutional weaknesses, such as limited supervisory independence and legal protection and a civil code that limits the scope for discretion. In addition to addressing these weaknesses, key items in LAC's agenda for reform will include (a) finding the proper balance in setting prudential requirements between financial stability and financial development, (b) ensuring that supervisory agencies can attract and retain the human resources they will need for effective systemic supervision, (c) finding ways to rely more on market signals and market discipline, (d) finding institutional arrangements that promote interagency coordination and adequately support systemic oversight, and (e) finding the most effective ways of coordinating supervision across borders.

Notes

1. This chapter draws heavily on the paper "Systemic Supervision" by Katia D'Hulster and Steven A. Seelig, which is part of the Edited Volume that accompanies this LAC flagship report. As discussed in chapters 6 and 10, past banking crises in Latin America originated for the most part with unsustainable macrodynamics accompanied by the collapse of fixed exchange rate regimes. In many cases, poor risk management, weak bank governance, and weak supervision worsened the vulnerability of banking sectors to these shocks. See Stallings and Studart (2003).
2. As reported in chapter 10, LAC supervisors are, by and large, well aware of the work ahead. The majority of supervisors who responded to the World Bank–Association of Supervisors of Banks of the Americas (ASBA) survey believe that recent global events will require a redefinition of the role and functions of supervisors, with a consequent need

for an in-depth build up of systemically oriented supervisory capacity.
3. For example, this is the conclusion reached by Stallings and Studart (2003) in their study of Latin American countries after the tequila crisis.
4. Granlund (2009) finds that in the European Union countries he looked at, most of the supervisory changes were focused on market stability and on changes in the organizational arrangements for supervision.
5. The "rules versus discretion" debate originated in the literature relating to monetary policy and dates back to the 1950s and 1960s. See, for example, Friedman (1959).
6. By contrast, according to a civil-code style of administrative law, the private sector is permitted to do whatever is not prohibited by laws and regulations.
7. For example, in the securities industry, the International Organization of Securities Commissions (IOSCO) has focused its standards on market conduct regulations and consumer protection, and to a much lesser extent on prudential standards. Consequently, on-site inspection, to the extent it exists at securities regulators, tends to be compliance focused. The recent experience in the United States, where securities firms were allowed to operate with virtually no capital but to engage in derivatives and structured products transactions with other financial institutions, confirms this vulnerability.
8. While economists tend to support greater reliance on capital market instruments, such as subordinated debt, many supervisors see such instruments as difficult to implement and believe that supervisors have in any case a better grasp of bank risks. For a thorough review of the literature on this topic, see Evanoff and Wall (2000).
9. The global crisis can be viewed as having, for the most part, vindicated these views. Despite market signals of potential problems, market discipline alone did not curb the buildup of risk in the system. Only when the crisis was a reality did market discipline become so severe that it forced regulatory and supervisory responses.
10. Measures of expectations regarding individual financial intermediaries include the change in spreads on credit default swaps and the changes in and volatility of stock prices (see Sharpe 1964).

11. An early proposal for LAC supervisors to use interest rates paid by financial institutions in the interbank markets is found in Rojas-Suarez (2001). A recent body of work has incorporated finance theory, market data, and a contingent claims approach to examining financial stability risks, an approach that has recently been applied in Chile. See Gray and Malone (2008) and Gray and Walsh (2008).

12. On subordinated debt issuance, the classic proposal is that of Calomiris (1999). As discussed in chapter 9, the availability of market-based insurance for financial intermediaries to buy may require some kind of private-public risk-sharing arrangement.

13. Indeed, many supervisory agencies have recently made great strides in overcoming their natural fears of opening up. For example, since the advent of risk-based deposit insurance premiums in the United States, analysts are readily able to estimate which banks are viewed as more risky by the Federal Deposit Insurance Corporation. Given the implications of administrative law in LAC, however, such disclosure may entail a legal liability for supervisors.

14. For example, in Uruguay, the banking supervisor (part of the central bank) publishes detailed financial information about each banking firm on a monthly basis with a degree of detail that allows analysts to fully understand the financial condition of individual banks. In fact, using the central bank's database, one financial reporter was able to predict when a small cooperative bank might become insolvent.

15. The coordination failures that need to be prevented are of the type famously alluded to by Citibank's former CEO Charles Prince: "You need to keep dancing until the music stops."

16. For example, financial stability reports are issued by central banks in Brazil, Chile, Colombia, and Mexico. The Peruvian supervisors also conduct a systemic risk assessment.

17. Stress testing was formally introduced into the supervisory process with the adoption of Basel II. However, the absence of data spanning full business cycles generally led to misleading estimates of capital adequacy. Moreover, market data failed to capture the crisis covariances and correlations given interconnectedness.

18. After the global crisis, stress tests were introduced in the United States by the Federal Reserve as a way to test whether the largest banks could withstand another systemic shock. See Hirtle, Scheurman, and Stiroh (2009). Similar tests were conducted in Europe by the Committee of European Banking Supervisors (CEBS). In mid-2010, the European Union (EU) announced its intention to conduct additional stress tests.

19. Twelve respondents to the World Bank–ASBA survey of supervisors confirmed that their agencies undertake systemic stress-testing exercises on a regular basis while nine respondents said they only perform this exercise occasionally. The remaining seven countries do not perform systemic stress tests but do not rule them out for the future. When regular stress tests are carried out, the common practice appears to be to carry them out on a three- to six-month cycle, but for the banking sector only. Authorities that do not perform regular stress tests indicate that they rely on the FSAP stress tests.

20. For an early discussion of the limits and perils of stress testing in a systemic context, see Haldane (2009a).

21. Five respondents to the World Bank–ASBA survey stated that they are considering a specific requirement for financial institutions to assess their exposure or contribution to systemic risk based on stress parameters provided by the supervisor. The institutions would then be required to adjust their capital and liquidity positions accordingly. Two countries stated that they already apply this procedure.

22. One such example of a complex financial conglomerate that ran into financial difficulties is CL Financial in Trinidad and Tobago. This firm had subsidiaries in insurance, banking, real estate, and real sector commercial activities in nine countries. See chapter 12 in this report and Powell (2010).

23. On quantitative approaches to map interconnectedness, see, for example, IMF (2010).

24. For example, about 60 percent of respondents to the World Bank–ASBA survey of supervisors reported that interconnectedness between financial institutions (in contrast to control) is a key part of their inspection process. But only four countries have taken this practice a step further and reported on interconnectedness within the financial system.

25. Thus, when assessing the obstacles to conducting systemic supervision, supervisors view the development of proper staff skills as the most important challenge. Although 11 respondents to the survey rate their agency's current

systemic supervision capacity as good relative to international standards, 5 rate it as fair, and 10 respondents think it needs strengthening.

26. In the World Bank–ASBA survey, only one supervisory authority states that it has a fully operating system of automatic corrective action triggers. Although another three Latin American supervisors have such systems in place, they admit the systems need strengthening.

27. Thus, a supervisory instruction may in several LAC countries be stopped by a successful court appeal until supervisors identify and prove noncompliance before a judge.

28. In the World Bank–ASBA survey of supervisors, only six agencies report that these powers are poor or nonexistent.

29. The United Kingdom and Germany have proposed shifting supervision from the Financial Sector Authority (FSA) into the central bank. The French have moved toward creating an FSA under the auspices of the central bank.

30. The case of AIG is an often-cited example of the failure of multiple supervisors, since its insurance activities were under the jurisdiction of the state insurance supervisors, its securities activities were under the Securities and Exchange Commission, and, through its ownership of a savings and loan, it was also regulated by the Office of Thrift Supervision. Thus, there have been calls for integrating the supervision of banking, securities, and insurance. See Garicano and Lastra (2010).

31. For example, Uruguay has created a council made up of the FSA, the monetary policy directorate (both in the central bank), and the minister of economy and finance to review developments and coordinate any necessary measures.

32. In the United States, a Financial Stability Oversight Council, made up of all the major financial sector regulators, has been created. Among other responsibilities, the council will determine which financial firms are "too big to fail." Similarly, in December 2010, the European Union created the European Systemic Risk Board. In addition, a joint committee of European supervisory authorities was established to ensure greater cooperation among supervisors.

33. In any case, the central banks' role as lender of last resort requires that they have real-time access to prudential supervisory information on all financial firms, especially in a crisis environment. The Bank of England's handling of Northern Rock during the early stages of the U.K. crisis provides a useful illustration of the problems that can emerge when real-time access to information is not the case. On these issues, see Goodhart and Schoemaker (1995) and Peek, Rosengren, and Tootell (1999).

34. For example, central bank staff should be encouraged to participate in on-site inspections while supervisory agency staff should be encouraged in directly participating in the drafting of financial stability reports.

Summary of Policy Directions for the Road Ahead | 14

This chapter concludes this flagship report with a summary review of the main themes of research and the main policy directions coming out of the report. The first section lays the groundwork by briefly synthesizing where Latin America and the Caribbean (LAC) region currently stands as regards both the stability and development of its financial systems. The next section reviews the broad set of issues that are likely to require further work before a specific policy agenda can be formulated. The two following sections summarize the key policy directions that can already be fleshed out at this stage. The first of those sections deals with the bright side, the next with the dark side. Beyond those discussions, this report cannot (and certainly does not) provide a list of country-specific, detailed policy recommendations. Given its regional perspectives and holistic approach, its aim is only to raise broad issues and suggest the directions of policy response.

Where is LAC?

LAC has made substantial progress as regards financial system stability. This progress, which in part explains the region's resilience to the recent global financial crisis, has

two roots: the much-improved macroeconomic policy frameworks and the enhanced quality of financial oversight. Regarding the macroeconomic underpinnings of financial stability, the main challenge is to build effective countercyclicality into fiscal policy while consolidating the hard-fought gains in monetary policy. As regards the financial oversight underpinnings, important gaps remain in traditional bank oversight, particularly with respect to the independence of bank supervisors and their legal protection, the regulation of capital adequacy, and the consolidated supervision of financial conglomerates (both domestically and across borders). At the same time, there is a substantial unevenness across LAC, with the smaller and lower-income countries generally lagging behind. Finally, LAC, as the rest of the world, faces the big and complex challenge of developing a robust systemic oversight framework. Given LAC's tumultuous macrofinancial history, it has to some extent a leg ahead in such matters; however, much remains to be done.

LAC has also made substantial progress as regards financial system development. First, the region experienced a general financial deepening, as told in chapter 2's broad developmental story, with capital markets and institutional investors playing an increasingly important role, and new markets and instruments springing up and making inroads. Consistent with this general deepening, the maturities of fixed-income instruments have lengthened considerably, yield curves have extended further into the future, and the region has experienced a broad-based, albeit not yet complete, return to the local currency (both in banking and bonds). At the same time, the patterns of financial globalization have become safer, with lower debt liabilities and higher reserve assets. Finally, substantial progress has been made as regards financial inclusion, particularly in the LAC-7 countries, which in fact now appear to be somewhat ahead of their peers.

Yet large, measurable gaps remain. First, the commercial banking sector underperforms in terms of both its size and its efficiency, with one probably having much to do with the other. Second, a substantial increase in consumer credit seems to have occurred, though much of that has been at the expense of other types of lending, including in the mortgage market (where LAC lags the most) and in small and medium enterprise (SME) finance. Third, the domestic equity market also underperforms in trading and liquidity, if not in capitalization. Finally, the insurance industry lags in the size of both premiums and assets. These gaps matter because (a) they are likely to limit the growth potential as well as the access to finance (however, finding out exactly to what extent will require further research, as discussed below), and (b) by limiting intertemporal consumption smoothing (as in the case of housing finance), they reduce welfare. But there is also substantial unevenness across the region. Indeed, looking on the brighter side, there are important success stories—such as banking, corporate bonds, and insurance in Chile; equity and mutual funds in Brazil; and public debt in Brazil, Colombia, and Mexico—that provide worthy examples to study and follow.

LAC's turbulent past is an important contributor to the mentioned gaps, but not all for the bad. Its history of financial instability appears to explain much of the banking

gap today and might also (although the story here is admittedly more murky) explain part of the domestic equity turnover gap. The history of low economic growth also appears to explain part of the banking gap as well as the relatively high interest rates in many LAC countries—a major hindrance to monetary policy. Yet the past is also a source of experience and strength for the future. In particular, the hands-on oversight and prudent banking with large buffers, which contributed to the resilience from the global crisis, are explained largely by history. The systemic experience and the region's active experimentation with systemically oriented instruments and policies are also at least partly a legacy of the past.

LAC also faces important challenges on two issues regarding which the region may not necessarily be performing worse than it should, but that are nonetheless central to the sound development of its financial systems and those systems' contribution to social and economic prosperity. The first such issue relates to the difficulties of establishing deep markets for long-term finance ("going long"), the second to the thorny rationale for risk bearing by the state.

As regards LAC's capacity to go long, in spite of the strong development of (and high fees charged by) its asset managers, the latter continue to concentrate their portfolios in the shorter-term and/or the more liquid securities. Moreover, they trade little. Although the annuities industry in some countries, such as Chile, is a potential success story of how to help channel demand toward the longer and the less liquid, difficulties emerge at the interface between pensions and annuities that most countries (to a greater or smaller extent) need to address. As regards housing finance, the budding progress achieved before the global crisis was largely interrupted by the crisis, with substantial uncertainty now looming regarding the best path to follow ahead.

As regards the risk-taking role of the state, following wide swings over the past three to four decades, the precrisis consensus view was to limit the risk-taking role of the state, by privatizing public banks or restricting them to second-tier operations while improving their financial discipline. Yet the important countercyclical role played by first-tier public banks during the global crisis has called this view into question, raising the premium on setting the rationale for risk absorption by the state on a sound footing.

The tough issues to think about

A first issue on which LAC will no doubt need to reflect further is the role of the state in financial development. The financial paradigms discussed in chapters 2 and 9 highlight the comparative advantage of the state (or markets) in solving collective (or agency) frictions. Yet the close interaction between the two classes of frictions complicates the fine allocation of roles at the same time as it boosts the case for complementarity and private-public partnership. In addition, the role of the state in taking risk must be reassessed based on risk aversion and collective action comparative advantages, rather than on agency frictions or externalities, as has commonly been the case. And states' intervention in finance needs to be justified, not based so much on ultimate objectives, but based instead on the best channels to reach these objectives. Indeed, if the same objectives can be met through less intrusive interventions—particularly by promoting participation and risk spreading by the private sector without the state assuming the risk itself—it should all be for the better. However, how best to translate these general principles into LAC's day-to-day financial reality remains a big challenge and, to a large extent, a theme for further thinking.

A symmetric issue, the role of the state in financial stability, also will deserve further thought. As explained in chapter 2 and discussed in chapters 11 to 13, the bright and dark sides of finance interact in much more complex ways than previously believed. In managing these interactions, states and markets need to interact closely and in ways that are often tense and potentially conflictive. Ex ante, states need to provide analysis and

information (a public good), induce financial market players and users to internalize externalities, and help steer markets in the right directions. At the same time, markets can (and need to) provide key signals to help guide states' policy actions. Ex post, states have a unique coordinating and risk absorbing role to play. Yet this role naturally breeds moral hazard and free riding. How best to manage these tensions and complexities in LAC's regional context is also something LAC (as everybody else, for that matter) will need to continue reflecting upon.

A third issue that will warrant revisiting is the role of finance in growth. This aim will first involve the question of how to promote the bright side of financial development without also promoting the dark side. The finance paradigms highlight the ways in which the two sides can interact. And they suggest that, unless the demons of the dark side are efficiently kept in check, at some point more finance might be bad (rather than good) for growth. In LAC, in view of the large developmental gaps, one might take the view that the region is far from reaching any such threshold, even if it exists. Taking this view too strongly would be unwise, however, given the growing interconnectedness and globalization of LAC financial systems. Moreover, one can also argue that potential perils down the road should already guide current policies. A second, related issue in LAC concerns the two-way direction of causality between finance and growth. The fact that LAC's financial development gaps in part reflect the mediocre growth of the past implies that much of the fixing of the regional underperformance in finance needs to take place outside finance, particularly in the growth, productivity, and competitiveness arenas. The history of mediocre growth also implies a need to focus more on financial policies that can help promote growth, as the latter will in turn help resolve the region's financial development gaps.

Exploring the border line and trade-offs between financial stability and financial development is a last broad generic issue worth inscribing in LAC's research agenda. While much has been written on stability issues after the global crisis, very little has as yet been said on the links between stability and development. Indeed, despite the new features of the international financial architecture (including the establishment of the Financial Stability Board and the G-20 process), it is still exclusively focused on financial stability and is thus clearly lacking in its ability to appropriately tackle the issues in the interface of financial development and financial stability. Finding the right balance between these two dimensions, which is a global challenge, acquires special tones in LAC. The current hands-on, silo-based, broad regulatory perimeter and innovation-cautious oversight have served the region well. However, some realignment may be needed as financial systems continue to mature and the intensity of cross-border competition increases. But the more room LAC opens for markets to play and innovations to be introduced, the more it will need to rely on a well-targeted ex ante internalization of systemic risks and an ex post capacity to provide liquidity and absorb risks. The current developmental gaps are likely to complicate finding the proper trade-off, not the least because they might feed pressures against the regulatory tightening associated with Basel III.

Policy directions: The bright side

Dealing with the banking gap should be the first order of business as regards the developmental policy agenda. To that end, a premium should be put on continuing to strengthen the contractual and institutional environment, which is responsible for at least part of this gap. As discussed in chapter 2, LAC has had an easier time reducing agency frictions, based on information-intensive technological innovations that can be readily imported, than it has had in making the necessary improvements in enforcement, creditor rights, or property rights, a taller order that includes the highly complex task of strengthening the judiciary. Although such contractual and legal weaknesses may not significantly hinder the development

of some financial services—for example, consumer lending or microlending—they can severely hamper other services that are arguably more crucial to economic growth and social welfare, such as the financing of SMEs, housing, and education and the availability of financial services (such as annuities) to ensure old-age income security. Given that progress on these matters will not come easily, the reform agendas must be designed and implementation efforts must be set in motion in earnest.

Beyond that, a research agenda needs to be developed to better understand the nature and implications of the banking gap. To what extent and in what manner are SMEs truly affected by lack of credit? To what extent is the problem instead with the lack of bankable projects? To what extent is lack of competition part of the problem? If so, what can be done about it? As research sheds further light on these questions, it shows that the policy agenda would need to be focused on promoting productivity-oriented credit (firms, students, infrastructure), which might include state interventions aimed at overcoming coordination failures as well as interventions that resort to well-targeted and well-priced credit guarantees to foster longer-term investments (including asset-backed securities or infrastructure bonds). Most importantly, however, sustainability is the name of the game: a slower but more sustainable, less fiscally risky catch-up is preferable to a more ambitious program of financial sector expansion that ends badly.

As regards the equity gap, a strengthening of the contractual environment will also help, as shown in chapter 7. But again, more research is clearly needed to assess impacts and uncover possible solutions. As regards impacts, the links between the lack of stock trading and the efficiency of stock price discovery need to be ascertained. And research is also needed to assess how the lower liquidity of the stocks of smaller firms affects their price. As regards solutions, while the region's atypically low turnover relative to the benchmark cannot be explained by size (because the benchmarking carried out in chapter 3 was all controlled for size), clearly size matters immensely when it comes to stock market development policy. With the clear exception of Brazil, this is indeed the major challenge for LAC. Although regional integration of stock exchanges might help overcome the major size constraints, it does not necessarily solve the constraints associated with the small size of stock issues. Furthermore, additional research is needed to ascertain whether regional integration of stock markets can achieve any special benefits that could not be effectively achieved through global integration. There is also a need to identify the governance frameworks that are appropriate to the larger as well as the smaller stock markets. While further improvements in market infrastructure are of course welcome, they will probably only help at the margin. In the end, it might be the case that more can be done through venture capital funds (that is, through relationship-based, non-liquid-equity finance) than through traditional market-based equity finance. If so, the emphasis should be put on ways to promote the growth of such funds.

With respect to the goal of lengthening financial contracts, the general strengthening of the contractual and institutional environment should again help. But, in addition, specific efforts should be geared at producing the basic information required for market completion. These efforts include (a) promoting credible, well-accepted inflation indexes that can be used to denominate longer-term contracts; (b) enhancing transparency, including through more standardized information and analysis on asset managers' performance, in a way that does not exacerbate their focus on short-term returns; and (c) further lengthening yield curves on public bonds and boosting their liquidity, so as to provide the necessary signals for the pricing of the longer private instruments.

There might also be room for strengthening regulations that encourage longer-term investing. For life insurance companies, prudential regulation that encourages a matching of maturities may suffice. For pension funds, life-cycle funds or regulations that

nudge defined-contribution funds into mimicking the investment behavior of defined-benefit funds could be necessary to lengthen their portfolios. In some cases, pension fund regulations may need to be revised to encourage investments in long instruments, such as infrastructure bonds, possibly with some partial public guarantees (see below). Clearly, however, there is a fine line not to be crossed between internalizing the positive externalities of long-term finance and undermining pension funds' fiduciary responsibility by obliging them to invest in the political pet projects of the day. In view of consumers' and workers' bounded rationality, regulations that, by default, channel their savings into investment portfolios that are the most appropriate for them should also generally be desirable. However, the scope of state intervention again clearly needs to be limited. A proper balance must be found between protecting those consumers who are clearly not equipped to manage their portfolios and encouraging those who are to do so, thereby enhancing market discipline.

As regards housing finance, the tricky balance to be ascertained here is that between monitoring, skin-in-the-game, and risk spreading, which underlies much of the current debate about covered bonds versus securitization. The failure of the originate-to-distribute model of U.S. housing finance has put much of the spotlight on ensuring sufficient skin in the game and mistrusting rating agencies (the key delegated monitor in the system). As a result, the scope for risk spreading may be reduced, hindering the development of a deep market for mortgage-backed securities and widening the scope for the development of covered bonds (where skin in the game is assured, because banks and their depositors keep the risk). While current efforts in many countries to strengthen the legal framework for covered bonds are of course welcome, a key question is therefore whether renewed efforts should be jointly pursued to reactivate the market for securitized instruments. In any event, the development of "mutualized" second-tier finance facilities to help spread risk and boost economies of scale deserves further attention, particularly for the underdeveloped mortgage markets. The necessary role of the state in limiting tail risks (at least as long as the monolines are not back in business) and ensuring liquidity of last resort will also need to be revisited.

More generally, to facilitate participation and risk spreading in a sound manner, a first avenue is to socialize some of the information gathering and dissemination (that is, to make it a public good) or to facilitate the use of common platforms. In some cases, the public provision of market indexes—for example, housing prices by city or rainfall statistics by region—might suffice to help markets develop. In other cases, the unbundling of collection and back-office functions from portfolio management (as is currently attempted in several countries for pension funds) might be needed to produce the economies of scale needed to raise affordability and, hence, to promote participation.

Another possible avenue to reduce participation costs (and boost returns to scale) is to mandate participation. For example, combining the existing second-pillar (mandatory) pension systems in the region with policies to promote the development of a vibrant annuities industry can go a long way toward promoting sustainable long-term finance. However, the relatively complex legal, regulatory, and informational problems that stand in the way of developing the market for life insurance products (including annuities) will need to be removed. To further facilitate the link between pensions and annuities, it may also be helpful to introduce well-designed state guarantees on annuities. In addition, the composition of asset holdings in the worker's pension fund upon retirement should be made as similar as possible to that of the life insurance company from whom the worker will buy his or her annuity.

As regards risk taking and spreading, a first avenue is to promote private sector participation in guarantee schemes where risk is mutualized, based on peer pressure. Such schemes are thriving in Europe and other parts of the world. The LAC region should review them carefully and analyze the extent to which they are exportable to the LAC environment and what can be done to facilitate their introduction. Where states can play a useful role in directly assuming risk through partial credit guarantee (PCG) programs, care must be taken to follow four basic principles: (a) program objectives, mandates, and reporting and disclosure requirements need to be refocused around risk-aversion and more explicitly linked to the agency or collective action frictions with which risk aversion interacts; (b) to ensure financial viability, guarantees should be adequately priced to reflect expected losses and other costs of running the PCG programs; (c) where PCG programs are self-sustaining, they should eventually be divested to the private sector; and (d) where there are hidden risks (fat-tailed or systemic) that free markets cannot handle, these risks should be explicitly recognized and also priced in to the extent possible. Auctioning the guarantees can help facilitate risk discovery. Where information is available, public guarantees can be specifically targeted just outside the private risk frontier to avoid competition and to enhance complementarity with private ventures.

The risks taken by public banks when they move further away from the private risk frontier can be bounded, and public governance protected, in a variety of ways. Earmarked capital brought in by the state to cover specific risks can help state banks assume risk in a responsible, bounded manner while protecting the banks' own capital from depletion. Public-private partnerships in which the state assumes most (but not all) of the risk at a fair price can help facilitate price and risk discovery. Recurrent strategic reviews can help strengthen the governance of second-tier banks engaging in higher-risk activities. Although it is helpful for second-tier development banks to be supervised by the bank supervisors, their supervision needs to be based on different criteria and methods than those used for regular banks, to appropriately acknowledge that development banks' activities should complement, rather than substitute, private financial service providers.

Finally, as regards the countercyclical role of public banks, their increased lending in downturns can play a useful role; this applies all the more so in LAC because it can take pressure off central banks that, in view of the political economy risks of reforming their charters, would have a hard time revising their role as lenders of last resort (more on this below). However, it does not necessarily follow that public banks must play an even greater role in normal times so as to be able to expand lending in the bad times. Instead, public banks that do not compete with private banks (especially those that are strictly second-tier) can more easily obtain from private banks the information they need to safely raise the coverage of the guarantees during downturns.

Policy directions: The dark side

On the dark side of finance, much will need to be done on the regulatory front to deal adequately with the growing interconnectedness of financial markets and institutions. The starting point should be a revisiting of the outer perimeter of regulation. LAC's very broad regulatory reach has served the region well thus far, although it has tended to put a heavy burden on the already stretched human and financial resources of regulatory agencies. And LAC is likely to face additional challenges as financial systems mature. Hence, policies that reduce the burden of oversight by delegating the oversight of the unregulated to the regulated might become desirable. At the same time, LAC needs to find effective ways to oversee the smaller financial institutions, such as the credit co-ops. One way is to leave them mostly unregulated but to strictly limit their funding to the contributions of their members. Another (not necessarily mutually exclusive) way to oversee them is to use auxiliary supervision (for instance, to rely on co-op federations). In that case, however, ways will need to be found to address the potential pitfalls of such delegated oversight.

As regards the inner perimeter, LAC's prevailing silo-based regulatory culture has also served the region well thus far. But again, to limit regulatory arbitrage and potential diseconomies of scope, governments may need to make changes as financial systems mature. Should the silo approach be retained, efforts will be needed to improve the oversight of the large and complex financial conglomerates that this approach unavoidably promotes, which currently incurs major weaknesses.

Improvements in the oversight of conglomerates will in turn need to be paired with a revisiting and, possibly, a major overhaul of the regulatory and resolution framework for financial conglomerates as well as the systemically important financial entities (SIFIs). The improvements (as yet largely untested) that have already been introduced across the region as regards the resolution of individual financial institutions will now need to be extended to the resolution of financial groups and SIFIs, including across borders. Although SIFIs will undoubtedly require tighter oversight, the region should avoid the U.S. example of formally anointing them as such. Instead, the intensity of supervision and tightness of regulation should be adjusted continuously (without sharp boundaries) according to criteria that apply to everyone.

At the same time, the region will need to revamp its liquidity regulations according to a more systemic perspective, to a large extent following the emerging guidelines provided by Basel III. It will also need to review its systemic liquidity access policies to better meet the challenges of the future. The systemic linkages increasingly taking place through funding markets highlight the possible need for lender of last resort (LLR) facilities to support critically important markets, and not just individual liquidity-distressed financial institutions. Although LAC central banks are understandably reluctant to move toward more flexible liquidity support arrangements, possible avenues to manage inherent conflicts might include the temporary relaxation of counterparty and collateral eligibility requirements, the strengthening of governance arrangements, the creation of private liquidity pools and insurance, and improved countercyclical operation of development banks.

Dealing with financial system dynamics will be another major component of LAC's systemic oversight reform. LAC will need to set its macroprudential policy objectives across a menu of progressively more ambitious goals, ranging from simply correcting the distortions brought about by traditional prudential norms to the most ambitious objective of dampening excessive fluctuations, and passing through the intermediate goal of simply making financial systems more resilient to fluctuations. The goals and design of macroprudential tools and policies will also need to reflect the fact that LAC's financial cycles have been more frequent and pronounced and have ended badly more often than in other regions. The region's current exposure to a potentially lethal mix of capital inflows and commodity price booms further raises the premium on quickly establishing or consolidating its macroprudential capacity. On the brighter side, however, by limiting the substitutability between currencies, the floating exchange rate regimes that now prevail in LAC should help limit regulatory arbitrage across borders. This should enhance the scope for a more active macroprudential home policy, even when the latter is asynchronous with that of rest of the world.

All in all, macroprudential policy should clearly not be viewed as a silver bullet. While it can assist monetary policy, particularly by smoothing out the potential conflicts between monetary and exchange rate policies, it should be viewed as a complement (not a substitute) for monetary (or fiscal) policies.

In putting together proper macroprudential tools, a number of design issues will need to be addressed, many of which are highly technical and go much beyond the scope of this report. One key architectural issue deserves special mention, however. While rules-based countercyclical prudential norms in principle would be more congenial to LAC's relatively weak institutions, a significant scope for discretion will unavoidably need to be built in, given the major uncertainties surrounding the impact of such policies. The region's credit lags are likely to further

complicate policy choices, as they make the task of differentiating between healthy catch-ups and unsustainable booms even more difficult.

Thus, putting in place a proper institutional setting should be the first priority. The region's experience with inflation targeting should provide a valuable guide toward implementing the financial stability committees that have already been introduced in several countries of the region. Ensuring the effectiveness, transparency, and accountability of these committees will be of the essence. In fact, defining who bears the final authority and responsibility for systemically oriented prudential decisions is even more crucial than for monetary policy in view of the potential costs (spoiling the party).

LAC's capacity to effectively implement the use of discretion in financial oversight will also largely be conditioned on putting in place an effective framework for systemic supervision. Key components of such a framework will include the seamless intermingling of bottom-up microsystemic supervision with top-down macroprudential supervision, an effective mix of market signals and publicly provided analysis and information, and the development of sophisticated tools to map boundaries and interconnectedness. All of the above, including the design of instruments to elicit market signals, is highly complex and will require much work and attention. At the same time, forming and retaining the qualified staff for designing the tools and implementing the reforms could be a severe problem. Where supervisory agencies are unable to attract the staff, they may need to form cooperative arrangements with central banks. In fact, greater cooperation between the supervisory and financial stability staffs are likely to be required even when they are both housed in the central bank. This cooperation should be based on appropriate decision-making and interagency coordinating arrangements, including allowing information to flow and encouraging staff to work together across agencies A strengthening of supervisory powers will be also needed across much of the region, all the more so where problems of supervisory legal protection and independence are already present.

The improvements in domestic coordination will need to be matched by similar improvements across borders. In fact, the importance of foreign banks in LAC further puts a premium on strengthening such cross-border supervisory coordination. A regional approach could help ensure information sharing and coordination among regional systemic supervisors and provide a unified front in dealing with the large developed countries. Alternative structures might include a college

of supervisors, a formal regional body (possibly under the auspices of an international financial institution), or an association of systemic supervisors similar to the International Association of Deposit Insurers. Wherever they are in force, laws that limit information sharing across borders will need to be amended.

Finally, the region should continue to benefit from international peer reviews that, in addition to contributing to the analytical process, can provide the ammunition the authorities may need to strengthen their resources, powers, and independence.

References

Adrian, T., and H. Shin. 2010. "Liquidity and Leverage." *Journal of Financial Intermediation* 19 (3): 418–37.

Adrian, T., and H. Shin. 2011. "Financial Intermediaries and Monetary Economics." In *Handbook of Monetary Economics*, ed. B. M. Friedman and M. Woodford, vol. 3, 601–46. San Diego, CA: Elsevier.

Aghion, P., and P. Bolton. 1997. "A Theory of Trickle-Down Growth and Development." *Review of Economic Studies* 64: 151–72.

Aizenman, J. Forthcoming. "The Impossible Trinity." In *The Encyclopedia of Financial Globalization*, ed. G. Caprio. San Diego, CA: Elsevier.

Aizenman, J., and G. K. Pasricha. 2010. "Determinants of Financial Stress and Recovery during the Great Recession." Working paper, Santa Cruz Institute for International Economics, University of California Santa Cruz, CA

Akerlof, G. 1970. "The Market for 'Lemons': Quality Uncertainty and the Market Mechanism." *Quarterly Journal of Economics* 84 (3): 488–500.

Alexander, G., C. Eun, and S. Janakiramanan. 1987. "Asset Pricing and Dual Listing on Foreign Capital Markets: A Note." *Journal of Finance* 42 (1): 151–58.

ALIDE (Latin American Association of Development Finance Institutions). 2009. "El Papel Contracíclico de la Banca de Desarrollo Frente a la Crisis Económica Internacional." Estudio básico para la Asamblea General de ALIDE 39, Curaçao, Antillas Holandesas.

Allen, F., and D. Gale. 2000. *Comparing Financial Systems*. Cambridge, MA: MIT Press.

Angeletos, G., G. Lorenzoni, and A. Pavan. 2010. "Beauty Contests and Irrational Exuberance: A Neoclassical Approach." NBER Working Paper 15883, National Bureau of Economic Research, Cambridge, MA.

Angelini, P., L. Clerc, V. Curdia, L. Gambacorta, A. Gerali, A. Locarno, R. Motto, W. Roeger, S. van den Heuvel, and J. Vlcek. 2011. "Basel III: Long-Term Impact on Economic Performance and Fluctuations." Document de Travail 323, Banque de France, Paris.

Anginer, D., A. de la Torre, and A. Ize. 2011. "Risk-Absorption by the State: When Is It Good Public Policy?" World Bank, Washington, DC.

Antolin, P., R. Hinz, H. Rudolph, and J. Yermo. 2010. *Evaluating the Financial Performance of Pension Funds*. Washington, DC: World Bank.

Anzoategui, D., M. S. Martínez Pería, and R. R. Rocha. 2010. "Bank Competition in the Middle East and Northern Africa Region." *Review of Middle East Economics and Finance* 6 (2).

Arcand, J. L., E. Berkes, and U. Panizza. 2011. "Too Much Finance?" Unpublished manuscript, Graduate Institute, Geneva.

Arizala, F., E. Cavallo, and A. Galindo. 2009. "Financial Development and TFP Growth: Cross-Country and Industry-Level Evidence."

RES Working Paper 4630, Inter-American Development Bank, Washington, DC.

Armendáriz de Aghion, B., and J. Morduch. 2005. *The Economics of Microfinance.* Cambridge, MA: MIT Press.

Arping, S., G. Loranth, and A. Morrison. 2010. "Public Initiatives to Support Entrepreneurs: Credit Guarantees versus Co-Funding." *Journal of Financial Stability* 6: 26–35.

Arrow, K. J., and R. C. Lind. 1970. "Uncertainty and the Evaluation of Public Investment Decisions." *American Economics Review* 60 (3): 364–78.

Arvai, Z., R. Rocha, and Y. Saadani. 2011. "A Review of Credit Guarantee Schemes in the Middle East and North Africa Region." Policy Research Working Paper 5612, World Bank, Washington, DC.

Ashbaugh-Skaife, H., D. W. Collins, and R. LaFond, 2006. "The Effects of Corporate Governance on Firms' Credit Ratings." *Journal of Accounting and Economics* 42 (1–2): 203–43.

Ashcraft, A., and T. Schuermann. 2008. "7 Deadly Frictions in Subprime Mortgage Securitization." PRMIA Philippines Credit Forum, Asian Institute of Management, Manila.

Athreya, K., X. S. Tam, and E. R. Young. 2010. "Loan Guarantee Programs for Unsecured Consumer Credit Markets." Working paper, University of Cambridge, Cambridge, U.K.

Banerjee, A., E. Duflo, R. Glennerster, and C. Kinnan. 2009. "The Miracle of Microfinance? Evidence from a Randomized Evaluation." Department of Economics, MIT, Abdul Latif Jameel Poverty Action Lab, Cambridge, MA.

Banerjee, A., and A. Newman. 1993. "Occupational Choice and the Process of Development," *Journal of Political Economy* 101: 274–98.

Barajas, A., G. Dell'Ariccia, and A. Levchenko. 2009. "Credit Booms: The Good, the Bad, and the Ugly." *IMF Research Bulletin* 10 (2).

Barth, J., G. Caprio, and R. Levine. 2001. "Banking Systems around the Globe: Do Regulation and Ownership Affect Performance and Stability?" In *Prudential Regulation and Supervision: Why Is It Important and What Are the Issues?* ed. F. Mishkin. Cambridge, MA: National Bureau of Economic Research.

———. 2008. "Bank Regulations Are Changing: For Better or Worse?" Policy Research Working Paper 4646, World Bank, Washington, DC.

BCBS (Basel Committee on Banking Supervision). 2010a. "Counter-Cyclical Capital Buffer Proposal." Consultative document 172, Bank for International Settlements, Basel, Switzerland.

———. 2010b. "Report and Recommendations of the Cross-Border Bank Resolution Group." BIS Papers No. 162, Bank for International Settlements, Basel, Switzerland.

———. 2010c. "Proposal to Ensure the Loss Absorbency of Regulatory Capital at the Point of Non-Viability." BIS Papers No. 174, Bank for International Settlements, Basel, Switzerland.

———. 2010d. "Basel III, A Global Regulatory Framework for More Resilient Banks and Banking Systems." BIS Papers No. 189, Bank for International Settlements, Basel, Switzerland.

Beck, T., 2011. "Bank Resolution: A Conceptual Framework." In *Financial Regulation at the Crossroads: Implications for Supervision, Institutional Design and Trade*, ed. P. Delimatsis and N. Herger, 53–72. Alphen aan den Rijn, Netherlands: Kluwer Law International.

Beck, T., and A. de la Torre. 2006. "The Basic Analytics of Access to Financial Services." Policy Research Working Paper 4026, World Bank, Washington, DC.

Beck, T., A. Demirgüç-Kunt, and R. Levine. 2007. "Finance, Inequality and the Poor." *Journal of Economic Growth* 12 (1): 27–49.

Beck, T., A. Demirgüç-Kunt, and M. S. Martínez Pería. 2008. "Banking Services for Everyone? Barriers to Bank Access and Use around the World." *World Bank Economic Review* 22 (3): 397–430.

———. 2011. "Bank Financing for SMEs: Evidence Across Countries and Bank-Ownership Types." *Journal of Financial Services Research* 39 (1): 35–54.

Beck, T., L. F. Klapper, and J. C. Mendoza. 2010. "The Typology of Partial Credit Guarantee Funds around the World." *Journal of Financial Stability* 6 (1): 10–25.

Beck, T., and R. Levine. 2005. "Legal Institutions and Financial Development." In *Handbook of New Institutional Economics*, ed. C. Ménard and M. M. Shirley, 251–78. New York: Springer.

Beck, T., R. Levine, and N. Loayza. 2000. "Finance and the Sources of Growth." *Journal of Financial Economics* 58 (1–2): 261–300.

Benartzi, S., and R. H. Thaler. 2007. "Heuristics and Biases in Retirement Savings Behavior." *Journal of Economic Perspectives* 21 (3): 81–104.

Benavente, J. M., A. Galetovic, and R. Sanhueza. 2006. "Fogape: An Economic Analysis." Unpublished paper, World Bank, Washington, DC

Berger, A. N., L. F. Klapper, and G. F. Udell. 2001. "The Ability of Banks to Lend to Informationally Opaque Small Businesses." *Journal of Banking and Finance* 25 (12): 2127–67.

Bernanke, B., and M. Gertler. 1990. "Financial Fragility and Economic Performance." *Quarterly Journal of Economics* 105 (1): 87–114.

———. 1995. "Inside the Black Box: The Credit Channel of Monetary Policy Transmission." *Journal of Economic Perspectives* 9: 27–48.

Berstein, S., and C. Cabrita. 2010. "Los Determinantes de la Elección de AFP en Chile: Nueva Evidencia a Partir de Datos Individuales." *Estudios de Economía* 34 (1): 53–72.

Bhattacharya, U., 1997. "Communication Costs, Information Acquisition, and Voting Decisions in Proxy Contests." *Review of Financial Studies* 10 (4): 1065–97.

Bhojraj, S., and P. Sengupta. 2003. "Effect of Corporate Governance on Bond Ratings and Yields: The Role of Institutional Investors and Outside Directors." *Journal of Business* 76 (3): 455–76.

Birdsall, N., A. de la Torre, and F. Valencia. 2010. "The Washington Consensus: Assessing a Damaged Brand." Policy Research Working Paper Series 5316, World Bank, Washington, DC.

Blake, D., A. Cairns, and K. Dowd. 2009. "Designing a Defined Contribution Plan: What to Learn from Aircraft Designers." *Financial Analysts Journal* 65 (1): 37–42.

Blake, D., B. N. Lehmann, and A. Timmermann. 2002. "Performance Clustering and Incentives in the UK Pension Fund Industry." *Journal of Asset Management* 3: 173–94.

Bordo, M. D., and O. Jeanne. 2002a. "Boom-Busts in Asset Prices, Economic Instability and Monetary Policy." CEPR Discussion Papers 3398, Centre for Economic Policy Research, London.

———. 2002b. "Monetary Policy and Asset Prices: Does 'Benign Neglect' Make Sense?" *International Finance* 5 (2): 139–64.

Borio, C., C. Furfine, and P. Lowe. 2001. "Procyclicality of the Financial System and Financial Stability: Issues and Policy Options." BIS Papers No. 1, Bank for International Investments, Basel, Switzerland.

Borio, C., and H. Zhu. 2008. "Capital Regulation, Risk-Taking and Monetary Policy: A Missing Link in the Transmission Mechanism?" BIS Working Papers 268, Bank for International Investments, Basel, Switzerland.

Brizzi, A. 2001. "Rural Development and Agriculture." In *Mexico: A Comprehensive Development Agenda for the New Era*, ed. M. Guigale, O. Lafourcarde, and V. H. Nguyen, 319–46. Washington, DC: World Bank.

Broner, F., T. Didier, A. Erce, and S. Schmukler. 2010. "Gross Capital Flows: Dynamics and Crises." Working Paper 1039, Bank of Spain, Madrid.

Broner, F., G. Lorenzoni, and S. Schmukler. Forthcoming. "Why Do Emerging Economies Borrow Short Term?" *Journal of the European Economic Association*.

Brunnermeier, M., A. Crockett, C. Goodhart, A. Persaud, and H. Shin. 2009. "The Fundamental Principles of Financial Regulation." *Geneva Report on the World Economy* 11, Geneva: International Center for Monetary and Banking Studies; London: Centre for Economic Policy Research.

Brunnermeier, M. K., and L. H. Pedersen. 2009. "Market Liquidity and Funding Liquidity." *Review of Financial Studies* 22 (6): 2201–38.

Burgess, R., and R. Pande. 2005. "Do Rural Banks Matter? Evidence from Indian Social Banking Experiment." *American Economic Review* 95: 780–95.

Caballero, R. J., and A. Krishnamurthy. 2008. "Collective Risk Management in a Flight to Quality Episode." *Journal of Finance* 63 (5): 2195–2230.

Caballero, R. J., and P. Kurlat. 2009. "The 'Surprising' Origin and Nature of Financial Crises: A Macroeconomic Policy Proposal." Prepared for the Symposium on Financial Stability and Macroeconomic Policy, Jackson Hole, WY, August 20–22.

Calderón, C., and L. Servén. 2011. "Macro-Prudential Policies over the Cycle in Latin America." LAC Finance Development Flagship, Office of the Chief Economist for Latin America and the Caribbean, World Bank, Washington, DC.

Calderón-Colín, R., E. E. Domínguez, and M. J. Schwartz. 2008. "Consumer Confusion: The Choice of AFORE in Mexico." IMF Working Paper 08/177, International Monetary Fund, Washington, DC.

Calomiris, C. 1999. "Building an Incentive-Compatible Safety Net." *Journal of Banking and Finance* 23, 1499–1519.

Calomiris, C. W., and C. P. Himmelberg. 1994. "Directed Credit Programs for Agriculture and Industry: Arguments from Theory and Fact." In *Proceedings of the 1993 World Bank Annual Conference on Development Economics*, 113–37. *World Bank Economic Review* (supplement), March 1.

Calomiris, C. W., and C. M. Kahn. 1989. "A Theoretical Framework for Analyzing Self-Regulation of Banks." Working paper, University of Illinois, Urbana.

———. 1991. "The Role of Demandable Debt in Structuring Optimal Banking Arrangements." *American Economic Review* 81 (3): 497–513.

Calvo, G., A. Izquierdo, and E. Talvi. 2003. "Sudden Stops, the Real Exchange Rate, and Fiscal Sustainability: Argentina's Lessons." NBER Working Paper 9828, National Bureau of Economic Research, Cambridge, MA.

Calvo, G., and C. M. Reinhart. 2002. "Fear of Floating." *Quarterly Journal of Economics* 107 (2): 379–408.

Campbell, J., and L. Viceira. 2002. *Strategic Asset Allocation: Portfolio Choice for Long-Term Investor.* Oxford, U.K.: Oxford University Press.

Caprio, G., J. Barth, R. Levine, and D. Nolle. 2007. "Comparative International Characteristics of Banking." Bank of England Conference Proceedings 2008, London.

Caprio, G., and P. Honohan. 2001. *Finance for Growth: Policy Choices in a Volatile World.* Washington, DC: World Bank; New York: Oxford University Press.

Cárdenas, M., and E. Levy-Yeyati. 2011. "Latin America Economic Perspectives: Shifting Gears in an Age of Heightened Expectations." Washington, DC: Brookings Institution.

Carvalho, F. A., and C. F. Azevedo. 2008. "The Incidence of Reserve Requirements in Brazil: Do Bank Stockholders Share the Burden?" *Journal of Applied Economics* 11 (1): 61–90.

Castaneda, P., and H. Rudolph. 2011. "Upgrading Investment Regulations in Second Pillar Pension Systems: A Proposal for Colombia." Policy Research Working Paper 5775, World Bank, Washington, DC.

Cerda, R. 2006. "Movilidad en al Cartera de Cotizantes por AFP: La importancia de Ser Primero en Rentabilidad." PUC Working Paper 309, Pontificia Universidad Católica, Santiago.

Chan, N. T. L. 2011. "Universal Banking—Hong Kong's Perspective." Central Banker's Speeches, Bank for International Investments, Basel, Switzerland.

Cheikhrouhou, H., R. Rocha, H. Rudolph, and C. Thorburn. 2006. "Financial Sector Dimensions of the Colombian Pension System." Policy Research Working Paper 5775, World Bank, Washington, DC.

Chinn, M., and H. Ito. 2008. "A New Measure of Financial Openness." *Journal of Comparative Policy Analysis* 10 (3): 309–22.

Christiano, L., C. L. Itut, R. Motto, and M. Rostagno. 2010. "Monetary Policy and Stock Market Booms." NBER Working Paper 16402, National Bureau of Economic Research, Cambridge, MA.

Claessens, S., G. Dell'Ariccia, D. Igan, and L. Laeven. 2010. "Lessons and Policy Implications from the Global Financial Crisis." IMF Working Paper 10/44, International Monetary Fund, Washington, DC.

Claessens, S., D. Klingebiel, and S. Schmukler. 2006. "Stock Market Development and Internationalization: Do Economic Fundamentals Spur Both Similarly?" *Journal of Empirical Finance* 13 (3): 316–50.

Claessens, S., M. A. Kose, and M. E. Terrones. 2011a. "How Do Business and Financial Cycles Interact?" IMF Working Paper 11/88, International Monetary Fund, Washington, DC.

———. Forthcoming. "Financial Cycles: What? How? When?" In *NBER International Seminar on Macroeconomics 2010*, ed. L. Reichlin and K. West, 303–43. National Bureau of Economic Research. National Bureau of Economic Research, Cambridge, MA.

Claessens, S., R. Lee, and J. Zechner. 2003. "The Future of Stock Exchanges in European Union Accession Countries." Corporation of London/Centre for Economic Policy Research, London.

Claessens, S., and N. Van Horen. 2008. "Location Decisions of Foreign Banks and Institutional Competitive Advantage." DNB Working Paper 172, Netherlands Central Bank, Amsterdam.

———. 2009. "Being a Foreigner among Domestic Banks: Asset or Liability?" MPRA Paper 13467, University Library of Munich, Germany.

Clarke, G., R. Cull, and M. S. Martínez Pería. 2006. "Foreign Bank Participation and Access to Credit across Firms in Developing Countries." *Journal of Comparative Economics* 34 (4): 774–95.

Columba, F., L. Gambacorta, and P. E. Mistrulli. 2009. "The Effects of Mutual Guarantee Consortia on the Quality of Bank Lending." MPRA Paper 17052, University Library of Munich, Germany.

Corbo, V., and K. Schmidt-Hebbel. 2003. "Macroeconomic Effects of Pension Reform in Chile." In FIAP: *Pension Reforms: Results and Challenges*, International Federation of Pension Funds Administrator, Santiago, Chile.

———. 2010. "The International Crisis and Latin America: Growth Effects and Development Strategies." CASE Network Studies and Analyses No. 429, Universidad Católica de Chile, Santiago de Chile.

Corporación Andina de Fomento. 2011. *Servicios Financieros para el Desarrollo: Promoviendo el Acceso en América Latina*. Reporte de Economía y Desarrollo, Corporación Andina de Fomento, Bogotá.

Cortes, M., M. Dijkman, and E. Gutierrez. 2011. "Micro-Systemic Regulation: A LAC Perspective." LAC Finance Development Flagship, Office of the Chief Economist for Latin America and the Caribbean, World Bank, Washington, DC.

Cull, R., and M. S. Martínez Pería. 2010. "Foreign Bank Participation in Developing Countries: What Do We Know about the Drivers and Consequences of This Phenomenon?" Policy Research Working Paper Series 5398, World Bank, Washington, DC.

Dahlquist, M., L. Pinkowitz, R. Stulz, and R. Williamson. 2003. "Corporate Governance and the Home Bias." *Journal of Financial and Quantitative Analysis* 38 (1): 87–110.

Dahlquist, M., and G. Robertsson. 2001. "Direct Foreign Ownership, Institutional Investors, and Firm Characteristics." *Journal of Financial Economics* 59: 413–40.

Debrun, X., and R. Kapoor. 2010. "Fiscal Policy and Macroeconomic Stability: Automatic Stabilizers Work, Always and Everywhere." IMF Working Paper 10/111, International Monetary Fund, Washington, DC.

de Carvalho, A. G., and G. Pennacchi. 2011. "Can a Stock Exchange Improve Corporate Behavior? Evidence from Firms' Migration to Premium Listings in Brazil." *Journal of Corporate Finance*, 1–21. Elsevier B.V.

de Grauwe, P. 2009. "The Crisis as a Paradigm Shift." In *Aftershocks: Economic Crisis and Institutional Choice*, ed. A. Hemerijck, B. Knapen, and E. van Doorne, 82–90. Amsterdam: Amsterdam University Press.

De Gregorio, J., and P. Guidotti. 1995. "Financial Development and Economic Growth." *World Development* 23 (3): 433–48.

Deidda, L., and B. Fattouh. 2002. "Non-Linearity between Finance and Growth." *Economics Letters* 74: 339–45.

de la Torre, A., C. Calderón, T. Didier, J. Messina, and S. Schmukler. 2010a. "From Global Collapse to Recovery: Economic Adjustment and Growth Prospects in Latin America and the Caribbean." World Bank Annual Meetings Report, Washington, DC.

de la Torre, A., C. Calderón, T. Didier, T. Kouame, M. I. Reyes, and S. Schmukler. 2011. "LAC Success Put to the Test." World Bank Annual Meetings Report, Spring. Washington, DC.

de la Torre, A., C. Calderón, T. Didier, E. Levy-Yeyati, and S. Schmukler. 2010b. "The New Face of Latin America and the Caribbean: Globalized, Resilient, Dynamic." World Bank Annual Meetings Report, Washington, DC.

de la Torre, A., E. Feyen, and A. Ize. 2011. "Benchmarking LAC's Financial Development," LAC Finance Development Flagship, Office of the Chief Economist for Latin America and the Caribbean, World Bank, Washington, DC.

de la Torre, A., J. C. Gozzi, and S. L. Schmukler, 2006. "Financial Development in Latin America: Big Emerging Issues, Limited Policy Answers," Policy Research Working Paper 3969, World Bank, Washington, DC.

———. 2007a. "Stock Market Development under Globalization: Whither the Gains from Reforms?" *Journal of Banking and Finance* 31 (6): 1731–54.

———. 2007b. *Innovative Experiences in Access to Finance: Market Friendly Roles for the Visible Hand?* Brookings Institution and the World Bank, Washington, DC.

de la Torre, A., E. Feyen, and A. Ize. 2011. "Benchmarking LAC's Financial Development," LAC Finance Development Flagship, Office of the Chief Economist for Latin America and the Caribbean, World Bank, Washington, DC.

———. 2007c. "Financial Development: Emerging and Maturing Policy Issues." *World Bank Research Observer* 22 (1): 67–102.

de la Torre, A., and A. Ize. 2010. "Regulatory Reform: Integrating Paradigms." *International Finance* 13 (1): 109–39.

———. 2011. "Containing Systemic Risk: Paradigm-Based Perspectives on Regulatory Reform." *Economía* 11 (1): 25–64.

de la Torre, A., M. S. Martínez Pería, and S. Schmukler. 2010. "Bank Involvement with

SMEs: Beyond Relationship Lending." *Journal of Banking and Finance* 34 (9): 2280–93.

de la Torre, A., and S. Schmukler. 2004. "Coping with Risks Through Mismatches: Domestic and International Financial Contracts for Emerging Economies." *International Finance* 7 (3): 349–90.

———. 2007. *Emerging Capital Markets and Globalization: The Latin American Experience.* Washington, DC: World Bank.

Delis, M., and G. Kouretas. 2011. "Interest Rates and Bank Risk-Taking." *Journal of Banking and Finance* 35: 840–55.

Dell'Ariccia, G., and R. Marquez. 2008. "Can Cost Increases Increase Competition? Asymmetric Information and Equilibrium Prices." *RAND Journal of Economics* 39 (1): 144–62.

de Meza, D., and D. C. Webb. 1987. "Too Much Investment: A Problem of Asymmetric Information." *Quarterly Journal of Economics* 102 (2): 281–92.

———. 1999. "Wealth, Enterprise and Credit Policy." *Economic Journal* 109 (455): 153–63.

Demirgüç-Kunt, A., E. Feyen, and R. Levine. 2011. "The Evolving Roles of Banks and Markets in Economic Development." Working Paper, World Bank, Washington, DC.

Demirgüç-Kunt, A., and R. Levine. 1999. "Bank-Based and Market-Based Financial Systems: Cross-Country Comparisons." Policy Research Working Paper 2143, World Bank, Washington, DC.

Demirgüç-Kunt, A., and L. Servén. 2010. "Are All the Sacred Cows Dead? Implications of the Financial Crisis for Macro and Financial Policies." *World Bank Research Observer* 25(1): 91–124.

de Nicolo, G. D., P. Honohan, and A. Ize. 2005. "Dollarization of Bank Deposits: Causes and Consequences." *Journal of Banking and Finance* 29 (7): 1697–1727.

Dewatripont, M., and J. Tirole. 1994. "A Theory of Debt and Equity: Diversity of Securities and Manager-Shareholder Congruence." *Quarterly Journal of Economics* 109 (4): 1027–54.

Diamond, D. W., and P. H. Dybvig. 1983. "Bank Runs, Deposit Insurance, and Liquidity." *Journal of Political Economy* 91: 401–19.

Diamond, D., and R. Rajan. 2000. "A Theory of Bank Capital." *Journal of Finance* 55: 2431–65.

Didier, T. 2011a. "Information Asymmetries and Institutional Investor Mandates." Policy Research Paper 5586, World Bank, Washington, DC.

———. 2011b. "Issues on SME Financing in Chile." Technical note prepared for the 2010/2011 Chilean FSAP, World Bank, Washington, DC.

Didier, T., C. Hevia, and S. Schmukler. 2011. "How Resilient Were Emerging Economies to the Global Crisis?" Policy Research Working Paper 5637, World Bank, Washington, DC.

Didier, T., R. Rigobon, and S. Schmukler. 2011. "Unexploited Gains from International Diversification: Patterns of Portfolio Holdings around the World." NBER Working Paper 16629, National Bureau of Economic Research, Cambridge, MA.

Didier, T., and S. Schmukler. 2011a. "Financial Development in Latin America: Stylized Facts and the Road Ahead." LAC Finance Development Flagship, Office of the Chief Economist for Latin America and the Caribbean, World Bank, Washington, DC.

———. 2011b. "Financial Globalization: Some Basic Indicators for Latin America and the Caribbean," LAC Finance Development Flagship, Office of the Chief Economist for Latin America and the Caribbean, World Bank, Washington, DC.

Dimson, E., P. Marsh, and M. Staunton. 2006. "The Worldwide Equity Premium: A Smaller Puzzle." Paper prepared for the 33rd European Finance Association Annual Meeting, Zurich, August 23–26.

Djankov, S., R. La Porta, F. Lopez-de-Silanes, and A. Shleifer. 2008. "The Law and Economics of Self-Dealing." *Journal of Financial Economics* 88 (3): 430–65.

Domonski, D. 2005. "Foreign Banks in Emerging Market Economies: Changing Players, Changing Issues." *BIS Quarterly Review*, December.

Domowitz, I., J. Glen, and A. Madhavan. 1998. "International Cross-Listing and Order Flow Migration: Evidence from an Emerging Market." *Journal of Finance* 53 (6): 2001–27.

Drehmann, M., C. Borio, L. Gambacorta, G. Jiminez, and C. Trucharte. 2010. "Countercyclical Capital Buffers: Exploring Options." BIS Working Paper 317, Bank for International Investments, Basel, Switzerland.

Dupas, P., and J. Robinson. 2009. "Savings Constraints and Microenterprise Development: Evidence from a Field Experiment in Kenya." NBER Working Paper 14693, National Bureau of Economic Research, Cambridge, MA.

Easterly, W. 1993. "How Much Do Distortions Affect Growth?" *Journal of Monetary Economics* 32: 187–212.

Edison, H., and F. Warnock. 2004. "U.S. Investors' Emerging Market Equity Portfolios: A Security-Level Analysis." *Review of Economics and Statistics* 86 (3): 691–704.

Eichengreen, B., and R. Hausmann. 1999. "Exchange Rates and Financial Fragility." In *Proceedings*, 329–68. Kansas City, MO: Federal Reserve Bank of Kansas City.

———. 2002. "How to Eliminate Original Financial Sin." *Financial Times*, November 22.

Eichengreen, B., R. Hausmann, and U. Panizza. 2005. "The Mystery of Original Sin," in *Other People's Money: Debt Denomination and Financial Instability in Emerging Market Economies*, ed. B. Eichengreen, and R. Hausmann. Chicago: University of Chicago Press.

Epstein, L. G. 1999. "A Definition of Uncertainty Aversion." *Review of Economic Studies* 66 (3): 579–608.

Errunza, V. 2001. "Foreign Portfolio Equity Investments, Financial Liberalization, and Economic Development." *Review of International Economics* 9 (4): 703–26.

Escriva, J. L., E. Fuentes, and A. Garcia-Herrero. 2010. "A Balance and Projections of the Experience in Infrastructure of Pension Funds in Latin America." Research Department Working Paper 10/02, Banco Bilbao Vizcaya Argentaria, Vizcaya, Spain.

Evanoff, D. D., and L. D. Wall. 2000. "Subordinated Debt and Bank Capital Reform." Working Paper Series 24, Federal Reserve Bank of Atlanta, GA.

Eyzaguirre, N., R. Valdes, S. Phillips, and L. Cubeddu. 2011. "Regional Economic Outlook: Western Hemisphere—Watching Out for Overheating." Washington, DC: International Monetary Fund.

Ferguson, N. 2008. *The Ascent of Money: A Financial History of the World.* New York: Penguin Press.

Fernández de Lis, S., and A. García-Herrero. 2010. "Dynamic Provisioning: Some Lessons from Existing Experiences." ADBI Working Paper Series No. 218, Asian Development Bank Institute, Tokyo.

Feyen, E., R. Lester, and R. Rocha. 2011. "What Drives the Development of the Insurance Sector: An Empirical Analysis Based on a Panel of Developed and Developing Economies," World Bank Policy Research Working Paper 5572, World Bank, Washington, DC.

Frankel, J. A., and G. Saravelos. 2010. "Are Leading Indicators of Financial Crises Useful for Assessing Country Vulnerability? Evidence from the 2008–09 Global Crisis." NBER Working Paper 16047, National Bureau of Economic Research, Cambridge, MA.

Friedman, M. 1959. *A Program for Monetary Stability.* New York, NY: Fordham University Press.

FSB (Financial Stability Board). 2010. "Reducing the Moral Hazard Posed by Systemically Important Financial Institutions." FSB Recommendations and Time Lines, October 20. http://www.financialstabilityboard.org/publications/r_101111a.pdf.

Galati, G., and R. Moessner. 2011. "Macroprudential Policy: A Literature Review." BIS Working Paper 337, Bank for International Settlements, Basel, Switzerland.

Gale, W. G. 1991. "Economic Effects of Federal Credit Programs." *American Economic Review* 81 (1): 133–52.

Galindo, A., and L. Rojas-Suarez. 2011. "Provisioning Requirements in Latin America: Where Does the Region Stand?" IDB Policy Brief 119, Inter-American Development Bank, Washington, DC.

Galor, O., and J. Zeira. 1993. "Income Distribution and Macroeconomics." *Review of Economic Studies* 60 (1): 35–52.

Garicano, L., and R. M. Lastra. 2010. "Towards a New Architecture for Financial Stability: Seven Principles." *Journal of International Economic Law* 13 (3): 597–621.

Geanakoplos, J. 2009. "The Leverage Cycle." Discussion Paper 1715, Cowles Foundation for Research in Economics, Yale University, New Haven, CT.

Gelos, G. 2009. "Banking Spreads in Latin America." *Economic Inquiry* 47 (4): 796–814.

Gennaioli, N., A. Shleifer, and R. W. Vishny. 2010. "Neglected Risks, Financial Innovation, and Financial Fragility." NBER Working Paper 16068, National Bureau of Economic Research, Cambridge, MA.

Giannetti, M., and S. Ongena. 2009. "Financial Integration and Firm Performance: Evidence from Foreign Bank Entry in Emerging Markets." *Review of Finance* 13: 181–223.

Gill, I., T. Packard, and J. Yermo. 2004. "Keeping the Promise of Social Security in Latin America." Stanford, CA: Stanford University Press; Washington, DC: World Bank.

Glaser E., S. Johnson, and A. Shleifer. 2001. "Coase versus the Coasians." *Quarterly Journal of Economics* 116 (3): 853–99.

Goldsmith, R. 1969. *Financial Structure and Development*. New Haven, CT: Yale University Press.

Goodhart, C. 2010a. "How Should We Regulate Bank Capital and Financial Products? What Role for 'Living Wills'?" *Revista de Economia Institucional* 12: 85–109.

———. 2010b. "Is a Less Pro-Cyclical Financial System an Achievable Goal?" *National Institute Economic Review* 211: 81–90.

———. 2011. "The Emerging New Architecture of Financial Regulation." CFS Working Paper 2011/12, Center of Financial Studies, Goethe-Universität, Frankfurt.

Goodhart, C., and A. Persaud. 2008. "How to Avoid the Next Crash." *Financial Times*, January 30.

Goodhart, C., and D. Schoemaker. 1995. "Institutional Separation between Supervisory and Monetary Agencies." In *The Central Bank and the Financial System*, ed. C. Goodhart, 333–413. Cambridge, MA: MIT Press.

Gordy, M., and B. Howells. 2006. "Procyclicality in Basel II: Can We Treat the Disease Without Killing the Patient?" *Journal of Financial Intermediation* 15: 395–417.

Gorton, G., and A. Metrick. 2010. "Securitized Banking and the Run on Repo." Yale ICF Working Paper 09-14, International Center for Finance, Yale University, New Haven, CT.

Gourinchas, P. O., N. Govillot, and H. Rey. 2010. "Exorbitant Privilege and Exorbitant Duty." IMES Discussion Paper Series 10-E-20, Institute for Monetary and Economic Studies, Bank of Japan, Tokyo.

Gourinchas, P. O., and H. Rey. 2007. "International Financial Adjustment." *Journal of Political Economy* 115 (4): 665–703.

Gourinchas, P. O., H. Rey, and K. Truempler. 2011. "The Financial Crisis and the Geography of Wealth Transfers." NBER Working Paper 17353, National Bureau of Economic Research, Cambridge, MA.

Gozzi, J. C., R. Levine, and S. Schmukler. 2010. "Patterns of International Capital Raisings." *Journal of International Economics* 8 (1): 45–57.

Granlund, P. 2009. "Supervisory Approaches and Financial Market Development: Some Correlation Based Evidence." *Journal of Banking Regulation* 11: 6–30.

Gray, D., and S. Malone. 2008. *Macrofinancial Risk Analysis*. Wiley Finance Series. West Sussex, England: John Wiley and Sons.

Gray, D., and J. P. Walsh. 2008. "Factor Model for Stress-testing with a Contingent Claims Model of the Chilean Banking System." IMF Working Paper 10/124, International Monetary Fund, Washington, DC.

Greenwald, B., and J. Stiglitz. 1989. "Toward a Theory of Rigidities." *American Economic Review* 79 (2): 364–69.

Haines, G., J. Madill, and A. Riding. 2007. "Incrementality of SME Loan Guarantees." *Small Business Economics* 29 (1): 47–61.

Halac, M., and S. L. Schmukler. 2004. "Distributional Effects of Crises: The Financial Channel." *Economía* 5(1); 1–67.

Haldane, A. 2009a. "Rethinking the Financial Network." Speech delivered at the Financial Student Association, Amsterdam, April.

———. 2009b. "Why Banks Failed the Stress Test." Speech presented at the Marcus-Evans Conference on Stress-Testing, London, February 9–10.

Haldane, A. 2010a. "What Is the Contribution of the Financial System: Miracle or Mirage?" In *The Future of Finance and the Theory that Underpins It*, 87–120. London: London School of Economics Press.

———. 2010b. "The $100 Billion Question." Bank of England, London, March.

Hanson, S., A. Kashyap, and J. Stein. 2010. "A Macroprudential Approach to Financial Regulation." *Journal of Economic Perspectives* 25 (1): 3–28.

Harding, D., and A. R. Pagan. 2002a. "A Comparison of Two Business Cycle Dating Methods." *Journal of Economic Dynamics and Control* 27: 1681–90.

———. 2002b. "Dissecting the Cycle: A Methodological Investigation." *Journal of Monetary Economics* 29: 365–81.

Hargis, K. 2000. "International Cross-Listing and Stock Market Development in Emerging Economies." *International Review of Economics and Finance* 9 (2): 101–22.

Hellwig, M. 2010. "Capital Regulation after the Crisis: Business as Usual?" Max Planck Institute for Research on Collective Goods, Bonn.

Heysen, S., and M. Auqui. 2011. "Recent Trends in Banking Supervision in LAC." LAC Finance Development Flagship, Office of the Chief Economist for Latin America and the Caribbean, World Bank, Washington, DC.

Hirtle, B., T. Scheurman, and K. Stiroh. 2009. "Macroprudential Supervision of Financial

Institutions: Lessons from the SCAP." Staff Report 409, Federal Reserve Bank of New York, NY.

Holland, A., and C. Mulder. 2006. "Can Indexed Debt Absolve Original Sin? The Role of Inflation-Indexed Debt in Developing Local Currency Markets." In *Financial Dollarization: The Policy Agenda*, ed. A. Armas, A. Ize, and E. Levy-Yeyati. Palgrave Macmillan, New York, NY.

Holmstrom, B., and P. Milgrom. 1991. "Multitask Principal-Agent Analyses: Incentive Contracts, Asset Ownership, and Job Design." *Journal of Law, Economics, and Organization* 7: 24–52.

Holmstrom, B., and J. Tirole. 1998. "Private and Public Supply of Liquidity." NBER Working Paper 5817, National Bureau of Economic Research, Cambridge, MA.

Honohan, P. 2008. "Partial Credit Guarantees: Principles and Practice." Prepared for the Conference on Partial Credit Guarantees, Washington, DC, March 13–14.

Huang, R., and L. Ratnovski. 2011. "The Dark Side of Bank Wholesale Funding." *Journal of Financial Intermediation* 20 (2): 248–63.

IDB (Inter-American Development Bank). 2005. *Unlocking Credit: The Quest for Deep and Stable Bank Lending*. Economic and Social Progress Report. Washington, DC: IDB.

———. 2007. *Living with Debt: How to Limit the Risks of Sovereign Finance*. Washington, DC: IDB.

Ilyina, A., A. Guscina, and H. Kamil. 2010. "Does Procyclical Fiscal Policy Reinforce Incentives to Dollarize Sovereign Debt?" IMF Working Paper 10/168, International Monetary Fund, Washington, DC.

IMF (International Monetary Fund). 2010. "Meeting New Challenges to Stability and Building a Safer System." Global Financial Stability Report, IMF, Washington, DC.

Impavido, G., E. Lasagabaster, and M. Garcia-Huitron. 2010. "Competition and Asset Allocation Challenges for Mandatory Defined Contributions Pensions: New Policy Directions." World Bank, Washington, DC.

Innes, R. 1991. "Investment and Government Intervention in Credit Markets When There Is Asymmetric Information." *Journal of Public Economics* 46 (3): 347–81.

———. 1992. "Adverse Selection, Investment, and Profit Taxation." *European Economic Review* 36 (7): 1427–52.

Ioannidou, V., S. Ongena, and J. L. Peydró. 2009. "Monetary Policy, Risk-Taking and Pricing: Evidence from a Quasi-Natural Experiment." Discussion Paper 2009-31S, Tilburg University, Center for Economic Research, Tilburg, Netherlands.

Izquierdo, A., and E. Talvi. 2011. *One Region, Two Speeds? Challenges of the New Economic Order for Latin America and the Caribbean*. Washington, DC: Inter-American Development Bank.

Jaffee, D. M., and T. Russell. 1976. "Imperfect Information, Uncertainty, and Credit Rationing." *Quarterly Journal of Economics* 90 (4): 651–66.

Jeanne, O., and A. Korinek. 2011. "Managing Credit Booms and Busts: A Pigouvian Taxation Approach." NBER Working Paper 16377, National Bureau of Economic Research, Cambridge, MA.

Jenkins, H. 2000. "Commercial Bank Behavior in Micro and Small Enterprise Finance." Development Discussion Paper 741, Harvard Institute for International Development, Cambridge, MA.

Jiménez, G., S. Ongena, J. L. Peydró, and J. Saurina. 2008. "Hazardous Times for Monetary Policy: What Do Twenty-Three Million Bank Loans Say about the Effects of Monetary Policy on Credit Risk-Taking?" Working Paper 0833, Bank of Spain, Madrid.

Joh, S. W. 2003. "Corporate Governance and Firm Profitability: Evidence from Korean Firms before the Economic Crisis." *Journal of Financial Economics* 68 (2): 287–322.

Joint Forum. 2010. "Review of the Differentiated Nature and Scope of Financial Regulation: Key Issues and Recommendations." Bank for International Settlements, Basel, Switzerland.

Jorda, O., M. Schularick, and A. M. Taylor. 2010. "Financial Crises, Credit Booms, and External Imbalances: 140 Years of Lessons." NBER Working Paper 16567, National Bureau of Economic Research, Cambridge, MA.

Kacperczyk, M., C. Sialm, and L. Zheng. 2008. "Unobserved Actions of Mutual Funds." *Review of Financial Studies* 21 (6): 2379–2416.

Kang, J. K., and R. Stulz. 1997. "Why Is There a Home Bias? An Analysis of Foreign Portfolio Equity Ownership in Japan." *Journal of Financial Economics* 46 (1): 3–28.

Karlan, D., and J. Zinman. 2010. "Expanding Credit Access: Using Randomized Supply

Decisions to Estimate Impacts." *Review of Financial Studies* 23 (1): 433–64.

Kashyap, A., and J. Stein. 2004. "Cyclical Implications of the Basel II Capital Standards." Federal Reserve Bank of Chicago. *Economic Perspectives* 28: 18–31.

Kay, J. 2010. "Should We Have Narrow Banking" In *The Future of Finance and the Theory that Underpins It*, ed. A. Turner et al., 215–34. London: London School of Economics.

Keynes, J. M. 1936. *The General Theory of Employment, Interest and Money*. New York: Macmillan; Cambridge University Press.

Kindleberger, C. P. 1989. *Manias, Panics, and Crashes: A History of Financial Crises*, rev. ed. New York: Basic Books.

King, R. G., and R. Levine. 1993. "Finance and Growth: Schumpeter Might Be Right." *Quarterly Journal of Economics* 108 (3): 717–37.

Kiyotaki, N., and J. Moore. 1997. "Credit Cycles." *Journal of Political Economy* 105: 211–48.

Klapper, L., 2006. "The Role of Factoring for Small and Medium Enterprises." *Journal of Banking and Finance* 30 (11): 3111–30.

Klapper, L., and I. Love. 2004. "Corporate Governance, Investor Protection, and Performance in Emerging Markets." *Journal of Corporate Finance* 10 (5): 703–28.

Klapper, L., and R. Zaidi. 2005. "A Survey of Government Regulation Intervention in Financial Markets." Prepared for the World Development Report 2005, World Bank, Washington, DC.

Klein, M. 1996. "Risk, Taxpayers, and the Role of Government in Project Finance." Policy Research Working Paper 1688, World Bank, Washington, DC.

Kroszner, R., and R. Shiller. 2011. *Reforming US Financial Markets: Reflections Before and Beyond Dodd-Frank*. Cambridge, MA: MIT Press.

Lacker, J. M. 1994. "Does Adverse Selection Justify Government Intervention in Loan Markets?" Federal Reserve Bank of Richmond. *Economic Quarterly* 80 (1): 61–95.

Laeven, L., and F. Valencia. 2008. "Systemic Banking Crises: A New Database." IMF Working Paper 08/224, International Monetary Fund, Washington, DC.

Lane, P. R., and G. M. Milesi-Ferretti. 2001. "The External Wealth of Nations: Measures of Foreign Assets and Liabilities for Industrial and Developing Countries." *Journal of International Economics* 55 (2): 263–94.

———. 2007. "The External Wealth of Nations Mark II: Revised and Extended Estimates of Foreign Assets and Liabilities, 1970–2004." *Journal of International Economics* 73 (2): 223–50.

Lanyi, A., and R. Saracoglu. 1983. "The Importance of Interest Rates in Developing Economies." *Finance and Development* 20 (2): 20–23.

La Porta, R., F. Lopez-de-Silanes, and A. Shleifer. 2002. "Government Ownership of Banks." *Journal of Finance* 57: 265–301.

La Porta, R., F. Lopez-de-Silanes, A. Shleifer, and R. Vishny. 1997. "Legal Determinants of External Finance." *Journal of Finance* 52 (3): 1131–50.

Larraín, C, and J. Quiroz. 2006. "Estudio para el Fondo de Garantía de Pequeños Empresarios." Banco Estado, Santiago, Chile.

Lee, R. M. G. 1999. *What Is an Exchange? The Automation, Management and Regulation of Financial Markets*. Oxford, U.K.: Oxford University Press.

Lerner, J., and P. Tufano. 2011. "The Consequences of Financial Innovation: A Counterfactual Research Agenda." NBER Working Paper 16780, National Bureau of Economic Research, Cambridge, MA.

Levine, R., and S. Schmukler. 2006. "Internationalization and Stock Market Liquidity." *Review of Finance* 10 (1): 153–87.

———. 2007. "Migration, Liquidity Spillovers, and Trade Diversion: The Effects of Internationalization on Stock Market Activity." *Journal of Banking and Finance* 31 (6): 1595–1612.

Levy-Yeyati, E., 2011a. "The Currency Issue: A Note on Globalization, Offshoring and Dollarization in Latin America," LAC Finance Development Flagship, Office of the Chief Economist for Latin America and the Caribbean, World Bank, Washington, DC.

———. 2011b. "Financial Globalization in Latin America: Myth, Reality, and Policy Matters." LAC Finance Development Flagship, Office of the Chief Economist for Latin America and the Caribbean, World Bank, Washington, DC.

Li, W. 1998. "Government Loan, Guarantee, and Grant Programs: An Evaluation." Federal Reserve Bank of Richmond. *Economic Quarterly* 84 (4): 25–51.

Licht, A. N. 1998. "Stock Market Integration in Europe." CAER II Discussion Paper No. 15, Harvard Institute for International Development, Cambridge, MA.

Lo, A. W. 2009. "Regulatory Reform in the Wake of the Financial Crisis of 2007–2008." *Journal of Financial Economic Policy* 1 (1): 4–43.

Lombra, R., and M. Wasylenko. 1984. "The Subsidization of Small Businesses through Federal Credit Programs: Analytical Foundations." *Journal of Economics and Business* 36 (2): 263–74.

Lorenzoni, G. 2008. "Inefficient Credit Booms." *Review of Economic Studies* 75 (3): 809–33.

Mankiw, N.G. 1986. "The Allocation of Credit and Financial Collapse." *Quarterly Journal of Economics* 101 (3): 455–70.

Martínez Pería, M. S. 2011. "Financial Inclusion in Latin America." LAC Finance Development Flagship, Office of the Chief Economist for Latin America and the Caribbean, World Bank, Washington, DC.

McAndrews, J., and C. Stefanadis. 2002. "The Consolidation of European Stock Exchanges." *Current Issues in Economics and Finance* 8 (6).

McKinnon, R. I. 1973. "Money and Capital in Economic Development." Brookings Institution, Washington, DC.

McMillan, M., and D. Rodrik 2011. "Globalization, Structural Change, and Productivity Growth." NBER Working Paper 17143, National Bureau of Economic Research, Cambridge, MA.

Merton, R. C. 1969. "Lifetime Portfolio Selection under Uncertainty: The Continuous-Time Case." *Review of Economics and Statistics* 51 (3): 247–57.

Merton, R., and Z. Bodie. 2004. "The Design of Financial Systems: Towards A Synthesis of Function and Structure." NBER Working Paper 10620, National Bureau of Economic Research, Cambridge, MA.

Mesquita, M., and M. Torós. 2010. "Brazil and the 2008 Panic." In "The Global Crisis and Financial Intermediation in Emerging Market Economies," BIS Paper 54, Bank for International Settlements, Basel, Switzerland.

Mian, A. 2003. "Foreign, Private Domestic, And Government Banks: New Evidence from Emerging Markets." Working paper, Graduate School of Business, University of Chicago, IL.

———. 2006. "Distance Constraints: The Limits of Foreign Lending in Poor Countries." *Journal of Finance* 61 (3): 1465–1505.

Micco, A., and U. Panizza. 2005. "Public Banks in Latin America." Paper prepared for the conference on Public Banks in Latin America: Myth and Reality, Washington, DC. February 25.

Minsky, H.P. 1975. *John Maynard Keynes.* New York: Columbia University Press.

Mishkin, F. 2011. "Monetary Policy Strategy: Lessons from the Crisis." NBER Working Paper 16755, National Bureau of Economic Research, Cambridge, MA.

Montoro, C., and R. Moreno. 2011. "The Use of Reserve Requirements as a Policy Instrument in Latin America." *BIS Quarterly Review,* March, 53–65.

Montoro, C., and C. Tovar. 2010. "Macroprudential Tools: Assessing the Implications of Reserve Requirements in a DGSE Model." Draft, Bank for International Settlements.

Morrison & Foerster. 2011. "ICB Interim Report on UK Banking Reform." *News Bulletin,* April 29.

North, D. C. 1990. *Institutions, Institutional Change, and Economic Performance.* Cambridge, U.K.: Cambridge University Press.

Olivares, J. A. 2005. "Investment Behavior of the Chilean Pension Funds." European Conference Paper 360419, European Financial Management Association Conference (EFMA), Siena, Italy. June 8–11.

Opazo, L., C. Raddatz, and S. Schmukler. 2009. "The Long and the Short of Emerging Market Debt." Policy Research Working Paper 5056, World Bank, Washington, DC.

Ordover, J., and A. Weiss. 1981. "Information and the Law: Evaluating Legal Restrictions on Competitive Contracts." *American Economic Review* 71 (2): 399–404.

Ostry, J., A. Ghosh, K. Habermeier, L. Laeven, M. Chamon, M. Qureshi, and A. Kokenyne. 2011. "Managing Capital Inflows: What Tools to Use?" IMF Staff Discussion Note, International Monetary Fund, Washington, DC.

Panzar, J. C., and J. N. Rosse. 1987. "Testing for 'Monopoly' Equilibrium." *Journal of Industrial Economics* 35 (4): 443–56.

Park, Y. 2011. "The Role of Macroprudential Policy for Financial Stability in East Asia's Emerging Economies." ADBI Working Paper 284, Asian Development Bank Institute, Tokyo.

Peek, J., E. S.Rosengren, and G. M. B. Tootell. 1999. "Is Bank Supervision Central to Central Banking?" *Quarterly Journal of Economics* 114 (2): 629–53.

Penner, R. G, and W. L. Silber. 1973. "The Interaction between Federal Credit Programs and the Impact on the Allocation of Credit." *American Economic Review* 63 (5): 838–52.

Perotti, E., and J. Suárez. 2011. "A Pigouvian Approach to Liquidity Regulation." CEPR Discussion Paper 8271, Centre for Economic Policy Research, London.

Porzecanski, A. C. 2009. "*Latin America: The Missing Financial Crisis.*" Washington Office Studies and Perspectives Series No. 6. Economic Commission for Latin America, United Nations Economic Commission for Latin America, New York.

Powell, A. 2010. "LAC Central Banks ahead of the Curve? Financial Sector Regulation and Supervision." Presentation at the Inter-American Development Bank meeting in Lacea, Medellin, Colombia, November.

Raddatz, C. 2011. "Institutional Investors and Agency Issues in Latin American Financial Markets: Issues and Policy Options." LAC Finance Development Flagship, Office of the Chief Economist for Latin America and the Caribbean, World Bank, Washington, DC.

Raddatz, C. and S. Schmukler. 2008. "Pension Funds and Capital Market Development: How Much Bang for the Buck?" Policy Research Working Paper 4787, World Bank, Washington, DC.

———. 2011. "Deconstructing Herding: Evidence from Pension Fund Investment Behavior." Policy Research Working Paper 5700, World Bank, Washington, DC.

Raith, M. G., T. Staak, and C. Starke. 2006. "The Goal Achievement of Federal Lending Programs." Working Paper Series 06019, Faculty of Economics and Management, Magdeburg, Germany.

Rajan, R. 2010. *Fault Lines: How Hidden Fractures Still Threaten the World Economy.* Princeton, NJ: Princeton University Press.

Rajan, R., and L. Zingales. 2001. "Financial Systems, Industrial Structure, and Growth." Oxford Review of Economic Policy 17: 467–82.

———. 2003. *Saving Capitalism from the Capitalists: Unleashing the Power of Financial Markets to Create Wealth and Spread Opportunity.* New York: Crown Business Division of Random House.

Repullo, R., and J. Saurina. 2011. "The Counter-cyclical Capital Buffer of Basel III: A Critical Assessment." Discussion Paper 8304, Centre for Economic Policy Research, London.

Repullo, R., J. Saurina, and J. Trucharte. 2010. "Mitigating the Pro-Cyclicality of Basel II." CEPR Discussion Paper 7382, Centre for Economic Policy Research, London.

Repullo, R., and J. Suarez. 2009. "The Procyclical Effects of Basel II." CEPR Discussion Paper 6862, Centre for Economic Policy Research, London.

Rioja, F., and N. Valev. 2004. "Does One Size Fit All? A Reexamination of the Finance and Growth Relationship." *Journal of Development Economics* 74 (2): 429–47.

Robinson, M. S. 2001. *The Micro Finance Revolution: Sustainable Finance for the Poor.* Washington, DC: World Bank.

Rocha, R., D. Vittas, and H. P. Rudolph. 2011. *Annuities and Other Retirement Products: Designing the Payout Phase.* Washington, DC: World Bank.

Rocha, R., and C. Thorburn. 2006. *Developing Annuities Markets: The Experience of Chile.* Washington, DC: World Bank.

Rojas-Suarez, L. 2001. "Rating Banks in Emerging Markets: What Credit Rating Agencies Should Learn from Financial Indicators." Working Paper 01-6, Institute for International Economics, Washington, DC.

Roubini, N., and X. Sala-i-Martin. 1992. "Financial Repression and Economic Growth." *Journal of Development Economics* 39 (1): 5–30.

Rudolph, H. 2009. "State Financial Institutions: Mandates, Governance and Beyond." World Bank Working Paper 5141, World Bank, Washington, DC.

Samuelson, P.A. 1969. "Lifetime Portfolio Selection by Dynamic Stochastic Programming." *Review of Economics and Statistics* 51 (3): 239–46.

Santana, M. H. 2008. "The Novo Mercado." In *Focus 5—Novo Mercado and Its Followers: Case Studies in Corporate Governance Reform*, ed. M. H. Santana, M. Ararat, P. Alexandru, B. B. Yurtoglu, and M. R. Cunha, 2–39. Washington, DC : International Finance Corporation.

Saurina, J. 2011. "Working Macroprudential Tools." In *Macroprudential Regulatory Policies: The New Road to Financial Stability*, proceedings of the Thirteenth Annual International Banking Conference, Chicago, IL, September 23–24, 2010.

Schularick, M., and A. M. Taylor 2009. "Credit Booms Gone Bust: Monetary Policy, Leverage Cycles and Financial Crises, 1870–2008." NBER Working Paper 15512, National Bureau of Economic Research, Cambridge, MA.

Seelig, S. A., and A. Novoa. 2009. "Governance Practices at Financial Regulatory and Supervisory Agencies." IMF Working Paper 09/135,

International Monetary Fund, Washington, DC.

Sengupta, R., and C. P. Aubuchon. 2008. "The Micro Finance Revolution: An Overview." *Federal Bank of St. Louis Review* January/ February.

Sharpe, W. 1964. "Capital Asset Prices: A Theory of Market Equilibrium under Conditions of Risk." *Journal of Finance* 19: 425–42.

Shaw, E. 1973. *Financial Deepening in Economic Development.* Oxford, U.K.: Oxford University Press.

Shiller, R. 2006. *Irrational Exuberance.* Princeton, NJ: Princeton University Press.

———. 2008. *Subprime Solution: How Today's Global Financial Crisis Happened and What to Do about It.* Princeton, NJ: Princeton University Press.

Shin, H. S. 2010. *Risk and Liquidity.* Clarendon Lectures in Finance. Oxford, U.K.: Oxford University Press.

Shin, H., and Y. Shin. 2011. "Procyclicality and Monetary Aggregates." NBER Working Paper 16836, National Bureau of Economic Research, Cambridge, MA.

Shleifer, A., and R. W. Vishny. 1997a. "A Survey of Corporate Governance." *Journal of Finance* 52 (2): 737–83.

———. 1997b. "The Limits of Arbitrage." *Journal of Finance* 52 (1): 35–55.

———. 2011. "Fire Sales in Finance and Macroeconomics." *Journal of Economic Perspectives* 25 (1): 29–48.

Smith, B. D., and M. J., Stutzer. 1989. "Credit Rationing and Government Loan Programs: A Welfare Analysis." *Real Estate Economics* 17 (2): 177–93.

Sosa, S. 2010. "The Influence of 'Big Brothers': How Important are Regional Factors for Uruguay?" IMF Working Paper 10/60, International Monetary Fund, Washington, DC.

Spence, M. 1973. "Job Market Signaling." *Quarterly Journal of Economics* 87(3): 355–74.

Squam Lake Working Group on Financial Regulation. 2009. "Improving Resolution Options for Systemically Relevant Financial Institutions." Working Paper, Center for Economic Studies, Council on Foreign Relations, Washington, DC.

Srinivas, P. S., E. Whitehouse, and J. Yermo. 2000. "Regulating Private Pension Funds' Structure, Performance, and Investments: Cross-Country Evidence." Social Protection Discussion Paper 23302, World Bank, Washington, DC.

Stallings, B., and R. Studart. 2003. "Financial Regulation and Supervision in Emerging Markets: The Experience of Latin America since the Tequila Crisis." Economic Commission for Latin America and the Caribbean (CEPAL), Santiago, Chile.

———. 2006. *Finance for Development: Latin America in Comparative Perspective.* Washington, DC: Brookings Institution; Santiago, Chile: Economic Commission for Latin America and the Caribbean (Spanish).

Stiglitz, J. E., J. Vallejo, and Y. C. Park. 1993. "The Role of the State in Financial Markets." In "Annual Conference on Development Economics" (supplement). *World Bank Research Observer* 19: 1–61.

Stiglitz, J. E., and A. Weiss. 1981. "Credit Rationing in Markets with Imperfect Information." *American Economic Review* 71 (3): 393–410.

Stulz, R. 1999. "Globalization, Corporate Finance and the Cost of Capital." *Journal of Applied Corporate Finance* 12 (3): 8–25.

Svensson, L. 2010. "Inflation Targeting." NBER Working Paper 16654, National Bureau of Economic Research, Cambridge, MA.

Taylor, M. 1995. "Twin Peaks: A Regulatory Structure for the New Century." Centre for the Study of Financial Innovation, London.

———. 2009. "The Road from 'Twin Peaks' and the Way Back." *Connecticut Insurance Law Journal* 16 (1).

Terrier, G., R. Valdés, C. E. Tovar, J. Chan-Lau, C. Fernández-Valdovinos, M. García Escribano, C. Medeiros, M. K.. Tang, M. Vera Martin, and C. Walker. 2011. "Policy Instruments to Lean against the Wind in Latin America" IMF Working Paper 11/159, International Monetary Fund, Washington, DC.

Thompson, J. 2009. "On Systemically Important Financial Institutions and Progressive Systemic Risk Migration." Policy Discussion Paper No. 27, Federal Reserve Bank of Cleveland.

Turner, A. 2010. "What Do Banks Do? Why Do Credit Booms and Busts Occur and What Can Public Policy Do about It?" In *The Future of Finance and the Theory that Underpins It.* Center for Economic Performance. London: London School of Economics.

Vargas, H., C. Varela, Y. Betancourt, and N. Rodriguez. 2010. "Effects of Reserve Requirements in an Inflation Targeting Regime: The Case of Colombia." Borradores de Economía 587, Banco de la República.

Viceira, L. 2010. "Application of Advances in Financial Theory and Evidence to Pension Fund

Design in Developing Economies." In *Evaluating the Financial Performance of Pension Funds*, ed. R. Hinz, H. Rudolph, P. Antolin, and J. Yermo. Washington, DC: World Bank.

Viñals, J. 2011. "The Do's and Don't's of Macroprudential Policy." Paper presented at the European Commission and ECB Conference on Financial Integration and Stability, Brussels, May 2.

Weitzman, M. L. 1974. "Prices vs. Quantities." *Review of Economic Studies* 41: 477–91.

Wezel, T. 2010. "Dynamic Loan Loss Provisions in Uruguay." IMF Working Paper 10/125, International Monetary Fund, Washington, DC.

Williamson, S. D. 1994. "Do Informational Frictions Justify Federal Credit Programs?" *Journal of Money, Credit and Banking* 26 (3): 523–44.

Woodford, M. 2011. "Inflation Targeting and Financial Stability." Keynote address at the conference "The Future of Monetary Policy," Einaudi Institute for Economics and Finance, Rome, September 2010 (Revised August 2011).

World Bank. 1989. *World Development Report* Washington, DC: World Bank.

———. 2001. *Finance for Growth: Policy Choices in a Volatile World*. Washington, DC: World Bank; New York: Oxford University Press.

———. 2005. *Economic Growth in the 1990s: Learning from a Decade of Reform*. World Bank: Washington, DC.

———. 2006. *Emerging Capital Markets and Globalization: The Latin American Experience*. Washington, DC: World Bank.

———. 2007. *Finance for All? Policies and Pitfalls in Expanding Access*. Washington, DC: World Bank.

Yunus, M. 2003. *Banker to the Poor: Micro-Lending and the Battle Against World Poverty*. New York: Public Affairs.

Zervos, S. 2004. "The Transaction Costs of Primary Issuance: The Case of Brazil, Chile and Mexico." Policy Research Working Paper 3424, World Bank, Washington, DC.